"Dr. Alexander has gathered the major, minor, profound and pedestrian aspects of African American Holiness-Pentecostalism in a volume that seeks to provide a Rosetta Stone for scholars, students, denominational historians and the general public. She is clear to state that this work is an endearing labor of love to articulate her experience as an African American Pentecostal worshiper, scholar and minister. This volume is the seedbed of a crop of readable studies in African American Holiness-Pentecostal history, theology and culture. A worthy investment in understanding the why, who, what and how of a century-old community of denominations linked to the book of Acts and 312 Azusa Street. Kudos!"

Dr. Ida E. Jones, Howard University

"*Black Fire* offers an expansive historical overview of African American Holiness-Pentecostals and their often overlooked contributions to the early development, dissemination and current vitality of the modern Pentecostal movement from its inception to the present. Students and scholars of African American religion and culture will appreciate its rich content, as well as its nuanced attention to matters of race, class, gender and generation."

Karen Kossie-Chernyshev, Texas Southern University

"This particular book is especially welcome. African American Pentecostals have become a major force in American (and world) Christianity, but there is a serious lack of well-documented studies. Estrelda Alexander does an excellent job filling that lamentable gap."

Mark Noll, University of Notre Dame

"Pentecostalism is one of the most vibrant and important developments in modern Christianity. In this welcome and much-needed book, Estrelda Y. Alexander demonstrates convincingly that this global work of the Spirit has to a large extent emerged from and continues to be fanned into flame by the African American community. Outsiders who think a few more controversial variations of "black fire" sometimes look like 'strange fire' will be glad to learn that the African American church has able internal critics of its own outliers. Every Christian—indeed, everyone interested in the present and future of Christianity—needs to know this story."

Timothy Larsen, Wheaton College

Black Fire

One Hundred Years of
African American Pentecostalism

Estrelda Y. Alexander

IVP Academic

An imprint of InterVarsity Press
Downers Grove, Illinois

InterVarsity Press
P.O. Box 1400, Downers Grove, IL 60515-1426
World Wide Web: www.ivpress.com
E-mail: email@ivpress.com

InterVarsity Press® is the book-publishing division of InterVarsity Christian Fellowship/USA®, a movement of students and faculty active on campus at hundreds of universities, colleges and schools of nursing in the United States of America, and a member movement of the International Fellowship of Evangelical Students. For information about local and regional activities, write Public Relations Dept., InterVarsity Christian Fellowship/USA, 6400 Schroeder Rd., P.O. Box 7895, Madison, WI 53707-7895, or visit the IVCF website at <www.intervarsity.org>.

All Scripture quotations, unless otherwise indicated, are taken from the Holy Bible, New International Version®. NIV®. *Copyright ©1973, 1978, 1984 by International Bible Society. Used by permission of Zondervan Publishing House. All rights reserved.*

Cover design: Cindy Kiple
Interior design: Beth Hagenberg
Images: Getty Images

ISBN 978-0-8308-2586-8

Printed in Canada ∞

Library of Congress Cataloging-in-Publication Data

Alexander, Estrelda, 1949-
  Black fire: one hundred years of African American Pentecostalism/
Estrelda Alexander.
    p. cm.
  Includes bibliographical references (p.   ) and index.
  ISBN 978-0-8308-2586-8 (pbk.: alk. paper)
    1. African American Pentecostals—History. 2. United States—Church
history. I. Title.
  BR1644.3.A45 2011
    277.3'08208996073—dc22

2010052970

P	19	18	17	16	15	14	13	12	11	10	9	8	7	6	5	4	3	2	1
Y	27	26	25	24	23	22	21	20	19	18	17	16	15	14	13	12	11		

CONTENTS

FOREWORD

Black Fire: One Hundred Years of African American Pentecostalism is a treasure trove of scholarly insight and information on African American Pentecostalism. Being among the rare books able to craft a narrative chronicling and interpreting the century-long history of African American Pentecostalism, this book expands our knowledge of the diverse social and theological trajectories that constitute the tradition. Here, Estrelda Alexander introduces scholars and general readers to the triumphs and travesties of the African American Pentecostal phenomenon.

This work fits squarely within the school of scholarship plotted out by Walter Hollenweger, Leonard Lovett and others who emphasize the African roots of Pentecostalism, in general, and of African American Pentecostalism, in particular—while challenging interpretations that focus solely on white origins. Alexander here argues that roots of the movement—not just for African Americans but for white Pentecostals as well—lie within a robust African spirituality with its beliefs in a supreme being, in the sacredness of creation, in the supernatural, in rituals of life and in ancestor veneration. She locates the embodiment of that African spirituality in the United States within the African survivals found in slave religion or "slave Christianity" of the antebellum era that stressed trances, visions, Spirit possession and the holy dance, as well as their conversion rituals, music making, oral tradition, and the theme of enslaved Africans being the children of God. Yet she nuances the African-roots thesis by stressing the role of the nineteenth-century black Holiness movement and the input of black Holiness leaders, such as William Christian and Charles Price

Jones, to the theological roots of African American Pentecostalism, following a position argued by scholars such as William C. Turner, Cheryl Sanders and myself.

This work dives squarely into the debate over the founding of American Pentecostalism by advocating for the crucial role played by William J. Seymour, an African American, and the Azusa Street Revival, over which he presided. Refusing to dismiss the contributions of Charles Parham, a white American, she credits him in formulating the doctrine of initial evidence as central to the baptism of the Holy Spirit message Seymour originally preached. Rather than casting Parham as the founder, however, Alexander identifies him as a major catalyst in initiating what came to be known as the identifying mark of modern Pentecostalism—evidentiary tongues. Following Robert Mapes Anderson in distinguishing between Parham's "relatively small, localized movement" and Seymour's much larger, international movement, she places Parham at the front of the chronology of the movement but reserves identification of the role of founder for Seymour.

A major contribution of this work is that it confronts the topic of race unabashedly and interrogates the racial divide in American Pentecostalism, noting how white racism affected the formation and ongoing development of African American Pentecostalism. At various intervals throughout *Black Fire*, Alexander interrogates the polities and theologies of white Christianity that promote the racial oppression of African Americans—first as enslaved people and later as second-class citizens during the segregation era. She further examines evidence of racist attitudes of white Pentecostals, such as: Parham, who attempted to undermine Seymour's leadership at Azusa Street and in the broader movement; the segregating of African Americans within predominately white denominations such as the Fire Baptized Holiness Church; and the struggle of African Americans who belong to predominately white Pentecostal denominations, such as the Church of God (Cleveland, Tenn.), to overcome paternalism and racial exclusion within denominational ranks.

Additionally, Alexander explores the history of two failed experiments in interracialism: the Church of God in Christ under Charles Harrison Mason's leadership and the Pentecostal Assemblies of the World under the leadership of Garfield T. Hayward. Central to her discussion of race in American Pentecostalism is an acknowledgment of the theological writings of Seymour, Charles Harrison Mason, Robert Clarence Lawson, Ida Robinson and others who unabashedly critiqued racism in the United States while often attempting to maintain an openness to their white Christian brothers, which was rarely returned.

Gender is another prominent theme in this volume. Alexander takes great pains to inform the reader of the pivotal role women played from the earliest formation through the ongoing development of the movement. She begins by exploring the ministries of black, Holiness, women evangelists and goes on to examine the role of several black women, such as Lucy Farrow and Jenny Moore Seymour of the Azusa Street Revival. She highlights organizational innovations, such as the women-headed denominations produced by Bishops Mary Magdalena Tate and Ida Robinson, as well the denominational women's departments erected by leaders such as Lizzie Robinson and Lillian Brooks Coffey. The pastoral ministries of women are reviewed, especially the ministries of Carrie Gurry of Baltimore, Lucy Smith of Chicago, Rosa Horn of New York City and Elizabeth Dabney of Philadelphia. The reality of sexism, which remains intact today within the ranks of African American Pentecostalism, is woven throughout her discussion of gender.

In *Black Fire*, Alexander blends historical reconstruction with theological interpretation. In this endeavor, her discussion of Seymour's theological reformulation of Parham's initial evidence and theology of the Holy Spirit as more than glossolalia and Spirit baptism is crucial. She also analyzes the theological distinctions between so-called trinitarian and oneness Pentecostalism, paying careful attention to describe those doctrines of oneness Pentecostalism—such as regenerational baptism and theology of the Godhead—with the respect that allows the latter movement, which is considered by many as heretical, to have a full hearing.

Alexander concludes *Black Fire* with a discussion of the involvement of African Americans in various aspects of charismatic Christianity, including the Word of Faith theology, the megachurch phenomenon and black neo-Pentecostalism within mainline congregations. Within this discussion she highlights the contributions of leaders such as Frederick K. C. Price of Crenshaw Christian Center in Los Angeles, John Bryant of the African Methodist Episcopal Church, George A. Stallings of the Roman Catholic Church, Carlton Pearson and T. D. Jakes. What is most significant about this discussion is the degree of variety the leaders and their ministries exhibit in helping to shape the contours of the Pentecostal, charismatic, neo-Pentecostal continuum during the late twentieth and early twenty-first centuries.

Black Fire makes a substantial contribution to the growing cache of literature on global Pentecostalism by focusing on the specific, often neglected, contribution of African American Pentecostalism as a major factor in the construction of the movement. As the store of scholarship, popular writing and journalism on global Pentecostalism continues to expand, it is important that a book such as this profiles a significant stream within North American Pentecostalism, reminding us of the significant contribution African Americans have made to the global expressions of Pentecostalism, on one hand, while keeping us aware of issues within the movement that continue to be salient. Placed alongside such works as *African Pentecostalism* by Ogbu Kalu and *Asian and Pentecostal* edited by Edmond Tang and Allan Anderson, *Black Fire* contributes to a more nuanced and fuller depiction of the streams that have constructed and continue to construct and expand global Pentecostalism.

Black Fire tells the history of African American Pentecostalism in an engaging and thoughtful manner, narrating an intriguing story drawn with theological portraits, biographical sketches and denominational snapshots. With the genius of pioneers such as William L. Fulford, Magdalena Tate, Charles Harrison Mason, William Edward Fuller Sr. and Thomas Cox being lauded, the verve of many women and men who "dug out" churches being heralded, this work provides readers with a fascinating account of African American Pentecostalism that both informs and challenges.

David E. Daniels
Professor of Church History
McCormick Theological Seminary

PREFACE

All that generation also were gathered to their fathers; and there arose
another generation after them who did not know the LORD, nor yet the work
which He had done.

JUDGES 2:10 NASB

GROWING UP IN AN URBAN, BLACK, working-class oneness Pentecostal congregation in the 1950s and 1960s, I knew little of my heritage. This was my grandmother's church, and so by default this was my church. So when at seven years old I walked down the aisle to "accept Jesus as my Lord and Savior" and two years later when I received my Pentecostal Spirit baptism following weeks of tarrying at the Sunday evening tarrying service, I thought that this was how church had always been for everyone. I did not understand that many Christians considered mine a strange heritage and, even more, knew little or nothing about it.

By the time I began college at Howard University, I was still largely unaware of my Pentecostal heritage. Even though I joined the campus Pentecostal Fellowship, which met in the Seymour House, neither I nor most of my Pentecostal friends knew anything of the Azusa Street Revival, William Seymour, Charles Harrison Mason or any of the forefathers such as Garfield Haywood or Robert Lawson and foremothers such as Ida Robinson, Mary Magdalena Tate or Rosa Horne, who had contributed to our tradition. In essence, I was unaware of the specific role that African American individuals had played in shaping what was to become the largest and fastest-growing expression of global Christian spirituality.

As I went on to pursue graduate work—first in sociology, then in theology—I would come to see that the reasons for this lack are myriad and somewhat complicated. Historically, among African American Pentecostal leaders and congregations, the urgent felt need to evangelize a lost world has overshadowed any desire to develop a written legacy. Therefore, early leaders produced very limited primary sources. Second, the self-deprecating humility of Pentecostals, who lifted up "no one but Jesus" and attributed all accomplishments to the Holy Spirit, encouraged leaders to eschew giving glory or undue attention to any person. This attitude was accompanied by a lack of historical consciousness that saw no or little need to preserve even the few primary sources that had been produced since Jesus was coming soon and there would be no need for them in heaven.

Yet such lack was also due to the rampant racism—and classism—that overshadowed American society during the first half of the twentieth century. White leaders and scholars denigrated the black contribution to any important arena, leaving most of Pentecostal historiography woefully bereft of evidence of black involvement. Yet black religionists and scholars were also quick to dismiss the uncouth gyrations and tongue-talking gibberish of Pentecostals as a throwback to a primitive past they were eager to forget. Though black Pentecostals were not entirely anti-intellectual, they saw intellectual reflection on matters of religion as somehow unspiritual. This prejudice was coupled with a very limited number of African American Pentecostal scholars doing credible research on the movement's early years. So, while Pentecostalism has grown to be one of the most researched aspects of contemporary Christianity, it is only in the last quarter of the twentieth century—more than one hundred years after its explosion onto the American religious scene—that black scholars emerged from within Pentecostal denominations to begin to make a strong contribution to this discourse.[1]

The task of documenting one hundred years of untold history is monumental. It cannot be accomplished in one volume. This work simply begins to celebrate the breadth of the contribution of people of color to American Pentecostalism and only begins the attempt to correct the lack of attention they have received in the unfolding historiography of Pentecostal origins and development.

---

[1]James S. Tinney, "A Theoretical and Historical Comparison of Black Political and Religious Movements" (Ph.D. diss., Howard University, 1978).

Whatever the reasons for previous oversights, the new generation of African American Pentecostal scholarship has been spurred by both the awakened consciousness of the ongoing struggle for justice and identity among people of color and an increased level of theological awareness within the community. Black Pentecostal scholars have begun not only to produce a body of work but also to prod the elders and the academy to take seriously the need to preserve the artifacts from our heritage. Up until now, however, no single scholar has ventured to assemble the disparate stories that make up our collected legacy, and so the story has remained largely untold.

While I attempt to maintain a level of academic objectivity in this effort, I am not dispassionate. I have attempted this volume so that our children—the generation that sits in the pews of African American Pentecostal congregations, as well as millions more who have been touched and enriched by some facet of this movement—will not be unmindful of what their foremothers and fathers have endured and accomplished. Recovering the extraordinary history of African American Pentecostalism from the scattered resources that have been left us is no easy task. This revision to the revision of Pentecostal history will take several years, if not decades, to adequately unearth, document, and report and will require the persistent energy of those who love this movement and what it has given us. Some will not be satisfied with this meager beginning, but this work represents only a start to this enormous task.

1

INTRODUCTION

*If this . . . work is of men, it will come to nothing; but if it is of God,
you cannot overthrow it.*

ACTS 5:38-39 NKJV

IN EARLY APRIL 1906 TWO EVENTS OCCURRED within a short
period in the relatively young state of California that would have major
effects on its citizens. Though different in nature, observers considered
both to be acts of God. The first, a natural phenomenon—the infamous
San Francisco earthquake—measured 7.7 on the Richter scale. It was felt
as far as one hundred miles away, from southern Oregon to south of Los
Angeles and inland as far as central Nevada. Its tremors resulted in the
deaths of nearly one thousand people (the greatest loss of life from a natural disaster in the state's history) and resulted in extensive damage to or
destruction of a vast number of homes and businesses in the surrounding
communities, mostly from the fires the quake spawned. This devastation
affected people from all segments of society, catching up both rich and
poor in its destruction. Local, national, and international newspapers and
magazines sent numerous reporters to document and graphically depict its
destruction and aftermath to a world that eagerly awaited such news.[1]

However, the second event, occurring nearly four hundred miles away,
initially got little attention from the press. Indeed, it got little attention
from most of the residents of Los Angeles, the city where it unfolded, or

---

[1]See, e.g., "Half of City Lying in Ruins," *Los Angeles Times,* April 19, 1906, p. I14; "Earthquake
Shocks Almost Continuous," *Washington Post,* April 19, 1906, p. 2.

from the rest of the world. For those involved were primarily plain, lower-class folks some would describe as religious fanatics and who mattered little to the outside society. When reporters scooped the story, they ridiculed the event and its participants as some bizarre spectacle that, like others before it, would soon fade from the community's interest. They saw it more as a passing curiosity than a matter of real consequence.[2]

On the one hand, that earthquake, with all of its devastation, has been mostly forgotten, except in written history. On the other hand, the Azusa Street Pentecostal Revival was to prove to be an even more powerful, spiritual act of God. Its far-reaching impact would be felt not only in California in early 1906 and along the West Coast later that year but also throughout the United States and the entire Christian world over the next one hundred years, signaling the beginning of a movement that has changed the face of American and global Christianity. African Americans would play a major, yet largely ignored, role in the unfolding of that movement.

The roots of African American Pentecostalism draw from the deep wells of African spirituality, slave religion, the independent black churches that came out of reconstruction and the nineteenth-century black Holiness movement that unfolded among free Methodists and Baptists. Each of these elements contributed unique qualities that would give black Pentecostalism its collective character and make it a force deserving our attention. African spirituality contributed a foundational worldview that opened Pentecostal believers up to encounters with the Spirit as the life-sustaining source of their spiritual and social liberation. The experience of slavery and the system of religion that surrounded it developed within believers, often only once removed from that dreadful institution, communal resilience to craft and sustain an alternative reality in which mutual respect replaced the indignities of the surrounding racist society. The independent black churches provided and appreciated the ability of African Americans to build their own organizational structures and depend on their own meager resources to sustain them. And the black Holiness heritage contributed both the experience of sanctification as a distinct work of grace

---

[2]See, e.g., "Weird Babel of Tongues: New Sect of Fanatics Is Breaking Loose; Wild Scene Last Night on Azusa Street; Gurgle of Wordless Talk by a Sister," *Los Angeles Times,* April 18, 1906, p. 1; "'Holy Roller' Had It Bad," *Los Angeles Times,* August 14, 1906, p. 1; "Rolling and Diving Fanatics Confess," *Los Angeles Times,* August 14, 1906, p. 1.

and the language of Holy Spirit baptism, which would overlay the movement with a dynamic spiritually.

The inclusive atmosphere in which the Azusa Street Revival—and the movement it spawned—was ushered in demonstrated a profound understanding of the nature of the Holy Spirit's work in unifying the body of Christ. Yet the racial birthright of American Pentecostalism has long been hotly contested among African American and white Pentecostal leaders and scholars, who place its beginning variably at either New Year's Day 1901 in Topeka, Kansas, under the leadership of the white evangelist Charles Fox Parham, or April 1906 in Los Angeles, under the leadership of African American William Joseph Seymour. A third group attempts to mediate this impasse by suggesting that the upstart of the movement was completely a "work of the Holy Spirit" that essentially owes no allegiance to any human source but sprang up more or less spontaneously.

Charles Parham, a largely self-taught evangelist, faith healer and armchair theologian, formulated the doctrine of tongues as "initial evidence" of Holy Spirit baptism that is the theological foundation for modern Pentecostalism. This doctrine, that the "baptism" or "outpouring" of the Holy Spirit on the believer is an essential aspect of Christian experience as a direct fulfillment of the prophecy of the Old Testament book of Joel, would become the distinguishing feature of classical Pentecostalism. To Pentecostals this "in-filling" endows believers with supernatural empowerment to both live a holy life and to accomplish "works of righteousness" on behalf of the kingdom of God. Its adherents seek to establish a personal communion with God through ecstatic religious experience, including glossolalia, or speaking in tongues, as initial objective evidence of that outpouring and in-filling.

It was in one of Parham's 1901 prayer meetings that the first reported incidence of speaking in tongues as this initial evidence of Holy Spirit baptism occurred. Parham's attempts at building interest in the experience of speaking in tongues first found little resonance beyond a few disciples. His efforts at promoting revival fires never gained momentum beyond sporadic meetings throughout the Midwest that centered more on divine healing, yielding few who experienced Pentecostal Spirit baptism. Under his leadership the doctrine of initial evidence would remain little more than an untested formulation except among a few of his closest followers.

His attempts to use it as a springboard for a worldwide revival with tongues serving as a tool for evangelizing peoples of all cultures and languages never materialized. Yet he never forsook that vision, and he used his informal Bible schools to instruct young ministers in the new doctrine and arm fresh crops of workers with the perceived truth of the evidence of Holy Spirit baptism.

Parham's legacy to African American Pentecostalism is tainted, however, by the unfortunate racial insensitivity he exhibited on encountering the interracial climate of the Azusa Street Revival.[3] Beyond that, in a movement noted for rigid personal piety, Parham's reputation is further discredited by his alleged moral failings.[4] Still, he is recognized as igniting the spark that set the movement on its path as the most prolific religious movement since the Reformation, and until the near the end of the twentieth century, Parham's contribution was singularly celebrated by many scholars, who almost entirely neglected any contribution from African Americans.[5] At Parham's Houston school, leadership for the fledging movement arose from an unsuspected—even unlikely—source, falling to one of his disciples, William Joseph Seymour, a largely self-taught, black son of former slaves. As Robert Mapes Anderson, a major social analyst of the Pentecostal movement, characterizes the shift, "What had been under Parham, a relatively small, localized movement, was to assume international proportions through the Los Angeles ministry of an obscure, chunky [sic] black man."[6]

After sitting under Parham's tutelage for a short time, Seymour would go on to preside over the Azusa Street Revival, which catapulted the Pen-

---

[3]Two works give a thorough accounting of Parham's life and ministry. The more objective of these is James R. Goff, *Fields White unto Harvest: Charles F. Parham and the Missionary Origins of Pentecostalism* (Fayetteville: University of Arkansas Press, 1988). A more sympathetic accounting is done by Parham's wife: Sarah E. Parham, *The Life of Charles F. Parham: Founder of the Apostolic Faith Movement* (New York: Garland, 1985).

[4]See, e.g., James S. Tinney, "William J. Seymour: Father of Modern-Day Pentecostalism," in *Black Apostles: Afro-American Clergy Confront the Twentieth Century*, ed. Randall Burkett and Richard Newman (Boston: G. K. Hall, 1978), pp. 213-25; and Iain MacRobert, *The Black Roots and White Racism of Pentecostalism* (New York: St. Martin's, 1988).

[5]E.g., Vinson Synan's earliest history of the movement, *The Holiness-Pentecostal Movement in the United States* (Grand Rapids: Eerdmans, 1971); his later work, *The Holiness-Pentecostal Tradition: Charismatic Movements in the Twentieth Century*, 2nd ed. (Grand Rapids: Eerdmans, 1997), expands coverage of Seymour to little more than eight pages.

[6]Robert Mapes Anderson, *Vision of the Disinherited: the Making of American Pentecostalism* (New York: Oxford University Press, 1979), p. 61.

tecostal movement into national and world prominence. Most existing Pentecostal denominations—whether white, African American, Latino or any other race—trace their roots either directly or indirectly back to this revival, or at least pay obeisance to its influence on their development. It was there that people of every race and culture came together for what has been categorized as one of the most significant religious events in modern history. Many who became prominent leaders in the movement found their way to Azusa Street; many more were touched directly by someone who had been a participant.

Proponents who attribute the origins of the movement solely to the work of the Holy Spirit cite the fact that in the ten years from 1896 to 1906 several renewal movements sprang up in which tongues and other manifestations were centrally present. The Shearer Schoolhouse Revival in 1896 in Cherokee County, North Carolina, was part of the history of the Church of God (Cleveland, Tennessee). In the fall of 1904, Evan Roberts's ministry in Wales drew international attention and seekers from many parts of Europe and the United States. A revival focused on women and children also took place at the Mukti Mission of Pandita Ramabai in Pune, India, later, in 1905.[7] Certainly, any attempt to understand the place of the Pentecostal movement within the history of global Christianity must place it both within a wider discussion of these and other movements of the Spirit in the church's life.

Within the American context, however, the racial implications of these interpretations cannot be ignored. Race has been an issue in American religion since the first shipment of African slaves arrived on the shores of North America. Not only has the racial legacy and foundation of the movement been contested; but also, no segment of society, including the Christian church, has remained untouched by the stormy legacy of racial division and bigotry that has torn at the very fabric of American society for more than three hundred years and has surrounded the Pentecostal movement since its inception. This legacy has colored the organizational structure of most mainline denominations, and it should be expected that it

---

[7]Charles Conn, *Like A Mighty Army: A History of the Church of God, 1886-1995*, rev. ed. (Cleveland, Tenn.: Pathway, 1977), pp. 13-22. Eifion Evans, *The Welsh revival of 1904* (London: Evangelical Press of Wales), 1974. Ramabai's revival was focused on women. For more information, see Stanley M. Burgess, "Pentecostalism in India: An Overview," *Asian Journal of Pentecostal Studies*, 4, no. 1 (2001): 85-98.

would influence the development of American Pentecostalism.

Formed during the height of a period when racial separation tainted every sphere of American society, earliest Pentecostals of all races vigorously and conspicuously fought segregationist urges, initially developing a pattern of inclusiveness and interracial leadership that had been unprecedented in American religious history. The earliest Pentecostals openly touted the movement's racial inclusiveness, and in a short time several denominations came into being that not only had interracial constituencies but also drew their leadership from the ranks of capable men (and sometimes women) without regard to race, culture or social class. Yet these intense early impulses, which went far beyond tolerance to involve actual embrace of persons of diverse ethnic groups, soon capitulated to surrounding racial realities. After the initial period, race became an issue and separation was soon to be the norm.

Examples of this racial divide would repeatedly surface. Within four years the Azusa Street Mission had a largely black constituency. Though both blacks and whites at first continued to diligently maintain at least a semblance of cordial relationships, most newly birthed denominations were formed along racial lines, and several bodies that earlier had interracial constituencies followed suit, splintering into new, racially differentiated denominations. Within ten years of the movement's beginning, there were virtually two Pentecostal movements—one heavily white, the other almost entirely black.

The Fire Baptized Holiness Church began in 1895 as a biracial Holiness body, moving into the Pentecostal camp shortly after the Azusa Street Revival. It too would succumb to the movement's race politics when, in 1908, the majority of blacks withdrew from the larger white body, though both groups initially retained the name. Later the larger white group adopted the name Pentecostal Holiness Church. The two groups have maintained a collegial relationship. In 1914 the majority of the white ministers in the biracial Church of God in Christ (COGIC) voted to form the separate fellowship that became the Assemblies of God. White historians insist that the separation was amicable and that COGIC founder Charles Harrison Mason continued collegial relationships with the new body. Indeed, a few African Americans were part of the new body. Yet the split from COGIC was largely along racial lines, stemming primarily from the reluctance of some whites to serve under a black leader. Interestingly, of the major Pentecostal bodies in the United States, the Assemblies of God has remained the most racially segregated, with less than 2 percent of its constituency being African American. The oneness branch of Pentecostalism, represented by the Pentecostal Assemblies of the World, remained biracial for the longest period, working to ensure that not only its congregations but also its leadership reflected racial equality. But it too had become largely divided along racial lines by the late 1930s.

The racial divide has meant that, over one hundred years, the majority of African American Pentecostals have historically worshiped within black congregations within classical black Pentecostal denominations. Yet a small but significant number are part of larger white denominations, as part of either African American, predominantly white or multicultural congregations. The history of black involvement within predominantly white bodies, such as the Church of God (Cleveland, Tennessee), the Assemblies of God, the Pentecostal Holiness Church and the International Church of the Foursquare Gospel, provides a story of dual loyalties, often contentious relationships, ongoing racism and limited access to positions of leadership. Within these denominations blacks were often relegated to separate enclaves, existing as virtual subdenominations and operating separate governing bodies, political systems and ecclesial gatherings, while institutional oversight remained in white hands. Those who were able to weather the realities of disenfranchisement, which rendered them all but invisible, remained part of these bodies. Others, however, broke away and formed new bodies, as in the case of the black Fire Baptized Holiness Church and its white parent, the Pentecostal Holiness Church.

Though black involvement in all Pentecostal arenas rivaled and in some ways surpassed that of whites, most early Pentecostal history had been written by white scholars who have not only downplayed Seymour's contribution in deference to Parham's but have also ignored the contributions of many other African American Pentecostals. Scholars of black religion regularly used the term *cult* to describe all black emotive religious experience and lumped Holiness and Pentecostal groups with spiritualist and quasi-Christian sects such as Prophet Cherry, Father Divine or Daddy Grace. Many historians, like Elmer Clark, have been reluctant to lift up any contributions Pentecostals may have made to the historical, sociological or theological discourse, characterizing them as among those groups whose "membership [was] from those less than lower class in status, with untrained charlatans for leaders, and worshipers who not only shout, but speak in strange tongues." Further, they characterized black Pentecostals as being "without theology, though they use biblically interpreted terminology; without worship style, though they are demonstrative; without cultural emphasis, though they conform to an expected mode of morality."[8]

Outside the academy, relatively more-affluent blacks who populated the mainline denominations dismissed early Pentecostals as uncouth, overemotional and ignorant. Most had little actual contact with Pentecostals and based their perceptions on the reading of unflattering caricatures in popular media and biased scholarship. So for the first seventy-five years, black Pentecostals were all but shunned by these more respectable Christian bodies, and anything that remotely smacked of Holy Rollerism was dismissed as pure emotional gibberish and a throwback to primitivistic impulses among the underclass.

All the while, black Pentecostals went about quietly building a spiritual and material infrastructure that would position them to become a force to be reckoned with.[9] They were continually gaining in numbers and moving up from primarily Southern and urban storefront edifices to modern state-of-the-art sanctuaries seating several hundred to a few thousand members in multiple services each Sunday. They were also moving out of their sectarian enclaves to engage their communities and the rest of society with a message of radical transformation through the power of the Holy Spirit that not only fitted one for eternal salvation but made a difference in one's personal, tangible situation. The ascetic lifestyle fostered by the movement also ensured that Pentecostals would begin to achieve levels of economic and familial stability that would give them a new respectability in the eyes of many.

Throughout the movement's history, outstanding African American men and women have helped shape its contours such that no area of its life has been left untouched by their individual and collective thought, aesthetic and culture. From liturgical form, spirituality, and preaching style

---

[8]Elmer Clark, *The Small Sects in America* (Nashville: Abingdon-Cokesbury Press, 1949), p. 120.
[9]See Vinson Synan, "The Quiet Rise of Black Pentecostals," *Charisma* 11 (June 1986): 45-55.

to music and theology, the imprint and leadership of African Americans permeates the fabric of the movement in an undeniable yet often denied manner. Indeed, political scientist James Tinney contends that Pentecostalism originated as a black religious development that gave rise to African spirituality of the slaves.[10] This sentiment has been echoed by others such as Leonard Lovett, who asserts that "the twentieth-century Pentecostal movement in America originated from the womb of the Black religious experience."[11]

Yet some responsibility for the dearth of information regarding black Pentecostalism must be laid at its own door. Its leaders historically ignored any suggestion of the necessity of preserving their history or interpreting it to a broader culture. While not entirely shunning education, they eschewed theological training that would prepare them to communicate its rich history to the outside world. Further, during its first three-quarters of a century, the strong penchant for schism within the movement fractured it into more than one hundred denominations, associations and independent bodies, so that no collective voice could be raised on its behalf.

The scarcity of early scholarship meant that many of the black Pentecostal leaders were known only by their followers and a few scholars dedicated to keeping that history alive. William Christian, Henry Fisher, Charles Price Jones, Charles Harrison Mason, William Fuller, Mary Magdalena Tate, Ida Robinson, Garfield Haywood, Robert Lawson and a host of others significantly contributed to the rapid rise of Pentecostal spirituality within the African American community. It also led casual observers to view black Pentecostals as a homogenous group—members of a broad category identified as the sanctified church.

At the first decade of the twenty-first century, there are more than one hundred African American Pentecostal denominations. All Pentecostal-type bodies largely agree on the necessity of expressing a personal faith in the atoning work of Christ and on the expectation that believers would subsequently receive the baptism of the Holy Spirit. But the various segments of the movement—Holiness groups, trinitarian and oneness Pentecostals, and charismatics and neo-Pentecostals—differ on a variety of is-

---

[10]James S. Tinney, "The Blackness of Pentecostalism," *Spirit* 3, no. 2 (1979): 28-29.
[11]Leonard Lovett, "Perspectives on the Black Origins of the Contemporary Pentecostal Movement," *Journal of the Interdenominational Theological Seminary* 2, no. 1 (1973): 42.

sues that have formed over the century: whether speaking in tongues is *the* or *a* sign of Holy Spirit baptism, the nature of the Godhead, church polity, whether divorced persons can remarry and remain in the church or in leadership, and the role of women in the leadership of the church. Such differences, which stemmed in part from the openness of Pentecostals to receive new "revelation" from God to establish a new body based on one or more issues, along with sheer personality conflicts among ambitious leaders, fueled the proliferation of denominations. The largest of these is the Church of God in Christ, whose membership has been variously estimated at between four to six million adherents.

Less than a decade after Azusa Street, the oneness controversy would have widespread implications for African American Pentecostalism. Initially framed around the appropriate baptism formula, Apostolics, as they came to be known, contended that the trinitarian baptism formula "in the name of the Father and of the Son and of the Holy Spirit" should be replaced with "in the Name of Jesus." Over time, however, this dispute also came to involve understandings of the nature of the Godhead and salvation. This segment of the Pentecostal movement has continued to grow and divide until there are now more than fifty black oneness bodies. Many of these are largely geographical in their coverage and revolve around the leadership of a highly charismatic founder or leader. Further, though they all hold to major oneness distinctions regarding the mode of baptism, the nature of the Godhead and the necessary elements of salvation, adherence to particular doctrinal tenets have repeatedly led to schism and formation of new denominations.[12]

Other schisms would arise over women's role in leadership, and black women have encountered a range of responses to the question. Over time a number of women would break with parent organizations that denied them viable leadership roles to establish organizations, such as Mt. Sinai Holy Church and Church of the Living God, that afforded them freedom to exercise what they saw as their God-ordained place in ministry and allowed them to use their God-given gifts at every level, including serving as founders and presiding bishops. Other bodies placed varying levels of restrictions on women, ranging from refusing them ordination to locking

---

[12]See James C. Richardson Jr., *With Water and Spirit: A History of Black Apostolics* (Washington, D.C.: Spirit Press, 1980).

them out of ministry entirely. At both extremes and at every place in the middle, leaders have maintained that their solution is the biblical response. Lines of division would also be drawn over governmental polity, jurisdictional governance, control and management of growing assets, ethical issues such as the divorce and remarriage question, and leadership styles. Some schisms would occur purely over personality clashes among strong men who had little opportunity to use their distinctive gifts outside the church and were determined that God had designated them to have a major voice in the direction of their respective bodies.

By the 1960s, when a new manifestation of Pentecostal spirituality began to take root in the African American community, the pattern of differentiation by division had already been set. Black classical Pentecostals would soundly reject the charismatic and neo-Pentecostal movements as a bogus infringement on their spiritual territory. This new form of spirituality took two distinct yet related trajectories. First, a number of individual blacks aligned themselves with the white-led charismatic movement that was breaking out within mainline congregations and smaller faith communities throughout the country. These blacks remained in their home congregations, which maintained their traditional patterns of worship but added Pentecostal-like elements, such as speaking in tongues and manifestations of spiritual gifts, including interpretation, prophecy, words of knowledge and wisdom, and divine healing. Two and a half million African Americans would label themselves charismatic.[13]

Since the 1980s, some have viewed neo-Pentecostalism and the consequent rise of black megachurches as among the most significant developments. Overwhelming growth in black Pentecostal spirituality has been among nondenominational charismatics and neo-Pentecostals, and formerly staid congregations that once eschewed any association with the "uncouth" emotionalism of the sanctified church adopted that spirituality as their own while maintaining their respective doctrinal distinctions. Though the total number of black neo-Pentecostals is hard to ascertain, historian Vinson Synan estimates that a third of mainline black churches have embraced this spirituality. Significantly, the majority of black mega-

---

[13]"Global Statistics," in *The New International Dictionary of Pentecostal and Charismatic Movements,* ed. Stanley M. Burgess and Eduard van der Mass (Grand Rapids: Zondervan, 2002), p. 287.

churches (those with over two thousand members) could be characterized as neo-Pentecostal.[14]

Within the racially segregated context of American Pentecostalism, the new religious movement at first offered a community in which the "color line" was "washed away in the blood."[15] Within a few years, however, alignments within the new movement generally reflected those within larger society, as white middle-class Pentecostal/charismatic believers tended to identify themselves with conservative causes, while black Pentecostal/charismatic believers tended to feel at home with more moderate political agendas.[16]

During the late twentieth century another phenomenon began to emerge within the movement, as African American Pentecostal scholars from within, or other scholars with an affinity for the movement, began filling the vacuum in knowledge by producing numerous articles and, less often, full-length manuscripts on various aspects of the movement over its one-hundred-year history. The majority of these works treat a single aspect or individual personality within the movement.[17] Nevertheless, the

---

[14]John Rivera, "A Shift in Their Focus for Black Churches," *The Baltimore Sun*, August 25, 2002, 1A.

[15]Bartleman, *How Pentecost Came to Los Angeles* (Los Angeles: Frank Bartleman, 1925), p. 54.

[16]See, Corwin E. Smidt, "'Praise the Lord' Politics: Social Characteristics and Political Views of American Evangelical and Charismatic Christians," *Sociological Analysis* 50, no. 1 (1989): 53-72; William Thompson, "Charismatic Politics: The Social and Political Impact of Renewal" in *Charismatic Christianity: Sociological Perspectives*, ed. Stephen Hunt, Malcom Hamilton and Tony Walter (New York: St. Martin's, 1997), pp. 160-83; Andrew Walker, "Pentecostal Power: The 'Charismatic Renewal Movement' and the Politics of Pentecostal Experience," in *Of Gods and Men: New Religious Movements in the West*, ed. Eileen Barker (Macon, Ga.: Mercer University Press, 1983), pp. 89-108; Scott Billingsley, *It's a New Day: Race and Gender in the Modern Charismatic Movement* (Tuscaloosa: University of Alabama Press, 2008).

[17]Notable among these are Douglas J. Nelson, "For Such a Time as This: The Story of Bishop William J. Seymour and the Azusa Street Revival, a Search for Pentecostal/Charismatic Roots" (Ph.D. diss., University of Birmingham, U.K.). This seminal work brought Seymour's contribution as the early leader of the movement to the light of Pentecostal scholarship. Iain McRobert's early work, *The Black Roots and White Racism of Pentecostalism in the USA* (New York: St. Martin's, 1988), specifically deals with the early and ongoing racial division within the Pentecostal movement. The excellent and much-quoted 1975 dissertation by James Shopshire, "A Socio-Historical Characterization of the Black Pentecostal Movement in America" (Ph.D. diss., Northwestern University), explores the social implications of early African American Pentecostalism. More narrow works such as William Turner, *The United Holy Church of America: A study in Black Holiness-Pentecostalism* (Piscataway, N.J.: Gorgias, 2006); Ithiel Clemmons *Charles Harrison Mason and the Roots of the Church of God in Christ* (Los Angeles: Pneuma Life Publishing, 2001); and David Michel, *Telling the Story, Black Pentecostals in the Church of God* (Cleveland, Tenn.: Pathway, 2000), all provide detailed historical informa-

story of African Americans' significant contribution to the formation, growth and shape of overall American Pentecostalism over its first one hundred years has remained largely untold.[18]

By the beginning of the twenty-first century, Pentecostalism had become the fastest growing segment of Christianity within the African American community, the United States and the world. Adherents to the Pentecostal-charismatic movement are estimated to number approximately 600 million worldwide, and yearly growth is estimated at approximately 12 to 15 million. Many of the world's largest congregations are found among Pentecostal denominations and independent groups. Among African Americans it is the second largest Christian tradition, following Baptist. By 2005 an estimated 15 million African American Christians would categorize themselves as classical (trinitarian or oneness) Pentecostals, neo-Pentecostal or charismatics.[19] The telling of their story cannot be completely accomplished in a few hundred pages. The most I can hope to do is lay out the contours of some of the most important people and organizations around which the movement has evolved.

---

tion about these respective Pentecostal traditions. Cheryl Townsend Gilkes, *If It Wasn't for the Women: Black Women's Experience and Womanist Culture in Church and Community* (Maryknoll, N.Y.: Orbis, 2001); and Anthea Butler's recent work, *Women in the Church of God in Christ: Making a Sanctified World* (Chapel Hill: University of North Carolina Press, 2007), both detail the significant contribution of women for both the Holiness and Pentecostal traditions.

[18]Two important works attempt to fill this void. Arthur E. Paris, *Black Pentecostalism: Southern Religion in an Urban World* (Amherst: University of Massachusetts Press, 1982); and Cheryl J. Sanders, *Saints in Exile: The Holiness Pentecostal Experience in African American Religion and Culture* (New York: Oxford University Press, 1996).

[19]"Gobal Statistics," p. 286.

2

"EVERY TIME I FEEL THE SPIRIT"

PENTECOSTAL RETENTIONS
FROM AFRICAN SPIRITUALITY

For as I was . . . considering the objects of your worship, I even found an
altar with this inscription: TO THE UNKNOWN GOD. Therefore, the One
whom you worship without knowing, Him I proclaim to you.

ACTS 17:23 NKJV

SHORTLY AFTER THE AZUSA STREET REVIVAL shifted into full gear, William Seymour invited his mentor and colleague Charles Parham to come and see for himself how the Lord was using his student to continue his vision for an end-time revival. Seymour expected that Parham would be excited that his vision of believers fully embracing the understanding of Holy Spirit baptism with tongues was being dynamically lived out, validating Parham's doctrine of initial evidence with proof that God was "pouring out His Spirit on all flesh." Seymour also believed that Parham would approve of God's marvelous use of his former student for this great outpouring. Parham, instead, was repulsed by what he saw as worshipers' scandalous, unrestrained and disorderly race-mixing and the "Africanisms" they displayed. The disturbing sight of white people freely associating with blacks and Latinos in "crude negroisms" sickened him;[1] and he left the revival, insisting that most of those claiming Holy Spirit's baptism were subject to no more than "animal spiritism."[2] He called the famous "heavenly choir"—the singing in tongues about which many raved—a form of "Negro chanting," declaring it had nothing to do with Pentecostal Spirit baptism.[3]

Other white religionists as well as members of the secular press echoed Parham's sentiments toward what he saw as "heathenish" elements. A *Los Angeles Times* article, for example, referred to speaking in tongues as "weird babel."[4] Leading white fundamentalist pastors, unsympathetic to both emotive worship and racial mixing, derided the revival in their sermons. One called it "a disgusting amalgamation of African voodoo superstition and Caucasian insanity."[5] Others used similar epithets to link its perceived strange behaviors to a variety of causes. Early mainline black religionists were no less caustic in critiquing the revival's "primitive" folk elements and condemned all forms of religious dance, including the ring shout, insisting that "many . . . old church goers still cling to these heathenish habits . . . thinking that the more noise and motion they have the better Christians they are."[6] Indeed, religious scholarship is replete with denigrating references to practices found in lower-class black religion. In *The Small Sects of America*, written forty years after the revival, Elmer Clark insisted that all African American worship (not derived from a white Christian tradition) was tainted by roots in African spirituality, characterizing emotive exercises, shouting, trances and bodily movements that blacks attributed to the Holy Spirit as "primitive traits."[7]

---

[1]Charles Parham, *Apostolic Faith* (Baxter Springs, Ks.: n.p., 1925), pp. 9-10, quoted in Robert Mapes Anderson, *Vision of the Disinherited: The Making of American Pentecostalism* (New York: Oxford University Press, 1979), p. 190.
[2]Charles Parham, "The Apostolic Faith," *The Apostolic Faith* 1, no. 8 (1912): 6.
[3]Parham, "New Years Greetings," *The Apostolic Faith* 1, no. 1 (January 1912): 6.
[4]"Weird Babel of Tongues: New Sect of Fanatics Is Breaking Loose; Wild Scene Last Night on Azusa Street; Gurgle of Wordless Talk by a Sister," *Los Angeles Daily Times*, April 18, 1906, p. 1.
[5]"New Religions Come, Then Go," *Los Angeles Herald*, September 24, 1906, p. 7, cited in Cecil M. Robeck, "The Past: Historical Roots of Racial Unity and Division in American Pentecostalism," *Cyberjournal for Pentecostal-Charismatic Research* 14 (2005) <www.pctii.org/cyberj/cyber14.html>.
[6]Joe M. Richardson, "Christian Abolitionism: The American Missionary Association and the Florida Negro," *Journal of Negro Education* 40, no. 1 (1971): 43.
[7]Elmer T. Clark, *The Small Sects in America* (Nashville: Cokesbury, 1949), p. 142.

These "negroisms"—shouting, dancing, jerking, Spirit possession, fall-ing, visions and trances—have been a part of black and white revivalistic worship for decades. Certainly, many behaviors identified as retentions (or survivals) were also found among predominantly white nineteenth-century camp meetings and the bodies that sponsored or grew out of them. The worship of the Great Awakenings—especially extraordinary meetings such as the Cane Ridge Revival—though largely led by whites, attracted blacks precisely because they exhibited behaviors common in African tra-ditional religion.[8]

Any discussion of African retentions within African American Chris-tianity must consider several mitigating factors that diminish our ability to discern direct connections between the traditions. First, there is no one African religious tradition, just as there is no single African culture. The vast continent of Africa is the second largest in the world, spanning 11,725,385 square miles. Then, as now, the continent had numerous dis-tinct political divisions and cultural systems. African people were further clustered by tribal affiliations, with significant variety in cultural develop-ment and worldviews. There are more than one thousand ethnolinguistic communities in black (sub-Saharan) Africa, each with its own sociocul-tural heritage, yielding various national, regional and religious traditions, from which New World expressions arose. Though the majority of slaves came from Africa's western coast—most from the Gold Coast (now Ghana), Sierra Leone, Benin and Dahomey—they also came from Cam-eroon, Gabon, Ivory Coast, the Congo, Angola, Mozambique and Mada-gascar. Each of these regions had unique cultural and religious traditions. When viewed holistically, however, these disparate traditions reveal com-mon elements that support a diverse yet generically African understanding of reality, which, at its root, is ontologically different from the Western or European worldviews slaves were thrust into.

Second, for a number of reasons, nothing from Africa survived the Middle Passage without substantial transformation. The social context of U.S. blacks demonstrated the least degree of African retentions of all the slaves imported into the New World.[9] Further, no segment of Christianity

---

[8]Richard D. Shiels, "America's Pentecost," *Cross Currents* 42, no. 1 (1992): 90.
[9]Melville J. Herskovits, *The Myth of the Negro Past* (Boston: Beacon, 1958), centered his study on the Caribbean and South America. Between 1619, when the first slaves were introduced onto

among African Americans in the United States displays direct importation of African spirituality as found in such Caribbean traditions as Haitian Vodun, Brazilian Contomblé or Cuban Santeria. The Spanish and French slaveholders who controlled the Caribbean were much more open to slaves retaining some form of their religious identity and were not adverse to expression of that spirituality or felt no need to replace it with a "purer" Christian spirituality.[10]

AFRICAN SPIRITUALITY

The disparate cultures that informed traditional African spirituality ensured that no one cohesive system of belief characterized the religion of all of Africa. Nonetheless, several threads ran throughout the African religious cosmos and found themselves in slave worship and in black religious life. These elements came through the Middle Passage embedded, in some shape, in the slaves' psyche to such a degree that decades of unimaginably inhumane treatment could not completely wipe them out, and attempts to divorce the slaves from "primitive" understandings of reality proved less than successful. Each of these elements—universal belief in a supreme being; a pervasive sense of the reality of the spirit world; blurring of lines between the sacred and profane; practical use of religion in all of life; surrender of excessive individualism for community solidarity; reverence for ancestors and their symbolic communal presence; greater involvement of women in ritual and community leadership; and creative use of rhythm, singing and dance in life and worship—has had implications for African American spirituality.

---

the mainland at Jamestown, Virginia, and 1865, when legal slavery was ended by the Emancipation Proclamation, twelve million black Africans were shipped to the Americas. The overwhelming majority were shipped to Brazil; less than six hundred thousand were transported to North America, though several hundred thousand were born here. This number was relatively small compared to those imported to the Caribbean and South America, with slaves within the United States representing only 5 to 10 percent of those brought to the New World. Individual U.S. plantations had relatively small numbers of slaves in comparison to those in other countries. The average number of slaves on U.S. plantations was twelve, while in Brazil, for example, the average number was one hundred. U.S. slave importation ended comparably early and the increase in that slave population was mainly through rapid reproduction. So, while growth in the U.S. slave population kept pace with growth in other regions, it did not involve newly captured peoples coming from the homeland with cultural identities still intact in their souls and spirits.

[10]Albert J. Raboteau, *Slave Religion: The "Invisible Institution" in the Antebellum South* (New York: Oxford University Press, 1978), pp. 87-89.

The slaves who came to the New World did not fit the usual definition of heathen—people totally uncivilized or irreligious. Rather, their religious heritage incorporated facets that would resonate with Christian faith. Among the most relevant was universality of belief in a supreme being—the Great Spirit or holy God. This God was not one among many or chief among equals, but rather the eternal Creator of every other being, including lesser gods created for his bidding, other spirits, the universe, humanity and every animate or inanimate creature that exists. As in the Judeo-Christian tradition, this transcendent Creator deity is sustainer and controller of the universe. This God is omnipotent, omnipresent, omniscient and sovereign.

As omnipotent, this supreme God originates and sustains all creation; every other thing that exists is subject to the one God. Any power exercised by another being, individual or community has its source in God and cannot be exercised without God's enablement. Since God is omnipresent, there is no need to erect buildings to confine worship. Everything God created is sacred, and worship can take place anywhere: at the mountain, at the river, beside a tree, because God's presence and majesty can be seen in these things. Western missionaries unfamiliar with this worldview generally mistook marvel at God's creation and apprehension of God within it as idolatry—worship of creation. Within African cosmology, however, God is not, pantheistically or panentheistically, part of everything. God's presence is in everything. God's omniscience is understood as possessing the highest possible level of wisdom, including knowing the secrets and intent of the hearts of men and women. Nothing is hidden from God. As sovereign God of the universe, the supreme God is not part of the pantheon of divinities but holds a position unique to himself. God is not an ancestor or chief among ancestors, but the "great other, beyond, yet at the center of, all human understanding and actions."[11] Not just a god of power and wisdom, this God is, most of all, a personal being, helping to defeat enemies and interjecting God's self into peoples' lives. God is known by the names Oladumare or Olorun among Yoruba in Nigeria, Imana in Rwanda, Onayeme or Nyame among Ghanaian Ahanti, and Mwari in Shona or Bantu.[12]

---

[11]Eunice Kamaara, "The Influence of Christianity on African Society's Concept of God," *African Ecclesiastical Review* 40, no. 1 (1998): 48.

[12]See, e.g., William A. Brown, "Concepts for God in Africa," *Journal of Religious Thought* 39, no. 2 (1982-1983): 5-16.

This supreme God is served by a host of lesser, immanent gods who function like the angelic realm in Western religious conceptions. They stand between God and the rest of created reality, mediating God's power to the world and doing God's bidding. They do not carry out their will but God's. Within this cosmology a personal devil is no less real than the supreme God and is associated with bad magic. There is no dualistic or polytheistic equality between the forces of good and evil, however. The devil's power is not equal to that of God, for the devil is a created being. While the devil is respected for his power, the ultimate mediator of justice remains the supreme God.

The African worldview is open to the supernatural in all of life. The African indeed prays for and expects God's necessary, supernatural intervention in all of life's affairs. All of life, therefore, is infused with both wonder and fear. No word exists for religion because religious affections permeate all other aspects of life. God is involved in all reality, and the line between service to God and the worldly or temporal is blotted out. All of life is sacred and has a religious element. For this reason Arthur Fauset's observation that to the casual eye the appeal of religion to the black person is as natural as the appeal of water to fish belies several misunderstandings about the black religious context.[13] Within this context the charge of animism needs to be reexamined. Africans do not worship nature as God; rather, God indwells all of nature. They do not worship the tree; the tree is a beautiful manifestation of God's handiwork to be deeply admired. They do not worship the lion; the majestic lion epitomizes the grandeur of God's creative power.

African spirituality infuses all of life with a ritual component. It is concerned with not only the well-being of the eternal soul but also the totality of life's experiences. Still, all religious practice contains a profanely secular element; nothing is done purely for the sake of ritual. Every ritual act has practical implications, and every secular, life-sustaining act has a religious aspect. God's name is invoked in everyday situations, not just reserved for worship, ritual or prayer. What white missionaries saw as taking God's name in vain was, for the African, invoking the name of God in the presence of lived reality.

Rugged individualism is strange to the African mind, which surrenders

---

[13]Arthur H. Fauset, *Black Gods of the Metropolis: Negro Religious Cults of the Urban North* (Philadelphia: University of Pennsylvania Press, 1970), p. 1.

individualism—excessive egoism—for solidarity with the community and all of nature. African intercourse is concerned with interrelationships between the individual, God, spirits, ancestors and the living community. Life centers on the entire society's needs, and sin is, first, that which breaches community—between the individual and God, family, tribe, nation and with the rest of creation. Each person is implicitly related to every other member of the community—the living and the dead, the animate and the inanimate. The well-being of the individual is intimately connected with the well-being of all of creation.[14] When any part of that connection is out of balance, broken or distorted, it does not bode well for the individual or community since "to be human is to belong to the whole community . . . participating in [its] beliefs, ceremonies, rituals and festivals."[15] The idea of covenant is taken seriously, and breaking covenant is an egregious sin. In keeping with the orality of the community, no formal written agreement is necessary. A spoken covenant is as good as a written contract. A person's word is his or her bond. Yet rituals and ceremonies are built around the making of covenant. Salvation within African traditional religion is a holistic concept. God, the creator of everything, is able to redeem everything. That redemption, however, relates as much to the present physical reality as to the afterlife.

Ancestor veneration—the real/symbolic presence of ancestors among the living to guide and inspire—is a central focus of African spirituality. Not every deceased person is venerated; only those whose morally exemplary lives have significantly contributed to the entire community's survival are given the honor. Expressions of veneration run from pouring memorial libation to prayers or sacrifices offered to particularly pious deceased in the belief that they may ascend to becoming minor deities. Within this continuum, distinctions between veneration and worship are not always clear. Worship ascribes deity to a being as the object of adulation, investing that being with salvific capacity, while veneration is reverential respect for a being because of their wisdom and dignity, without ascribing supernatural power except as that derived from a supernatural deity. Honor is given on behalf of the ancestor, not to the ancestor. Libation is poured for

---

[14]John Mbiti, "Christianity and African Culture," *Journal of Theology for Southern Africa* 20 (1977): 26.
[15]John Mbiti, *African Religions and Philosophy* (Oxford: Heinemann, 1990), p. 2.

the ancestor, not to the ancestor, understanding that "God will witness your action and accept it," and expecting that, "as you do for your parents, your children will do likewise for you."[16]

> The ancestors like all human beings have an essentially spiritual essence. They are not dead or annihilated, but are living spirits (not deities) who bind the present generation to the past, intermediating between the natural realm and God. Like the Catholic saints, they are intercessors. When prayer or libation is offered to them, the ancestors are not the end. These acts are offered to them so they can offer them to God. But there is no deification or divinization of ancestors in spite of whatever great role they played in society. Eponymous ancestors or clan-founders as well as tribal spirits are never mistaken for gods . . . never identified . . . with gods. Ancestors are . . . human spirits . . . from created human beings, and . . . limited in power.[17]

Ancestral beliefs act as social control to regulate the moral behavior of individuals as well as the entire community. Rites to honor ancestors, which take place in private settings such as meals or in large public religious ceremonies, remind the community of those collective traits that are esteemed. Their deeds are recounted through song, story, myth, folklore and proverbs; and the understanding that they are aware of one's actions restrains antisocial behavior.

While within the African cosmology, ancestor veneration serves as a source of restraint, music serves as a source of release. All of African life, and every ritual, is infused with music and rhythm—singing and dancing. Not to sing or dance is not to be African. Africans sing while they work, while they pray; they sing to give and receive instruction. Music is essential to the African spiritual reality. In the African context spirit possession occurs when the music is at its highest pitch; drumming, singing and dancing are most intense; and the participants become completely absorbed. The deities will not come unless they are implored. They will not come unless there is song and rhythm.

Dancing is as important as singing. African ritual is permeated with

[16]Karenga, M. *Kwanzaa: A Celebration of Family, Community and Culture* (Los Angeles: University of Sankore Press, 1997), pp. 80-81.
[17]Ignatius M. Zvarevashe, "Shona (Bantu) Traditional Religion," *African Ecclesial Review* 22, no. 5 (October 1980): 295.

dance. Africans dance not only for social gatherings; but they also dance in worship; they dance before going to war and to celebrate victory in war. No one is too young or too old to dance. Not just the feet and the legs, but every part of the body dances—the arms, the hand, the shoulders and the head. Just as the song does, the dance conveys the community's stories. Dancing, like almost everything else in African culture, is communal. It is an expression of the collective story. No one is purely a spectator; everyone has a role in the dance.

Everyone—both men and women—are part of all African ritual life. The cosmology of African traditional religion is less male dominated than the Western context. Women have been historically played a number of significant roles in African traditional religion. They were priestesses, performing sacerdotal functions in worship, including admonishing, praying and leading in the worship of deities. They have been called on as healers, especially when those experiencing sickness were other women or children.[18] Women have often maintained the sacred objects of African worship. Outside of formal worship, they have been prophetesses and seers given to visions that were used to guide community decision making. Gender has always had a different connotation within the African context. Each gender had a role to play; each has been important for the maintenance of the community and the community's religious tradition. There have been both male and female images of the one supreme God. And God has been identified with male and female names. God, unashamedly, has had male and female qualities.

SLAVE CHRISTIANITY

The Africans who came to the New World were as strange to their captors as their captors were to them. Many who later owned these men and women had never been in contact with an African and knew little of them as human beings. Though some had read descriptions of the people of the "dark continent," depictions of these exotic creatures were less than exemplary, casting them as savage heathens, illiterate and largely unteachable. Some depicted both men and women as voraciously sexual with inordinate libidos and lacking the requisite soul to be fully human receptacles for salvation.

---

[18]John Mbiti, "The Role of Women in African Traditional Religion," *Cahiers des Religions Africaines* 22 (1988): 76.

Though "Christian" slaveholders treated their slaves more humanely than others, slavery was dehumanizing.[19] Slaves were legally considered nonpersons, except when they committed crimes. An Alabama court asserted, for example, that slaves "are rational beings, they are capable of committing crimes; and in reference to acts which are crimes, are regarded as persons. [But] because they are slaves, they are incapable of performing civil acts, and, in reference to all such, they are things, not persons."[20]

At least at first, the recent arrivals retained much of their African spiritual sensitivities. Though slaves, they still believed in a supreme being who was vitally concerned about them and reigned over a spirit world that, at God's bidding, was able to assist them. They made little distinction between what was sacred and profane, for all of life held both elements; religion was a practical help in all of life, and all of life was religious. Their sheer survival depended on retaining community solidarity, and this very solidarity was threatening to slave masters. Reverence for ancestors and their symbolic communal presence was also considered a vital component of that survival. Music—rhythm, singing and dance—was an ever-present component of their lives. Their survival as a people demanded that the ablest among them—women as well as men—be involved in ritual and community leadership.

The slaves and masters saw contradictions in each others' religions. Missionaries and slaveholders misunderstood many of the ritual practices that the slaves incorporated into everyday life and critiqued the slaves as severely superstitious and resorting to ignorant and uncivilized conjuring and nature worship. Masters who ascribed reverence of the natural world to pagan witchcraft were threatened by practices perceived as giving slaves a sense of empowerment, potentially inciting them to aggressive, defiant behavior. Masters took pains to eradicate these practices and erase them from the slaves' individual and collective memory in order to keep them as docile as possible and to weaken the communal bonds so vital to African spirituality. Individuals were separated from those of the same culture,

---

[19]For a full discussion of the role that Christian faith played in the life of the slaves, see Gayraud Wilmore, "The Religion of the Slave" in Wilmore, *Black Religion and Black Radicalism: An Interpretation of the Religious History of Afro-American People* (Maryknoll, N.Y.: Orbis, 1993), pp. 1-28; and Raboteau, *Slave Religion.*

[20]Helen T. Catterall, ed., *Judicial Cases Concerning Slavery and the Negro* (Washington, D.C.: Carnegie Institute, 1926), p. 247.

language or dialect. Families were broken apart, and not only were husbands separated from wives but also parents, children and siblings were sold to different masters—sometimes on adjoining farms, sometimes several miles or states away.

While loathing the heathen tendencies they perceived in slave religion, slaveholders' doubts of the slaves' full humanity meant that the earliest masters made little attempt to convert their chattel. Moreover, some masters felt that if slaves were converted, they would have to treat them more humanely or be forced by conscience to free them.[21] Once masters began to acquiesce to slave conversion, the Christian religion served different purposes for them than for their slaves. For the master, it bolstered an economic system and way of life by providing a biblical warrant for slavery under the context of the God-ordained social order. Within that order the slave remained at the bottom to assure that the structure would be sustained.[22] According to Peter Paris, the Christianity offered to slaves had a fivefold utilitarian goal. White preachers used carefully selected passages (1) to teach slaves that the lot they endured was part of that order, (2) to admonish "biblical" obedience to masters, (3) to convince slaves their desire for freedom was a satanic temptation, (4) to convince them that patient diligence in work and punishment of laxity were within God's design, and (5) to exhort them that forgiveness for wrongdoing was in the hands of God and the master.[23] Masters were more interested in religious indoctrination as a civilizing measure for the temporal sphere than in evangelism that offered salvation and made the slave a spiritual brother or sister with an equal stake in eternal reality. In almost every sermon they attempted to entice slaves to patiently and humbly abide their present, God-ordained lot to ensure their future betterment, but such tactics did little to assuage emotional and spiritual angst over the present misery of slave existence.

For slaves the Christian faith was a source of comfort, providing affirmation of their dignity as children of the one supreme God while reinforc-

---

[21]For an excellent discussion of the religious context of the slaves, see Raboteau, *Slave Religion.*

[22]See, Elizabeth Fox-Genovese and Eugene D. Genovese, "The Divine Sanction of Social Order: Religious Foundations of the Southern Slaveholders' World View," *Journal of the American Academy of Religion* 55, no. 2 (1987): 211-33.

[23]See, e.g., Peter J. Paris, "The Christian Way through the Black Experience," *Word and World* 6, no. 2 (1986): 125-31; and Fox-Genovese and Genovese, "Divine Sanction of Social Order."

ing hope of either divine intervention in this life or a better existence and divine retribution in the life to come. They drew liberative elements from the biblical narrative and found comfort in the familiar African rituals that were played out in appropriations of that narrative that resonated with their status as captives in a strange land awaiting rescue by the great emancipator. Though early missionaries (who themselves were sometimes slaveholders) sought to placate audiences and make them malleable by holding out the promise of heaven for quietly and patiently enduring their humiliating lot on earth, objects of their evangelism were quick to discern inconsistencies in their conception of the Christian faith. They understood intrinsically what African American church people and scholars have often highlighted as the contradiction between the biblical Christianity that promotes equality of all humanity before God and the wanton disregard for black personhood encountered in their masters' definition of them as less than fully human.[24]

Some slaveholders, however, could see the humanity of their slaves and were genuinely concerned for their authentic spiritual needs. Yet early efforts by sincere Christians to convert slaves[25] met with only limited success since they employed an evangelism strategy focused on instruction by catechesis and slaves' acceptance of formal religious propositions. They also fell short because they failed to critique the system of enslavement so abhorrent to their hearers.[26] The slaves largely rejected this Christianity as disingenuous and rejected the God of the slave masters, who would condone their inhumane treatment, as a false god. It did not make it more attractive that whites contended that heaven would be as segregated as their earthly existence. While blacks would no longer be subjugated, they would not be housed in the same compartment as whites. There would be a Negro or "kitchen" heaven where slaves would be housed. Though it too would be glorious, it would be com-

---

[24]E.g., the Three-Fifths Compromise struck during the 1787 Philadelphia Convention between southern and northern states stipulated that three-fifths of the slave population would be counted for purposes of distribution of taxes and the apportionment of the members of the House of Representatives.

[25]Such as those of the Society for the Propagation of the Gospel in Foreign Parts, established by the Episcopal Church in 1701 to evangelize slaves and Native Americans.

[26]See, e.g., "250 Years of the SPG," *International Review of Mission* 40, no. 3 (1951): 331-36. The society itself owned slaves in the West Indies.

pletely separate from where whites would be lodged.[27]

Slaves did not wholeheartedly embrace the Christian faith in this form. Neither did they flatly reject it. Though they saw hypocrisy in their masters' distorted belief system that offered them a "loving" God who would subjugate them and denigrate their humanity, they gleaned kernels of truth they could hold to. For them the Jesus of the Bible was a different person than the harsh God the master declared required their subservience. This Jesus was as concerned about their welfare as that of the master. The God they embraced was an emancipator, like the God of their African faith, ready to deliver them from slavery's cruelties.

As in Africa, religion was an ongoing part of the life of the slaves, and they practiced it openly. Slaves stole away during their "free" time in brush arbors and fields to practice their "invisible religion," where, far from the master's disdaining eye, they could give vent to a deeper spirituality. These practices ensured that in spite of attempts of slave owners to suppress elements of traditional spirituality, many—such as openness to engagement of the supernatural, communal participation in ritual practices, reverence for ancestors, creative use of music and freedom for women to actively participate in ritual leadership—survived in the vivid memories of their psyches and reappeared in whatever context they found themselves.

Anthropologists, sociologists and historians have debated the significance of African survivals in black religion. In the famous Frazier-Herskovitz debate of the 1940s, renowned black sociologist E. Franklin Frazier contended that slavery destroyed any connection with an African past, stripping slaves of their social heritage so that African American culture developed independently of any of its influence.[28] White anthropologist Melville J. Herskovitz countered that there was cultural continuity from Africa to the New World, which influenced African American worship as well as the southern white camp meeting, instead of the converse.[29] Historian Carter G. Woodson, pointing out parallels between African belief systems and the Jewish background of Christianity exem-

---

[27]Lewis V. Baldwin, "A Home in Dat Rock: African American Folk Sources and Slave Visions of Heaven and Hell," *Journal of Religious Thought* 41, no. 1 (1984): 40.

[28]See E. Franklin Frazier, *The Negro Family in the United States* (Chicago: University of Chicago Press, 1939), pp. 3-15.

[29]Herskovitz, *Myth of the Negro Past;* John Blassingame, *The Slave Community: Plantation Life in the Antebellum South* (New York: Oxford University Press, 1972).

plified in parallels between African and Christian creation myths, suggested that there was so much affinity between African religion and the Christian tradition that slaves could relabel elements that had been practiced in Africa for centuries as Christian.[30] More recently John Mbiti agreed with Herskovitz that there are "parallels from the life of the African peoples who were cast into the Diaspora in the New World," and "in spite of their loss of languages and . . . traditional setting, African religion . . . remained in their blood."[31] His sentiments were echoed by historian John Blassingame, who contends that slaves hung on to their religion as a form of resistance, insisting that many of the earliest black ministers in the missions of the Baptist churches, for example, were former river-cult priests from traditional religions of Africa.[32]

Once masters overcame their reluctance to accept slaves into the Christian faith, they were determined to stamp out any vestiges of perceived heathen religions that might intrude into Christian worship. Under the watchful eye of the master or overseer, slaves mimicked the white Christianity of their owners and participated in emotionally restrained worship that made no room for elements they had retained within their bosoms. Attendance at the masters' worship services, however, was not their only religious involvement.

Survivals were so intricately woven into the psyche of the slaves that they found expression in whatever religious tradition the slaves attached themselves to, and later black leaders who objected to their presence and sought to imbue the black church with a measure of respectability took steps to eradicate them. These leaders put as much distance as possible between themselves and anything that would remind them and their white antagonists of a heathen past. In the North, independent African Baptists and Methodists patterned worship after the white churches they emerged out of. Richard Allen, founder of the African Methodist Episcopal Church, for example, denounced emotional displays in worship and took

---

[30]Carter G. Woodson, *The Negro in Our History* (Washington, D.C.: Associated Press, 1941), p. 35.

[31]John Mbiti, "God, Sin, and Salvation in African Religion," *Journal of the Interdenominational Theological Center* 16, nos. 1-2 (1988-1989): 60.

[32]Mbiti, "God, Sin, and Salvation in African Religion," p. 60; Melville Herskovitz, "Social History of the Negro," in *A Handbook of Social Psychology*, ed. Carl Murchison (Worcester: J. Clark, 1935), p. 256.

pains to ensure that emotive forms were excluded from the liturgy and worship of his nascent denomination.

Despite these contradictions, slaves resonated with much of the Christian faith. They were already open to belief in the supernatural, so evil spirits, the devil, angels and the Christian God made sense to them. Within slave culture, however, Christian faith existed side by side with other supernatural expressions, such as conjuring and magic. Further, while some slaves came to denounce traditional practices as evil, others embraced elements of both traditions—sometimes forming entirely new quasi-Christian traditions.

Conversion rituals paralleled communal rites of passage in African traditional society. Like these rituals, conversion was a communal affair, with both a private and a public element. Baptism paralleled African water rituals. The secretive and largely oral nature of slave religion means that little written detail of actual slave practices are extant. Fragments from slave narratives and oral histories of their descendents provide some indication of the content of that worship.

Music was a constant feature of slave religion, and the extraordinary repertoire of Negro spirituals attests to its significance. The slaves sang to communicate messages of hope and endurance to each other. They sang encoded messages of defiance against an unjust system of servitude. They sang to reassure each other of an ultimate emancipation from their dire situation. They sang to give and receive instruction. They sang to themselves (often silently) as they ran away. They sang for every occasion and about everything. Rhythm was an outstanding feature of slave music, and the drum was a central element in making that rhythm. The importance of this truth did not escape even the slave masters, who feared and outlawed drums in worship and social intercourse because of the perceived power their rhythm held over the slave. Where there was no drum, however, any item could be improvised to produce rhythm, a stump or bark from a tree, the ground, the floor of the praise house. And when there was no external rhythm the slaves sang in rhythm. Their bodies swayed, bowed and moved in every direction as if controlled by an inner mechanism that needed no outside source to keep in perfectly in step with the tenor of the moment and the situation.

In a largely oral religious tradition there was no Bible or holy books, no

Book of Common Prayer with written creeds and liturgies, no polity or hymnals to transmit the tradition and out of which to conduct worship.[33] Instead, salient elements were handed down the generations through verses of song, riddles, proverbs and even dance. For, as Joseph Washington asserts, "religion in African communities [was] written in the members' hearts, minds, histories [and] rituals."[34] This orality held important implications for the development and spread of Pentecostalism, which for most of its own history has been conceived of as largely an oral tradition. Even today the global Pentecostal movement has seen it greatest growth within cultures that incorporate an oral communication mode.

The extent to which masters went to squelch the teaching of slaves to read has been often overstated. Yet many slaves remained illiterate, semiliterate or at least unable to read their master's language. The slave's illiteracy or semiliteracy, however, did not reduce the importance of the "sacred book" within the community. Many black preachers learned long passages by heart. Those who could not read listened to those who could or from others who had committed passages to memory. But the stories they encountered there they reinterpreted and contextualized within their own struggle. The oral tradition of the African cult provided the slaves with a reliable means of communication. Some particularly gifted slaves were able to commit to memory entire biblical passages, sermons or hymns they had heard in white church services. The most gifted among them imbued these elements with remembrances from African culture or incidental anecdotes derived from their enslavement. What they crafted from these elements bore the unique character of slave sermons full of hope for ultimate emancipation, which they could repeat with embellishment to a gathering of their peers.

Prayer was another constant of slave religion, and slaves prayed about everything. They prayed for protection from the evil magic of the conjurer. They prayed for healing from the variety of physical, mental and emotional diseases afflicting them. They prayed for respite from the master's inhumane demands and the equally inhumane consequences of failing to meet even the harshest or most demeaning of these demands. In these

---

[33]Iain MacRobert, *The Black Roots and White Racism of Early Pentecostalism* (New York: St. Martin's, 1988), p. 11.
[34]Joseph R. Washington, *Black Sects and Cults* (Garden City, N.Y.: Doubleday, 1972), p. 25.

prayers they implored God to touch and soften the master's heart. Mostly they prayed for emancipation and that God would avenge the injustice they received at the master's hands. Many of the slaves' prayers were communal, very unlike the formal prayers of their masters. But there were also impromptu individual prayers throughout the day—long and short conversations with God about everything. Their songs were prayers, their communications with each other were prayers, their thoughts were prayers, and their moans and shouts were prayers; for the supernatural God was never perceived to be far away. And sometimes the prayer was only the invocation of the name of his Son—Jesus![35]

AFRICAN SPIRITUALITY WITHIN PENTECOSTALISM

By the time the Azusa Street Revival erupted in 1906, the blacks who made up a substantial portion of the congregation were similar to other descendents of slaves and heirs to three hundred years of harsh subjugation and discrimination that might have destroyed a lesser stock of people. Though, like the rest of the African American community, they had endured extreme hardship, they retained belief in one supreme God, whom they were convinced was involved in every aspect of their lives. They also retained an appreciation for the pervasiveness of the spiritual realities that surrounded them. For them religion was a mainstay, not just something one practiced in church on Sunday but the element that sustained their everyday life. Their communal solidarity was stronger than ever because the survival of the community depended on it. They still gave great honor to their forebears and retained a place for women in ritual and community leadership. And music was an integral part of who they were as a people, both in worship and in life. These individual elements of African spirituality can be singularly found in all African American Christian expressions.

Yet the constellation of these elements in African American Pentecostalism strongly ties that movement to its African roots, infusing it with a quality different in degree if not nature from other traditions that had often taken pains to distance themselves from such "heathenish" and uncouth roots. Contemporary scholars contend that not just black Pentecostals but also the entire American Pentecostal movement is influenced by

---

[35]For a deeper discussion, see James M. Washington, *Conversations with God: Two Centuries of Prayers by African Americans* (San Francisco: HarperSanFrancisco, 1995).

African spirituality through a common root in the experience of the Azusa Street Revival, since Seymour, the Azusa Street Revival leader and son of former slaves, and many of those who made up that early congregation were products of this heritage.[36]

James Tinney insists that the entire Pentecostal movement has roots derived from African sources and "thrives best among persons in the African Diaspora (or those who have come into contact with persons of African descent)."[37] For Tinney, the "truly African" nature of Pentecostalism is visible in worship style, philosophy of faith, practices and an organizational structure, embodying three specifically African themes: spirits, magic and eschatology.[38] Tinney saw the persistence of song, dance, percussion and tongue-speaking in Pentecostal worship as representing African spirituality[39] and tied Pentecostal theology, as primal as scholars might perceive it, directly to African philosophy.[40] Without linking Pentecostalism directly to Africa, Steven Land lists African American and Wesleyan spiritualities as the two most important spiritualities forming early Pentecostalism.[41] He suggests that the "spirituality of former slaves joined with the specifically Catholic spirituality of John Wesley to produce the movement's distinctive spirituality."[42] Specifically, Land contends that "[black] spirituality was the immediate mediator of [the Azusa Street Revival] in the person of William Seymour."[43] Alan Anderson concurs, "The African roots of Pentecostalism help explain its significance in the Third World today."[44] Walter Hollenweger asserts that the same orality that is foundational to African culture is a central characteristic of the Pentecostal spiri-

---

[36]Political scientist James Tinney, theologians Steven J. Land and Allan Anderson, missiologist Walter Hollenweger, and religionists Iain MacRobert and Roswith Gerloff see an African link to black Pentecostal spirituality, attempting to frame discussions that take this influence seriously.

[37]James S. Tinney, "The Blackness of Pentecostalism," *Spirit* 3, no. 2 (1979): 27.

[38]Ibid., p. 28.

[39]Ibid., p. 31.

[40]Ibid.

[41]Stephen J. Land, *Pentecostal Spirituality: A Passion for the Kingdom* (Sheffield: Sheffield Academic Press, 1993), p. 47.

[42]Ibid., 35.

[43]Ibid., p. 52.

[44]See Allan Anderson, *The Origins, Growth and Significance of the Pentecostal Movements in the Third World*, paper presented to the postgraduate seminar, University of Leeds, November 1997, http://artsweb.bham.ac.uk/aanderson/Publications/origins.htm.

tuality that sparked the movement's initial growth.[45] Iain MacRobert asserts that the common Pentecostal practices of rhythmic hand clapping, the antiphonal participation of the congregation in the sermon, the immediacy of God in the services and baptism by immersion are all "survivals of Africanisms."[46]

While turn-of-the-century mainline black churches denounced African survivals as uncouth and heathenish, the working- and lower-class people who filled Holiness and Pentecostal pews held on to these remnants, imbued them with Christian understandings and incorporated them into their lives and worship. They were unashamedly emotive and exuberant in their use of music and rhythm. They were open to supernatural encounters with God through the Spirit. And they understood all they did as somehow having sacred significance. Further, their unorthodox inclusion of all classes of people into their community and leaders, and specifically their inclusion of women at every level, was scandalous but very African.

The idea of sanctification in which every part of a person's being was set aside for God's use, not only in sacred ritual but in the mundane living of everyday life, resonated not only with the African blurring of the line between sacred and profane but also with the practical use of religion in all of life; and it made both the Holiness and Pentecostal movements attractive to blacks. Even more important, the God that Pentecostalism offered to blacks was the God of power who was intimately interested in their practical as much as their spiritual well-being. Within this realm, religion was much more than a Sunday-go-to-meeting experience. It permeated all of their mundane reality, imbuing it with since of sacred attachment.

AFRICANISMS AT AZUSA STREET

According to Douglas Nelson, whose seminal dissertation reintroduced Seymour as a prominent early Pentecostal leader, the Azusa Street pastor would not separate himself from the slave spirituality he experienced as a child in Louisiana.[47] Since the revival began only forty years after emanci-

---

[45]Walter J. Hollenweger, *Pentecostalism: Origins and Developments Worldwide* (Peabody, Mass.: Hendrickson, 1997), p. 23.

[46]MacRobert, *Black Roots and White Racism*, p. 29.

[47]J. Douglas Nelson, "Such a Time as This: The Story of Bishop William J. Seymour and the Azusa Street Revival, a Search for Pentecostal/Charismatic Roots" (Ph.D. diss., University of Birmingham, U.K., 1981), pp. 157-58.

pation, many blacks in attendance were former slaves or the children or grandchildren of former slaves. Those who had not experienced slavery personally inherited at least a reminiscence of the "invisible religion" from their forebears. Lucy Farrow, for example, born fifteen years before emancipation, had either been born as a slave or was sold into slavery. Though there is no detailed knowledge of her birthplace, mother Prince had been born during slavery. Julia Hutchins and J. A. Warren, other leaders in the revival, were from the same era.

Such openness to the Spirit of God and to an inclusive ecclesiology created scenes like those Parham encountered at the Azusa Street Revival and, without the interracial element, would characterize much of African American Pentecostal worship for decades. Certainly Parham's characterization of the meetings was colored by racial bias, but he was not the only critic who found the cultural undertones of the saints' behavior reprehensible. Secular periodicals pointed out similarities between worship at Azusa Street and pagan rites; religious critics specifically objected to certain aspects of the worship, which they compared to "heathen" ritual.

The most visible element African religion within the revival was its spiritual openness. People of every race, culture and age yielded themselves to intense engagement with the Spirit of God, which displayed itself in ways many other Los Angeles congregations would have considered strange. When the Spirit came, they danced the holy dance reminiscent of the ring shout, ran, jumped, fell, rolled and exhibited other physical gyrations. Men, women and children had trances and visions and spoke prophetic orations.

Just as in African spirituality, music was a constant in the revival. The saints sang the hymns of their Holiness forebears that told of expectation of the coming Spirit and testified to their newfound piety and fervor. But they also sang the Negro spirituals that had been fused from the meeting of African spirituality and Christian hope in the midst of continued discrimination.[48] But no longer under the master's whip or the threat of imminent harm or total deprivation of their rights and dignity, they imbued the spirituals with new meanings drawn from their experience of hope within this different but continued oppression. And they sang new songs

---

[48]Spirituals such as "Swing Low, Sweet Chariot" and "Ev'ry Time I Feel the Spirit," e.g., became a regular part of the African American Pentecostal repertoire.

given to them by the Spirit. They sang in known and unknown tongues. And when words were not enough to vent their spiritual longing or exhilaration, they hummed, moaned or yelled out wordless melodies. Such singing was always communal—African style. There was no robed, trained choir; there were no hymnals. The leader of the moment lined out the song and the congregation joined in antiphonal symphony. And that singing was accompanied by whatever instrument was on hand—tambourine, maracas or washboard.

Healing rituals took a variety of forms: anointing with oil, laying on of hands and praying over material objects, such as prayer cloths as points of contact for those in distress, paralleled the use of artifacts in African traditions. Christian faith healers took the place of medicine men and women, using perceived supernatural power for communal good. In both traditions neither sickness nor death was seen simply as a natural matter. They were given spiritual connotations. Demonic roots were often ascribed to physical, mental and emotional illness. Prayer was offered as much for deliverance from the forces of evil as for healing.

The unusually heavy involvement of women in the revival led some observers to characterize early Pentecostalism as essentially "women's religion."[49] While this is certainly an exaggeration, the prominence of women at Azusa Street drew from both biblical sanction and African cosmology. It was not just the involvement of women but also the freedom women were given to participate in every aspect of the worship and life of the congregation that harkened back to African sensitivities. Because of this, some of the earliest and harshest criticism of the revival and the movement was lodged at the openness showed to women—an openness much in keeping with African spirituality and communal life.

Indeed. Parham's and others' criticism of the revival noted elements that a non-African observer might have viewed as out of place with Christian propriety, such as the way in which men and women openly embraced each other or "inappropriately" approached each other to lay hands and pray for healing and deliverance. Women led, preached and exhorted the entire community. They gave prophetic utterances, spoke in tongues and

---

[49]Ethnographer Elaine Lawless is one scholar who uses this characterization; see her introduction to *God's Peculiar People: Women's Voices and Folk Tradition in a Pentecostal Church* (Lexington: University of Kentucky Press, 1988), p. 6.

interpreted, and prayed. But such openness to women's involvement was entirely consistent with African communal understandings that valued their contribution to the community. Ithiel Clemmons contends that it is exactly this characteristic communal aspect of African American spirituality that made the Azusa Street Revival so different from earlier evangelical revivals. He further contends that this communal sense (rather than speaking in tongues) even today makes Pentecostalism—especially African American Pentecostalism—so significant.[50]

AFRICANISMS IN DEVELOPING DENOMINATIONAL STRUCTURES

The uniquely African spirituality of Pentecostalism did not wane with the drawing to a close of the Azusa Street Revival. Instead, later black Pentecostal leaders picked up on the themes of this spirituality and incorporated them into to the fabric of the numerous denominations that developed over the course of the movement's one-hundred-year history. Some of these leaders were both deliberate and vocal in their support of African spirituality; others were less so, but not less resolute to incorporate elements of their heritage into their context.

Church of God in Christ (COGIC) founder Charles Harrison Mason was among the most adamant of the early Pentecostal leaders that black Christians needed to acknowledge their African heritage, and he took pains to provide biblical sanction for African rudiments in COGIC culture. Because of his passion, the denomination's worship continually exemplified a texture with as much foundation within African and slave religion as within Scripture—a distinction Mason found unwarranted. But Mason was not the only Pentecostal leader to openly embrace African spirituality. Though he and colleague Charles Price Jones were later to disagree on the necessity of glossolalia as evidence of Spirit baptism, Jones was as adamant as Mason about the importance of Africa in the heritage of black Christians. In 1902 he authored a volume of poetry, *Appeal to the Sons of Africa*, in which he recalled the linkage of U.S. blacks to the

---

[50]Ithiel Clemmons, "New Life through New Community: The Prophetic Theological Praxis of Bishop William J. Seymour of the Azusa Street Revival" (address delivered at Regent University School of Divinity, April 18, 1996).

motherland.[51]Another Holiness leader, William Christian, made explicit claims of African heritage and the value of African spirituality in the catechism of his denomination, the Church of the Living God (Christian Workers for Fellowship), going as far as asserting that "the saints of the Bible," including Jesus and David, "belonged to the black race."[52]

In 1915, William T. Phillips left the Methodist Episcopal Church to found the Ethiopian Overcoming Holy Church of God, expressing within the organization's name his pro-African sentiments. Though he was to later change the designation to reflect a more inclusive ecclesiology, Phillips's denomination earlier constituted itself as a religion to meet black folk's spiritual needs within the segregated American South. After World War I, Elias Dempsey Smith, founder of Triumph the Church and Kingdom of God, became enamored of Ethiopianism and Marcus Garvey's "Back to Africa" movement. In 1920, he made a pilgrimage to that nation, where he was given a traditional royal reception including a lavish banquet.[53]

Black Pentecostalism incorporates African use of music and rhythm as key experiences of worship. As with the slaves and at Azusa Street, music remains a constant, in individual performance and congregational singing, accompanying prayer and collection of the offering, and punctuating and emphasizing strategic points in the sermon. Kinetic spirituality—the body and movement—stands as a central symbol in both contexts.[54] Not to move (raising hands, clapping or swaying) in some visible way indicates that a person is not part of what the community is experiencing and signals a lack of spirituality; it gives evidence that he or she is an outsider and might be a candidate for conversion. The importance of rhythmic engagement in Pentecostal worship is inescapable.

One of the most persistent elements of African spirituality in Pentecostalism is dance. Dancing is conceived of as both a release of spiritual en-

---

[51]Charles Price Jones, *Appeal to the Sons of Africa: A Number of Poems, Readings, Orations and Lectures, Designed Especially to Inspire Youth of African Blood with Sentiments of Hope and Nobility as Well as to Entertain and Instruct All Classes of Readers and Lovers of Humanity* (Jackson, Miss.: Truth, 1902).

[52]"A Catechism: The Church of the Living God," www.mesacc.edu/~kefir/club/african_american /catechism.html. See also Walter Hollenweger, "A Black Pentecostal Concept: A Forgotten Chapter of Black History," *Concept* 30 (June 1970): 16-19.

[53]See a more detailed discussion of Triumph the Church and Kingdom of God in chap. 3, and of the Apostolic Overcoming Holy Church in chap. 6.

[54]John Wilson and Harvey K. Clow, "Themes of Power and Control in a Pentecostal Assembly," *Journal for the Scientific Study of Religion* 20, no. 242 (1981).

ergy and an invitation for the Spirit to take control of the worshiper. For where there is rhythm, there is the common element of dance. In one tract, Mason questions rhetorically, "Is it right for the saints of God to dance?" answering with a resounding yes and insisting that while shouting and the holy dance descended from the slaves' "ring shout," it is at the same time a true biblical form of worship.[55] Zora Neale Hurston, noted African American anthropologist, saw the significance of the influence of African spirituality in combined elements of openness to the Spirit and the creativity that shouting represents, commenting, "There can be no doubt shouting is a survival of African 'possession' by the gods . . . as a sign of special favor from the spirit that it chooses to drive out the individual consciousness temporarily and use the body for its expression."

Hurston further saw the communal importance of shouting within Pentecostal worship services, contending that "shouting is a community thing. It thrives in concert. It is the first shout that is difficult for the preacher to arouse. After that one they are likely to seep over the church. This is easily understood, for rhythm is increasing with each shouter who communicated the fervor to someone else."[56]

One of the most pronounced African retentions within the COGIC's worship remains the ceremonial healing ritual Mason promoted among the saints. Craig Scandrett-Leatherman points out that in both African spirituality and COGIC culture, health is both physical and social; restoration is enacted in corporate ritual that invests symbolic medicine with strong power to heal. While he concentrates on the important role plant and gourd roots played for Mason, the COGIC founder confirmed that many ritual healing practices begun at Azusa Street, such as laying on of hands, prayer cloths and anointing with oil, have as much referent in African traditional religion as in Scripture, and he unashamedly displayed his collection of healing roots, which he described as "mystical wonders of God."[57] Though criticized by some for bringing magic into the church by

---

[55]C. H. Mason, , "Is It Right for the Saints of God to Dance?" in *History and Formative Years of the Church of God in Christ with Excerpts from the Life and Works of Its Founder—Bishop C. H. Mason*, ed. James Oglethorpe Patterson, R. Ross German and Julia Mason (Memphis: Church of God in Christ Publishing House, 1969), p. 36.

[56]Zora Neale Hurston, *The Sanctified Church* (Berkeley, Calif.: Turtle Island, 1981), p. 91.

[57]Craig Scandrett-Leatherman, "The Cultural Roots and Multi-Cultural Mission of Afro Pentecostalism: Bishop Charles Harrison Mason, Slave Religion in His Heart and Roots on His Desk" (paper presented to the thirty-fifth annual meeting of the Society for Pentecostal Studies,

using these tactics, Mason consistently insisted that COGIC spirituality keep its allegiance to African and slave religion intact and prominent.

Though the early involvement of women in all levels of Pentecostal ministry and the distinctive COGIC structure for ministry roles of men and women may be seen as inconsistent with each other, both are structural elements within African spiritual systems. Following the Azusa Street model, many early Pentecostal bodies gave women almost complete freedom to carry out a variety of ministries in the local congregations, in evangelistic work throughout their surrounding communities and on the mission field. The COGIC's stratified structure of gender-related functions with a dual yet parallel political system gave women a measure of power within ritual settings and church governance. Within both the COGIC and the broader Pentecostal movement, older women enjoy a measure of reverence, afforded by the title church "Mother," and are vested with political status and (private) veto powers as well as significant economic control.[58]

THE PERSISTENCE OF AFRICANISMS IN PENTECOSTAL WORSHIP

Though the Azusa Street Revival and the COGIC are perhaps the most visible examples of African retentions within Pentecostal worship, the influence of African spirituality can be found throughout the one-hundred-year history. The orality and communal essence of African spirituality resonates in the call-and-response communication of preaching and gospel singing. Tinney points to parallels between black Pentecostal and other expressive preaching and the African tradition of the "griot." Characteristics of the black sermon such as antiphonal structure in which the preacher and audience form a joint choir, with the preacher becoming the lead singer and the congregation the chorus are more pronounced within Pentecostal worship. The longer and louder the preaching goes on, the more the audience talks back, and the rhythm of the preaching forms a cadence of its own.

African American Pentecostalism remains a communal affair. Testimony and tarrying services, congregational singing, preaching (the antiphonal call and response) are all a part of that communal tapestry. No

Fuller Theological Seminary, Pasadena, Calif., March 25, 2006).
[58]Ibid.

one testifies alone. Though one person has the floor, the entire congregation is involved. Pentecostal testimony service parallels the African practice of storytelling by the griot. Testimonies are not just my testimony of what God has done for me but also our testimony of what God has done for us—in our family, our church, our community and our history. They are the testimony of how God, through the centuries, has brought deliverance, as he did the children of Israel in Egypt and as he did in bringing a remnant through the middle passage, as he delivered us from slavery and from the Jim Crow experience in America. The biblical narrative is often woven into the telling as if it were the story of the speaker. For to claim their experience is to make it the experience of the congregation. That testimony is supported by "amens" and "hallelujahs" affirming that the story that is being delivered is not a singular story but a corporate one. It affirms both the universal experience of oppression as well as the universal hope for deliverance.

Communal feasts are a regular part of the church year, not only reserved for special occasions or times of the year. In keeping with the African sensitivities, there is a practical and spiritual element to communal meals. While inexpensive dinners served after Sunday worship service often provide necessary income for the congregation and respite for the faithful who have toiled all week and still "pressed their way" to church on Sunday, they are a time for the saints to gather and fellowship.

The most common act is infused with a sense of community, ceremony and celebration in which color as much as music plays a significant role. This too has both sacred and practical implications, and has both ritual and social import, serving as a reminder of heritage and signaling who is truly part of the community. White, the symbol of holiness and purity, is employed on a number of occasions—communion, baptisms, women's day and funerals. Other colors such as purple, denoting royalty, or blue have their own particular significance.

Even the shout takes on a communal aspect as brothers and sisters dance alongside the person shouting in the Spirit, upholding him or her physically while affirming the spiritual reality of the experience. Harvey Cox insists that "there is an irony is all of this. The very features that Parham . . . anathematized at Azusa Street—the trance, the ecstasy of the 'colored camp meeting,' the interracial fellowship—were precisely what enabled Pentecostalism to speak with such power in the 20th century."[59] The sense of the sacredness of all of life and of everything in life allows Pentecostals to embrace, utilize and enjoy rhythm in every arena, and to incorporate that rhythm as part of the worship of God through use of a variety of instruments that others may have deemed inappropriate. According to Hurston, the observation that "all black music is dance music" finds a parallel in the understanding that every instrument could be employed in worshiping God—the drum, the horn, the washboard, the tambourine."[60] Furthermore, all of one's body, including the dancing feet, is a sacred vessel of praise.

With the dance, the tarrying ritual brings the communal structure and "dynamic pneumatology" of the ring shout into Pentecostal worship. These join emotions with posture to produce a primal mode of prayer not usually fully enacted within a congregation's most public venues. Instead, both the shout and tarrying are given fullest expression in more intimate settings hidden from the purely curious and reserved for the initiated, true believers.[61] Tinney vividly describes the tarrying process:

> The seeker prays, loud and long as hard and as fast as he can to get this power. He sweats and cries and screams and physically throws himself, demanding that God do what he wants. He commands the power of God as his own. It is a violent scene—one which is carefully hidden from the casual visitor.[62]

In tarrying, the seeker approaches God through the repetition of specific words—"Jesus, Jesus, Jesus, Jesus," or phrases—"Thank you, Jesus; Thank you, Jesus; Thank you, Jesus; Thank you, Jesus" in rapid succession, to the point of exhaustion. This unifying experience was familiar to most blacks who were part of the Pentecostal movement prior to the advent of the less formal structures of the charismatic movement.[63]

---

[59]Harvey Cox, *Fire from Heaven: The Rise of Pentecostal Spirituality and the Reshaping of Religion in the Twenty-First Century* (Reading, Mass.: Addison-Wesley, 1995), p. 100.

[60]Hurston, *Sanctified Church*, p. 103.

[61]David Daniels provides an important discussion of the import of the tarrying ritual with COGIC worship in "Live So God Can Use Me," *Asian Journal of Pentecostal Studies* 3, no. 2 (2000): 299-301.

[62]Tinney, "A Theoretical and Historical Comparison of Black Political and Religious Movements" (Ph.D. diss., Howard University, 1978), pp. 239-40.

[63]Daniels, "Live So God Can Use Me."

Though adherents would not name it as such, Scandrett-Leatherman saw that such a "foreign" element as ancestor veneration within Pentecostal worship was essential for connecting the traditions.[64] Founders of local congregations or entire denominations are specifically venerated, and their claims of specific revelation in dreams and visions hold a sacred place among present and future generations. Elaborate portraits or even statuary of long-deceased founders grace vestibules of the most modest sanctuaries like the portraits of saints in a Catholic chapel or artifacts of ancestors in African ritual. Throughout the year, narrative exploits are invoked in hagiographies that are recited on numerous "special" occasions. Their songs, no matter how esoteric, are given special reverence in congregational singing. Annual founder's day festivities celebrate their contributions. Parishioners listen intently to the retelling of how the Lord spoke to Bishop So-and-So, telling him (or her) specifically where, when and how to start the church and giving him promises of success. The sacrifices of these leaders, the persecution they endured and the victories they won remind the congregation of their collective past and destiny. Recalling their exploits reengages these men and women in the ongoing life of the community as speakers recount, "I remember, when I heard Bishop preach, and surrendered my heart to God," or "If Bishop were here, he would admonish us to hold on."

Practical elements of veneration are evident in the honorary designation "temple" that enshrines the memory of founders of so many Pentecostal edifices and congregations.[65] More than the name, the very places founders graced become important. A brochure from the 2007 COGIC convocation, for example, declares that "with exuberant praise and spirit-filled worship, the sounds of Pentecost will fill the air as saints stand on the sacred ground of their forefathers in witness to the faithfulness of God."[66]

Veneration is shown to living elders in episcopal systems that allow pastors and bishops to remain in places long after they have passed the usual

---

[64]Scandrett-Leatherman, "The Cultural Roots and Multi-Cultural Mission of Afro Pentecostalism."

[65]While Mason Temple in Memphis, for example, honors the name of the COGIC founder, several other congregations in major cities, including Norfolk, Kansas City, Milwaukee and Tulsa, and small towns such as Conway, South Carolina; Bartow, Georgia; and Altheimer, Arkansas, carry the same name.

[66]Church of God in Christ convocation brochure, 2007.

age of retirement and when they are, sometimes, unable to function at full intellectual capacity. Special gifts of money are often given in tribute and congregants vie for the honor of making the largest contribution. But in even more simple ways, elders speak first and are afforded greater authority and honor than younger community members. The special designation of older women as church mothers and older men as deacons is also a reflection of the same African sensitivities. Such respect finds additional biblical warrant in instructions to "give honor to whom honor is due" (Rom 13:7) as well as Old Testament Wisdom literature which suggest that special reverence is due to God's prophets and those elderly members of the community who exhibit great wisdom.[67]

DISTINCTIONS FROM AFRICAN TRADITIONAL RELIGION

The parallels found in African religions and black Pentecostalism should not obscure what Pentecostals claim as biblical authenticity in their worship. Blacks were attracted to certain practices because they resonated with familiar elements of traditional religion, but they understood these as being part of the early Christian tradition and saw them as supported within Scripture.

The experience of spirit possession is an excellent example of such distinction. The phenomenon runs through both traditions; the idea of possession by the gods, spiritual power and spirit baptism is older than Christianity itself and is a central theme in religious experience throughout the Diaspora.[68] Pentecostal understandings of Holy Spirit baptism differ, however, from the understanding of spirit possession in African traditional religion. In African spirit possession, participants seek to restore the disrupted community to a state of harmony. The goal is restoration to the past order of things.[69] Spirit possession in African traditional religion denotes being controlled by the ancestors, secondary spirits or lesser gods—not possession by the high God, who is essentially other, ultimately transcen-

---

[67]See, e.g., Leviticus 19:13 and Proverbs 23:22.

[68]Archie Smith Jr., "Reaching Back and Pushing Forward: A Perspective on African American Spirituality," *Theology Today* 56, no. 1 (1999): 44-58; Cheryl J. Sanders, "African-American Worship in the Pentecostal and Holiness Movements," *Wesleyan Theological Journal* 32, no. 2 (1997): 105-20. Sanders points out that "Spirit possession is an important feature of virtually all the diasporic religions of New World Africans" (p. 114).

[69]Hurston, *Sanctified Church*, p. 63.

dent and removed from mundane matters of life. Within the former, possession is by a lesser god, since the high God is completely transcendent and inaccessible.[70]

Pentecostals contend that God's Spirit powerfully indwells personal and communal life, and intervention of the sacred is expected and sought—rather than cajoled—to create a new individual and community. The Spirit is made manifest, and its glory reveals something essentially other. What separates the African American Holiness and Pentecostal tradition from the purely African spirituality, however, is belief that the possessing spirit bears the exclusive identity of the Holy Spirit—the third member of the Trinity. Possession by the Spirit is openness to God as one comes to share in the ultimate reality who is still essentially other in a personal and intimate way.

The Pentecostal faithful insist that there is a qualitative difference between their experience of being "possessed by the Spirit" and the traditional experience of being "spirit possessed." For them, when a man or woman is possessed by the Spirit, an encounter with the ultimately sacred is expected and sought; the goal is rebirth, regeneration and renewal.[71] Unlike the understanding of traditional religion, the sacred does not mount those affected; there is still distance between the subject and the object. In African traditional religion, to be possessed by the Spirit implies merger of the sacred and the profane. In the Pentecostal experience of Holy Spirit baptism, the Spirit is always still the Spirit of God. The liminal state that results from such baptism brings with it a sense of empowerment but never results in a merging of the self with ultimate reality.[72]

Early Pentecostals saw the Holy Spirit not just taking possession of individuals but also of the entire community. No greater assessment could be made of a worship service than that the Holy Ghost "took control." Testimony after testimony of this phenomenon poured into the *Apostolic Faith*, the periodical that the Azusa Street Mission staff began publishing in

---

[70]Ibid., pp. 61-63.
[71]For a discussion of understandings of possession by the Spirit within African American Pentecostalism, see Annette Beverly Collins, "African American Pentecostalism as an Ecstatic Movement" (D.Min. thesis, University of Chicago, 1996).
[72]See, e.g., Bobby Alexander, "Correcting Misinterpretations of Turner's Theory: An African-American Pentecostal Illustration," *Journal for the Scientific Study of Religion* 30, no. 1 (1991): 26-44.

1906, such as one telling of how "one afternoon the Holy Spirit took possession of the meeting and set aside the program, giving freedom to all
who had received their personal Pentecost to witness and speak or pray in
tongues."[73] Yet black Pentecostals understood intrinsically, as James Cone
insists, that the "divine Spirit" who descends on them "is not some metaphysical entity but rather the power of Jesus who breaks into the lives of
the people giving them a new song to sing in confirmation of God's presence with them in historical struggle."[74]

Importantly for Pentecostals, with possession comes power. Believers
cast Holy Spirit baptism as "a gift of power on the sanctified life" and an
empowerment for service. Either the Holy Ghost "came in mighty power"
to a congregation, the power came upon a person, or they came under the
power. In any case, those involved would testify that they themselves were
left powerless, that is, unable to function under their own strength. This
was power to preach more effectively, thwart the plans of the devil, evangelize and triumph over sinful habits.[75] The saints never equivocated about
the source of that power. They were clear; this was no nebulous encounter
with some ephemeral essence. "We only have power with God through
Jesus. He puts the Spirit in us that He might recognize Himself. . . . All
we get from God we get through Jesus."[76]

The Pentecostal attempt to tap into and harness spiritual power for the
good of the individual and the community finds direct parallels in African
religion. The African worldview that lay at its roots provided openness to
the supernatural. But it also provided a strong critique of the heavily rational
post-Enlightenment Christianity of the white church. Given that worldview, it was problematic to black Pentecostals that the white church could
not see the ethical contradiction in the biblical imperative to love our neigh-
bor as ourselves and the holding of an entire class of men and women first in
chattel slavery and then in Jim Crow conditions that stripped them of their
dignity and nullified their right to live as authentic, free human beings.

The experience of trance, closely tied to the experience of being possessed by the Spirit as a mechanism for communicating with and receiving

[73]"From Other Pentecostal Papers" *Apostolic Faith* 1, no. 8 (1907): 3.
[74]James H. Cone, "Sanctification, Liberation and Black Worship," *Theology Today* 35, no. 2 (1978): 139-40.
[75]"Questions Answered" *Apostolic Faith* 1, no. 11 (1907-1908): 2.
[76]"Prayer," *Apostolic Faith* 1, no. 12 (1908): 4.

from God, is another parallel with African religion. One testimony in the *Apostolic Faith* declared,

> I wanted to pray but the Lord tied my mouth. The power began to come in waves. The Lord took full possession. I fell over like a dead man. I was dead to the world. I tried to pray while lying on the floor, but when my tongue was loosened, it was in a different language. . . . Jesus had come to me.[77]

CONCLUSION

The earliest Pentecostals stood only a generation and a half away from slavery, with the psychic remembrance of slave religion lodged in their souls. Despite Parham's protestations of animalisms, the tendency of both some white Pentecostals and mainline black religionists to dismiss suggestions of ties to African spirituality and deliberate efforts of upper-class blacks to conform black worship styles to that of the "more dignified" white congregations they had left, the spirituality of the African sacred cosmos has persisted for over one hundred years of the movement's history. It can be found most openly in the lower-class storefront congregations of inner cities and metropolitan suburbs, but it also exists within large congregations throughout the country. The very elements early black church leaders had attempted to repress—the shout, possession by the Spirit, emotive worship—rang true to the blacks who found their way to early Pentecostal meetings and attracted them to a way of being that allowed them to tenaciously hold on to their ancestors' "old time religion."

While Hurston astutely saw the rise of the sanctified churches in America not as the beginning of a new religious movement but as older forms of black religions reasserting themselves against the new modern realities,[78] ultimately, no direct link can be made between African American Pentecostalism and African traditional religion. Yet survivals from the slaves' religious experience and their descendents through the centuries, which were played down by respectable black religionists, rebounded as vital elements in black Holiness and Pentecostal worship. Conversion to Christianity did not force people to shed their traditional religiosity and go naked into their new religion. Rather, it allowed them to incorporate

---

[77]Untitled item, *Apostolic Faith* 1, no. 5 (1907): 1.
[78]Hurston, *Sanctified Church,* p. 103.

that African worldview, culture and spiritual identity into a new religious context. For them, as for their Africans ancestors, the biblical world was not a two-thousand-year-old historical reality but a world of yesterday, today and tomorrow.[79]

The same African spirituality that retained a place for itself in slave worship and community survived attempts by masters and more elite black religionists to destroy its vestiges from the slaves' psyche and was retained in whatever new Christian form they created—including Pentecostalism. These conditions within the North American context did not provide the same context for full adoption of African spirituality as could be found in the more welcoming Caribbean and South American religious climate, which bred quasi-Christian and new forms of religion. It was precisely the African spirituality of recently emancipated people, however, that was open to such a phenomenon as tongues speaking and Spirit possession, as well as more pragmatic dimensions of communal worship and more egalitarian structures that are the hallmark of African American Pentecostalism. Finally, as Roswith Gerloff contends, after all is said, these "non-white or African derived movements are simply closer to the New Testament narrative and the pattern of thought within the Bible than are many European interpretations of doing theology after Christopher Columbus."[80]

---

[79]John Mbiti, "God, Sin, and Salvation in African Religion," p. 60.
[80]Roswith Gerloff, "The Holy Spirit and the African Diaspora: Spiritual, Cultural and Social Roots of Black Pentecostal Churches," *EPTA Bulletin: Journal of the European Pentecostal Theological Association* 14 (1995): 85.

3

SAVED AND SANCTIFIED

THE LEGACY OF THE NINETEENTH-CENTURY BLACK HOLINESS MOVEMENT

May the God of peace Himself sanctify you entirely; and may your spirit and soul and body be preserved complete, without blame at the coming of our Lord Jesus Christ.

1 THESSALONIANS 5:23 NASB

MORE THAN FIFTY YEARS BEFORE the Azusa Street Revival, language of sanctification and baptism in the Holy Ghost came into prominence as Christians in the United States and Europe who had been enamored of the spiritual piety and fervor of early Methodism and the Great Awakenings attempted to recapture that bygone religious passion. The earliest Holiness rousings echoed throughout existing congregations as enthusiasts attempted to import revivalist piety into flocks that they perceived had grown cold with the cares of the world. Finding less than wholehearted acceptance for their sentiments in their home congregations, many "come outers" left established denominations to form associations that promoted camp-meeting-style revivals where the faithful gathered, sometimes for weeks at a time, to hear heartfelt sermons, sing fervent choruses and experience the physical manifestations that they felt signaled God's imprimatur on sanctified lives.

The interracial fellowship that African Americans found in Holiness worship was different from what they encountered in everyday life. It provided respite from the racism of their surrounding communities and a platform for black itinerant preachers and laypersons to ply their ministries, often among largely white audiences. The eager faithful gathered regularly to hear enthusiastic messengers of either race exhort them on the beauty of holiness and encourage them to live the sanctified life. Outside these gatherings, however, existing racial mores prevailed, and the social intercourse between brothers and sisters so welcomed and celebrated in worship services were less than acceptable. Moreover, where Holiness proponents dared cross racial barriers in worship, they met with derision, threats and even violence, which sometimes caused them to back away from their interracial experiment. And, convinced that sanctification should bring a change in social consciousness in as well as outside the sanctuary, blacks began to form their own Holiness bodies.

Though often lumped under the rubric "sanctified church," black Holiness and Pentecostal bodies primarily share similarities in piety, language and starting points that revolve around three related expectations—sanctification, divine healing and a life a personal piety. "Entire sanctification" or "Christian perfection" was understood as the act of God, subsequent to regeneration, by which believers were made free from original sin, or depravity, and brought into a state of perfect love toward God. Labeled the second of three stages of salvation—or the "second blessing"—it was understood to follow new birth and precede baptism in the Holy Spirit, providing believers with victory over intentional or voluntary sin.

The notion of sanctification was not foreign to Methodist and Baptist believers, who saw it as a state that unfolded over the entire life span of a few exceptional Christians who would invest the spiritual energy to engage in protracted periods of prayer, focused Bible reading and generous amounts of good works. Holiness proponents, however, believed the experience to be available to every believer who earnestly yearned for it, claiming it as act of grace poured out without partiality on the spiritually hungry. Factions within the movement differed on whether sanctification was instantaneous, progressive or both. But all understood that as a result of sanctification, the believer would be able to live a life reflecting a higher moral character—essentially free of all voluntary sin.

For Holiness believers, divine healing was held as a benefit of the atoning work of Christ. And, while moderate Holiness believers held that all illnesses could be healed, radical leaders went as far as teaching that true believers had no need for conventional medicine but could completely trust in prayer and faith as a cure for even the most serious conditions. Several were willing to follow that conviction to the point of death.

The life of personal piety was lived out in obedience to a set of holiness codes that governed most aspects of a believer's personal and private life. The faithful lived by proscriptions on appropriate dress for saints (especially for women), acceptable and unacceptable social activities, marriage and family life, and even acceptable occupations as they attempted to achieve that piety. The penalties for breaching these proscriptions were severe and included silencing the violators within a congregation or community, and even possible excommunication.

As the movement evolved, the language grew to include the notion of baptism of the Holy Ghost. This deeper experience of God further purified the believer and endued him or her with the power to sustain the benefits of sanctification so that one could live a consistent life of holiness and boldly engage in the work of the Lord with more boldness and power. But Holiness believers stopped short of demanding that Holy Spirit baptism had to be accompanied by any external evidence. Though many, especially African American, leaders did not deny the desirability of such an experience, they quickly pointed out that not every believer would receive it. Unlike their later Pentecostal siblings, they were equally insistent that there was no distinction in the spiritual maturity of those who had spoken in tongues and those who did not.[1] Both of these movements draw from the common heritage of the earlier revivalistic fervor of the First and Second Great Awakenings.

BLACKS AND THE GREAT AWAKENINGS

In the years immediately following the Civil War, the religious climate of America evidenced fervor unmatched in the young nation's history. It touched every strata of society but was most evident among the working class and poor, including the newly freed slaves who searched for spiritual

---

[1]See, e.g., Charles Price Jones, *The Gift of the Holy Spirit in the Book of Acts* (Chicago: National Publishing Board, Church of Christ [Holiness] U.S.A., 1996), originally published in 1903.

succor amid dire social conditions. Impoverished and still subject to discrimination and disenfranchisement, black Americans found little other resources to sustain them through such challenges.

These were not the first fervent spiritual stirrings that resonated with blacks, however. In the late seventeenth and early eighteenth centuries, Puritan preachers such as Cotton Mather and John Elliot targeted blacks for conversion. The First Great Awakening (1730-1760) began in the North, largely among Congregationalists, Presbyterians and Baptists. From there, evangelistic efforts pushed the revival into the South, bringing with it an emphasis on the power of immediate, personal religious experience and preaching that relied on emotional appeals aimed at convincing hearers of their personal guilt before God and need of repentance rather than on eliciting intellectual assent to ethical propositions.

Though one of its most renowned preachers, Jonathan Edwards, owned slaves, he was the first minister at Northampton, Massachusetts, to baptize black people and admit them into full membership. Many blacks were converted under his preaching, which held out the promise of a degree of personal liberty. But this "liberty" was not social or political liberty on a par with that of whites. Rather, it was solely spiritual. Edwards agreed with other New Englanders of his day that adult blacks and Native Americans had innate capacities only slightly more developed than children. Black people flocked to hear the message of salvation, becoming converts in record numbers. From 1735 to 1741, Edwards baptized eleven blacks. Eventually, seven of these, along with three others, were admitted to full membership in his congregation.[2] Yet this awakening began shattering socioreligious barriers, as a few white women and free black people were allowed to shed their subordinate social status long enough to exhort religious gatherings. Once converted, slaves as well as free black people were able to take an active part in the services as exhorters and preachers.

The practical outworking of the Calvinist understanding of predestination fit with the institution of slavery, holding that while all might have a sinful nature, some (blacks) were predestinated by God to be slaves, while others (whites) were predestined to be masters, and nothing could change that situation. In a religious sense, though Edwards understood that both

[2]For a discussion of Edwards's view of slaves, see Kenneth P. Minkema, "Jonathan Edwards' Defense of Slavery" *Massachusetts Historical Review* 4 (2002): 23-59.

blacks and whites were equally in need of salvation, the quality of salvation offered them was inherently different. For him, the hierarchical social order divinely imposed on this world would also be strictly observed in heaven. There would be different "degrees of glory" for whites and blacks.[3]

George Whitefield, a colleague of John and Charles Wesley, emerged from within the Great Awakening preaching a fervent salvation message while affirming slavery and contending that it was not sinful or immoral. Still, Whitefield decried harsh treatment of slaves by some masters and exhorted his followers to treat them more humanely but sanctioned the institution as an economic necessity and means of introducing blacks to salvation. In 1749, he supported the introduction of slavery into Georgia, a state where it had previously been prohibited, and later used slaves to run an orphanage in that state. Still, his preaching among blacks was highly effective, and his campaigns made many black converts.[4]

Seventy years later, at the height of the American slave trade, the revivals of the Second Great Awakening attracted black people because the emotive style resonated with their African spiritual heritage and because of the multiracial worship, in which some revivalists openly agitated against slavery. Yet again, openness to spiritual inclusiveness did not always translate into social inclusiveness. For example, famed revivalist Charles Finney opposed slavery, arguing on the one hand that regeneration and oppression of one's brothers were inconsistent. On the other hand, he did not promote racial equality, cautioned against using radical and inflammatory language, and did not see abolition and segregation as incompatible.[5]

The racial implications of the Second Great Awakening—its abolitionist sentiments and emphasis on emotive, ecstatic religion—dramatically affected the spirituality of both slave and freedman. Preachers of the Great Awakenings did not share early slave master's convictions that blacks

---

[3]Jonathan Edwards, "The Miscellanies," in *The Works of Jonathan Edwards*, ed. Kenneth P. Minkema et al. (New Haven: Yale University Press, 1997), 13:437-39.

[4]Two works that discuss Whitefield's views and practices regarding slavery are Arnold Dallimore, *George Whitefield: The Life and Times of the Great Evangelist of the Eighteenth Century*, vol. 2 (Edinburgh: Banner of Truth Trust, 1980); and Edward J. Cashin, *Beloved Bethesda: A History of George Whitefield's Home for Boys, 1740-2000* (Macon, Ga.: Mercer University Press, 2001).

[5]James H. Moorhead, "Social Reform and the Divided Conscience of Antebellum Protestantism," *Church History* 48 (1979): 416-30.

lacked the spiritual capacity to benefit from the experience of conversion. It was that capacity for the "experience" of conversion rather than intellectual capacity that made the religion of the Great Awakenings even more attractive. Further, the same type of "religious exercises"—jerking, rolling, fainting and shouting—that were also native to African traditional religion and that would become a hallmark of early Pentecostalism were a regular feature of these revivals. Along with shifting the base of American religion from propositional truth to a spirituality of experience, the Great Awakenings introduced the "itinerant" evangelist who, like Whitefield, traveled the country preaching in any available venue and holding crowds of repentance seekers spellbound as they attacked not only personal sin but societal decay and promised heavenly reward for the converted faithful. Criteria for the call to ministry also changed. No longer was intellectual capacity and seminary training required. Instead, evidence of spiritual piety, knowledge of the stories of the Bible, giftedness in oratory skills and that indefinable characteristic of charisma was what was needed to ensure the success of these religious endeavors. Nearly half a century later, these same characteristics would be the hallmark of what Pentecostal leaders considered preparation for ministry.

THE LEGACY OF METHODISM

As a young Anglican priest, John Wesley seemingly failed as a missionary to Georgia, experienced his own personal conversion and then spearheaded one of the most widely successful evangelistic movements in British—or American—history. Wesley only desired to call those within his beloved Anglican Church to repentance and holiness of life and remained an Anglican all of his life. The Methodist societies he organized were so named because they adhered to his methods—division of converts into a class-meeting system, quarterly visitations or conferences, circuit-riding lay preachers and itinerancy. His most important theological contribution to the legacy of the Holiness and Pentecostal traditions is the doctrine of "entire sanctification" or "going on to perfection." For Wesley, such perfection meant, to be "sanctified throughout," even "to have a heart so all-flaming with the love of God."[6] Such perfection, which began at conver-

---

[6]John Wesley, "Plain Account of Christian Perfection," in *The Works of John Wesley*, ed. Thomas Jackson (1872; reprint, Grand Rapids: Baker, 1996), 11:385.

sion, was a goal of the Christian journey but did not become a reality until near the end of one's life. This tension between sanctification as a crisis event and as an ongoing process remained a part of Wesley's theology and would repeatedly evidence itself, first in the struggle between mainline Methodists and Holiness proponents, and again in the schism between Holiness Pentecostals and those within the finished-work camp.

The singularly important contribution of Methodism to the African American context was its strong abolitionist stand. Both John and his brother Charles, the prolific hymn writer, were abolitionists. When the two came to Georgia in 1735, they landed in what was then an antislavery state. The Methodist movement that sprung from their efforts produced great abolitionist leaders in Britain and America. Encouraged by the Wesleys, for example, William Wilberforce, the British parliamentary leader and philanthropist campaigned ardently against slavery until the time of his death. His efforts led to the passage of British antislavery legislation and strongly influenced antislavery sentiment in the United States.[7]

John Wesley often referred to slave trade as that "execrable sum of all villains"[8] and fought against British and America slavery in sermons, letters and books.[9] Prohibitions on "buying and selling" slaves was written into early Methodist polity,[10] and Wesley's 1774 work *Thoughts upon Slavery* refuted moral arguments for it.[11] At one point, he rhetorically asked, "Did the Creator intend that the noblest creatures in the visible world should live such a life as this?"[12] While conceding that slavery was not illegal and was "authorized by law," so that a Christian could claim legal justification for holding slaves, Wesley countered that it was, nevertheless, immoral and inconsistent with natural justice.[13]

---

[7]For a discussion of Wilberforce's campaign against slavery, see Eric Metaxas, *Amazing Grace: William Wilberforce and the Heroic Campaign to End Slavery* (San Francisco: HarperOne, 2007). This legislation abolished the slave trade in the British Empire, but not slavery itself.

[8]John Wesley, "Letter to William Wilberforce," February 24, 1791.

[9]See, for example, John Wesley and Albert C. Outler, *The Works of John Wesley*, vol. 3 (Nashville: Abingdon, 1984), p. 453.

[10]Quoted from "The Nature, Design and General Rules of Our United Societies," in *Book of Discipline of the United Methodist Church, 1980* (Nashville: Methodist Publishing House, 1980), p. 69.

[11]John Wesley, "Thoughts upon Slavery," in *The Works of John Wesley*, ed Thomas Jackson (1872; reprint, Grand Rapids: Baker, 1978), 11:59-79.

[12]Ibid., 11:68.

[13]Ibid., 11:70.

When the Methodist Episcopal Church (MEC), as direct heir to British Methodism, was founded in America in 1784, it officially opposed slavery. By the early nineteenth century, its antislavery fervor was weakened by wealthy southerners. Later, though clergy were expected not to own slaves, conflict arose in 1840 when a Methodist bishop inherited a couple of slaves and refused to sell them on humanitarian grounds. The General Conference did not immediately expel him; but four years later, when it voted to remove him from his bishopric unless he freed his slaves, the question was raised regarding the conference's authority to discipline bishops, which ultimately divided the church into the proslavery Methodist Episcopal Church South (MECS) and the antislavery Methodist Episcopal Church, primarily in the North.

By the late nineteenth century, the stance of the northern Methodists had weakened somewhat, and in 1860 and 1869, respectively, the Free Methodists, founded by B. T. Roberts, and the Wesleyan Methodists, founded by a group of ministers and laymen, separated from the Methodist Episcopal Church largely over the slavery issue. The Free Methodists went beyond simply denouncing the practice of slavery; they supported freedom for all slaves, and many of its members were actively involved in the Underground Railroad. But ironically, even these newly founded denominations maintained segregated churches, pretty much resembling their mainline brothers and sisters, where blacks were admitted to membership but restricted to carefully segregated areas. Freedmen as well as slaves regularly suffered other indignities, including separate class meetings, separate worship services and segregated altars. Repeated experiences of racism throughout this period were enough to convince blacks to begin to form separate denominations where they could worship freely without the experience of these indignities.

INDEPENDENT AFRICAN METHODISM

Within this context, three black Methodist bodies and a number of Baptist and independent groups came into being.

African Methodist Episcopal Church. In 1786, former slave and licensed MEC exhorter Richard Allen was appointed assistant minister of Philadelphia's racially mixed St. George's Church. Within that position he was allowed to preach to black parishioners in the early morning meetings within a segregated section built for that purpose. But within a year, he and his companions made the mistake of leaving the segregated section to pray at the main altar. For that infraction they were pulled from the altar while in prayer. Following that incident the group of freed men and women left that congregation, where they had been long-time members, to form the Free African Society, a mutual aid society that served its member's spiritual and material needs. Along with spiritual succor and fellowship, the society provided practical assistance such as burial insurance and support for widows and children.

Though Allen was determined to remain with the Methodist church, a large contingent of the society desired to align themselves with the Episcopal Church because much of the city's free black community was affiliated with that denomination. Absalom Jones, a lay minister among those pulled from the altar, led that group into a merger with the Episcopalians. He was later ordained the first black Episcopal priest and assumed the pastorate of the new congregation. The ten members who remained with Allen became the nucleus for Bethel African Methodist Episcopal Church, which officially opened in 1794. With Allen as pastor, "Mother Bethel" became the founding congregation of the African Methodist Episcopal (AME) Church, which grew to be the largest independent black Methodist denomination and oldest independent black institution in the country.

African Methodist Episcopal Zion Church. Though St. John's Street Methodist Episcopal Church in New York City was racially mixed, its "segregated Sabbaths" relegated black worshipers to limited sacred space and refused them access to positions of leadership. Several black members first received permission to hold separate prayer meetings while staying under the covering of the Methodist Episcopal Church. But, in the same year that Allen was forming the AME Church, a group of black people within the congregation responded to a pattern of discrimination by leaving to form St. Thomas's African Methodist Episcopal Church, which became the focal point for the development of the second major black Methodist denomination, the African Methodist Episcopal Zion (AMEZ) Church.

This group had no single leader, but several men such as Peter Williams, James Varick and Christopher Rush decided to incorporate the new congregation in 1801 while continuing to depend on white elders to lead in worship. Eventually several other black congregations formed, and in

1820, after unsuccessfully attempting to become a separate black conference within the Methodist Episcopal Church or secure black pastors for
their congregations, leaders voted to separate from the MEC.[14] Abolitionist sentiment ran strong in the AMEZ church from its inception, and famous abolitionist members included Harriet Tubman, Frederick Douglass
and Sojourner Truth. Like their sister denomination, AMEZ churches
served as Underground Railroad stations. This activism and its early emphasis on racial justice and other social causes won it the moniker "freedom church." During its earliest years it was called the African Methodist
Episcopal Church in America, but the group adamantly resisted Allen's
overtures to come under his leadership. The word "Zion" was added to the
title during the church's general conference in 1848 to distinguish itself
from the Philadelphia-based body.

Colored Methodist Episcopal Church. Some southern white Methodist
slaveholders continued to work toward the conversion of their slaves. And
even after the MECS separated from the MEC over the issue, a cadre of
blacks remained with that body, though never offered full participation in
its congregational or denominational life. In 1866, a year after the end of
the Civil War, black members approached the General Conference for
permission to establish a separate conference as a new branch within the
MECS, but with their own polity. While this arrangement worked for a
while, the post–Civil War climate of the South created a situation where
both the black and white members of the MECS felt that it was best if its
black members be along to form a separate body. So in 1870 the Colored
Methodist Episcopal (CME) Church was founded in Jackson, Mississippi,
with the blessing of the parent body. The polity of the new body remained
essentially the same as the parent body, and Henry Miles and Richard
Vanderherst were elected as the first two bishops.[15] In 1956, the denomination changed its name to Christian Methodist Episcopal Church since
the predominantly African American body has historically been open to
any person "desiring to flee from the wrath to come."[16]

---

[14]The Methodist Episcopal Church generally supplied white pastors for these black congregations.

[15]C. H. Phillips, *The History of the Colored Methodist Episcopal Church in America: Comprising Its
Organization, Subsequent Development and Present Status* (Jackson, Tenn.: C.M.E. Church
Publishing House, 1925), pp. 25-26.

[16]"Historical Statement of Denomination," Welcome to the Department of Education, CME

BEGINNINGS OF THE HOLINESS MOVEMENT

By the mid-nineteenth century the revivalistic impulse of early Methodism had settled into what appeared to some as mere method, and some fervent believers of both races sensed a growing coldness coming into the church and a lack of holiness in the lives of its people. Those persons who desired to recapture earlier Methodist fervor bemoaned not only the demise of religious passion but also the spiritual and moral purity identified with it. They attempted to recapture the "vital piety" of which Wesley spoke through prayer, preaching and intense study of the Scripture. Holiness leaders related to the Wesleyan understanding of entire sanctification; going on to perfection was a key tenet of their spiritual endeavor. But they reinterpreted Wesley's use this of this terminology to see sanctification as an instantaneous crisis experience that rendered the individual impervious to sin.

In 1867, John S. Inskip, John A. Wood, Alfred Cookman and other white Methodist ministers convened the first "Holiness camp meeting" at Vineland, New Jersey. At the height of the meeting, attendance reached ten thousand. Out of it, the National Camp Meeting Association for the Promotion of Holiness was formed with the intention to conduct a similar gathering the next year. The next year the second camp meeting, in Manheim, Pennsylvania, drew nearly twenty-five thousand from across the United States. Out of this movement grew innumerable Holiness papers, local camp meetings and associations, missions, and colleges.

Holiness fervor gradually spread beyond Wesleyan Methodism to include people from a variety of affiliations. Congregationalists such as Thomas Upham; Asa Mahan, president of Oberlin College; and Charles Grandison Finney, an evangelist associated with Oberlin, promoted Holiness ideas. Presbyterian William Boardman was a leader in the Keswick movement in England, and his work *The Higher Christian Life*[17] became a classic expression of the movement. Influenced by Boardman's ideas, Quaker lay speaker and author Hannah Whitall Smith and her husband, Robert Pearsall Smith, were also to become leaders.

One of the earliest issues facing the movement was abolition, and numerous people, publications and institutions that supported the abolition-

---

Church, http://netministries.org/see/charmin/cm01103.
[17]William E. Boardman, *The Higher Christian Life* (Boston: H. Hoyt, 1859).

ist stance came from Holiness ranks. The early editors of the *Guide to Holiness* were abolitionists. Oberlin College went so far as to advocate "civil disobedience" in the face of the fugitive slave laws (leading to the Oberlin-Wellington Rescue Case—an important event in the history of American civil liberties). The founding of the college as a racially integrated institution was a high point of the egalitarian and racially inclusive Holiness social ethic. The Wesleyan Methodist Church was explicitly abolitionist at its founding.

Gilbert Haven, an ardent Holiness reformer and Union Army chaplain, not only took on abolitionist and feminist causes but also advocated interracial marriage. Haven was elected an MEC bishop in 1872, served as a benefactor of Clark College during Reconstruction[18] and succeeded Bishop Davis Wasgatt Clark as president of the Freedman's Aid Society of the Methodist Episcopal Church. LaRoy Sunderland, a founder of Houghton College, withdrew from the Methodist Episcopal Church in 1840 after being tried and defrocked for antislavery writings. Sunderland helped found the Wesleyan Methodist Church and was a founding member of William Lloyd Garrison's American Anti-Slavery Society but ended his life as an agnostic.[19] In 1860, Anthony Bewley, an outspoken Methodist missionary and antislavery proponent from Tennessee, was lynched by an angry Texas mob that suspected him of being a John Brown sympathizer and slave agitator plotting to burn Texas towns and murder the citizens.[20]

KESWICK HOLINESS INFLUENCE

The Wesleyan Holiness understanding of entire sanctification differed markedly from another strain of Holiness thought that came to be known as the "higher life," or Keswick movement. The latter designation grew out of a series of conferences, beginning in 1875 in Keswick, England, under the leadership of people such as William Boardman[21] and Robert and Hannah Smith.[22] Both groups held that sanctification began at the

---

[18]Now Clark Atlanta University.

[19]For a discussion of Sunderland's career, see Edward D. Jervey, "LaRoy Sunderland: Zion's Watchman," *Methodist History* 6, no. 3 (1968): 16-32. For a discussion of his abolitionist activities, see Herman E. Thomas, "Abolition and the Wesleyan Methodist Connection in America," *AME Zion Quarterly Review* 111 (January 1999): 18-29.

[20]Charles Elliott, "Martyrdom of Bewley," *Methodist Review* 45 (October 1863): 626-45.

[21]See Boardman, *Higher Christian Life.*

[22]Hannah Smith is the author of the classic *The Christian's Secret of a Happy Life* (London:

moment of justification, and "the principle of sin with which man is born remains in the justified believer,"[23] but Keswick theology differed from that of Wesleyan Holiness doctrine in a number of ways. First, it denied the possibility of the eradication of the sinful nature, emphasizing rather endowment with power for greater Christian service. Second, it distinguished between a "state" of holiness and a "condition" of holiness, the latter being that those who have been sanctified are not made holy but only made completely victorious over the sin nature, which still remains in their hearts.

These two movements were never completely estranged from each other, however, and Holiness proponents from both sides regularly read each others' literature, sang each others' hymns and made the journey over the ocean to attend and address each others' meetings. By the 1890s, Holiness advocates within both camps began to identify the second blessing with "Pentecost" or the "baptism of the Holy Spirit," though the initial evidence of tongues was never implied. Instead, according to Keswick devotees, such baptism would be manifested in greater power to work on God's behalf. For Wesleyans it signified greater power to lead a life free of sin.

The terminology of Pentecost gained acceptance in church names and hymn collections several years before the Azusa Street experience of tongues. Phineas Bresee, for example, formed his denomination as the Pentecostal Church of the Nazarene, though once the impact of the Azusa Street Revival began to spread through the Holiness movement, Bresee dropped the term "Pentecostal" from the church's name to avoid any hint that he might support the nascent movement.

Though distinctions between the Holiness and Keswick schools are not immediately apparent to those outside the movement, their specific formulations would play a major role in one of the first deep schisms within the Pentecostal movement. William Durham's formulation of two stages of salvation provided for in the "finished work of Calvary,"[24] which was to divide him from William Seymour's Wesleyan-Holiness formulation, which had its roots within the Keswick tradition.

Fleming H. Revell, 1873).

[23]See W. Ralph Thompson, "An Appraisal of the Keswick and Wesleyan Contemporary Positions," *Wesleyan Theological Journal* 1, no. 1 (spring 1966): 14.

[24]See Allen L. Clayton, "The Significance of William H. Durham for Pentecostal Historiography," *Pneuma: The Journal of the Society for Pentecostal Studies* 1, no. 1 (fall 1979): 27-42.

HOLINESS ROUSINGS WITHIN MAINLINE AFRICAN METHODISM

Though these bodies provided a safe spiritual haven for black Methodist believers, the civilizing efforts of bishops such as Daniel Alexander Payne in the AME Church were seen as attempts to kill the Spirit and keep worshipers from experiencing God's full presence. In response, many common people felt a need for something more than existing Methodist worship could offer. Affinity for Holiness teaching and practice in the upper echelons of African Methodism was rare; but some leaders, such as AME bishop Abraham Grant, did have such an affinity, which in Grant's case may have been related to the fact that he was converted in a camp meeting in 1868. Grant was a prominent educator: vice president of Paul Quinn College, a founder of Payne Theological Seminary, a trustee of Wilberforce University and colleague of Booker T. Washington.[25] He also associated with Holiness preacher Amanda Berry Smith.[26] Likewise, within the AMEZ Church, Bishop Alexander Walters strove to join social justice with personal piety in a way that did not give undue stress to either. Walters, a noted nineteenth-century civil rights advocate who cofounded the National Afro-American Council with T. Thomas Fortune and served as editor of the *New York Age,* was a close associate of Holiness preacher Julia Foote, whom he called "a great preacher, an uncompromising advocate of holiness."[27]

BLACK BAPTIST ROOTS WITHIN THE HOLINESS MOVEMENT

Though the majority of earliest Holiness proponents in the country were Wesleyan, several independent black Baptist congregations were swept into the tide of Holiness rhetoric and experience. Though Arminian conceptions such as that of sanctification were not a natural outgrowth of Baptist theological understanding with its deep Calvinist foundations, much of the teaching found an affinity among those Baptists who were open to it.

---

[25]Booker T. Washington, "Letter to William Howard Taft, Jun 7, 1908," in *The Booker T. Washington Papers,* ed. Louis R. Harlan, Raymond Smock and Nan Woodruff (Urbana: University of Illinois Press, 1980), 9:560.

[26]African Methodist Episcopal Church and Abraham Grant, *Deaconess Manual of the African Methodist Episcopal Church* (s.l., 1902).

[27]Alexander Walters, *My Life and Work* (New York: Fleming H. Revell, 1917), 46.

Several of the earliest leaders of the black Holiness movement, including Charles Price Jones, Charles Harrison Mason, William Christian and presumably William Seymour, had roots within the Baptist tradition. These men had been nurtured in the Baptist culture from an early age and had experienced conversion within that tradition. They had sought to make a place of ministry for themselves and were fairly successful doing so. Yet they later sensed a longing for a deeper experience of God and contended that they found it in the experience of sanctification. When they independently sought to share that experience with their Baptist brothers and sisters, they found that any insinuation that the Baptist spirituality of their faith community was somehow deficient was received with less than open acceptance.

Jones had been converted and licensed to preach in a Baptist church, attended a Baptist Bible college where he later served as a trustee, pastored three Baptist congregations, served as editor of a Baptist periodical and was an officer in the state Baptist convention. On graduating from Arkansas Baptist College in 1891, Jones, who described himself as having been "almost a fanatical Baptist," "began to be impressed with the inconsistencies of our Baptist Churches."[28] He was introduced to the doctrine of sanctification through the writing and preaching of white Baptist evangelist Joanna Patterson Moore, who worked among the freedmen, not only preaching on eternal salvation but also attempting to help improve their temporal social conditions. The two became friends, and the relationship, as well as Moore's writings, profoundly influenced Jones.

Mason grew up in a devout Baptist home, was converted and licensed to preach in a Baptist church, attended Baptist educational institutions, and pastored Baptist congregations. Both men rose to some prominence within their respective Baptist conventions before being forced out over the issue of sanctification.

William Christian had been pastor of a Baptist church in Fort Smith, Arkansas. Christian had been a colleague of Mason while they were both Baptists. Christian reportedly had a divine revelation in which God instructed him that the Baptist church was in error in that it taught a sectarian gospel.

While the Methodist churches initially made room for the Holiness be-

---

[28]John M. Giggie, "The African American Holiness Movement," *Society* 44, no. 1 (November/December 2006): 54.

lievers, Baptist Holiness advocates fared less well almost from the beginning. Many, including Jones, Mason and Christian, were expelled from their congregations and conventions for suggesting that the doctrine of sanctification was a missing element in Baptist piety. While other Baptists did not deny the reality of sanctification, they defined it differently than Holiness proponents. The definition put forth by Elias Camp Morris, first president of the National Baptist Convention and an influential leader among both black and white Baptists, summarized the meaning of sanctification as most Baptist leaders generally understood it: For them, "the word 'sanctify' means to set apart, or appoint to service." It was "a call to service, a getting ready for a meeting in which to worship God; a laying aside of secular matters, that . . . the whole being may be devoted to the service of God."[29]

For Baptists, sanctification did not mean total purging from sin, as Wesleyan leaders proposed, but that individuals were "turn[ed] to God with their whole hearts, and to put themselves in absolute obedience to his commands."[30] Morris's close friend J. H. Eason, another national Baptist leader, echoed this understanding by defining sanctification as "an unfolding series of spiritual events that never fully cleanses an individual" but successively, though not completely, "purif[ies] him ever more of sin."[31]

Partly due to sentiments like these, the Holiness movement among Baptists was never as organized as that among the Methodists. While efforts such as those put forth by some south Georgia Baptists in late in the nineteenth century resulted in structures such as the Holiness Baptist Association formed in 1894, for the most part Baptist Holiness proponents found themselves in loose organizations that never fully coalesced. Instead, believers assimilated Holiness doctrine into existing Baptist structures, adding concepts of sanctification, perfection and Holy Spirit baptism to elements of Baptist polity and spirituality.

THE EMERGENCE OF INTEGRATED HOLINESS DENOMINATIONS

The revivalistic, camp-meeting-style worship of the Second Great Awak-

---

[29]Elias C. Morris "Sanctification," sermon delivered before the Arkansas Baptist State Convention, 1899.
[30]Ibid.
[31]John M. Giggie, "African-American Holiness Movement," *Society* 44, no. 1 (2006): 55.

ening and the less formal worship practices of the Holiness movement resonated with the cultural sensitivities of black people much more than the quietist style of the mainline congregations to which many had been previously exposed. This vibrant worship made room in the church for active involvement of less-educated clergy and laypeople than was possible in more structured congregations.

While such divisions into separate "white" and "black" denominations occurred among most of the other mainline denominations, the earliest Holiness denominations showed a degree of racial openness that was rare, and African Americans were part of the Holiness movement from its inception. The National Camp Meeting Association for the Promotion of Holiness endorsed and promoted several black evangelists. Amanda Berry Smith, for example, spoke more often at white revival meetings than among black colleagues. Still, even in "interracial" Holiness meetings accommodations often were conformed to the existing racial mores. Seating was often segregated, and separate areas of the altar were reserved for whites and blacks.[32]

Predominantly white Holiness bodies made attempts to attract, hold and fully involve blacks in their membership and leadership. Often the level of effort reflected the personal sensitivities and convictions of the founder and how well he was able to hold to and communicate those convictions in the face of mounting pressure to bow to the Jim Crow social ethic. Groups such as the Evening Light Saints who were convicted that racism was sinful were more prone to actively integrate blacks in to their communal and worship life. Other groups saw the need to evangelize the black masses but felt no compunction against segregating them into enclaves where they could worship in their own way, without being compelled to mix socially.

THE SALVATION ARMY

The Salvation Army represents one of the first groups to attempt to integrate blacks into the existing structure of its congregations. When William and Catherine Booth founded the Christian Mission in London in 1868, they never foresaw that the Salvation Army, as it came to be known,

---

[32]Paul Harvey, *Freedom's Coming: Religious Culture and the Shaping of the South from the Civil War Through the Civil Rights Era* (Chapel Hill: University of North Carolina Press, 2005), p. 130.

would explode throughout the European continent and reach North American shores within five years. Neither did they foresee the difficulty that would ensue in their attempts to live out a commitment to social equality among people of different class, ethnic and cultural backgrounds. Such a goal would not be easy to achieve and would meet with varying degrees of success within the numerous settings in which the Army had planted itself.

Many poor white, working-class, rank-and-file Salvation Army converts recoiled at the idea of attracting large numbers of blacks into full fellowship within their congregations. Yet denominational leaders sought an integrated church and attempted to draw blacks into its ranks. Beginning with its earliest U. S. efforts as the Christian Mission, the group was already known for its breach of common social piety—using loud street meetings and weird street parades, singing hymn lyrics to popular tunes, and openly allowing women to preach and exhort. It added the insult of holding integrated worship services, taking them into full membership in its congregations and launching campaigns specifically targeted at attracting them to the organization.

The earliest black Salvationist in the United States was James Jermy, an Afro-Britisher who migrated first to Canada and then to Cleveland, Ohio, around 1871. Jermy worked as a carpenter and meat cutter by day, but though not officially authorized to undertake mission work for the Army, labored among poor blacks in both locations during the evening. He eventually set up five outposts (as Salvationist mission congregations were called). But, with no material support from the fledgling denomination, his short-lived ministry experienced limited success and ended abruptly four years later, when Jermy did not obtain support from headquarters. The congregation faltered and Jermy returned to England, where he took leadership of a Clapton corps.[33]

In the late 1800s, seventeen-year-old Lieutenant Eleza Shirley, who had worked closely with Salvation Army founder William Booth in England, came to the United States to join her father, who had migrated to the country in 1879. Shirley's initial work was also not officially sanctioned by headquarters, but she was determined to continue evangelistic ministry in her

[33]Warren L. Maye, *Soldiers of Uncommon Valor: The History of Salvationists of African Descent in the United States* (Nyack, N.Y.: Salvation Army, 2008), pp. 15-22.

new homeland. Spurred by a promise from Booth that he would support her work should she become successful and the sheer energy of her youthful religious passion, Eliza and her parents conducted street meetings in Philadelphia, eventually opening two stations in the city. Though white, the Shirleys used spirituals and other black secular songs and hymnody to attract a congregation among the city's black residents that was to draw not only the support but also the attention of Salvation Army leaders.[34]

The Shirleys' work was the impetus for the beginning of authorized North American Salvation Army efforts, when Booth sent George Scott Railton, the first officially sanctioned missionary, to oversee the work in this country.[35] Railton's concern for the salvation of the "African" in this country was matched by an equally passionate commitment to gender equality. In 1890, he arrived in New York with seven "Hallelujah Lassies" led by ten-year veteran Emma Westbrook, to "show what women, inspired by the power of the Holy Ghost, could do."[36] After meeting with the Shirleys in Philadelphia to present them with the official Army flag, Railton moved on to the Midwest before Booth recalled him to England. On remembering his encounter with the Shirleys, Railton was to concede that the meeting he attended with them was the largest he had seen, with more than two hundred soldiers and fifteen hundred blacks and whites in attendance.[37]

The Booths replaced Railton with Frank Smith, a political and social activist who was commander of the London corps.[38] Smith's concern for reaching the black community led him to open a station on the edge of a black neighborhood in New York as the national headquarters. From this location the Army attracted residents of both races, bringing them together into a racially mixed congregation. Yet Smith saw little return on his initial labors because blacks remained leery of white evangelization efforts. But while his early efforts produced few black converts, the blacks he successfully recruited were often featured in the testimony and music segments of Salvation Army services. One of these was W. S. Braithwaite, a

---

[34]Ibid., pp. 26-30.

[35]Diane Winston, *Red-Hot and Righteous: The Urban Religion of the Salvation Army* (Cambridge, Mass.: Harvard University Press, 2000) 19.

[36]Maye, *Soldiers of Uncommon Valor*, pp. 27-28.

[37]Ibid., p. 30.

[38]Winston, *Red-Hot and Righteous*, p. 35.

former medical student, lawyer and Harvard graduate who, over the years, rose to the rank of captain.[39] In 1885, Smith tapped the former African Methodist Episcopal Zion clergyman, possibly the most educated member of the Salvation Army of the time, to spearhead the "Great Colored Campaign and Combined Attack." The British Guyanese native's efforts were concentrated throughout the Northeast and Midwest. Meetings were held in the Northeast and Michigan to recruit soldiers and raise support for this effort. He opened two corps in Virginia in the late 1880s, and by 1886 one of them, in Fredericksburg, boasted the first predominantly black Salvation Army corp. The second was in Alexandria, near Washington, D.C. Braithwaite left the Salvation Army a short time later, when another Salvationist leader leveled "mysterious charges" against him.[40] Undaunted by the loss of this charismatic leader, Smith launched a second campaign, the "Colored Skins and White Hearts Crusade."[41] This campaign proved to be no more successful.

Though Smith encouraged white Salvationists to welcome blacks into existing stations where possible, he, like other Salvation Army leaders, felt there were areas of the country where existing racial mores made this impossible. When he returned to England in 1886, Booth sent two more officers with a heart to reach the black masses, his son, Ballington, and his daughter-in-law, Maude. The couple had success in expanding the Army on several fronts.

By the early 1900s, most efforts to attract blacks had largely waned, and little was being done to promote blacks who had been recruited to officer status. Further, strong racial antagonism made it difficult to conduct successful campaigns in the South, and Army leaders urged patience for those who wanted to do so. Still, its publications, *Good News* and *War Cry*, were two of the few Holiness periodicals to give serious attention to the concerns of African Americans. Army leaders were some of the most outspoken critics of racist practices such as lynching, and the Army used its peri-

---

[39]Maye, *Soldiers of Uncommon Valor,* pp. 43-45.

[40]Ibid., pp. 44-45.

[41]An article titled "Wanted for the Southern Expedition" appeared on the front page of the December 12, 1885, edition of the *War Cry,* the official Salvation Army periodical, which advertised, "Wanted, men and women, with colored skins, and white hearts, 'ready to endure hatred and hardships for Jesus'" (cited in Lillian Taiz, *Hallelujah Lads and Lasses: Remaking the Salvation Army in America, 1880-1930* [Chapel Hill: University of North Carolina Press, 2001], p. 195 n. 23).

odical *War Cry* to speak out against the atrocity.[42]

Even with concentrated effort, an emphasis on equality of all members and worship so emotive that the secular press sometimes compared it to "Negro meetings,"[43] Salvationists had only limited success in reaching blacks. The goal remained as official policy, but within a short number of years, efforts in this direction continued to wane so that by the early 1900s they had come almost to a complete halt. But even while the Army was actively recruiting blacks, it succumbed to some of the same racist practices as other bodies. In England, Booth compared the poor masses he found in London to "African savages."[44] In North America, the Army's campaigns into the southern states "respected" the racial mores of that area. Several racially defined congregations were established and blacks in the Midwest were relegated into a separate Central District.

Moving into twentieth-century America, the Salvation Army continued its outreach to blacks while at the same time maintaining many of the discriminatory practices that would hallmark the society. Its social service centers, the residential facilities maintained for indigent men, were segregated until the early 1950s. To add insult to injury, the *War Cry* often printed unflattering caricatures in poetry and stories that used "darkie dialect" and depicted blacks in condescending and paternalistic terms.[45] Still, conservative black leaders such as Booker T. Washington praised the Army for its attention to blacks and hailed their "methods and work" as having a "peculiar value" for the uplift of blacks.[46] Even as early Salvationists attempted to reach blacks, paternalistic attitudes often surfaced in the wording of their appeals to other whites for support. Even while Smith, for example, spoke of a desire to be "by the help of God . . . among the first white Christians . . . who would faithfully and wholly break down the wall of partition separating whites and blacks," he also talked about the need to

---

[42]*War Cry*, July 14, 1894, pp. 8, 21; July 21, 1894, p. 8; December 28, 1895, cover, p. 2; May 1899, p. 8 (cited in Maye, *Soldiers of Uncommon Valor*, p. 290 n. 66).

[43]Winston, *Red-Hot and Righteous*, p. 41.

[44]Ibid.

[45]See, e.g., *War Cry*, Feb 14, 1885, p. 1; May 2, 1885, p. 2; June 23, 1988, p. 2; September 18, 1888, p. 9; Jan 31, 1890, p. 4; May 2, 1891, p. 3; and May 20, 1899, p. 10 (cited in Winston, *Red-Hot and Righteous*, 261 n. 65).

[46]Booker T. Washington, "A Kind Letter from Principal Washington," *The Conqueror*, October 1896, p. 475 (cited in Maye, *Soldiers of Uncommon Valor*, p. 48).

not only "liberate and save" the race, but to "civilize" them.[47] Samuel Logan Brengle, who participated in the 1904 International Congress, characterized the blacks he saw there as "ignorant natives of Africa," who were from "the most backward and depraved of nations."[48] Much of the segregationist policies and practices came about because Army leaders did not want to offend lower-class whites, who made up the bulk of their constituency. But Army leaders were never quite comfortable with these policies and continually wrestled with ways to overturn them.

THE CHURCH OF GOD (ANDERSON, INDIANA)

From its inception in 1881 as the Evening Light Saints, the Church of God (Anderson, Indiana)—or the Church of God Reformation Movement, as it is also known—has been among the most racially diverse Christian bodies in the United States. The legacy is due in large extent to the theological commitment of its founder, Daniel S. Warner. From its earliest history Warner's group welcomed blacks, and both black and racially mixed congregations were in existence as early as 1896.

The Evening Light Saints held that interracial worship was a sign of the true church and gave racial prejudice a theological critique. Further, not only were services interracial in attendance, but both blacks and whites ministered regularly in these mixed meetings.[49] In the early Church of God, blacks and white openly worshiped together, even in the Deep South. And instead of testifying that they were saved, sanctified and filled with the Holy Ghost, the Evening Light Saints were more likely to assert that they were "saved, sanctified, and prejudice removed."[50] This conviction was part of Warner's vision for a church without hierarchical denominational structures and restoring New Testament unity, including unity among the races, even where it meant blatantly disregarding existing mores.

Coming into existence during Reconstruction, the Church of God encouraged its ministers to courageously challenge existing racial mores and the treatment of black folks. In one instance, for example, the traveling female evangelist Lena Shoffner preached at an 1897 camp meeting ser-

---

[47]Ibid., p. 46.
[48]Ibid., p. 57.
[49]B. Scott Lewis, "William J. Seymour: Follower of the 'Evening Light,'" *Wesleyan Theological Journal* 39, no. 2 (2004): 171.
[50]Ibid., p. 172.

vice in which she employed the passage in Ephesians 2:14, "Christ has broken down the dividing wall of hostility." As she preached, someone in the congregation untied the rope separating blacks and whites, and worshipers of both races approached the altar to pray.

Such brazen flaunting of societal norms often brought open hostility from surrounding communities and proved to be personally dangerous for Church of God members. Undeterred even by violence, Church of God members maintained their strong interracial position as the core of their message of the unity of all believers, which appealed to blacks, who experienced racism in every other segment of society. Shoffner's simple act, for example, incurred the wrath of some in the neighboring community, who gathered to throw rocks and try to disrupt the meetings, going so far as dynamiting some of the camp meeting buildings.[51]

The racial openness and gender inclusiveness of the Evening Light Saints went beyond congregational leadership. In one instance, a black woman, Jane Williams, founded a congregation in Charleston, South Carolina, and brought it into the Church of God in 1886, making it the denomination's first black congregation.[52] That congregation functioned as headquarters for spreading the Church of God movement in the southern states. But even with the denomination's generally open attitude toward integrated congregations, some blacks chose to set up their own churches. So by the 1890s, there were a number of African American congregations in Augusta, Georgia. Between 1910 and 1940, two million African Americans moved away from the blatant racism and Jim Crow policies of the rural South to find a better social and economic life for themselves and their families in the industrialized areas of the Midwest, Northeast and West. This movement, called the Great Migration, forever changed the fabric of African American culture from one that was largely rural and southern to one that was largely urban. Blacks within the Church of God moved to the north and began worshiping in some white congregations; but by 1915 and 1916, they had already set up predominantly black congregations in cities like Chicago and Detroit.[53]

---

[51]Merle D. Strege, *A Look at the Church of God for Children: The Story of the Church for Children 1880-1930* (Anderson, Ind.: Warner Press, 1987), 1:8.

[52]Cheryl J. Sanders, *Saints in Exile: The Holiness Pentecostal Experience in African American Religion and Culture* (New York: Oxford University Press, 1996), pp. 22, 33.

[53]Strege, *A Look at the Church*, pp. 1-8.

Possibly, along with its emphasis on the sanctified life, the denomination's racial inclusiveness was partly what attracted Azusa Street leader William Seymour to the body. While with the Evening Light Saints, Seymour experienced entire sanctification and was exposed to a level of racial inclusiveness unlike any he had witnessed in his relatively short life. Further, he encountered the communal missionary homes where members worked together to support each other and carry out ministry. These homes were to later serve as a model for the communal living arrangement that was in place for a season at the Azusa Street Mission. Yet the Church of God (Anderson) was among those Holiness bodies that did not adopt a Pentecostal theology, insisting instead that "the convincing evidence of the Spirit-filled life is holiness" and that "the Pentecostal outpouring in Acts 2 was more mission-centered than person-centered. The purpose was empowerment for the divine mission."[54]

FIRE BAPTIZED HOLINESS CHURCH

The 1894 decision by the Methodist Episcopal Church South to adopt a statement opposing the growing Holiness movement set off a chain of events that galvanized the more radical elements to establish new Holiness groups.[55] Many of these, like the contemporary Pentecostal body known as the Pentecostal Holiness Church, went through several iterations before evolving into a coherent denomination. The earliest iteration of that group came into existence in 1895 as the Fire Baptized Holiness Association in Iowa. Three years later, Benjamin H. Irwin, a former Baptist preacher from Nebraska, organized the body into the national Fire Baptized Holi-

---

[54]"Our Beliefs: The Spirit-Filled Life," Church of God, Anderson, IN, www.chog.org/portals/0/pdfs/Our%20Beliefs.pdf.

[55]A statement from the 1894 General Conference of the Methodist Episcopal Church South declared, for example, that "there has sprung up among us a party with holiness as a watchword; they have Holiness associations, Holiness meetings, Holiness preachers, Holiness evangelists, and Holiness property. Religious experience is represented as if it consists of only two steps, the first step out of condemnation into peace and the next step into Christian perfection. The effect is to disparage the new birth, and all stages of spiritual growth from the blade to the full corn in the ear. . . . We do not question the sincerity and zeal of these brethren; we desire the church to profit by their earnest preaching and godly example; but we deplore their teaching and methods in so far as they claim a monopoly of the experience, practice, and advocacy of holiness, and separate themselves from the body of ministers and disciples." Quoted in Vinson Synan, *The Holiness-Pentecostal Movement in the United States* (Grand Rapids: Eerdmans, 1997), p. 40.

ness Church at Anderson, South Carolina. By then there were churches in eight U.S. states and two Canadian provinces.

During that same period, North Carolina Methodist Holiness evangelist Abner Blackmon (A. B.) Crumpler founded the first congregation of the Pentecostal Holiness Church in Goldsboro. Crumpler had come into contact with the Holiness movement in 1880s in Missouri and was sanctified in a Holiness camp meeting. In 1897, Crumpler organized the North Carolina Holiness Association. By 1900, having been dismissed from the Methodist Episcopal Church, Crumpler formed a new body, the Pentecostal Holiness Church. A year later, as the term *Pentecostal* began to be associated with the doctrine of initial evidence, Crumpler truncated the name of his organization to the Holiness Church to distance himself from the new doctrine. His group merged with the Fire Baptized Holiness Church in 1911 after both had accepted the Pentecostal doctrine and moved into the Pentecostal camp.

Irwin's Fire Baptized Holiness Church had been interracial from its inception, holding interracial conventions and supporting integrated congregations throughout the South. Holiness views on race were distinctly different from other southern Christians. The Fire Baptized Holiness Church proved exceptional with regard to interracial worship. In fact, some of its evangelists, like Richard Baxter Hayes, attracted the anger of other whites for challenging racial norms. In one incident, after asking a few African Americans to lead in song at an 1898 revival in Carlton, Georgia, a man with a stick approached Hayes for "showing Negro equality." Hayes's meeting tents were burned down several times, a Baptist minister punched him in the face, he was shot at and he regularly faced hostile crowds.[56]

Though black people were admitted to the Fire Baptized Holiness Church with full equality, no other black achieved the prominence of William E. Fuller. Fuller was converted in 1892 at the age of seventeen and joined New Hope Methodist Church in Mountville, South Carolina, where he shortly became a class leader and a steward. A year later, he was called to preach. During the next few years, Fuller immersed himself in a

---

[56]Randall Stephens, "'There is Magic in Print': The Holiness-Pentecostal Press and the Origins of Southern Pentecostalism," *Journal of Southern Religion* 5 (2002): http://jsr.fsu.edu/2002/Stephens.htm.

life of personal prayer. Over the next two years, he sought and received the experience of sanctification—the baptism of the Holy Ghost and fire— while praying in a corn field.

Not convinced that his experience had a biblical foundation, Fuller began searching for scriptural sanction for it. This search led him to begin reading J. M. Pike's *Way of Faith*. Through it, Fuller learned of the Fire Baptized Holiness Association and initially sensed that he had found not only support for his newly embraced faith but also fellowship between black and white Christians, and an opportunity to minister. In reality, however, the actual level of fellowship Fuller found turned out to be less than he had originally expected. For some time before he attended a FBH meeting, he had been corresponding with B. H. Irwin, and the two men had struck up a collegial ministerial relationship. Accordingly, Fuller made plans to attend a FBH conference and wrote of his intention to do so. In 1897, When Fuller showed up at the Topeka Kansas National Holiness Movement, however, Irwin was surprised that the person he had been so easily corresponding with was a black man and was not quite sure what to do with him. Following that episode, the entirely white body decided "to accept him into the organization, but not into the fellowship."[57]

But in 1900, in a crisis of faith, Irwin left the church. His successor, Joseph King, recognized Fuller's giftedness as a preacher and organizer and empowered him to evangelize and establish churches throughout the region. In 1905, Fuller, who was only thirty and had become one of the earliest and most prominent black members of the group, was appointed as one of four members of the executive board. The prolific church planter stayed with the interracial body until 1908 and continued establishing churches throughout the South. In that year, a contingent of blacks under his leadership left the parent body to form what would become the Fire Baptized Holiness Church of God, an entirely black denomination.[58] The body was later renamed the Fire Baptized Holiness Church of God of the Americas.

---

[57]Andrew Lewter, "Re-Imagining Pentecostalism" (paper presented to the conference on African American Pentecostalism, "All the World: Black Pentecostalism in Global Contexts," Harvard University Divinity School, Cambridge, Mass., March 2005).

[58]"Fuller, William Edward, Sr.," in *Biographical Dictionary of African-American, Holiness Pentecostals, 1880-1990*, ed. Sherry S. DuPree (Washington, D.C.: Middle Atlantic Regional Press, 1989), pp. 96-97; and *Souvenir Journal* (one hundredth church anniversary, Fire Baptized Holiness Church of the Americas, Greenville, S.C., June 9-14, 1998), p. 15a.

ITINERANT BLACK HOLINESS EVANGELISTS

Holiness culture provided a rich field for gifted black itinerant preachers to ply their vocational calling without being tied to the pulpit of a traditional congregation. The only criterion for acceptance was a felt call of God and evidence of effective ministry. Though few blacks rose to prominence as Holiness leaders, some enjoyed a degree of exposure at the numerous camp meetings that rapidly sprung up throughout the country. Interestingly, many of the most-sought-after of these black preachers were women.

Amanda Berry Smith. African Methodist Episcopal lay preacher Amanda Berry Smith was among the most famous of the Holiness evangelists, addressing white camp meeting congregations at least as often as she did blacks. In 1878, friends suggested she go to England to work with the churches there. While there, she made friends with two prominent Keswick women, Hannah Whitall Smith and Mary Broadman, opening an opportunity to attend the Keswick Conference for the Promotion of Higher Life and for invitations to preach throughout the United Kingdom as the first black woman to work as an international evangelist.

The next year she traveled to India, where she spent two years holding meetings and working with churches in large cities such as Bombay and Calcutta and in numerous smaller towns and villages. Her ministry in India was curious not only because she was a woman minister within this highly male-dominated culture but as also as a black former slave within a highly stratified caste system. After returning to England for a short time, she spent nearly eight years (1881-1889) in Liberia and Sierra Leone helping with churches and establishing temperance societies. Smith was never appointed by her AME Church, and her twelve years of missionary work was largely taken on by faith with limited MEC support supplemented by donations from friends and supporters. While on the continent, Smith, branched out beyond preaching in local churches and camp meetings or leading temperance meetings, going beyond working with AME efforts to include working with people such as Bishop William Taylor, the famed Methodist missionary leader, who said that she "had done more for the cause of missions and temperance in Africa than the combined efforts of all missionaries before her."[59]

---

[59]Hallie Quinn Brown, *Homespun Heroines and Other Women of Distinction* (New York: Oxford University Press, 1988), p. 131.

Throughout Smith's work, she was concerned with two causes: the status of women in society and the need for the education of Africa's children—male and female. Along with preaching the gospel, she spent a great deal of the eight years on the continent attempting to ameliorate both. Her work was not without controversy. Though she tasted great victories, she also incurred strong opposition to her presence as a woman on the mission field and suffered bouts of depression. Smith remained a member of the AME Church throughout her life, though her relationships with AME congregations were often distant and the source of some of her harshest criticism. Nineteenth-century AME leaders explicitly went against all that Smith stood for, desiring to conform to middle-class standards of decorum and civility, suppressing emotive worship, relying on an educated clergy, and evoking a rigid class structure and middle-class gender norms. Further, Smith was criticized for supporting Holiness teaching on sanctification, not contributing her gifts and talents to support the burgeoning AME women's effort in the church, and focusing her attention on ministering to whites rather than to blacks.

Julia Foote. Julia Foote became the first African American woman to gain ordination as a deacon in the African Methodist Episcopal Zion Church. But that was not until 1894, only six years before her death in 1900 and following a long and fruitful preaching career. She had sought ordination earlier, but though she had been a renowned evangelist throughout most of her life, she was denied it.[60] Convinced that she was sanctified and called of God to preach, Foote began her ministry conducting services in her home without her pastor's approval. She was disfellowshiped from her local congregation. Though Foote was the first woman ordained an AMEZ deacon, Mary Jane Small, wife of AMEZ bishop John B. Small, became the first woman elder when she was ordained by the Philadelphia and Baltimore Annual Conference in 1895.

Foote, the daughter of former slaves, was born in Schenectady, New York, in 1823. In 1851, she temporarily ceased her evangelistic work due to the loss of her voice and the need to care for her invalid mother. Eighteen years later, she reported experiencing divine healing and began to preach

[60]See Julia Foote, "A Brand Plucked From the Fire: An Autobiographical Sketch by Mrs. Julia A. J. Foote," in *Sisters of the Spirit*, ed. William L. Andrews (Bloomington: University of Indiana Press, 1986), pp. 161-234.

again. On one occasion in 1878, an estimated five thousand people heard her preach at a Holiness meeting in Lodi, Ohio. Foote moved to Boston with her husband and joined the AMEZ Church of Reverend Jehiel C. Beman, a leading antislavery advocate. Convinced she had been divinely called to preach, she sought Beman's permission to do so but instead was barred from preaching and then excommunicated from his church. Undaunted by this rebuttal, Foote conducted evangelistic campaigns throughout the Northeast, as far west as Ohio and up into Canada.

Foote challenged women who felt called to ministry but were reluctant because of prejudice. "Sisters, shall not you and I unite with the heavenly host in the grand chorus?" she asked. "If so," she continued, "you will not let what man may say or do, keep you from doing the will of the lord by using the gifts you have for the good of others."[61]

EVOLUTION OF THE BLACK HOLINESS MOVEMENT

While small numbers of black Holiness believers made a home for themselves in white Holiness bodies and individual black itinerant preachers found some success within the broader Holiness movement, there was still some limitation on the full acceptance of black believers within the larger context. Many of the groups were centered in the South, and adherents steeped in paternalistic racial attitudes struggled, with the assistance of their sanctifying experience, to overcome inbred prejudice and fully embrace their black brothers and sisters. But southern social conventions made it all but impossible to do so in every instance. Racial inclusion of these congregations' worship was not hailed by the surrounding communities but became an occasion for harassment—and in some cases violence. And there was almost always racial disparity in available accommodations for those attending joint meetings, with blacks having to settle for lodging and food of poorer quality than that of their white colleagues. Travel arrangements to these meetings were also often less comfortable for blacks, who were forced to ride in segregated sections of public transit systems.

Further, inclusion did not always mean equality. White leaders struggled to yield their prejudices to the sanctifying work of the Spirit, with varying degrees of success. Their less-than-equal treatment within wider

---

[61]Ibid., p. 112.

Holiness ranks did not go unnoticed by the black people, who sought various remedies to make themselves feel completely at home in a less-than-totally welcoming situation. Early black Holiness leaders were neither entirely successful in bringing reform to black mainline bodies, nor did they feel completely at home within them. At first they simply attempted to return existing African Methodist and independent Baptist congregations to their pietistic roots. Nonetheless, as they gradually took on the more stringent stances of the radical Holiness movement, they incurred the displeasure of their mainline brothers and sisters. By the last quarter of the nineteenth century, the schism between Holiness proponents and established denominations widened to the point that separation became inevitable. This turn forced many Holiness proponents to "come out" and establish organization more suitable to their spiritual sensitivities.

African American Holiness proponents began to pull out of both white Holiness bodies and African American mainline bodies to form separate black Holiness denominations. These new groups reflected the spiritual imprint of their parent denominations, the moral imprint of the individuals who birthed them and shaped their early existence, and the social imprint of interaction with everyday reality of discrimination. Adherents shared core beliefs about the need for a personal experience of salvation as well as a subsequent initial experience of sanctification that progressively led to a life of perfection. They also exhibited a strong sense of black identity, often incorporating, at least implicitly, themes of liberation and social justice into their statements of belief and practical outworking. But each of the new groups offered its own interpretation of what it meant to live a holy life, largely shaped by the prophetic individuals who stood at their helm and pointed to a new understanding.

REFORMED ZION UNION APOSTOLIC CHURCH

Unlike numerous other Holiness groups formed at the end of the nineteenth century, the earliest black Holiness denomination did not result from schism in an existing group but came about largely because one man, James R. Howell, was dissatisfied with what he felt was "ecclesiasticism" of other black churches.[62] It would not, however, remain free of schism.

---

[62]James R. Howell, *History of the Reformed Zion Union Apostolic Churches of America* (Lawrenceville, Va.: Brunswick, 1998), p. 1.

After failing to secure an African Methodist Episcopal Church pastorate because he lacked the requisite education, the native Philadelphia abolitionist was sent as a missionary to Virginia to evangelize newly freed blacks.[63] In 1864, Howell moved to the Tidewater area of that state, working as a carpenter by day and as a preacher on Sundays and in the evening. Finding this field less than fruitful, he established himself in Boydton, Virginia (a rural community one hundred miles south of Richmond) and began traveling throughout the state and neighboring North Carolina, evangelizing and looking for a place to establish his ministry.

Despite his lack of education, the persuasive speaker's charismatic delivery soon rallied lay leaders of several disparate congregations that had left the Episcopal, Methodist and Baptist congregations of their former owners. In 1869, he organized these Zion societies (a designation used because he was convinced that the Bible portrayed Zion as "the dwelling place of God among men") as the Zion Union Apostolic Church. Though not adopted until 1874, the plan of union Howell drafted in 1866 closely followed the AME discipline. By 1869, there were eight established societies and at least six more being organized. Several of them were named after existing AME congregations including Bethel, the mother church in Philadelphia; New Hope; and Salem. That October a second meeting was held to complete the work of organizing a Zion Union Society and electing Howell to a four-year term as president of the "Zion Union Apostolic Church of America."

Howell's heavy-handed leadership would eventually bring about a temporary dissolution of the new body. Not only had he imposed the organization's name on the rest of the body; but he also insisted that the polity change from congregational to episcopal and had himself elected as bishop for life. By 1874, the internal friction completely disrupted the body, and Howell resigned as its leader. But Howell's authoritarian style was not the only issue. Several within the body specifically wanted less emotive worship and a more structured organization, the very elements Howell had previously denounced. In 1877, this faction forced a vote during which the Union Zion Apostolic Church elected to merge with the Episcopal Church. No such merger ever occurred.

---

[63]Ibid., p. 3.

When the church reorganized (between 1881-1882) under the present name, Reformed Zion Union Apostolic Church, the four-year term for presiding bishop was reinstated. With Howell again taking that office, the friction between him and several factions within the body resumed. As a result, several congregations left to return to their former Methodist or Baptist roots. Others left to become independent congregations. Several leaders who disagreed with Howell or whom he felt to be undermining his authority were stripped of their pastorates and disfellowshiped from the denomination. By 1882, however, Howell stepped down from his position and again left the denomination, severing all communication with the group and leaving virtually no information regarding the rest of his life. While by 1923, RZUAC congregations could be found only in Virginia and North Carolina, by 1965, the denomination had sixteen thousand members in fifty churches stretching as far north as Philadelphia; Hackensack, New Jersey; and Detroit. After numerous schisms, today the denomination is primarily a southern church.

THE CHURCH OF CHRIST (HOLINESS)

As Ithiel Clemmons correctly points out, in contradistinction to other black independent traditions, the Church of Christ Holiness (COCHUSA) arose out of intragroup conflict within the black Christian community rather than as a reaction to white racism. Yet its founder, Charles Price Jones, was keenly aware of the racial reality in which his black constituency found themselves, and he used his knowledge of Scripture and slave spirituality to keep the notion of God's intervention in that reality ever before them.

Jones was born near Rome, Georgia, in 1865, which was the year after the Civil War ended, and was steered toward faith at an early age by his mother, a deeply religious Baptist former slave. When she died in 1883, Jones was seventeen. He left Georgia to work at odd jobs throughout the South, landing in Memphis, where he stayed for four years. In 1887, he moved to Cat Island, Arkansas, where he was converted and joined the congregation at Locust Grove Baptist Church. A year later, he was preaching in local congregations and three years later was licensed to the ministry. Shortly, Jones matriculated at Arkansas Baptist College.

Ordained in 1888, within four years, Jones served in three pastorates—

the newly organized Pope Creek Baptist Church, in Groat County, Arkansas; St. Paul Baptist Church in Little Rock; Tabernacle Baptist Church; and the College Church of Selma University in Alabama. In 1892, Jones was elected corresponding secretary of the state Baptist convention and appointed as a trustee of his former alma mater. Jones excelled in preaching, was hailed as a great revivalist and sought out to conduct meetings throughout the Mississippi Valley. Still, he sensed a need for a deeper experience of God. This would come in 1894 through the experience of sanctification, which he declared moved him from "doctrinal assurance" to "spiritual assurance, heart peace, rest of soul, the joy of salvation in the understanding of a new heart, a new mind, a new spirit, constantly revived and comforted by the Holy Ghost."[64]

By 1895, Jones was called to the oldest black congregation in Jackson, Mississippi, Mt. Helm Baptist Church. There he began teaching the doctrine of sanctification; attacking Baptist and Methodist practices he considered worldly, including involvement with fraternal orders, fashionable standards of consumption and allegiance to secret societies; and called on his followers to mark their spiritual birth as sanctified Christians by "pitching their secret order pins . . . out the church windows."[65] Jones had sought to bring the Mt. Helm congregation into the Holiness movement, but some members soundly objected to his new stance. At the same time, he and others began to promote the Holiness message within the General Baptist Association of Mississippi, with whom he was affiliated. Many with that body also found it hard to buy into the new teaching, and friction arose within the group.

Charles Harrison Mason was born in 1866 to former slave parents. The family moved to Plummersville, Arkansas, when Charles was twelve. He was raised in his parents' Missionary Baptist tradition, was converted at a young age and grew up intending to be a minister. As a young man he forsook that goal, but after a bout with tuberculosis from which he was miraculously healed, and perceiving that healing as a reprieve and reiteration of his divine call, he was licensed to preach by his Baptist church in 1893. Mason initially attended Arkansas Baptist Col-

[64]Otto B. Cobbins, ed., *History of the Church of Christ (Holiness) USA, 1895-1965* (New York: Vantage, 1966), pp. 23-24.
[65]Ibid., p. 83.

lege but left after only three months, asserting that he saw "no salvation in schools and colleges"[66] and opting to enter the college's ministerial institute, where he received a certificate. He received his Baptist preaching license in 1893. Within four years, Mississippi Baptists ordered him to vacate his pulpit for the offense of preaching Holiness doctrines, especially the doctrine known as "sanctification." Seeking to find a place for his own church, he received permission to use an abandoned gin house for a revival in 1897; this was the origin of what became the Church of God in Christ.

As young men, both Jones and Mason were highly respected in black Baptist circles. They were protégés of the college's founder, Elias Camp Morris, who was by this time president of the Arkansas Baptist Convention and later first president of the National Baptist Convention. Additionally, Jones was also a protégé of Charles Lewis Fisher, president of the college. Their meeting began what promised to be a fruitful spiritual connection and personal friendship. They joined other black Holiness proponents including J. A. Jeter, D. J. Young and W. S. Pleasant to conduct a revival in Lexington, Mississippi, and then throughout the Mississippi Valley, in which many experienced divine healing and several were sanctified. The group established new congregations and drew existing congregations into a loose-knit fellowship. During the Lexington meeting, the formal structure of an organization initially called the Church of God in Christ was set in place, and throughout the following decade the four men established new congregations and persuaded existing congregations to adopt the Holiness doctrine of sanctification and join the ecumenical group that included Baptists and a variety of Methodist congregations throughout the Mississippi Valley.[67]

Jones began publishing the semimonthly periodical *Truth*, in which he promoted his Holiness understanding throughout the Mississippi Valley. Through such media and numerous revivals and camp meetings, Holiness fervor continued growing among black Baptist congregations in the valley. In 1897, Jones and Mason convened AME, Colored Methodist Episcopal (CME) and Baptist clergy and lay Holiness proponents

[66]Mary Mason, *The History and Life Work of Elder C. H. Mason, Chief Apostle, and his Co-laborers*, ed. Mary Mason (s.l.: s.n., 1924), p. 24.
[67]Ibid., p. 25.

from nine eastern states to refute denominationalist "slavery" and create a "communion of the Holy Spirit" among like-minded believers. Jones also insisted that these churches should adopt biblical names rather than geographic or sentimental designations. These teachings were unacceptable to many of his Baptist colleagues, who began to close their pulpits to Jones and his sympathizers. After a two-year battle, Jones was ousted from Mt. Helm Baptist Church and the Jackson Baptist Association. Mason suffered a similar fate with his Christ Association of Mississippi of Baptized Believers.

While Jones was the catalyst in forming the association, it was Mason who envisioned the name "Church of God in Christ" through what he contended was a direct revelation from God. Jones was elected the new organization's overseer, and Mason was appointed overseer of the Tennessee work. Along with the Wesleyan understanding of sanctification, the two shared the radical Holiness stance on divine healing that at first precluded use of conventional medical care. They also shared particular interest in developing the spiritual and practical needs of their communities.

Despite their close affinity, an issue would arise to drive a wedge between the two seemingly inseparable colleagues. Once the Azusa Street Revival broke out, Jones and Mason decided that the latter should go to Los Angeles to investigate whether what was occurring was a move of God or simply fanaticism. Mason returned from Azusa Street not only convinced that the Pentecostal experience of Holy Spirit baptism was genuine but also having had the experience himself and insisting that such an experience was normative for Holiness believers. Such an assertion was untenable to Jones, who insisted that, though he had never spoken in tongues, he had been baptized in the Holy Ghost in 1894, twelve years before the Azusa Street Revival was under way. By this he simply meant that he had had a supernatural infusion of God's power for holy living— not the Pentecostal experience of Holy Spirit baptism coupled with glossolalia. More importantly for Jones, the greatest evidence was an infusion of love in the heart of the believer.[68]

Separation from Mason did not signal Jones's complete rejection of speaking in tongues. In his first tract on the issue, *The Gift of the Holy*

---

[68]Jones laid out his understanding of Holy Spirit baptism in *Gift of the Holy Spirit*, p. 17.

Spirit in the Book of Acts, Jones validated the experience as genuine but rejected insistence that all who received Holy Spirit baptism received tongues as initial evidence of such an infilling. Jones insisted that every true believer was heir to the Holy Spirit, that receiving the Holy Spirit was an integral part of conversion and that no specific gift signified the Spirit's presence.[69]

Both Jones and Mason's groups claimed rights to the name Church of God in Christ until 1915, when Mason, insisting that God had personally revealed the name to him, had it incorporated. Though the congregations that had maintained the Holiness distinctive began to use the name Church of Christ Holiness, a protracted court battle ensued. In 1920, when Jones's group lost the suit, it chartered the name Church of Christ (Holiness) U.S.A.[70]

Though Jones was a dynamic speaker and prolific hymn writer, the Church of Christ (Holiness) never showed the dynamic growth of its sister denomination. At its height, membership never totaled more than several hundred thousand, while the membership of the Church of God in Christ had grown to several million. In its more than one-hundred-year history, there have only been four presiding bishops of the Church of Christ (Holiness) U.S.A. Jones held the position from 1928 until his death in 1949. At that time, Rudd Conic assumed the position and held it until 1992, when Maurice Bingham of Jackson, Mississippi, took the position. In 1996, the leadership was split so that the denomination is now led by a senior bishop and a president.

Another major split within COCHUSA came in 1920, when Bishop King Hezekiah Burruss founded the Churches of God, Holiness, in Atlanta, Georgia, using the congregation he founded in that city in 1914 as headquarters. Within three years there were twenty-two churches in eleven states, Cuba, the Canal Zone and the British West Indies. Burruss led the denomination for fifty years, until his death in 1963. Three years later, by 1965, the younger body grown to 25,600 members in 32 congregations, mostly along the East Coast.[71] The doctrine is identical to that of the par-

---

[69]See sermon 1, "The Baptism of the Holy Spirit," in Jones, *Gift of the Holy Spirit*, pp. 5-12.
[70]Cobbins, *History of the Church of Christ (Holiness)*, p. xx.
[71]"Church of Christ (Holiness) USA," *The Encyclopedia of American Religions*, ed. Melton J. Gordon (Tarrytown, N.Y.: Triumph, 1991), 1:223, 319.

ent body. A second group, the Evangelical Church of Christ (Holiness), was founded in 1947 by William C. Holman. This break was primarily administrative; the doctrine and practice are the same as that of the parent body. In 1990, membership in this group was approximately five hundred members in four churches in Washington, D.C.; Los Angeles; Omaha; and Denver. There were also two mission churches in Los Angeles.[72]

THE GOSPEL SPREADING CHURCH OF GOD

One of the most colorful figures in the black Holiness movement also worked with Jones for a short period. Elder Lightfoot Solomon Michaux founded his first congregation, the Gospel Spreading Church, in 1919 in Newport News, Virginia, and organized the Gospel Spreading Tabernacle Building Association. Michaux split with Jones in 1921, when Jones attempted to assign him to another congregation in nearby Hampton, Virginia.[73] Michaux founded the Gospel Spreading Church of God in that same city in 1928.

Michaux's radio ministry, which started as a local broadcast on station WJSV in Alexandria, Virginia, in 1929 had spread to fifty stations on the CBS network that broadcast his sermons and songs weekly to twenty-five million people across the country by 1934. During the Depression the *Washington Post* called him "the best known colored man in the United States."[74] Despite the inferior wattage of rival preacher Sweet Daddy Grace,[75] Michaux and Grace used their broadcasts to hurl epithets at each other throughout the 1930s. Described by one writer as "stocky, gold-

---

[72]Sherry Sherrod DuPree, *African-American Holiness Pentecostal Movement: Annotated Bibliography* (New York: Garland, 1992), p. 257.

[73]Lillian Ashcraft Webb and Lightfoot Michaux, *About My Father's Business: The Life of Elder Michaux*, Contributions in Afro-American and African Studies (Santa Barbara, Calif.: Greenwood, 1981), pp. 19-21.

[74]John Mangin, "Gods of the Metropolis: The Rise and Decline of the Black Independent Church," *Next American City* 3 (2003): http://americancity.org/magazine/article/gods-of-the-metropolis-the-rise-and-decline-mangin/.

[75]Grace himself was a renowned and outlandish pulpiteer whose United House of Prayer for All People was a rival organization to Michaux's. Grace distinguished himself by his mass baptisms using a fire hose and is alleged to have claimed some sort of deity for himself. For more on Grace, see Danielle Brune, "Sweet Daddy Grace: The Life and Times of a Modern Day Prophet" (Ph.D. diss., University of Texas, Austin, 2002); and Marie W. Dallam, "By Daddy Grace Only: Bishop Grace and the Foundational Years of the United House of Prayer" (Ph.D. diss., Temple University, 2006).

toothed and grey-haired,"[76] Michaux was dubbed "The 'Happy Am I'
preacher"[77] by the popular press.

Michaux took pains to maintain the distinction between Pentecostals
and the Holiness movement. His wife, Mary, hated what she considered
the ravings of the lower-class "tongue people" and vowed never to allow
them or their practices into her husband's church.[78] Yet many who came
into the Holiness movement through movements such as that of Michaux,
Jones or Elias Smith would later go on to embrace Pentecostal spirituality
and assert the need to move past sanctification to accept Holy Spirit baptism with tongues.

A social reformer and entrepreneur as well as preacher, Michaux ran an
employment bureau and the Happy News Café, a local restaurant. In 1942,
he collaborated with Howard University professor Albert Cassell to build an
affordable apartment complex for Washington's black residents, who were
often excluded from other areas by the city's racially restrictive housing cov-
enants. When completed in 1946, the five-hundred-unit Mayfair Mansions
project was one of the earliest and largest complexes conceived and designed
for working- and middle-class blacks. His Gospel Spreading Church also
operated an amusement park and beach on ground located near the place
where the first slaves that came to the United States landed. He used the facility for revivals and other religious activities, including his famous mass-
baptismal services in which he immersed hundreds at one time. President
Dwight Eisenhower was an honorary deacon of Michaux's Washington congregation; supporters included Eleanor Roosevelt and Mamie Eisenhower.

THE CHURCH OF THE LIVING GOD (CHRISTIAN WORKERS FOR FELLOWSHIP)

The influence of Baptist foundations would be seen again in the denomination founded by former slave and Baptist pastor William Christian in
Fort Smith, Arkansas, in 1889. Christian had been an associate of C. H.
Mason, and in 1888, like his associate, found himself out of fellowship
with the Baptist church over embracing the doctrine of sanctification, his

---

[76]"Religion: Happy Am I," *Time*, July 11, 1934, www.time.com/time/magazine/article/0,9171
,762188,00.html.
[77]Ibid.
[78]Mangin, "Gods of the Metropolis."

objection to what he felt was the tendency of Baptist and Methodist churches in misleading seekers about what was required for salvation, and what he saw as the commercialization of religion. He chided black pastors for enticing parishioners to purchase household goods, apparel and even Bibles produced by white northern manufacturers, with these pastors unjustly profiting from their positions at the expense of their members.[79]

Reportedly, after having a series of divine revelations, Christian left the Baptist church to form a new organization. Though the Christian Workers for Fellowship (CWFF) is Holiness in doctrine, his group distinguished itself from other Holiness bodies by incorporating elements of Judaism. His congregations, for example, are temples, not churches, and his members understand themselves as black Jews. Like the Jewish community, the Church of the Living God originally celebrated the Sabbath and worshiped on Saturday rather than Sunday. Further distinguishing himself from his Holiness colleagues, Christian's group used water and unleavened bread in the Lord's Supper, which was administered to a believer only once. Within the CWFF, the Lord's Prayer is held to be the only prayer that Christians should pray.[80]

But Christian's group held on to some Holiness tenets, including believers' baptism by immersion and washing of the saints' feet. Like many Holiness groups, CWFF does not see speaking in tongues as an initial sign of Holy Spirit baptism but only one of the several gifts that come to a believer with Holy Spirit baptism. While the CWFF allows operation of this gift within its worship, it only permits speaking in tongues in recognizable languages.[81]

Born in Mississippi nearly ten years before emancipation and reared as a slave during the earliest years of his life, Christian's awareness of southern racial dynamics and led him to intentionally address racial inequality in the tenets and structure of his new body. The CWFF statement of faith was crafted, in part, to address racial disparity Christian had experienced

---

[79]William Christian, *Poor Pilgrim's Work: In the Name of the Father, Son and Holy Ghost*, no. 3 (Texarkana, Tex.: Joe Erlich's Print, 1896), p. 10.

[80]"About Prayer," The Church of the Living God C.W.F.F. Temple #29, http://cotlg29.org/AboutPrayer.php.

[81]Wardell Payne, ed., *Directory of African American Religious Bodies: A Compendium by the Howard University School of Divinity*, 2nd ed. (Washington, D.C.: Howard University Press, 1995), p. 165.

and asserts, "We believe in the Fatherhood of God and the Brotherhood of man" and "We believe that all men are born free and equal."[82] The statement refuted racist teachings, including the claims of some late nineteenth-century Baptist preachers that "Negroes were not men, but the outcome of a human father and a female beast,"[83] by asserting that "the saints of the Bible belonged to the black race."[84] In other writings, Christian expanded his theology to insist that, since Jesus had no earthly father, he belongs to all people and could be considered "colorless," but because he came from the lineage of Abraham and David, Jesus, as well as many other biblical saints, was black.[85]

Prior to forming the church, Christian had been a Freemason. Presumably, since membership in secret societies such as the Masons is incompatible with Holiness doctrine he withdrew from that organization. Several elements of the church's culture, however, are reminiscent of such fraternal organizations. Some "secret" doctrinal tenets are only known by members of the church.

Within ten years of its formation, Christian's group claimed a membership of ten thousand and had nearly ninety congregations in eleven states. Christian served as chief bishop of the denomination until his death in 1928. His wife, Ethel, served with her husband at the head of the organization until his death in 1928, at which time she took over leadership. Over the century, several changes have developed in the denomination's organizational structure. The body is no longer Sabbatarian. Worship in the temples, which are designated by number, is held on Sundays, and pastors are referred to as "elder."

In 1953, a schism in the denomination led William F. Fizer to form the Church of God (Which He Purchased with His Own Blood) after being excommunicated from the parent body. Fizer had concluded that grape juice or wine, not water, should be used in the Lord's Supper, which should be held weekly, thus denying one of the major distinctive practices of the

[82]Statement of Faith, Church of the Living God (CWFF), www.ctlgcwff.org/articles.htm.
[83]George Eaton Simposn, "Black Pentecostalism in the United States," in *Native American and Black Protestantism: Modern American Protestantism and Its World*, 9, ed. Martin E. Marty (Munich: K. G. Saur, 1993), p. 148.
[84]Walter Hollenweger, "A Black Pentecostal Concept: A Forgotten Chapter of Black History," *Concept* (June 1970): 18-19.
[85]Ibid., p. 34.

Church of the Living God. The first annual convention of the Church of God (Which He Purchased with His Own Blood) was held in 1954. The church represents a unique blend of religious elements from a number of traditions. Without putting emphasis on speaking in tongues, in deference to its Holiness heritage, the denomination teaches that the Holy Ghost is given to those who obey the Lord; and though it promotes the practice of divine healing, unlike the parent body, use of conventional medical practices is also affirmed. Following the Jewish orientation, unleavened bread is used for Communion. In 1997, the denomination whose headquarters are in Oklahoma City had seven churches, eight hundred members and ten ministers. These are also members in Nigeria and the Philippines.[86]

TRIUMPH THE CHURCH AND KINGDOM OF GOD IN CHRIST

Apostle Elias Dempsey Smith had been an African Methodist Episcopal pastor but, like other Holiness converts, sought what he felt was a deeper relationship with God. The denomination Smith founded, variably called the Triumph Church, insists it was called into existence through divine revelation to Smith. In it, an eagle, a lion and a brown-skinned young woman dressed as a bride appeared to him. According to Smith, God revealed the particular significance of each element. The eagle meant to Smith that his church would be the highest religious group in existence, the lion indicated that his message would be stronger than any other and without "carnal ordinances" like those of other preachers and the bride represented the church and the entire world who, when married to the bridegroom, holds the ability to birth all of her needs.[87] Though the revelation was given in 1897 with instruction to start a new church, it was not until five years later, in 1902, that the first congregation called Triumph the Righteous Church was formed as a Methodist congregation in Baton Rouge, Louisiana. Yet even then Smith reportedly kept its content secret for several years, only making its substance public in 1904.

Before he solidified his organization, Smith temporarily joined forces with C. H. Mason, founder of the Churches of God in Christ. By 1912, the two parted ways, for while Mason favored interracial cooperation and fellowship,

---

[86]William Jordon Fizer, *Bible Doctrine* (Oklahoma City: the Author, s.d.).

[87]Triumph the Church and Kingdom of God in Christ, "Church History," www.triumph thechurchnatl.org/ChurchHistory.htm.

Smith made a distinction between the "church militant of whites and the peace loving church of blacks."[88] Further, Smith rejected Mason's Pentecostal emphasis on speaking in tongues. Mason, in turn, rejected Smith's conception of "body redemption"—the contention that justification eliminated the necessity of physical death for the redeemed. Smith further contended that the "everlasting Gospel" he preached was to "prepare and call mankind, both soul and body, into everlasting existence on earth together."[89]

Triumph Church teaches a seven-step plan of salvation: conversion, justification, sanctification, baptism of the Holy Ghost with fire, redemption of the body, perfection and eternal life. For Smith, all of these are necessary in order for a person to be completely saved. Smith understood that there was a definite experience of the baptism of the Holy Ghost and fire that was "obtainable by a definite appropriation of faith on the part of the fully cleansed believer, but did not put emphasis on speaking with tongues."[90]

The first National Congress of Triumph Church was held in Birmingham, Alabama, in July 1915. At this assembly Smith was named "Apostle, Priest and King" and the name of the church was changed to Triumph the Church and Kingdom of God in Christ. Smith chartered his body as denomination in 1918 in Washington, D.C. After World War I, Smith was among a number of black religious leaders who became involved in Marcus Garvey's "Back to Africa" movement and Ethiopianism. In 1919, he hosted the head of the Universal Negro Improvement Association at the denomination's international convention, and a year later he traveled to Ethiopia, which he referred to as Abyssinia. On his arrival, Smith was given the reception of a king, including a lavish banquet. Shortly after this elaborate ceremony, he died suddenly, amid some conjecture that he may have been poisoned or killed in some other way by his hosts.[91]

Prior to his trip to Africa, Smith relocated the denomination's headquarters to Birmingham, Alabama. In 1936, the church had only two con-

---

[88]Ibid.

[89]"Welcome," Triumph the Church and Kingdom of God in Christ, www.triumphthechurch natl.org.

[90]"Basis of Union," Triumph the Church and Kingdom of God in Christ, www.triumph thechurchnatl.org/Basis of Union.htm

[91]"Smith, Elias Dempsey," in *Biographical Dictionary of African-American, Holiness Pentecostals, 1880-1990*, ed. Sherry S. DuPree (Washington, D.C.: Middle Atlantic Regional Press, 1989), p. 255; "Elias Dempsey Smith," in *Encyclopedia of African American Religions*, ed. Larry G. Murphy, J. Gordon Melton and Gary L. Ward (New York: Routledge, 1993), p. 706.

gregations and thirty-six members. By 1972, it had grown to 475 congregations and 54,000 members in the United States, Africa and the Philippines. Today it has congregations is thirty-six states and in Liberia, West Africa. After his death, leadership of the denomination shifted from one person to a board of seven bishops.

CHRIST HOLY SANCTIFIED CHURCH OF AMERICA, INC.

In 1903, members of the Christ's Sanctified Holy Church based in Jennings, Louisiana (a white body), traveled to West Lake, Louisiana, to evangelize that black community whose residents had primarily been members of the Colored Methodist Episcopal Church. Rather than seeking to bring sinners Christ, the group specifically set out to share the Holiness message of sanctification to Christians who were not yet sanctified.

A year later, the work had been so successful that Joseph Lynch and several other former CME communicants embraced the doctrine of sanctification that the white "missionaries" had taught and chartered a separate organization, the Colored Church South, but soon changed its name to the Christ's Sanctified Holy Church Colored. By early 1906, before news of the outpouring of the Holy Spirit at Azusa Street, this small community reportedly had experienced an equally powerful outpouring of the Holy Spirit, which resulted in members receiving their Pentecostal Spirit baptism. By that time, black church members dropped the word "Colored" from their title and, though the two groups remained separated, returned to using the same name as their parent body, Christ's Sanctified Holy Church, whose doctrine was almost identical.

Judge and Sarah King had been converted years earlier in the Baptist Church but later joined the Methodist Church; and by 1890, after being exposed to the doctrine of sanctification through the preaching of traveling Methodist evangelists, they had joined the Holiness movement. In 1910, the Kings established a CHSC congregation in Keatchie, Louisiana, near Shreveport. That group merged with the West Lake group, and once he assumed leadership of the newly merged organization, King changed the name to Christ Holy Sanctified Church, switching the order of the terms "Sanctified" and "Holy" to differentiate his group from the white body.

CHSC doctrine highlights the distinction between classical Pentecostal and Holiness understandings of Holy Spirit baptism. While the CHSC encourages its members that "being baptized with the Holy Spirit adds to believer's power," it does not promote speaking in tongues as the single initial evidence, but only one evidence of the experience. Further, the centrality of the doctrine of sanctification is attested to in the church's polity which differentiates between two types of membership. Those who are justified and are waiting for sanctification are probationary members. Those who have experienced sanctification are admitted as full members.[92]

William Seymour visited King's congregation as he traveled from Los Angeles to preach in Tennessee. After hearing about the group, Seymour stopped at Sarah King's mother's home, where he explained what those in King's congregation had experienced when they received the Holy Spirit.[93] In an essay, titled "The New Birth," Seymour would come to assert a theology much like that of the CHSC, rejecting the insistence of many Pentecostals that tongues was the initial and most important evidence of Holy Spirit baptism.[94] The CHSC teaches that the primary purpose of Holy Spirit baptism is threefold: evangelizing with accompanying supernatural signs; giving a "necessary dimension" to a worshipful relationship with God; and enabling the full expression of fruit, gifts and ministries of the Holy Spirit for the edifying of the body of Christ.[95]

Judge King served as presiding bishop of the organization for thirty-six years, from 1910 to 1945. When he died, his son Ulysses, who had assisted his father for some time, assumed leadership of the organization and served until his death in 1985. He was succeeded by Elmer McBride who served until 1991. James E. Williams served from 1991 to 1998. Billy R. Brown followed him, serving from 1998 to 2005. In 2006, Georgia E. Jones, the first woman, assumed office and served until her death in 2008. At some point, headquarters for the body was moved to Fort Worth, Texas. Statistics of the Christ Holy Sanctified Church are difficult to obtain. By the late 1950s, however, there were approximately 600 members in 30

---

[92]Payne, *Directory of African American Religious Bodies*, p. 160.

[93]"A Brief Synopsis of the History of the Christ Holy Sanctified Church," Christ Holy Sanctified Church of America, www.chschurch.org/history.

[94]William Seymour, "The New Birth," in *Doctrines and Disciplines of the Azusa Street Apostolic Faith Mission of Los Angeles, Cal. With Scripture Readings by its Founder W. J. Seymour* (Los Angeles: s.n., 1915), p. 8.

[95]"Doctrine," Christ Holy Sanctified Church of America, Inc., www.chschurch.org/what_we_believe.

churches.[96] Reportedly, today there are approximately 250 congregations. The denomination operates an industrial school, Christ Holy Sanctified School. Its headquarters is now in Sacramento, California.[97]

CHURCH OF GOD (SANCTIFIED CHURCH)

The first congregation of the Church of God (Sanctified Church) was originated in 1900 by members of a Baptist congregation in Columbia, Tennessee, led by Charles Grey, a former member under Jones and Mason's Church of God in Christ. When Jones incorporated the Church of Christ (Holiness) U.S.A. after the 1907 split, Grey continued his work independently, splintering from the parent body largely over church polity. Specifically, his group maintained a congregational structure, with the local church calling its own pastor rather than an episcopal form, in which the pastor is assigned by a bishop, as in the parent body. For the next twenty years, Grey drew a number of congregations, but this group remained unincorporated until 1927, when the Church of God (Sanctified Church) consolidated the work under a board of elders.

Centered in the Holiness movement, the Church of God (Sanctified Church) statement of faith is insistent that "sanctification is that instantaneous act of divine grace, whereby we are made holy [and] must be definitely experienced to fit us to see the Lord." Regarding baptism of the Holy Spirit, however, it simply states, "[We] believe in the present ministry of the Holy Spirit by whose indwelling the Christian is able to live a Godly, holy, and sanctified life."[98] According to the doctrine of the church, "every true believer is heir to the gift of the Holy Ghost," which is "the gift of God in Christ Jesus to the children of God sanctifying, quickening, guiding into all truth, and giving power to obey God's word and by witnesses." Further the group insists that "the initial receiving of the Holy Ghost occurs at conversion," since "the Holy Ghost baptized the whole church on the Day of Pentecost, thereafter, He is referred to as a gift."[99] The move to incorporate in 1927 led to further controversy and a schism. The founder, who was against such structure, left to form the Original Church of God Sanctified.

---

[96]DuPree, *African American Holiness Pentecostalism*, p. 141; and Payne, *Directory of African American Religious Bodies*, p. 159.
[97]DuPree, *African American Holiness Pentecostalism*, p. 141.
[98]"Articles of Faith," Church of God Sanctified, www.cogsanctified.org/articles.htm.
[99]Ibid.

CONCLUSION—THE LEGACY TO BLACK PENTECOSTALISM

By the time the Pentecostal movement exploded onto the scene in 1906, radical Holiness revivals could be found on six continents.[100] More than a dozen of the one hundred and fifty Holiness bodies that formed throughout the late nineteenth century ultimately become part of twentieth-century "Holiness-Pentecostal" churches.[101] Several of these, including the Church of God in Christ, the United Holy Church, and the Fire Baptized Holiness Church, were black denominations. They brought with them a commitment to the experience of sanctification lived out in a life that eschewed all visible vestiges of sin and sustained by a rigid inner purity. The strict holiness codes that prescribed a life separated from worldliness in dress, in personal habits, vocational pursuits, and social activities and relationship translated well into the new movement and, in some cases, provided a foundation for even more strictures governing almost every aspect of personal life as well as involvement with other believers and the outside world.

Holiness believers had embraced the emphasis of divine healing being available to all Spirit-filled believers. Their revivals and camp meetings were replete with instances and testimonies of miraculous reversals in seemingly incurable conditions. Some radical Holiness believers went as far as shunning use of all conventional medical treatment, and faith-healing homes replaced doctors' offices, drug stores and hospitals as the places believers looked for recovery. When healing didn't come, the most radical adherents were willing to die holding to the commitment to trust only in God for deliverance from their ills, seeing in death their ultimate delivery from all earthly distress. This emphasis translated well into the Pentecostal movement and became a mainstay of its doctrine.

The Holiness movement sustained a promise of greater participation for women than had been experienced in any previous period of American religious history. Armed with an understanding of the empowering work of the Holy Spirit through sanctification, women forged new places of equality alongside male colleagues. Like them, these women traveled

---

[100]Jay R. Case, "And Ever the Twain Shall Meet: The Holiness Missionary Movement and the Birth of World Pentecostalism, 1870-1920," *Religion and American Culture* 16, no. 2 (2006): 125.

[101]For an overview of these denominations, see Charles E. Jones, *Guide to the Study of the Holiness Movement* (Lanham, Md.: Scarecrow Press, 1974).

across the country and the world, preaching revivals, pastoring churches and taking on a full range of ministerial and lay leadership roles that previously would have been out of bounds for them. Prominent white women such as Phoebe Palmer, who led the Tuesday Morning Meeting for the Promotion of Holiness; Alma White, founder of the Pillar of Fire denomination; renowned evangelist Maria Woodworth-Etter; and faith healer Carrie Judd Montgomery were joined by black Holiness proponents such as Julia Foote, Amanda Berry Smith and others as prominent participants in the growing movement. These women incorporated the spirituality of revivalism into a new paradigm for ministry that did not recognize the common social boundaries of the day but effectively gave vent to their vocational and spiritual aspirations.

For the African American Pentecostal movement, the greatest legacy of the Holiness movement was unprecedented racial inclusion. Integrated worship services were a hallmark of the Holiness movement, and black and white preachers and exhorters frequented each other's meetings with regularity. This inclusiveness did not always carry over into the social arena outside of these meetings, and black congregants were more often than not subjected to the harsh realities of Jim Crowism when they returned to the regular activities of daily life. Still, the Holiness experiment in interracialism was, at least initially, to set a pattern, which several black Pentecostal leaders attempted to emulate, with varying degrees of success.

As Holiness spirituality gave way to Pentecostal fervor, not everyone who embraced notions of sanctification or baptism of the Holy Spirit was willing to concede that there was specific, verifiable evidence that such baptism had occurred. Even some who conceded that such evidence might be plausible refused to impose a condition for that evidence on fellow believers. Those who took this relatively moderate stand continued to identify with the Holiness movement. While some went as far as to adopt the language of "baptism in the Holy Ghost" into their doctrinal understandings, they never accepted the Pentecostal definition of Holy Spirit baptism with speaking in tongues as the sine qua non of authentic religious experience.

The most extreme Holiness groups, including the Church of the Nazarene, forbade glossolalia (speaking in tongues). Others, such as A. B. Simpson's Christian and Missionary Alliance, adopted a "seek not, forbid not" posture that neither promoted nor forbade the experience, allowing—

but not encouraging—constituents who had the experience some freedom
to employ tongue speaking within their fellowship. Still others relegated
tongue speech to private devotion, severely restricting or banning their use
in regular publish worship.

The rejection of Pentecostal claims by these Holiness proponents did
not bolster the growth of the parent movement, and the Holiness movement never realized the phenomenal growth of its Pentecostal sister. So,
after one hundred years, following the birth of the Pentecostal movement,
the combined membership of the black Holiness bodies is considerably less
than that of the collective membership of Pentecostal bodies. By the beginning of the twenty-first century, most Holiness bodies number in the ten
thousands, and the combined constituency of the ten major black Holiness
bodies in the United States total less than five hundred thousand. At the
same point, at least two individual Pentecostal denominations have constituencies that large, and the collective membership is several million.

While tongues play an important role in Pentecostal spirituality, the
resistance of Holiness groups to the Pentecostal insistence on the experience as normative has been repeatedly overlooked, as scholars have lumped
these sister movements together under the designation "sanctified church."
In doing so, they have not paid as careful attention to this facet of the black
religious experience as they have given to other elements of American religion; and as a consequence, they have failed to discern a distinction that
is important for understanding the distinctive cultures of the two groups.

Table 3.1. Characteristics of Representative Black Holiness Denominations

Denomination	Year Est.	Founder	Parent Body	Constituency
Reformed Zion Union Apostolic Church	1877	James R. Howell		16,000
Church of Christ Holiness USA (COCHUSA)	1895	Charles Price Jones	COGIC	10,460
Church of the Living God (Christian Workers for Fellowship)	1889	William Christian		20,000
Triumph the Church and Kingdom of God in Christ	1902	Elias Dempsey Smith		54,307

Denomination	Year Est.	Founder	Parent Body	Constituency
Gospel Spreading Church of God	1928	Lightfoot Solomon Michaux		
Christ Holy Sanctified Church	1903	Judge King	Christ Sanctified Holy Church	
Church of God (Sanctified Church)	1900	Charles Grey	COGIC	5,000
Churches of God, Holiness	1920	Hezekiah Burruss	COCHUSA	25,600
Original Church of God Sanctified	1927	Charles Grey	Church of God (Sanctified Church)	25,600
Evangelistic Church of Christ	1847	William C. Holman	COCHUSA	
Church of God (Which He Purchased With His Own Blood)	1953	William F. Fizer	Church of the Living God (CWFF)	800 (1991)

4

THE COLOR LINE
WAS WASHED AWAY
IN THE BLOOD

WILLIAM J. SEYMOUR AND
THE AZUSA STREET REVIVAL

When the Day of Pentecost had fully come,

they were all with one accord in one place.

ACTS 2:1 NKJV

NOTWITHSTANDING CONTENTIONS FROM SOME contemporary scholars that the modern Pentecostal movement resulted from a direct work of the Holy Spirit, the human contribution of William Seymour and the early-twentieth-century Los Angeles revival he led is so important to Pentecostalism's spread that charismatic scholar Peter Hocken asserts,

> If the developments associated with Charles Parham had not been followed by the outbreak at Azusa Street, the former would have probably only been another variation on the baptism of the Holy Spirit as a personal experience . . . hav[ing] no greater claim to validity than many interpretations of individual experiences in Holiness circles.[1]

---

[1]Peter J. Hocken, *The Glory and the Shame: Reflections on the Twentieth-Century Outpouring of the Holy Spirit* (Guildford, U.K.: Eagle Press, 1994), p. 53.

Yet for seventy years, Seymour's role was obscured by race politics of a movement whose initial prophetic witness of radical equality was compromised in an attempt to gain respectability within the broader evangelical context. Resultantly, Seymour's value to the movement has, historically, been underplayed to the extent that even many black Pentecostals remained unaware of his contribution until a resurgence in scholarship prompted, in part, by the civil rights movement, brought him to light.

The son of freed slaves, Seymour was born in 1870 in Centerville, Louisiana, a community whose pre–Civil War burgeoning farm economy was depleted by the war and emancipation, reducing a thriving system to a shadow of its former self and influencing freed slaves as much as former owners. The repressive culture of Reconstruction in Louisiana kept former slaves, who were legally free, in de facto servitude. Curfews kept them sequestered in their residences for much of the evening; special licenses were required to obtain employment; those who did not work were heavily fined; and black codes subjected them to violent attacks, including beating and lynching for the smallest infraction of white-defined civility.

Seymour's family lived with devastation and poverty, which increased after his father's death during William's teens, as he assumed the place as male head of the family. Little is known of Seymour's childhood religious exposure. Several sources indicate he was raised as a Baptist; others contend he was reared as a Catholic.[2] In either case, his community would have been largely Catholic. Before emancipation, masters were required to baptize slaves in the Catholic Church, and after the war, many freedmen continued to be, at least nominally, Catholic. Born five years after emancipation, William was baptized as an infant in the Roman Catholic Church in Franklin, Louisiana,[3] and would imbibe that culture during his formative years. But Louisiana, and Seymour, was influenced strongly by a rich variety of Afro-spiritual sects who combined traditional religion and Catholicism, contriving a spirituality that blended Christian liturgical ingredients and African understandings of reality, including engagement with

---

[2]See, e.g., Vinson Synan, *The Holiness-Pentecostal Tradition: Charismatic Movements in the Twentieth Century* (Grand Rapids: Eerdmans, 1997), p. 93; Cecil M. Robeck Jr., *The Azusa Street Mission and Revival: The Birth of the Global Pentecostal Movement* (Nashville: Thomas Nelson, 2006), p. 24.

[3]Larry Martin, *The Life and Ministry of William Seymour* (Pensacola, Fla.: Christian Life Books, 2006), pp. 53-54.

the supernatural and heavy doses of music and dance. Some scholars suppose that Seymour was either illiterate or completely self-taught. Though no one is sure how much education he actually completed, Seymour reportedly attended a freedman school, at least for a time.[4] Later, the lie of his illiteracy was put to rest by the detailed sermons and articles he wrote for the *Apostolic Faith* newspaper and the doctrinal statements he developed for the Apostolic Faith Mission.[5]

Seymour abandoned the poverty and racial tension of the Bayou state in his early twenties and headed north, stopping first at Memphis, Tennessee, where he served as a porter for a local businessman and then as a driver for the Tennessee Paper Company. By 1893, he was in the Midwest moving through Indiana, Ohio, Illinois, and possibly Missouri and Tennessee, working as a hotel waiter. By age twenty-five, he had settled in Indianapolis, a former Underground Railroad stop. By the time Seymour arrived in Indianapolis, however, the city and the state were less welcoming to blacks, having taken on the racial complexities of other northern areas. Blacks who moved to Indiana had to register with the state, and by the 1920s, several years after Seymour was in the city, Indianapolis had become a center of Ku Klux Klan activity.[6] While there, his job as a hotel waiter provided for his material needs. To provide for his spiritual needs, he joined Simpson Chapel Methodist Episcopal Church, where he had a conversion experience.[7] Soon, however, he found himself unsatisfied with the congregation's spiritual tenor as well as the racial climate developing in the Methodist Church and sought what he felt was a deeper experience of God as well as a more accepting environment for himself as a black man. Yet the time that he spent with this congregation would give him an appreciation for order within the church that would later be evident in the polity of the Azusa Street Mission.

---

[4]Robeck, *Azusa Street Mission and Revival*, pp. 24-25.

[5]See, e.g., William J. Seymour, "River Of Living Water" *Apostolic Faith* 1, no. 3 (1906) 2; and several essays that appear in *Doctrines and Disciplines of the Azusa Street Mission* (s.l.: s.n., 1915).

[6]See, e.g., Sarah Frances Chenault, "The Ku Klux Klan in Indiana," in *Negro Anthology*, ed. Nancy Cunard (New York: Negro Universities Press, 1969), pp. 170-72; and Richard K. Tucker, *The Dragon and the Cross: The Rise and Fall of the Ku Klux Klan in Middle America* (Hamden, Conn.: Shoe String Press 1991).

[7]Charles Shumway, "A Critical History of Glossolalia" (Ph.D. diss., Boston University, 1919), p. 173n8.

By 1900 Seymour was in Chicago and within a year had moved to Cincinnati, again working as a waiter. There he came into contact with the radical Holiness teachings of Martin Wells Knapp, founder of God's Bible School and the God's Revivalist movement. Knapp espoused a doctrine of divine healing and premillennialism, promoted Holiness revivals and missions, and helped form the International Holiness Union and Prayer League, which eventually became part of the Wesleyan Church. Knapp died in 1901, but the school continued. Whether Seymour ever encountered Knapp is unknown, but reportedly before Knapp's death, Seymour attended classes at the school that bore his imprint.[8]

In Cincinnati, he also came in contact with Daniel S. Warner's Church of God Reformation movement—the Evening Light Saints. While with the Saints, Seymour claimed the experience of sanctification and was exposed to a level of racial inclusiveness unlike any he had witnessed. The Saints saw interracial worship as a sign of the true church, and people of both races worshiped and ministered regularly in their services. More importantly, they gave racial prejudice a theological critique. Instead of testifying that they were "saved, sanctified and filled with the Holy Ghost," Saints asserted that they were "saved, sanctified, and prejudice removed."[9] Their radical criticism of racism extended beyond the church to American society. In 1901, for example, one of its leaders, William Sched, published, *Is the Negro a Beast?* to counter racist claims made in Charles Carroll's widely circulated *The Negro a Beast.*[10]

In the Evening Light Saints, Seymour found a place of full acceptance and affirmation without the debilitating sting of segregation. The group licensed and ordained him, sending him off to join the army of itinerant tent-making evangelists scattered throughout the country, and Seymour imbibed the heady spiritual fervor that had captivated the movement. During this period, he encountered the group's communal missionary homes where members worked together to support each other and carry

---

[8]J. Douglas Nelson, "For Such a Time as This: The Story of Bishop William J. Seymour and the Azusa Street Revival, A Search for Pentecostal/Charismatic Roots" (Ph.D. diss., University of Birmingham, U.K., 1981), pp. 163-64.

[9]Lewis, "William J. Seymour: Follower of the 'Evening Light,'" *Wesleyan Theological Journal* 39, no. 2 (fall 2004): 171.

[10]William Sched, *Is the Negro a Beast?* (Moundville, W.V.: Gospel Trumpet, 1901); Charles Cornval, *The Negro a Beast* (St. Louis: American Book and Bible, 1901).

out ministry. This communal living arrangement would later be modeled at the Azusa Street Mission . Other evidence of Seymour's exposure to the Evening Light Saints surfaced in the Azusa Street Mission's doctrinal distinctives. Like the Saints, Seymour's view of sanctification incorporated imagery of "cleansing the sanctuary," and a diagram of the sanctuary cleansing found in *Doctrines and Disciplines of the Azusa Street Mission* exactly copied one used by Daniel Warner.[11]

The highpoint in Seymour's spiritual sojourn in Cincinnati was countered with a personal nadir. While there Seymour contracted smallpox, a highly contagious, often fatal disease from which he was unsure of recovery. Yet even that negative episode had far-reaching spiritual implications for both Seymour and the future movement. While he lay in bed ill, he dreamed that God told him he would heal him if he would preach the gospel. Answering affirmatively, he was healed almost entirely, except for the loss of sight in his left eye from corneal ulcerations, which required him to wear a glass eye for the rest of this life.

Seymour first moved to Houston in 1902, looking for relatives with whom his family had lost contact during slavery. Using the city as a base, he traveled and preached throughout Texas and Louisiana. In summer 1904 he reportedly traveled to Jackson, Mississippi, to meet black Holiness leaders Charles Price Jones and Charles Harrison Mason. Though nothing much is known of this supposed meeting, presumably Seymour's contact with Jones, a fairly well-educated man, would strengthen his understanding of Holiness doctrine and allow him to witness a black man at the helm of a fairly successful religious movement. Whether the two maintained a relationship over the years is unknown. As the Pentecostal movement shifted into full swing, however, Jones sharply criticized the doctrine of initial evidence and any assertion that one had to speak in tongues to be assured of having the baptism of the Holy Spirit,[12] and his influence on Seymour may be detected in the Azusa leader later backing away from insistence on such evidence once the movement moved into full force.[13]

---

[11]Daniel S. Warner and H. M. Riggles, *The Cleansing of the Sanctuary* (s.l.: Faith Publishing, 1903), cited in Lewis, "William J. Seymour: Follower of the 'Evening Light,'" pp. 179-80.

[12]See Charles Price Jones, *The Gift of the Holy Spirit in the Book of Acts* (Chicago: National Publishing Board, Church of Christ [Holiness] U.S.A., 1996 [originally published in 1903]), pp. 9-12.

[13]Mason would later visit the Azusa Street Revival and have his own Pentecostal experience. In the following years, Mason and Seymour would become close friends and supporters of each other.

Back in Houston Seymour met Pastor Lucy Farrow, the woman who would introduce him to the doctrine and experience of Pentecostal Spirit baptism and began attending her Holiness church. After a period, when Farrow decided to travel and work with the Charles Parham family, she tapped him as interim pastorate of the small congregation. Farrow had already been working as a cook for Parham's Bible school and had been able to hear the lectures he delivered about the doctrine of initial evidence. Her pastoral relationship with Seymour opened a door for him to sit under Parham's teaching, and reportedly, the two men quickly struck up a relationship and an appreciation for each other's gifts as evangelists and preachers. Their introduction touched off a series of events that would change the face of American Christianity, ensuring each a place in religious history. Their meeting brought Seymour, once again, face-to-face with racial prejudice. In early spring 1906 Seymour found himself in a peculiar situation at Parham's school. Texas law precluded him from being a full-fledged student sitting in the classroom with white students. So Seymour, possibly along with other African Americans, positioned himself outside the door to glean as much as he could of Parham's doctrine.[14]

State law was not the only reason Seymour was excluded from the class. Parham had developed a convoluted Anglo-Israel theology that saw Anglo-Saxons as a superior race descended from the ten tribes of Israel.[15] He reworked the biblical creation narrative, contending that God created two distinct types of humans—a dominant and a lesser race. According to him Cain's marriage to a descendant of the sons of God caused the flood and other evils, including disease, that have plagued humankind throughout history. More importantly for him, society was now composed of three classes of human beings. Hindus, Japanese, high Germans, Danes, Scandinavians and Anglo-Saxons, as descendents of Abraham, "retained experiential salvation and deeper spiritual truths." Russians, Greeks, Italians, low Germans, French, Spaniards and their descendants were the Gentiles "who scarce ever obtain the knowledge of truth." And black, brown, red and yellow races were heathens whom he was unsure were redeemable.[16]

---

[14]Nelson, *For Such a Time as This*, p. 167.
[15]Charles F. Parham, "The Ten Lost Tribes," in *The Sermons of Charles F. Parham* (New York: Garland, 1985), pp. 105-8. First published as *A Voice Crying in the Wilderness* (Baxter Springs, Kans.: Apostolic Faith Church, 1910).
[16]Ibid., p. 107.

Despite these misgivings he seemed intent on having Seymour help expand his teachings and revival to Houston's black community. In the af-
ternoons the two could be found doing evangelistic outreach in the black
section of town. In the evenings, though forced to sit in the section reserved for blacks, Seymour joined other black worshipers in Parham's multiracial evangelistic services.

Among Seymour's other Houston Holiness associates was a young
Black woman, Neely Terry, who would be pivotal in bringing him to Los
Angeles. The former Baptist had moved with a small contingent of her
congregation to the Nazarene Church after accepting the Holiness doctrine. While visiting relatives in Houston, Terry visited Farrow's church at
least once while Seymour filled in and was impressed with his ministry.
On returning to Los Angeles, she found that her pastor, Julia Hutchins,
was looking for a man to assist her. Terry convinced Hutchins that Seymour was the right man, and an invitation was issued.[17]

Seymour arrived in Los Angeles midwinter 1906, and Hutchins's congregation was anticipating his ministry. But when his preaching emphasized the Pentecostal experience of speaking in tongues as evidence of
Holy Spirit baptism, he found himself at odds with Hutchins, who rejected the contention. She and members of her congregation saw themselves as having already experienced Holy Spirit baptism and felt that it
needed no physical evidence.[18] It is unsure how long Hutchins's congregation tolerated his ministry. Some historians suggest he only preached one
sermon and that when he returned for the evening service, he was locked
out of the church. Others suggested that he preach several messages over
a short period.[19] Before long, however, he was asked to leave and arrangements for his lodging were canceled.

---

[17]James S. Tinney, "William J. Seymour: Father of Modern-Day Pentecostalism," in *Black Apostles: Afro-American Clergy Confront the Twentieth Century*, ed. Randall Burkett and Richard
Newman (Boston: G. K. Hall, 1978), p. 218.

[18]By that time, the Holiness movement was divided. Some, such as Hutchins, upheld the notion
that Holy Spirit baptism needed to follow sanctification but was to be accepted by faith and
acted on, requiring no outward sign or confirmation. Others, such as Parham and Seymour,
were convinced that though it was through faith that one received the baptism of the Holy
Spirit, without some form of concrete evidence to confirm it, one could never be sure whether
one actually had received such Spirit baptism.

[19]James Tinney draws the former conclusion in "A Theoretical and Historical Comparison of
Black Political and Religious Movements" (Ph.D. diss., Howard University, 1978), p. 231, and
Robeck draws the latter in *Azusa Street Mission and Revival*, p. 62.

Notwithstanding her misgivings, Hutchins did not entirely break fellowship with Seymour or rely solely on her own judgment to assess the validity of his claims. Instead, without promoting Seymour's theology, she provided an audience for his message, attempting to settle its truthfulness by arranging a meeting for him with local Holiness leaders, including T. M. Roberts, president of the Southern California Holiness Association. Unconvinced by his argument, Roberts forbade Seymour to continue teaching on the local Holiness circuit. Though Seymour complied without attempting to contact other Holiness congregations, the meeting's exposure gave his ideas voice among a number of Holiness preachers. Not all dismissed his contention out of hand, and the exposure ensured that news of the teaching made the rounds of the Los Angeles Holiness community. Some would later come to his meetings not as seekers but as skeptical observers; some came attempting to correct Seymour and curtail the spread of his message. Others came drawn by the sheer strangeness of the tongues phenomenon. Nonetheless, some eventually accepted the doctrine and received the Pentecostal experience; and a few remained as supporters. Between the time she first encountered Seymour and the early days of the Azusa Street Mission, Hutchins had a change of heart. She would become one of Seymour's supporters and, as a regular participant in the Azusa Street Revival, sought and received the Pentecostal experience. Later, she not only took the Pentecostal message from Azusa Street to Africa but also encouraged others to become missionaries to that continent.

BONNIE BRAE STREET PRAYER MEETING: THE REVIVAL BEGINS

Once locked out of Hutchins's church, Seymour initially found himself with few allies, little material resources, no fare back to Houston and no place either to preach or reside. Neely Terry, the woman who had suggested the invitation, probably felt both some loyalty and a sense of obligation to him, since it was her suggestion that first brought him to the city. Perhaps with only a little urging from Terry, Brother Lee, a member of Hutchins's group, acted out of Christian charity to solve at least one of Seymour's problems. Though still somewhat skeptical of Seymour's doctrine, he offered the evangelist a place to stay until he could find other accommodations. This invitation would later seem to have been providential, for Lee would become the first of Seymour's initially small group to receive the Pentecostal evidence of speaking in tongues.

With Seymour at least temporarily having his need for shelter met, Terry influenced her cousin Ruth Asberry and her husband Richard to open their modest home at 214 Bonnie Brea Street as a place to continue his ministry.[20] Knowing no one else in Los Angeles, Seymour accepted Lee's invitation for lodging and the Asberrys' invitation as the base for teaching a Bible study. The timing of the move of the meeting to Bonnie Brae Street is disputed to be as early as late February and as late as early April.[21] Either way, the opening of the Asberry home set the stage for the outbreak of revival. There, a band of mostly black women household workers began to gather to seek God for a new experience of the Spirit.

Seymour himself had not yet had the experience, and initially his teaching bore little fruit, except to intensify the little congregation's hunger for the experience. For several days no one at the meeting was able to lay hold of it; but the meeting slowly continued to grow, and the saints faithfully studied and prayed. It would be at the Lee home, just down the block, that the initial spark of the Azusa Street Revival would flare. One evening while sharing a meal, Edward Lee asked Seymour to pray with him. As he did Lee became the first of the group to receive the Pentecostal experience of tongues. When he and Seymour arrived at the prayer meeting, they shared the news of his experience with those who had gathered. This was just the spark necessary for turning up the fire of revival to red-hot temperature.[22]

On April 9, 1906, seven of those attending the Bonnie Brae Street Meeting experienced speaking in tongues. Seymour would not receive his Pentecostal experience until three days later.[23] The prayer meeting continued for several days, and one by one, as more people began to experience speaking in tongues, the small group grew to fill the double parlor of the house to overflowing. Within days, as news of the meeting spread through the community, attendance grew such that it spilled out onto the porch.

[20]Since the church that served as the original site for the Azusa Street Revival was subsequently demolished, the Bonnie Brae Street site remains as the only physical memorial to the beginning of the Pentecostal movement.
[21]Robeck, *Azusa Street Mission and Revival,* p. 62, contends that Seymour probably preached most of the sermons during the first weeks.
[22]Shumway, *Critical History of Glossolalia,* pp. 174-75.
[23]Untitled article, *Apostolic Faith* 1, no. 4 (1906): 1.

The street in front of the house was filled with seekers, and onlookers were drawn by the strange sights and sounds.

AT THE REVIVAL

When news of the outbreak of tongues traveled through the Los Angeles Holiness community and the committed and curious flocked to see, it became apparent that the Bonnie Brae Street house was too small. The group found and rented a converted livery stable at 312 Azusa Street that had once served as the sanctuary of the Stevens African Methodist Episcopal Church. When they took possession of the building, evidence of the former use as a stable was visible. And though the two-story building was usable, it was in ill repair. The saints gathered daily in a large room on the first floor for worship. The second floor held several smaller rooms that served a number of uses. The "Upper Room" was an anteroom where those desiring to "pray through" to conversion, healing or baptism of the Holy Spirit could receive concentrated attention by altar workers. There was a missions office and several small apartments where members of the congregation lived from time to time, much like Seymour had witnessed with the mission homes, or guest ministers would be housed while attending the revival. At one point the Seymours, along with Lucy Farrow, resided there.

The first three and a half years were the most intense. Day and night, seven days a week, for more than seven years, they came from all over the country and the world to take part in an unparalleled move of God reminiscent of the Upper Room on the Day of Pentecost. Daily camp-meeting style worship lasted for several hours, and it generally ran from ten in the morning until at least midnight and sometimes for several hours past that. These ecstatic services were characterized by impromptu sermons by a number of people, prophesying, singing in English and in tongues, conversions, divine healing and exorcisms. No count was taken, but most reports estimate that, at least in the early days of the revival, attendance ran in the hundreds and that the mission was scarcely large enough to contain the anxious seekers. Many stood for several hours around the perimeters of the walls; others stood outside on the porch or listened in through the glassless windows.

Soon word of the revival caught the attention, albeit mostly negative, of the secular press, and the local media began to notice this little-regarded section of town inhabited by a less-regarded group of people. They sent reporters to observe and critically—often sarcastically—report the goings on to the city and the world. Headlines such as "a weird babel of tongue" among people who "practice the most fanatical rites, preach the weirdest theories and work themselves into a state of trance in their peculiar zeal" were designed to draw public attention and expand readership.[24] These stories, along with those published in the *Apostolic Faith*,[25] word of mouth reports, letters and other correspondences from attendees to loved ones and acquaintances, drew a steady crowd almost from the beginning.[26] Some were only curiosity seekers; some were skeptics who came to convince Seymour and his followers to abandon their fanatical antics and heretical beliefs. Some just wanted a closer relationship with God. Others wanted to add yet another spiritual experience to their lives.

Within months the mission began publishing its own newspaper, the *Apostolic Faith*, which was sent out free of charge, and distribution quickly soared from five thousand to fifty thousand copies. The four-page tabloid of the thirteen issues, published monthly, more or less, from September 1906 until its demise in May 1908, was filled with testimonies of Holy Spirit baptism, healing, deliverance and other miraculous occurrences. It carried "word for word" interpretations of messages given in tongues at Azusa Street and other revival sites and stories of those going out from the revival to carry the Pentecostal message across the country and around the world. Sermons and teachings provided instruction in doctrine and correction of heretical teachings beginning to circulate through the movement.

Leaders and common people sent stories from other Pentecostal revivals around the country and the world. Many who would later become important to the movement sent items. Thomas Ball Barratt wrote from Norway about the outbreak of revival there. G. B. Cashwell, a Holiness evangelist from North Carolina, described the success of his meeting throughout the Southeast; Charles Harrison Mason, founder of the

---

[24]"Weird Babel of Tongues: New Sect of Fanatics Is Breaking Loose; Wild Scene Last Night on Azusa Street; Gurgle of Wordless Talk by a Sister," *Los Angeles Times*, April 18, 1906, p. 1.

[25]*Apostolic Faith* was the monthly newsletter produced by the Azusa Street Mission. It was disseminated to a mailing list of approximately three thousand people between 1906 and 1908, when Florence Crawford had a disagreement with Seymour and left the ministry, taking the mailing list with her.

[26]Within six months, several thousand people had visited the services.

Church of God in Christ, gave a testimony of his conversion to a Pentecostal understanding of Holy Spirit baptism. Florence Crawford kept the congregation abreast of what was unfolding in the Northwest. Sam and Ardell Mead, two seasoned missionaries to Africa, spoke of how baptism in the Holy Spirit had given their ministry new vitality. But there were also testimonies from just plain folk who had in some way been touched by the fire of Pentecost either at the revival at Azusa Street or at a camp meeting or in their local congregation. Story after story told of Holy Spirit baptisms, healings and other miracles.

Interestingly, while the *Apostolic Faith* took pains to include information from other pockets of revival, many existing Holiness and new Pentecostal papers largely ignored what was going on at Azusa Street. An examination of papers such Alexander Boddy's *Confidence*, published between 1908 and 1926 from Sunderland, England; M. M. Pinson's *Word and Witness*, established around 1911; *The Pentecost*, published 1908 to 1910 by J. Roswell Flower; and the *Latter Rain Evangel*, published by William Piper in Chicago from 1908, show very little attention to the Azusa Street meetings.[27]

A prominent feature of the meetings was their radically egalitarian nature. Though most worshipers were from the lower and working classes, there was no stratification either by class, race, gender or age in involvement or leadership in the services. Men and women, adults and children, black, white, yellow, and red freely worshiped God and admonished each other to holiness of life through speaking in tongues and interpretation, prophecy, testimony, song, prayer, miraculous signs and preaching. Each one, in order, as they felt directed by the Holy Spirit, gave vent to the fire that was shut deep within their bones and glorified God for their newfound freedom and empowerment. Women and men freely participated as they felt God leading them. Even children who felt inspired by God had a voice in the worship and received Pentecostal Holy Spirit baptism.[28] Ecclesiastical creden-

---

[27]Boddy published a report of his 1912 trip and meeting with Williams and Jennie. See "At Los Angeles," *Confidence* (1912): 1. For more on early Pentecostal periodicals, see Wayne E. Warner, "Periodicals," in *The New International Dictionary of Pentecostal and Charismatic Movements,* ed. Stanley M. Burgess and Eduard van der Mass (Grand Rapids: Zondervan, 2002), pp. 974-82; and J. Roswell Flower, "Publishing the Pentecostal Message: A Pioneer Editor Tells How Early Papers Published the Story," *Assemblies of God Heritage* 2, no. 3 (1982): 1, 8.

[28]Indeed, one of the strongest critiques of the revival was the freedom that men and women, as well as people of various races, exhibited in praying for, embracing, and otherwise interacting with one another.

tials or education played no part in determining a person's role in the meetings. Rather, people felt led directly by the Holy Spirit to testify, sing, exhort, pray or preach. Seymour and others of those in "leadership" gave them freedom to do so. People of different races and cultures came together to experience this "new religion" and worshiped side-by-side without the constraint of segregated seating, evident even in mixed-race meetings of the period. This degree of racial harmony led Frank Bartleman to report in his later memoirs that "the color line was washed away in the blood [of Jesus]."[29] Another characterization put it more explicitly:

> It was something very extraordinary . . . white pastors from the South were eagerly prepared to go to Los Angeles to Negroes [sic], to fellowship with them and to receive through their prayers and intercessions the blessings of the Spirit. And it was still more wonderful that these white pastors went back to the South and reported that they had been together with Negroes [sic], that they had prayed in one Spirit and received the same blessing.[30]

Ministry was largely a lay matter, based on perception of a call that relied on personal testimony rather than ecclesial endorsement. A congregation's affirmation of such testimony revolved around perceived Spirit empowerment, a personal sense of God-ordained destiny and endowment with specific spiritual gifts for effective ministry. For them, the Spirit, rather than church hierarchy, was arbiter of a person's fitness for ministry.

There was no distinction of ministerial credentials in the dramatic demonstrations. Black washerwomen prayed with prominent white pastors. Young girls prophetically confronted seasoned men with messages that brought them to repentance and renewed spiritual vitality. Lay people laid hands on clergypersons of all ranks, praying for them to receive healing, sanctification and Holy Spirit baptism. Some of these early Pentecostals were simply "ordained by the Lord" with no human agency affirming ministerial status, asserting that the fruit of their accomplishments determined whether they were truly called. Some were informally set apart by laying on of hands within a group in a home meeting or other nontraditional setting; but again, they sought no formal credentials. Others held

---

[29]Frank Bartleman, *How Pentecost Came to Los Angeles* (Los Angeles: Frank Bartleman, 1925), p. 54.

[30]Walter Hollenweger, *The Pentecostals: The Charismatic Movement in the Churches* (Minneapolis: Augsburg Press, 1972), p. 24.

credentials from local mission churches. Some who had been licensed or ordained with established denominations were forced to forfeit their credentials once they accepted the Pentecostal experience.

As people prayed for the sick and reported reversals in their physical, mental, emotional or spiritual conditions, testimonies in the *Apostolic Faith* attested that "people are healed at the Mission almost every day."[31] Adherents were quick to clarify, "We are not divine healers any more than we are divine saviors. Healing is done through the Almighty God."[32] Other spiritual gifts were manifested as men and women prophesied, gave words of wisdom or knowledge, exhorted, and interpreted messages spoken in tongues.[33] People reported dreams and visions of God encouraging them or giving direction for their lives or that of the congregation.

Many observers—including some who formerly had only been curious or skeptical—stayed to experience Holy Spirit baptism with tongues. Once convicted, some Holiness ministers left the revival to preach their newfound reality. Many of these were forced to leave their existing bodies after embracing the new doctrine, even as others steered their congregations and denominations toward the Pentecostal movement.

The revival's heightened spiritual climate also drew a surplus of interest from spiritualist mediums, hypnotists and others who dabbled in mystical experiences. Seymour was not unaware of their presence, but their dark power proved no match for the faith of the saints, who contended that those who had experimented with the occult were being set free by God's power. Indeed, the *Apostolic Faith* boasted that "spiritualists have come to our meetings and had the demons cast out of them and have been saved and sanctified."[34] Another *Apostolic Faith* article testified:

> A brother who had been a spiritualist medium . . . so possessed with demons that he had no rest, and was on the point of committing suicide, was instantly delivered of demon power. He then sought God for the pardon of his sins and sanctification, and is now filled with a different spirit.[35]

---

[31]Untitled article, *Apostolic Faith* 1, no. 5 (1907): 1. See also, "The Precious Atonement," *Apostolic Faith* 1, no. 1 (1906): 2; Salvation and Healing, *Apostolic Faith* 1, no. 4 (1906): 2.

[32]Untitled article, *Apostolic Faith* 1, no. 2 (1906): 4.

[33]See, e.g., "A Message Concerning His Coming," *Apostolic Faith* 1, no. 2 (1906): 3; "A Testimony in Tongues," *Apostolic Faith* 1, no. 8 (1907): 2

[34]Untitled article, *Apostolic Faith* 1, no. 4 (1906): 2.

[35]Untitled article, *Apostolic Faith* 1, no. 1 (1906): 1.

SPREADING THE REVIVAL

While Azusa Street was home to many ordinary people, some who attended had already made names for themselves in Holiness and evangelical circles. For example, Alfred Garrison (A. G.) and Lillian Garr arrived in the spring of 1906 and within several days experienced the baptism with tongues. Reportedly, not only did the Garrs attend the Azusa Street meetings themselves; but they also temporarily closed their church so members of the congregation could attend services with them. And after a short time, Garr permanently closed his church and urged the congregation to join with Seymour's meeting.[36] Some historians suggest Garr's move helped turn a revival populated by a few, mostly African American, house servants into the large multiracial meeting that the Azusa Street Revival became.[37] By either account the Garrs found themselves without a pastorate and eagerly seeking to be involved again in ministry leadership. Certainly they, like so many other ministers at the Azusa Street Revival, were given an opportunity to testify and exhort as they felt directed by the Spirit, yet they held no position at the Azusa Street Mission. Not surprisingly, with no place to serve in official leadership, they stayed at the revival for only a short while. Within a week of Alfred's Pentecostal baptism in the Holy Spirit, the couple announced that they felt called as missionaries to India. Almost immediately, an offering of several hundred dollars was raised for their support. In late June 1906, Alfred and Lillian left to begin what was to become a spiritually fruitful, yet personally costly, missionary journey.[38]

Charles Harrison Mason came to Azusa Street partially on the prodding of his colaborer Charles Price Jones to ascertain whether the news they had been receiving back east was founded on truth or error. Once

---

[36]Steve Thompson and Adam Gordon, *A Twentieth Century Apostle: The Life of Alfred Garr* (Wilkesboro, N.C.: MorningStar, 2004), p. 61. Frank Bartleman, *How Pentecost Came to Los Angeles*, p. 53, is also among those who make this suggestion.

[37]Thompson and Gordon, *Twentieth Century Apostle*, pp. 61-62.

[38]Despite great spiritual victories, the Garrs paid a heavy personal price. They experienced deprivation and the necessity to depend on God for their daily meager sustenance. When the Garrs arrived in Hong Kong in 1907, Lillian was pregnant with their second daughter, who was delivered stillborn. The first daughter, Virginia, succumbed to smallpox at the age two. Their premature son weighed only three pounds at birth and was initially given only a slight chance to live because of lactose intolerance. After returning from the mission field, Lillian died in Los Angeles in 1916 at the age of thirty-eight. For more information on the Garrs, see Thompson and Gordon, *Twentieth Century Apostle*.

he visited the revival, Mason accepted the Pentecostal message and experienced Pentecostal Spirit baptism. When he returned east to tell Jones and their constituents about his new understanding, Jones rejected the doctrine and experience, and the two eventually severed ties. The organization that Mason went on to build became the Church of God in Christ, the largest African American Pentecostal denomination in the world.

Though his initial racial prejudice almost short-circuited his acceptance of the Pentecostal baptism, the coming of G. B. Cashwell to the Azusa Street Revival and his eventual receipt of the experience would greatly influence the movement's early growth. Cashwell had previously been in mixed-race Holiness meetings, so these were not new to him. But he had not witnessed blacks at such high levels of leadership as they held at Azusa Street. He struggled for a time before going forward to the altar.[39] Like so many others, once he received his Holy Spirit baptism he stayed at Azusa Street only a short time, leaving to conduct a succession of evangelistic services in Tennessee, Georgia and North Carolina. In these meetings, leaders of several Holiness bodies heard his message of initial evidence of tongues, and several new Pentecostal bodies came into being.[40]

John G. Lake met Seymour while attending Parham's meetings in Houston and reported receiving the baptism of the Holy Spirit under Parham's ministry at Zion, Illinois. But he visited the Azusa Street Mission prior to taking the Pentecostal message to South Africa in 1908 and revisited Azusa Street at least once to report on the progress of that work. He attempted to carry at least part of the interracial vision of Azusa Street to that country and was disturbed that he could not conduct interracial meetings or baptize blacks and whites together. Lake's South African ministry would become one of the most prolific Pentecostal works on the continent. Within five years he established 500 black and 125 white Pentecostal

---

[39]Gaston B. Cashwell, "Came 3,000 Miles for His Pentecost," *Apostolic Faith* 1, no. 4 (1906): 3.

[40]A. J. Tomlinson, general overseer of the Church of God (Cleveland, Tennessee), heard Cashwell during his Tennessee campaign, received the experience of glossolalia and subsequently moved that body into the Pentecostal camp. In one campaign in Dunn, North Carolina, J. H. King, who later became bishop of the Pentecostal Holiness Church, experienced speaking in tongues and was influential in getting that body to move into the Pentecostal camp. Also because of his North Carolina campaign, the United Holy Church, a black Holiness body, adopted a statement of faith that placed the group in the Pentecostal family.

churches. Though Lake's ministry produced seemingly more tangible fruit than the man he so much admired, Lake later commented that Seymour had "more of God in his life than any man I had ever met."[41] He would remember his first encounter with Seymour this way, "God Almighty had put such a hunger in [his] heart that when the fire of God came it glorified him. I do not believe that any other man in modern times had a more wonderful deluge of God in his life than God gave to that dear fellow."[42]

Individuals and teams spread out across the country and world speeding the Pentecostal message, called to specific mission fields by prophetic pronouncements, dreams, visions and messages in tongues. A primary mechanism for hearing a call was attestation that a tongue speaker was conversing in a known language through the gift of xenolalia (the ability to supernaturally speak in a known language that was previously unlearned).[43] Seekers and believers in the congregation were excited to hear their mother tongue spoken, ready to affirm it as an authentic language and eager to give an "interpretation" of what was being spoken. In some cases that interpretation was a simple "praise to the Lord." In a few cases, it was a strong rebuke or admonition to a single individual or the entire group. In other cases it was a call or confirmation to ministry or missions.

Armed with these interpretations and confirmations, several set out for the mission field without the benefit of language study. The second edition of the *Apostolic Faith* reported, for instance, that "missionaries for the foreign fields, equipped with several languages, are now on their way."[44] Julia Hutchins, for example, was said to have received the "Uganda language . . . of the people to whom she is sent." And that gift seemed to have been affirmed because "a brother who has been in that country understands and has interpreted the language she speaks."[45] Some, like Hutchins and Farrow, reported using xenolalic languages on the mission field.[46] Hutchins saw her language endowment as confirmation of God's call to her to go to Africa that had come several years earlier. Her trip gave no

[41]John G. Lake, *Adventures in God* (Tulsa: Harrison House, 1981), p. 19.
[42]Frank Bartleman, *Azusa Street* (South Plainfield, N.J.: Bridge, 1980), p. xviii.
[43]One example of this phenomenon is the Garr's story in "Good News from Danville, Va.," *Apostolic Faith* 1, no. 1 (1906): 4.
[44]"Fire Still Falling," *Apostolic Faith* 1, no. 2 (1906): 1.
[45]"Testimonies Of Outgoing Missionaries," *Apostolic Faith* 1, no. 2 (1906): 1.
[46]See, e.g., "Tongues Go into Africa" *Los Angeles Times*, May 18, 1907, p. Il1.

occasion to prove the gift, since English was the official language of the area of Liberia in which she ministered. Reportedly, however, during Farrow's tenure in the same country, she preached at least two messages in Kru, and some of the Kru people to whom she ministered received the English language with their Holy Spirit baptism.[47] Many, however, returned to Los Angeles disappointed when they could not communicate in their new language. Once in China, Lillian Garr found the Mandarin dialect she received at Azusa Street inadequate for communicating to the Chinese people. When their efforts in utilizing tongues in evangelism and preaching failed, A. G. Garr abandoned his insistence that tongues was a missionary tool, and Lillian then began to study the Chinese language, devoting several hours a day to learning its grammatical rules, syntax and pronunciation.[48]

No part of the world was untouched by the revival. Stories poured in from every corner of the globe to the *Apostolic Faith*, reporting that

> the Pentecost has crossed the water on both sides to the Hawaiian Islands on the west, and England, Norway, Sweden and India on the east. . . . We rejoice to hear that Pentecost has fallen in Calcutta, India. . . . We have letters from China, Germany, Switzerland, Norway, Sweden, England, Ireland, Australia and other countries from hungry souls that want their Pentecost.[49]

SEYMOUR'S LEADERSHIP

With all that was going on at the revival, Seymour clearly emerged as the leader of the congregation and the meeting. He was instrumental in bringing the mission into being and, for sixteen years until his death in 1922, served as its pastor. Seymour kept a low profile, his leadership exhibiting humility that some mistook for weakness; yet he displayed inner strength when needed to handle the myriad difficult situations arising within the congregation. On several occasions he was challenged to defend not only his position as pastor but also his authority as head of the fledgling mission and movement. While "Brother Seymour" (as the saints referred to him)

---

[47]Untitled article, *Apostolic Faith* 1, no. 12 (1908): 1.

[48]Grant Wacker, *Heaven Below: Early Pentecostals and American Culture* (Cambridge Mass.: Harvard University Press, 2001), p. 50.

[49]"Pentecostal Missionary Reports," *Apostolic Faith* 1, no. 6 (1907): 1.

pastored the flock, many contended that "the Lord was, in reality, the leader."[50] Throughout extended periods of the services, Seymour reportedly could be found with his head behind a makeshift pulpit of empty shoe boxes, lost in prayer yet cognizant of everything that was going on.[51] As time passed, it became evident that he was, indeed, the leader of the little mission, if not of the revival itself.

Though many gave impromptu sermons as prompted by the Spirit, Seymour was the main preacher. He apparently did not fit the Bible-thumping caricature often ascribed to Pentecostal preachers, but his messages were powerful enough that the altars of the mission were regularly filled with those seeking repentance, sanctification, Holy Spirit baptism or healing.

As the congregation increased, Seymour introduced greater structure, appointing a committee to oversee the congregation's administrative needs and selecting, credentialing and appointing people to lead within the congregation. Hiram Smith served as Seymour's associate pastor, helping sign credentials for other workers, baptizing new converts and exercising general oversight of the mission.[52] Phoebe Sargeant and Jennie Moore were appointed as city missionaries.[53] Glenn Cook served the mission's business manager; Clara Lum was Seymour's secretary and coedited the *Apostolic Faith* newspaper.[54] But these were only the head of a cadre of volunteers who cooked and served meals, prayed at the altar, and carried out all the tasks needed to sustain the work of the growing mission. He also selected, credentialed and appointed people to serve in leadership roles throughout the movement developing around the mission. Florence Crawford, for example, was appointed as the state supervisor of California, and Cook as her assistant. G. W. Evans was appointed as a field director to spearhead revival meetings along the West Coast and organize new congregations that would come under the leadership of that local congregation.

In 1915 Seymour developed the *Doctrine and Disciplines of the Azusa Street Mission*. This publication not only laid out the foundational beliefs

---

[50]Eyewitness Frank Bartleman makes such a contention in *How Pentecost Came to Los Angeles*, p. 58.
[51]Ibid.
[52]Robeck, *Azusa Street Mission and Revival*, p. 173.
[53]The specific responsibilities of these two women in this position is unclear.
[54]Edith Blumhofer and Grant Wacker, "Who Edited the Azusa Mission's *Apostolic Faith*?" *Assemblies of God Heritage* 21 (2001): 17.

of the congregation and its founder; but it also detailed liturgies and orders of worship for ordination, Communion, weddings and funerals, extending fellowship to new members and other special services. The document provides the clearest exposition of Seymour's doctrinal understanding of salvation, sanctification, Holy Spirit baptism and the nature of the church. It also outlined Seymour's understanding of a number of practical issues such as acceptable criteria for dissolution of marriage and for remarriage, criteria for selecting ministers within the church, and church discipline. Before its publication, excerpts had appeared in volumes of the *Apostolic Faith* as early as 1907. The doctrinal stances Seymour portrays in the work reflect his early Holiness affiliation, especially with the Evening Light Saints, while his liturgical formulations clearly indicate an earlier tie to Methodism.[55] The breadth of structure of these liturgies—replete with specific biblical passages, written prayers and words of institution—shows an exposure to, and appreciation of, traditions outside the Holiness or Pentecostal movements. The grammatical structure puts to bed the lie that Seymour was largely illiterate. It portrays a man who valued education and had at least a rudimentary understanding of complex theological ideas. Within this document he envisioned the establishment of educational institutions: primary and secondary schools as well as colleges, universities, Bible schools and seminaries to train ministers.[56]

While the revival continued, several who came and received their Pentecostal experience moved on to plant their own congregations within a short distance of the mission. First New Testament Church, the Eighth and Maple Mission, the Upper Room Mission, Peoples' Church, and the Vernon Mission were all within walking distance of Azusa Street. But these congregations differed from Azusa Street primarily in their more homogeneous racial makeup. Undaunted by what some pastors may have seen as a competition for members, Seymour embraced the new congregations, celebrated the spread of the revival, invited prayer on their behalf and even advertised their meetings. As much as possible, Seymour continued a congenial fellowship with these pastors, preaching in their churches when asked and inviting them to preach at the Azusa Street Mission even

---

[55]E.g., the polity outlined in the *Doctrines and Disciplines of the Azusa Street Mission* clearly followed the structure used within the African Methodist Episcopal discipline.
[56]*Doctrines and Disciplines of the Azusa Street Mission*, p. 84.

during his absence. Testimonies from these congregations were published in the *Apostolic Faith*. Seymour went as far as organizing a weekly meeting where these leaders could gather for prayer, mutual support, counsel and Bible study. Many of their congregations grew and expanded at what appeared to be the Azusa Street Mission's expense.

SEYMOUR'S THEOLOGICAL TURN

As important as Seymour's administrative and spiritual gifts may have been, an often overlooked aspect of his leadership was his attempt at constructing a Pentecostal theological framework. His earliest preaching in Los Angeles seems to have centered on the phenomenon of speaking in tongues accompanying authentic Holy Spirit baptism, and the Azusa Street Mission and Revival were certainly open to the display of that and other ecstatic phenomena. Articles in the *Apostolic Faith* as well as writings in *Doctrines and Disciplines* show, however, that Seymour gradually moved away from insisting that speaking in tongues was the most valid initial visible evidence of Holy Spirit baptism or any insinuation that every Spirit-filled believer had to show such evidence.[57] Instead, he insisted that love was as sure a sign of Holy Spirit baptism as tongues and that without such love tongues was an insufficient sign of the Spirit's indwelling of an individual.[58] Further, for him, the experience of Spirit baptism was not an essential element in conversion but rather an added blessing or impartation of grace. According to Seymour, therefore,

> When we set up tongues to be the Bible evidence of baptism in the Holy Spirit and fire only, we have left the divine Word of God and have instituted our own teaching. . . . While tongues is one of the signs that follows God's Spirit-filled children, they will have to know the truth and do the

---

[57]See, e.g., "Is the speaking in tongues the standard of fellowship with the Pentecost people?" *Apostolic Faith* 1, no. 12 (1907-1908). In an untitled article in the January 1907 issue of the *Apostolic Faith,* the editor declared, "We have seen missions and churches banded together to stop what they call a 'tongues' salvation. But, dear ones, this is not a salvation of tongues. It is in the Blood . . . of Jesus Christ that cleanses from all sin." See also *Doctrines and Disciplines of the Azusa Street Mission,* pp. 51-53.

[58]Seymour said explicitly that "the baptism of the Holy Ghost means to be flooded with the love of God and power for service, and a love for the truth as it is in God's Word" (*Doctrines and Disciplines of the Azusa Street Mission,* p. 92). In an article in the *Apostolic Faith* 1, no. 11 (1908-1909): 2, titled "Questions Answered," Seymour responded to the query of "What is the real evidence of that [one] has received the baptism with the Holy Ghost?" by asserting that it was "Divine love, which is charity."

truth. . . . All God's children . . . can pray . . . for an outpouring of the Spirit upon the holy sanctified life and can receive a great filling of the Holy Spirit and speak in tongues. But we don't put our faith on [the gift of tongues] as essential to our salvation.[59]

Seymour fully expected that his stand might place him at odds with some Pentecostal brothers and sisters and wrote about that possibility. An article in the *Doctrines and Discipline* anticipated their objections by proclaiming,

How does our doctrine differ from the other Pentecostal brethren? First they claim that a man or woman has not the Holy Spirit, except that they speak in tongues. . . . That is contrary to the teachings of Christ. If we would base our faith on tongues being the evidence of the Holy Ghost it would knock out our faith in the blood of Christ and our inward witness of the Holy Spirit bearing witness with our Spirit.[60]

He was certain that many had settled for false hope in an outward physical sign without having an inward change in their spiritual condition, which he refuted by asking, "How do you know when you have the gift of the Holy Ghost? He, the Spirit of Truth will guide you into all truth. . . . The gift of the Holy Ghost is more than speaking in tongues. He is wisdom, power, truth, holiness. He is the person that teaches us the truth."[61] Seymour's concern was, seemingly, tied to the outworking of Holy Spirit baptism rather than any mechanical formulaic test of its reception. As Ithiel Clemmons asserts, "At the heart of Seymour's pastoral vision w[ere] the principles of [h]oliness and [u]nity."[62]

THE REVIVAL'S DETRACTORS

From its earliest days, when every seat was full and people stood around the perimeters to get a taste of what was going on inside, the revival was not without critics. The very aspects touted by some were denounced by others. Racial inclusiveness, for example, was held up by some as a new paradigm

[59]*Doctrines and Disciplines of the Azusa Street Mission*, p. 9.
[60]Ibid., pp. 51-53.
[61]Ibid., p. 51.
[62]Ithiel Clemmons, "New Life through New Community: The Prophetic Theological Praxis of Bishop William J. Seymour of the Azusa Street Revival" (address delivered at Regent University School of Divinity, April 18, 1996).

the Spirit was forging while others found it disgusting or, at least, illegal and lacking in social decorum. While some saw the lack of hierarchical structure as freeing, others called it chaos. The emphasis on tongues and other ecstatic expressions in worship were hailed by some as a fresh move of the Spirit and denounced by others as heretical fanaticism. Criticism came from three major sources, which apparently held little in common with each other except that they found the revival and the movement it was ushering in problematic. The secular press led the assault, but it was closely followed by leaders in the Holiness movement, who were only a step ahead of other, generally more fundamentalist religious leaders.

The secular press. While Seymour's formulations and the goings on at Azusa Street were certainly discussed among Holiness leaders and laity, they generally withheld public critique during the earliest days of the revival. The earliest written ridicule came from the local press around Los Angeles, who sent reporters within days of the revival's move to Azusa Street. The *Los Angeles Times*, whose 1906 circulation was forty-five thousand, used these stories to titillate its readers. In its first story on the revival, only several days after it moved into the Azusa Street setting, the paper reported that those who gathered there were "a bizarre new religious sect . . . 'breathing strange utterances and mouthing a creed which it would seem no sane mortal could understand.'"[63] Furthermore, it alleged that "devotees . . . practice the most fanatical rites, preach the wildest theories, and work themselves into a state of mad excitement."[64] One of the major issues that disturbed the secular press was the freedom the revival allowed for what would have been considered socially inappropriate contact between genders.[65]

The racial undertones of reports from the secular press were inescapable. Though dismissing the entire revival as a gathering of religious fanatics, what struck many reporters was the unabashed racial mixing, which the same story characterized as "Whites and Negroes mixing in a religious frenzy."[66] Rarely did articles give Seymour the respect of referring to him by name. One *Times* article simply called him the "major domo" and "an

[63]"Weird Babel of Tongues: New Sect of Fanatics Is Breaking Loose; Wild Scene Last Night on Azusa Street; Gurgle of Wordless Talk by a Sister," *Los Angeles Times*, April 18, 1906, p. II1.
[64]Ibid.
[65]"Men and Women Embrace," *Los Angeles Times*, September 3, 1906, p. II1.
[66]Ibid.

old colored exhorter, blind in one eye."[67] In every city the revival spread, the press was curious and tried numerous schemes to get the lowdown on the inner workings of the movement. In Portland, Oregon, for example, reporters induced a young man to pretend to be a seeker so they could get a scoop from him. During one service, he came and knelt with a bottle of whiskey in his pocket, but reportedly he himself became a believer and the reporters never got their story.[68]

Holiness leaders. As Pentecostalism emerged from the Holiness movement, many Holiness believers excitedly received news about what was unfolding in the former livery stable, came to Azusa Street and received their Pentecostal experience. While many who shared their experience with their pastors and fellow believers found their new spiritual vitality openly accepted, others were greeted with derision and were forbidden to speak about it or exercise their newfound gift, and some were disfellowshiped by their congregations. Some of these came back to join the Azusa Street Mission. Others started new Pentecostal fellowships throughout the city.

Some Holiness leaders were unconvinced that this was a genuine move of God and saw the movement as not just heretical and fanatical but also as demonic, and they laid out their arguments against it in print. Phineas Bresee called what was happening at Azusa Street, "of small account . . . insignificant both in numbers," and having "about as much influence as a pebble thrown into the sea"; and he saw what little influence the revival was having as "mostly harmful, instead of beneficent."[69] As the movement grew, Bresee's Pentecostal Church of the Nazarene dropped the word "Pentecostal," adopting the title Church of the Nazarene. It remains staunchly opposed to Pentecostal manifestations within its ranks to the present day.

A. B. Simpson's Christian and Missionary Alliance (CMA) took a more balanced stance. When a number of CMA members experienced speaking in tongues and a revival broke out within the denomination, Simpson sought the experience for himself. Finally, however, after not receiving it, he contended that speaking in tongues was only one evidence

---

[67]"Weird Babel of Tongues," p. II1. The depiction of Seymour's eye was confirmed by Frank Bartleman in *Azusa Street*, p. 38.

[68]"Pentecost in the North," *Apostolic Faith* 1, no. 6 (1907): 5.

[69]Phineas Bresee, "Editorial: The Gift of Tongues," *Nazarene Messenger* 11, no. 24 (1906): 6.

of Holy Spirit baptism. Simpson did not forbid speaking in tongues but instructed his followers to "seek not—forbid not" the experience,[70] and he remained among a number of Holiness leaders who did not renounce ties with his Pentecostal brothers and sisters.

Black Holiness leader Charles Jones broke with his colleague Charles Harrison Mason after the latter returned from the revival embracing the new movement. With the split, Mason and the majority of the members left to form a new Pentecostal body, while Jones retained leadership over the remainder, becoming the Church of Christ (Holiness).[71] Jones took pains to formulate doctrinal statements that refuted the new understanding of Holy Spirit baptism, insisting that "every true believer is heir to the Holy Ghost as God's gift that is not for a select few," and that "Holy Spirit baptism ratified acceptance with God and was the guarantee of man's eternal inheritance in Christ."[72] Specifically, for Jones, "no one gift is the specific sign or evidence of the Holy Spirit's presence." Rather, the presence of faith, hope and love in the believer's life was three essential evidences that a person was filled with the Spirit. Jones went even further to insist that while the Bible endorsed speaking in tongues as a gift, no one really speaks in tongues unless he speaks a language understood by man.[73]

Seymour had come to know radical Holiness leader and noted Greek scholar William Baxter Godbey from their days at Knapp's Bible School. Godbey used his facility with Greek and Latin to feign a Pentecostal Spirit baptism at an Azusa Street meeting long enough to be invited to preach by Seymour. Citing that experience, Godbey insisted that Pentecostal leaders were "Satan's preachers, jugglers, necromancers, enchanters, magicians, and all sorts of mendicants." He claimed the movement was the result of spiritualism.[74]

The leaders of the Burning Bush Association derided one of its promi-

---

[70]The Christian and Missionary Alliance statement of faith states its position regarding tongues: "We do not believe that there is any scriptural evidence for the teaching that speaking in tongues is the sign of having been filled with the Holy Spirit, nor do we believe that it is the plan of God that all Christians should possess the gift of tongues. This gift is one of the many gifts and is given to some for the benefit of all. The attitude toward the gift of tongues held by pastor and people should be 'Seek not, forbid not.'"

[71]See further discussion on this split in chap. 5.

[72]Jones, *The Gift of the Holy Spirit in the Book of Acts*, p. 16.

[73]Ibid., p. 23.

[74]W. B. Godbey, *Tongue Movement, Satanic* (s.l.: Pillar of Fire, 1918), p. 4.

nent members, A. G. Garr, for his defection to the Pentecostal movement. They declared that he was "led away by the people . . . who profess to receive an unknown tongue as an evidence of a third blessing . . . [so that] the light has left his eye, the fire is gone and he has lost the Holy Ghost."[75]

Since racial inclusiveness was a hallmark of the still relatively young Holiness movement, these criticisms did not generally carry the racial undertones of the secular press. One exception was Alma White, founder of the Pillar of Fire movement. Seymour, on his way to Los Angeles, stopped in Denver to visit White, who taught sinless sanctification but denied the authenticity of a third work of grace or speaking in tongues. White was unimpressed with Seymour's doctrine and seemed personally offended by everything about the young preacher, later remarking, "I had met all kinds of religious fakers and tramps, but . . . he excelled them all."[76] The Holiness leader was among those who linked Seymour and Pentecostalism with demon possession. In her 1910 work, *Demons and Tongues,* she referred to the Azusa Street Revival as "the most hellish outburst of demonical power that has ever been known under the name of religion." She lodged a personal attack against Seymour, accusing him of leading people into "Satan's slime pits, sealing their doom for damnation."[77]

White's attacks on Seymour appear to be, at least in part, racially motivated. She at some point became affiliated with the Ku Klux Klan. Fifteen years later she published *The Ku Klux Klan in Prophecy,*[78] a work that attempted a biblical justification of the existence and work of the racist and anti-Semitic organization. But her disdain for Seymour had, perhaps, yet another root. Her husband Kent eventually accepted the Pentecostal experience of speaking in tongues. His defection from her theological camp caused a rift in the marriage that was never healed.

Other religious leaders. Some of the strongest criticism came from two factions of the Christian community that, at first glance, would be least suspected. Though fundamentalist leaders shared with their Pentecostal counterparts a high view of Scripture and a disdain for modernist ideas, their literal biblical hermeneutic and cessationist theology precluded seri-

---

[75]"A. G. Garr," *The Burning Bush,* July 19, 1906, p. 4.
[76]Alma White, *Demons and Tongues* (Zarephath, N.J.: Pillar of Fire, 1910), pp. 68-69.
[77]Ibid., p. 70.
[78]Alma White, *The Ku Klux Klan in Prophecy* (Zarephath, N.J.: Pillar of Fire, 1925).

ous consideration of the nascent movement as a legitimate move of God. Congregationalist preacher G. Campbell Morgan, pastor of London's Westminster Chapel, referred to the revival and its ecstatic experiences as the "last vomit of Satan."[79] Bible teacher, preacher, pastor and author Harry A. Ironside, who later became pastor of Chicago's famous Moody Church and was influential in popularizing North American Protestant dispensationalism, referred to the phenomenon exhibited at the revival as "absurd delusions."[80] Ironside called the Azusa Street meetings, "pandemoniums where exhibitions worthy of a madhouse or collection of 'howling dervishes' were causing a heavy toll of lunacy and infidelity."[81] He contended that there was a "long list of shipwrecks concerning the faith to be attributed to [the movement's] unsound instruction."[82]

Rueben Archer (R. A.) Torrey, instrumental in the leadership of Moody Bible Institute and Moody Church and founder of Biola Bible College, supplied the theological formulation upon which Pentecostalism was based.[83] Torrey's notion of "baptism for service" clearly articulated a stream of revivalism that would directly influence Pentecostalism. His 1895 book, *Baptism with the Holy Spirit*, linked Spirit baptism with the doctrine of sanctification. Yet Torrey decried Pentecostals' interpretation of his conceptions. He did not accept the gift of tongues as valid and declared that the movement was "emphatically not of God, and founded by a Sodomite."[84] Clarence Larkin, American Baptist pastor and dispensationalist Bible teacher, joined the strong critique, seeing the revival of "what is called the 'gift of tongues'" as "another sign of the times" and cautioning that

> the conduct of those possessed, in which they fall to the ground and writhe in contortions, causing disarrangements of the clothing and disgraceful scenes, is more a characteristic of demon possession, than a work of the Holy Spirit. . . . All about us are "Seducing Spirits" . . . [that] will become more active as the Dispensation draws to its close.[85]

---

[79]Synan, *Holiness-Pentecostal Movement*, pp. 143-44.
[80]Harry A. Ironside, *Holiness, the False and True* (Neptune, N.J.: Loizeaux Brothers, 1912), pp. 38-39.
[81]Ibid., p. 39.
[82]Ibid.
[83]See Rueben A. Torrey, *Baptism with the Holy Spirit* (New York: Fleming H. Revell, 1895).
[84]Synan, *Holiness-Pentecostal Tradition*, p. 146.
[85]Clarence Larkin, *Dispensational Truth or God's Plan and Purpose in the Ages* (Glenside, Penn.: the Author, 1918), p. 102.

These responses both positively and negatively affected the revival. When participants took the Pentecostal message and experience back to their congregations and denominations, they fully expected to be welcomed with open arms, but some were surprised that such a welcome was not forthcoming. The more liberal mainline churches reacted in two ways: they dismissed what they saw as machinations of ignorant, uneducated and "disinherited" people given to hyperspiritualism with no respectable outlet for feelings of desperation, or they ignored the revival entirely. Whatever the source, detractors' tirades only spurred the curious, enticing them to come and see for themselves what was going on at Azusa Street and the other Pentecostal missions that had begun to spring up from it.

CRITICISM FROM WITHIN

Parham's Denunciation. Once the revival got underway, Seymour, a relative novice, remained in close association with Parham, kept him informed of events in Los Angeles and asked advice regarding how to handle situations as they arose.[86] Parham wrote back encouraging Seymour and informing him that he would come to Los Angeles as soon as he could. He also sent Seymour help in the form of two experienced preachers—Lucy Farrow and male colleague J. A. Warren. But Parham did not make his way to Los Angeles for several months. He arrived in Los Angeles in October 1906, presumably hoping to make Seymour's work part of a wider network of Apostolic Faith believers under his leadership. But first he attempted to challenge the overzealousness and unseemly behavior he found at the revival.[87]

Parham had previously seemed to be genuinely pleased about what was going on. In a letter in the first edition of *The Apostolic Faith*, reminiscent of a Pauline salutation, he apparently approved of Seymour's efforts, saying,

> I rejoice in God over you all, my children, though I have never seen you; but since you know the Holy Spirit's power, we are baptized by one Spirit into one body. Keep together in unity till I come, then in a grand meeting let all

[86]Gary B. McGee, "Tongues, The Bible Evidence: The Revival Legacy of Charles F. Parham," *Enrichment Journal* (summer 1999): http://enrichmentjournal.ag.org/199903/068_tongues.cfm.
[87]Ibid.

prepare for the outside fields. I desire, unless God directs to the contrary, to meet and to see all who have the full gospel when I come.[88]

The lead article in the paper's second edition looked forward to Parham's coming and detailed his role as a forerunner to the revival. It portrayed Parham as the man that God had used to "bring back the Pentecostal Baptism to the church," and that he was "surely raised-up of God to be an apostle of the doctrine of Pentecost."[89] Throughout the early months of the revival, Seymour repeatedly credited the movement's origins to Parham, asserting that the revival and mission were extensions of his Apostolic Faith movement. He excitedly anticipated his former teacher's visit, expecting him to put his stamp of approval on what he saw and that "a mightier tide of salvation [would] break out" with his visit.[90]

When Parham arrived in mid-fall, he fully expected control of the meeting to be given over and had two goals in mind. Initially, he was excited that Seymour's group might become part of the organization, intending to incorporate them within a network of Apostolic Faith missions. First, he wanted to tame what he considered to be unbridled but generally harmless religious enthusiasm. As Parham entered the mission, however, he was appalled by what he saw as improper race mixing and the "animalisms" of the unsightly, overemotive worship.[91] Whether he first privately expressed his concerns to Seymour is unknown. But afforded the opportunity to preach, he took the occasion to berate the congregation about what he found.

A number of motivations possibly lay behind Parham's obvious aversion to the scene he found at Azusa Street. First, Parham was generally averse to the more emotive elements of revivalism such as those that exhibited themselves in the Azusa Street meeting. His teaching at his Bible schools and his writings clearly expressed his opposition to what he saw as extremes that manifested themselves in "all the chattering, jabbering, wind sucking, holy-dancing-rollerism" that he considered "the result of hypnotic, spiritualistic and fleshly controls."[92]

---

[88]"Letter from Bro. Parham" *Apostolic Faith* 1, no. 1 (1906): 1.

[89]Untitled article, *Apostolic Faith* 1, no. 2 (1906): 1.

[90]Ibid.

[91]Charles F. Parham, "Free Love," *Apostolic Faith* (December 1912): 4.

[92]Charles Parham, *The Everlasting Gospel* (Baxter Springs, Kans.: Apostolic Faith Bible College, 1911), p. 53.

Second, he may have been taken aback by the apparent success Seymour was having at propagating the doctrine he had formulated, when his own attempts had seemingly failed. For even after several attempts to spark an ongoing revival, Parham never managed to parlay his efforts into a sustained campaign. His student was apparently managing to do so with little strain. Parham had probably envisioned Seymour as being an emissary of his theology to the black race. Yet the heavy black influence over the Azusa Street Mission and meetings were an affront to Parham's lesser-known ideology of white superiority. To Parham, blacks were designed to take a supportive role, not to lead whites. And certainly his black former student was in no position to lead him.

In late summer Mabel Smith Hall, one of Parham's protégés, arrived at the revival. While there, she stayed in contact with Parham, writing him about what was going on in the meetings. Probably because of this close affiliation, Seymour tapped her to help arrange for the approaching visit and a big meeting of all the saints in which Parham would take part, but that meeting never materialized. Seymour, whose humble demeanor betrayed a resolute spirit, felt strongly that God had divinely positioned him to lead the Azusa Street Revival, if not the movement that was unfolding around him. He was not about to turn its leadership over to anyone. Rebuffed by Seymour's seeming defiance, Parham set up separate meetings at the local YMCA. After a short while he turned these meetings over to Warren Carothers, who had become his field director, and again took to the evangelistic trail. But Parham was not done with Seymour or his revival. He took pains to discredit both in meetings throughout the country. Denouncing the revival as counterfeit and insisting that two-thirds of the people claiming to have had a Pentecostal experience were either hypnotized or "spook-driven," Parham also personally rebuked Seymour as being "possessed with a spirit of leadership."[93] He further contended that

> I found conditions even worse than I had anticipated . . . spiritualistic controls, saw people practicing hypnotism at the altar over candidates seeking baptism, though many were receiving the real baptism of the Holy Ghost. . . . I found hypnotic influences, familiar spirit influences, spiritualistic

---

[93]James R. Goff, *Fields White unto Harvest: Charles F. Parham and the Missionary Origins of Pentecostalism* (Fayetteville: University of Arkansas Press, 1988), p. 130.

influences, mesmeric influences, and all kinds of spells, spasms, falling in trances. . . . The Holy Ghost does nothing that is unnatural or unseemly, and any strained exertion of body, mind or voice is not the work of the Holy Spirit, but of some familiar spirit, or other influence.[94]

Though Seymour maintained his humble demeanor, he did not ignore Parham's tactics. Mission leadership temporarily changed the name to the Mission Pacific Apostolic Faith Movement to distinguish it from Parham's work. When Seymour continued to receive inquiries regarding Parham's leadership, an article in the December 1906 *Apostolic Faith* stated: "Some are asking if Dr. Chas. F. Parham is the leader of this movement. We can answer, 'no, he is not the leader of this movement of Azusa Mission. We thought of having him to be our leader and so stated in our paper, before waiting on the Lord.'"[95] Parham's stature among Pentecostal leaders might have given credence to his critique of the revival, but any damage he may have caused was short-circuited. His influence on the Azusa Street meetings came to an abrupt end, and his position as founder of the movement became open to challenge when, within a few weeks after his visit, he was arrested and charged with immoral conduct.[96] When word of Parham's problems reached Carothers, he disbanded the Los Angeles work, returning to Texas to try to salvage the ministry there.

Joseph Smale. Another significant source of criticism came from some who had come to Azusa Street or other Pentecostal meetings and embraced and received but later denounced the Pentecostal experience. Some had risen to some prominence as leaders in the movement but after receiving "greater revelation" would no longer support what they saw as the spiritual excess of the new movement. Former Baptist Joseph Smale, pastor of the New Testament Church, never fully accepted the Pentecostal experience, though he had been on the fringes of the movement for some time. Smale had earlier received criticism for embracing the experience of

[94]Sarah Parham, *The Life of Charles F. Parham* (Birmingham, Ala.: Commercial Printing, 1930), p. 163.
[95]"Pentecost with Signs Following: Seven Months of Pentecostal Showers. Jesus, Our Protector and Great Shepherd," *Apostolic Faith* 1, no. 4 (1906): 1.
[96]James R. Goff Jr., "Charles Fox Parham," in *The New International Dictionary of Pentecostal and Charismatic Movements,* ed. Stanley M. Burgess and Eduard van der Mass (Grand Rapids: Zondervan, 2002), 956.

sanctification. Resultantly, he was at first sympathetic to the Azusa Street Revival, which several members of his congregation regularly attended, and he gave space in his worship services for testimonies of what was unfolding there. During one of these times, on Easter Sunday 1906, Jennie Evans Moore shared her Holy Spirit baptism experience with the congregation, following her testimony with a demonstration of the gift of tongues. This incident generated an influx of some of Smale's members into the Azusa Street congregation, at least temporarily.

Though he never received Pentecostal Spirit baptism, Smale attempted to introduce a degree of freedom into his worship services that would allow Pentecostal expression. At one point, however, sensing this expression getting out of hand, Smale tried to exercise control within his worship services, and his criticism of the gifts of tongues became increasingly severe, but still tempered. Smale conceded that "some of my people have it without a doubt and they are good conscientious Christians, but the devil, as well as God, is having a hand in this."[97]

Perhaps one of the most devastating defections came from one who had been prolific in spreading its message. G. B. Cashwell's preaching throughout the Southeast and his publishing of the *Bridegroom Messenger* drew hundreds, including many important future leaders and their congregations, into the movement. The "Apostle of Pentecost to the South," Cashwell joined G. F. Taylor to oppose Holiness leader A. B. Crumpler's stand against moving the Holiness Church of North Carolina into the Pentecostal camp and helped redraft the constitution of the body to include an article on initial evidence. But Cashwell quickly became disillusioned at the failure of his expectations for the movement, including the delayed second coming and the ineffectiveness of xenolalia within the missionary context. Reportedly, he was also disappointed at not being elected to head the Pentecostal Holiness Church after spearheading its move into the Pentecostal camp. By 1909 Cashwell had left the movement, though for some time he continued to hold revivals in independent congregations throughout the South until his death in 1916.[98]

---

[97]Robeck, *Azusa Street Mission and Revival*, p. 203

[98]For a discussion of Cashwell's life, ministry and influence on the movement, see Douglas Beacham, *Azusa East: The Life and Times of G. B. Cashwell* (Franklin Springs, Ga.: LSR, 2006).

HARASSMENT

The seedy neighborhood surrounding the mission was not unaccustomed to noise or excitement, for within it were a number of bars and other less reputable establishments whose patrons were not noted for proper decorum. But the constant coming and going at the revival, and the high volume of activity it brought, was too much for many of those who had grown used to the usual clamor. Without amplification the noise of the speakers and seekers found ample, natural intensification through the paneless windows. Local police kept busy answering complaints of "hideous" noises emanating from the building into the early hours of the morning. They responded by posting officers outside to keep noise to a tolerable level and threatened to issue citations when it did not stop.[99] Neighbors and community leaders were as disgusted with the inordinate, unseemly race and gender mixing as with the noise and late hours. One complaint to police was about "the manner Negro elders had" of "laying on of hands [on young white women]."[100]

Beyond criticism and the betrayal of those once-loyal brothers and sisters, attendees were regularly subjected to harassment by police and other civic officials and ostracized by friends, family, employers, coworkers, and members and pastors of their home congregations. Some harassment involved simple verbal assault or social isolation. Other times it resulted in physical altercation or violence. Whether the lack of acceptance came from the community, the police or home congregation, the Azusa Street faithful perceived it as harassment by the devil and his workers; and it only heightened their conviction that they were doing God's work, spurring them to even bolder efforts in spreading what they saw as the end-time gospel. As an article in the *Apostolic Faith* details:

> Some workers were preaching on the street corner in Los Angeles and a poor drunkard had just been saved, when a policeman . . . ordered them to stop, and took two of them off to jail. The sister sang all the way to the jail and shouted and prayed while they were there. They soon were anxious to get rid of them and let them go. Meantime the other workers returned to the mission and told how the workers had been arrested and they all went

---

[99]"Rolling and Diving 'Fanatics,'" *Los Angeles Times*, June 23, 1906, p. 17.
[100]"Tongue Gift is Denounced: Ministers of Akron Criticise Queer Sect," *Los Angeles Times*, January 7, 1907, p. 13.

to the altar and prayed and arose praising God; and soon in walked the ones who had been arrested. We are ready not only to go to prison, but to give our lives for Jesus.[101]

SCHISM AND DECLINE

Following the revival's three-year heyday, the spiritual fervor ebbed and waned for the next four years. Prominent ministers and everyday people visited, and schism and controversy, fueled as much by personality conflicts and style as by doctrinal differences, continued to plague the congregation. Each ensuing controversy took its toll until, at the end, the Azusa Street Mission was a small African American congregation that remained faithful to the Pentecostal message but had lost its influence in the broader movement.

Marriage and remarriage. One of the earliest controversies arose over a matter that usually brings joy to a congregation—the marriage of their pastor. In May 1908, William Seymour married Jennie Moore in a private ceremony conducted by his friend and colleague Edward Lee. Lee's wife, Mattie, and Richard Asberry, host of the Bonnie Brae Street meetings, were the only witnesses. After the nuptials the couple moved into one of the modest apartments above the mission, though Jennie continued to own a home on Bonnie Brae Street. Reportedly, the couple adopted a daughter, who by 1914 was nine years old.[102] The marriage set off a chain reaction that had ongoing consequences for the mission's future. Though Seymour was beloved by his members, from the beginning, Jennie was less trusting of white people, less optimistic about the prospect of true racial harmony in the movement and a source of agitation among white members. While she was a preacher and gifted worker who contributed much to the mission's ministry, some were disappointed at the turn of events, but not all for the same reasons.

One person apparently disturbed by the marriage was Clara Lum, who edited the *Apostolic Faith* with Seymour and Florence Crawford. The three regularly worked closely together, and their working relationships eventually blossomed into strong friendships. Lum and Crawford's friendship

---

[101]"Arrested for Jesus' Sake," *Apostolic Faith* 1, no. 1 (1906): 4.
[102]Shumway, "Critical History of Glossolalia," p. 179. Though nothing more is known about the girl, some sources suggest that she later became a part of the Church of God in Christ.

was driven in part by a shared interest in rescue mission work, but Lum and Seymour's relationship appeared to have a deeper quality to it. Reportedly, the two had entertained the idea of marriage. When Seymour consulted his friend Charles Harrison Mason about the possibility, however, that hope came to an abrupt end. Mason cautioned him that such a marriage between a black man and a white woman would be controversial and disastrous for the ministry. Not surprisingly, Lum objected to Seymour's subsequent decision to, instead, marry Jennie Evans Moore. After the marriage, Lum left the mission, following Crawford to Portland. She never married.

Though Florence Crawford sympathized with her friend, her main objection to Seymour's marriage was that she shared the radical understanding of the imminence of Christ's return with many early Pentecostals. Crawford, however, held the extreme position that such activities as marriage and raising a family were counterproductive to evangelism. She sensed an urgent need to reach as many as possible with the Pentecostal message before Christ's return. To her, any digression from that commitment, such as the marriage, signaled compromise on the standard of Holiness. For Crawford, Seymour's marriage was no exception.

Further, Crawford may have felt that her prominent place in the ministry was threatened by the new alliance between Seymour and Moore. There may have been some foundation to this fear, for after the marriage Jennie played an ever-expanding role in the mission's leadership. She regularly preached in the worship services, filled in for Seymour as pastor when he was away and occasionally traveled on his behalf. From time to time, she also accompanied him when he traveled. At any rate Crawford too left the ministry shortly after the marriage and moved to Portland, Oregon, where she established her own Apostolic Faith Mission.

Seymour disagreed with Crawford on the issue of marriage and divorce, and their disagreement caused problems for him on two fronts. On the one hand, in line with predominant Holiness and Pentecostal teaching, Seymour took what might appear a harsh stand on the issue of remarriage of people who had previously been divorced. In an issue of the *Apostolic Faith* he wrote, "This Apostolic Faith stands for one wife and one husband. Our God is going to have a clean people, a people that will stand for the whole counsel of God. Praise God for a people that are willing to stand for the

Gospel and die for it if need be."[103] On the other hand, he attacked notions like Crawford's that discounted the need to be married altogether. In an article titled "The Marriage Tie," infused with multiple scriptural references, Seymour tersely asserted, "God commended [marriage] . . . and God is in it." He further insisted, "[Marriage] is honorable in all," and "the forbidding of marriage is a doctrine of devils."[104] In another piece, titled "Bible Teaching on Marriage and Divorce," he even more adamantly declared, "It is no sin to marry."[105] Seymour's arguments did not convince Crawford, who still saw it as compromise on sanctification. Her move to Portland was one of the first casualties of the fallout over the subject, and it had severe ramifications for the mission. She convinced several congregations she had started or overseen under Seymour's direction to leave his fold and took some of his best workers with her.

Loss of the **Apostolic Faith** *newspaper.* As a result of Lum's departure, the revival received one of its greatest blows: the loss of the expertise to produce the *Apostolic Faith* newspaper and the loss of the two most important of the twenty-two mailing lists used to distribute it. The national and international lists had been the lifeblood of the newspaper. Their loss left Seymour with several smaller local lists that were not enough to sustain the newspaper. Lum, one of Seymour's closest associates at the mission, was by nature and training a gifted editor. After receiving the Pentecostal experience of Holy Spirit baptism, she was convinced that God had added a supernatural "anointing" for writing.[106]

The first issue of *Apostolic Faith* did not appear until several months after the revival began, when Seymour took note of Lum's editorial skill and enlisted her to work with him and Crawford. Indeed, the idea to begin a newspaper chronicling the events of the Azusa Street Revival may been suggested by Lum. Since she had served as associate editor for Charles Hanley's highly successful *Firebrand,* she appreciated the utility such a publication could provide and had the experience and ability to handle such an undertaking. Further, her contacts within the Holiness community would be invaluable. It was Lum, for example, who solicited Hanley

---

[103]Untitled article, *Apostolic Faith* 1, no. 9 (1907): 1.
[104]"The Marriage Tie," *Apostolic Faith* 1, no. 10 (1907): 3.
[105]"Bible Teaching on Marriage and Divorce," *Apostolic Faith* 1, no. 5 (1907): 3.
[106]Blumhofer, "Clara E. Lum," *Assemblies of God Heritage* 21, no. 2 (summer 2001): 16.

for money to purchase a typewriter.[107] As secretary and coeditor of the *Apostolic Faith* from 1906-1908, she was involved in every aspect of that periodical's production. She wrote some articles and edited many more. She developed and maintained the mailing lists, eventually reaching fifty thousand names of local, national and international constituents. Published on a monthly basis, more or less, it reached across the country and the world and was distributed free of charge, supported by offerings from the congregation and the paper's recipients.

One of Lum's duties was recording some of Seymour's sermons in shorthand. Many of these found their way into the *Apostolic Faith*. All but a few of her own articles in the newspaper were unsigned. But due to her unique skills, her portraits of the actual worship at the Azusa Street Mission are among some of the most graphic extant depictions of what was said and done at the revival. Even during her time at Azusa Street, the *Apostolic Faith* was not the only periodical to which Lum contributed. In an article titled "Miss Clara Lum Writes Wonders," in the August 1906 *Missionary World*, she described the heavenly chorus,

> There is singing in the Spirit . . . the music is not learned. No one can join in unless it is given to them [by the Spirit]. They sing in different tongues at the same time, and the different parts are song. Sometimes, one is singing in English, thus interpreting while the others are singing [in tongues].[108]

Those who had previously worked with Lum at *Missionary World* said she was "one of the most earnest and efficient workers and members" of their community. Glenn Cook, the mission's former business manager who later became a leader in the oneness Pentecostal movement, called her a "wonderful helper" in editing the paper.[109] The last edition of the *Apostolic Faith* that Lum helped Seymour produce from Los Angeles was the June 1908 issue, published a month after the Seymour marriage and the same month that Lum moved to Oregon. With her went much of the expertise to edit and produce the newspaper. Of the two women, Lum was probably responsible for removal of the lists since the newspaper continued to be published from Los Angeles several months after Crawford's depar-

---

[107]Ibid., p. 18.
[108]"Miss Clara Lum Writes Wonders," *Missionary World*, August 1906, p. 2.
[109]Blumhofer and Wacker, "Who Edited the Azusa Mission's *Apostolic Faith*?" p. 17.

ture. After the removal of the lists, the two continued to produce a newspaper from Portland. Initially they made no mention of the fact that the place of publication had changed or that Seymour was no longer involved in its production. Indeed, it would be several months before they would divulge this information. According to J. C. Vanzandt, an occasional Azusa Street attendee who reportedly was never a supporter of the revival, Seymour produced one final newspaper from Los Angeles, in which he insisted, "I must for the salvation of souls let it be known that the editor is still in Los Angeles . . . and will not remove the *Apostolic Faith* from Los Angeles without letting subscribers and field workers know."[110] Seymour made a final attempt to convince Crawford and Lum to return control of the mailing list and newspaper to the Azusa Street Mission. He and Jennie traveled to Oregon to confront the two, but to no avail. Finally in the summer of 1909, a full year after the move had been made to Oregon, the seventh volume published in that state conceded that "we said that [the newspaper] was moved from Los Angeles. We should have stated we are starting a new *Apostolic Faith* in Portland."[111] But it was too late. The damage had been done, and Seymour and the Azusa Street Mission had lost a vital link to the outside world. To be sure, a plethora of new periodicals filled the void, and the mission and the revival were never able to regain the momentum they had experienced in the earliest period.

William Durham and the finished work of Calvary. Prominent Chicago pastor William H. Durham was drawn to the Azusa Street Revival in 1907, having had his interest pricked by the drastic spiritual change he perceived in an elder in his congregation. Subsequently, he traveled to Los Angeles to observe what God was doing. Instead of the chaos Parham had noted, Durham was, at first, enthralled by what he encountered and filed this glowing testimony of its effects on him.

> As soon as I entered . . . I became conscious that God was there. . . . I was in His holy presence. . . . No man had anything whatever to do with what was happening. The Holy Ghost seemed to have full control, and yet the order seemed perfect. My soul was melted down before the Lord; but to me the

---

[110] J. C. Vanzandt, *Speaking in Tongues: A Discussion of Speaking in Tongues, Pentecost, Latter Rain, Evidence of Holy Spirit Baptism and a Short History of the Tongues Movement in America and Some Foreign Countries* (Portland, Ore.: J. C. Vanzandt, 1926), p. 37

[111] *Apostolic Faith* (Portland) 7 (May-June 1909), cited in Vanzandt, *Speaking in Tongues*, p. 34.

most wonderful thing was yet to happen. . . . And there I saw, more plainly than ever before, the difference between having the presence of the Spirit of God with us and having Him living within us in person, and I resolved then and there that I would never cease seeking, till I had received Him in Pentecostal fullness, and by the grace of God I kept that resolve.[112]

Seymour received Durham openly, prophesying that he "would become an apostle of the new movement," and wherever he preached, the Holy Spirit would fall on people.[113] Shortly after receiving his Pentecostal experience, Durham returned to Chicago for four years, making that city the Midwest Azusa Street and leading thousands into the movement. Many who later became Pentecostal leaders experienced Spirit baptism at Durham's church. Eudorous Bell would become the first general superintendent of the Assemblies of God. A. H. Argue became leader of the Pentecostal Assemblies of Canada. Andrew Urshan would accept the oneness doctrine and become a leader in that movement. Howard Goss, another future oneness leader, would work with Bell to found the Assemblies of God before helping to found the oneness group that eventually became the United Pentecostal Church. Young Robert and Aimee Semple, who had previously had their own Pentecostal experiences, would come under Durham's influence. After Robert's death on the mission field in China, Aimee would go on to found the International Church of the Foursquare Gospel.

All the while, Durham stayed in contact with Seymour. The two held a mutual respect and affection for each other, and the Azusa Street saints were equally fond of Pastor Durham. People traveling from the revival to the East Coast and across the Atlantic regularly stopped in Chicago at North Avenue Church for spiritual succor. In fall 1906, Jesse and Mabel Smith, for example, left Azusa Street and stopped in Chicago on their way to Chelsea, Massachusetts, preaching nightly to overflowing crowds at North Avenue Church. They were responsible for several members of Durham's congregation receiving the Pentecostal experience, and they also convinced Durham to visit the Los Angeles revival. Sometime before marrying Seymour in 1908, Jennie Moore also visited Durham's mission and preached. In an item in the *Apostolic Faith* Moore briefly described in

---

[112]William H. Durham, "Personal Testimony of Pastor Durham," *The Pentecostal Testimony* (1909): 6.

[113]Vinson Synan, *Holiness-Pentecostal Tradition*, p. 132

glowing terms the revival she found there, calling it a "blessed place."[114] Moore's warm reception prompted her to invite Durham to revisit the Azusa Street Mission any time he would be back in Los Angeles.

During the four years Durham was away from Azusa Street, he refined his singularly important contribution to the fluid Pentecostal theology evolving around him—the doctrine of the "finished work of Calvary." Durham was thoroughly convinced that he saw a genuine manifestation of God's Spirit in the mission and the revival. Yet he was also convinced that Seymour's Wesleyan understanding of entire sanctification—the lynchpin of Holiness-Pentecostal theology—was in error.[115] The distinction between these two understandings hinged on the Wesleyan Holiness teaching of two distinct stages of grace—salvation and sanctification—prior to reception of Holy Spirit baptism. Both stages were instantaneous and integral in the believer's salvation, together resulting in the believer being completely cleansed of known sin so they could receive Holy Spirit baptism. Durham's finished-work understanding saw salvation unfolding through only two stages—conversion and baptism of the Holy Spirit. He proposed that at the moment one became a believer by faith, the process of sanctification began because of the finished work of Christ on Calvary. For Durham there was no need for a second, instantaneous, blessing of sanctification; ongoing, progressive sanctification continued throughout the believer's life. He or she would continue to grow in Christian virtue; there was no change in nature that rendered the believer impervious to sin.

By the time he left the revival and returned to Chicago, however, he had already begun to promote this understanding from his pulpit. Early in 1911 he moved his ministry to Los Angeles, turning over the Chicago mission to Frank Ewart. Durham intended to use this new location as a base to establish a firm root for this new teaching. He went first to Elmer Fisher's Upper Room Mission; but after a short stint there, his provocative message and combative attitude made him no longer welcome, and Fisher forbade him from preaching in his pulpit. Shortly afterward, Jennie (now

---

[114]Untitled Article, *Apostolic Faith* 1, no. 12 (1908): 1.

[115]Durham insisted that salvation and Holy Spirit baptism involved a two-stage process and that sanctification was progressive. Seymour held the Wesleyan Holiness understanding that salvation and sanctification were two instantaneous experiences that would be followed by baptism in the Holy Spirit.

Mrs. Seymour), remembering her warm reception in Durham's congregation, invited him to fill her husband's pulpit while he was absent on a preaching tour. Durham's series of messages, however, would ultimately prove to be detrimental to the health of the mission and would had devastating effects for an already tenuous situation.

When Durham returned to Azusa Street at Jennie's invitation, most whites had already left, leaving the mission a small, mostly black congregation. Frank Bartleman contended that Durham was "sent from the Lord . . . with a message for the Pentecostal saints in Los Angeles,"[116] and his charismatic preaching stirred a new excitement. Large crowds again began to be drawn, and Bartleman contended that, with Durham's arrival, the revival "returned to its glory days."[117] Durham, however, took the occasion to denounce the doctrine of entire sanctification. In Seymour's absence, he prodded members of the Azusa congregation to decide if they wanted to follow him or Seymour, and a majority of the remaining whites aligned themselves with him so that the resulting schism saw Seymour's remaining white attendees decrease even more.

The rupture proved to be larger than a rift between two pastors. Factions outside their congregations rose up on both sides. Durham's supporters, planted in the Keswick view of sanctification, denounced the doctrine of entire sanctification as heretical. Wesleyan believers, who still included Charles Parham, returned the favor. Florence Crawford condemned Durham's teaching and forbade him to preach in her church. Parham went so far as to issue the challenge that, "if this man's doctrine be true, let my life go out to prove it, but if our teaching . . . is true, let his life pay the forfeit."[118]

Durham's ministry at his rented Los Angeles facility flourished for several months, while Azusa Street Mission attendance declined. But his meteoric rise came to an abrupt end, when a year later at age thirty-nine, he died of pneumonia. Parham saw his death as vindication of the Wesleyan position and resolutely responded, "How signally God has answered."[119] Nevertheless, Durham's formulation took root in many independent Pen-

[116]Bartleman, *Azusa Street*, p. 150.
[117]Ibid.
[118]Edith Blumhofer, *The Assemblies of God: A Popular History* (Springfield, Mo.: Radiant Books/ Gospel Publishing, 1985), p. 43.
[119]Goff, "Charles Fox Parham," p. 152.

tecostal congregations and denominations formed after 1911. While his teaching never became acceptable among earlier denominations rooted within the Wesleyan Holiness movement, it resonated with many from the Keswick or Higher Life Holiness wings.[120] The majority of these congregations later affiliated as the Assemblies of God. Interestingly, Durham's teaching found little resonance among African American Pentecostals. Consequently, there are no major African American Pentecostal denominations within the finished-work wing of Pentecostalism.[121]

Frank Bartleman. One of those who aligned himself with Durham was former Holiness evangelist and avid Seymour supporter Frank Bartleman. Once Durham was locked out of the Azusa Street Mission, Bartleman helped him secure a new facility and promoted the finished-work teaching among his own colleagues. He had been a staunch supporter of Seymour at the beginning of the revival but, in the end, numbered himself among his detractors, faulting Seymour for comprising on the standard of holiness by introducing worldly structure into the revival that quenched the Spirit.

Though Bartleman had visited the Bonnie Brae Street prayer meeting, he was not a faithful attendee. After the revival began in earnest, however, he was attending Smale's New Testament Church one day when an unidentified woman[122] who had been present a few nights earlier at the Bonnie Brae Street prayer meeting and had received the Pentecostal experience there arose and began to speak in tongues. Within four days Bartleman was at the Azusa Street Mission. Though he apparently did not experience speaking in tongues during the period, he occasionally preached there. Even while a regular at the Azusa Street services, the restless evangelist was also visiting other Holiness congregations where he sensed revival fires were ready to break-out. His later eyewitness account of the Azusa Street Revival is one of the earliest written about this period of the movement and shows a great deal of respect for "Brother Seymour," whom he said was "recognized as the nominal leader in charge," though he was also

---

[120]Though the Keswick movement also promoted sanctification as a second work of grace in the life of the believer, it saw this work as more progressive than instantaneous and viewed it as a setting apart for God's service.

[121]The two major finished-work denominations are the Assemblies of God and the International Church of the Foursquare Gospel. There are no major African American Pentecostal bodies within the finished-work Pentecostal family.

[122]Presumably Jennie Moore.

quick to add that "we had no pope or hierarchy."[123]

By the time he left the mission, four months after its start, Bartleman had become disenchanted with Seymour's leadership, accusing his former colleague of worldliness and compromise. He was disgruntled with what he saw as Seymour's "apostacizing of the movement" by introducing structure into the revival, and being particularly disturbed that a sign reading "Azusa Street Mission" had been hung outside the door, a move he saw as signaling the beginning of the mission and revival's demise. To him,

> From that time the trouble and division began. It was no longer a free Spirit for all as it had been. The work had become one more rival party and body, along with the other churches and sects of the city. No wonder the opposition steadily increased from the churches. We had been called to bless and serve the whole body of Christ everywhere.[124]

Bartleman accused the Azusa Street congregation of becoming sectarian, believing God had warned against making a "party" spirit of the Pentecostal work. He determined that such a spirit had been "the curse and death of every revival body sooner or later": "To formulate a separate body is but to advertise our failure, as a people of God. It proves to the world that we cannot get along together, rather than causing them to believe in our salvation."[125]

Still not having experienced Pentecostal tongues, Bartleman left the mission in August 1906, setting up a rival congregation at Eighth and Maple Streets, just blocks away, taking several white members of the Azusa Street Mission with him. He received the experience a short time later, and Seymour never broke fellowship with him. Bartleman later insisted, "There was never any jealousy or rivalry" between the two congregations and contended that Seymour thought highly of him until the end.[126] Such an assessment seems to be confirmed by the fact that the *Apostolic Faith* continued to report on the work being accomplished through Bartleman's mission.[127] Being an evangelist rather than a pastor at heart, Bartleman

[123]Frank Bartleman, *How Pentecost Came to Los Angeles: As It Was in the Beginning*, 2nd ed. (Los Angeles: the Author, 1925), p. 58.
[124]Ibid., p. 68.
[125]Ibid.
[126]Ibid., p. 72.
[127]"Fire Still Falling," *Apostolic Faith* 1, no. 2 (1906): 1. By then, however, Bartleman had already turned the mission over to Pendleton.

remained restless. After a short period he turned leadership of his mission over to William Pendleton, a former Holiness pastor who had earlier moved most of his congregation to the Azusa Street Mission, and went back out on the evangelistic circuit.

Bartleman promoted the infant movement in tracts and articles in Holiness and Pentecostal publications. Though his assessments are colored by an apparent sense of his own import, his accounts put the Azusa Street Revival on the map months before the mission could begin producing the *Apostolic Faith*. His later eyewitness recollections provide one of the few firsthand records of its unfolding. Though centered on his own role, Bartleman's depictions give a colorful, informative glance of its worship, subsequent evangelistic efforts and evolution of the Pentecostal movement. His defection from the mission was not in and of itself harmful to the work of Seymour or the revival. It was, however, another instance of the slow, continuing decline of allegiance to Seymour among the revival's white participants and a signal of the dissolving racial harmony that had been a significant element of the revival.

THE WANING YEARS OF THE MISSION AND SEYMOUR'S PERSONAL DECLINE

While Azusa Street Mission's leadership was racially mixed, a number of blacks played prominent roles on Seymour's "staff," and it was primarily black members of the congregation who remained with Seymour after most whites had left and he had broken with the Latinos.[128] Besides Lucy Farrow, who had returned to the mission after her missionary trip, Julia Hutchins was joined at the mission by her husband and her niece, Leila McKinney, both of whom accompanied her to Liberia. Ophelia Wiley, who had traveled extensively with Florence Crawford as a missionary to the Northwest, probably remained at the mission. Sister Prince, who was called a "mother in Israel," probably served on the administrative board until her death. Richard and Ruth Asberry remained loyal members of the congregation until the building was condemned and Jennie Moore's health failed.

---

[128]Though Seymour's congregation initially had several Latino and Latina members, such as Susie Valdez or Abundio de Lopez, whom Seymour ordained in 1909 and who were involved in all areas of ministry, the Latino members left to form their own ethnic congregations. There is some indication that earlier friction had developed between Seymour and the Latino members of the congregation prior to their leaving.

As the revival drew to an end around 1914, there were more than twenty denominations and several hundred congregations in the United States identifying themselves as Pentecostal and holding the doctrine of tongues as initial evidence of Holy Spirit baptism. In the twenty years following the close of the revival, several more denominations and several thousand congregations in the United States had been established and several hundred more existing congregations had switched to the Pentecostal camp. By that time, the Pentecostal message had been heard all over the world.

For several years after the end of the revival, Seymour remained in demand as a speaker among a small circle of supporters. But as the years advanced, this circle grew smaller and invitations became fewer. One of Seymour's greatest hopes for the movement was that it would be unified and never develop barriers based on race, gender, class or some insignificant theological distinction. He had previously taken steps to ensure this would be so, organizing a weekly meeting of pastors throughout the Los Angeles area to come together to pray, study Scripture, and share their struggles and triumphs. Using the Azusa Street Mission as a meeting site, men like Smale and Pendleton regularly joined with him for fellowship and succor and to promote a unified spirit among their disparate Pentecostal congregations. In 1917, several years after the mission's revival fires waned, Seymour again called a meeting of Pentecostal leaders in or near Los Angeles to pray and fellowship. This time, the turnout was scandalously small considering his former prominence and the fact there had been no impropriety or heresy to discredit him as a leader of a movement that was barely eleven years old.

Throughout the later period, Seymour continued to travel around the country, encouraging existing congregations and planting new ones. In 1911, for example, he visited the town of Handsome in southwestern Virginia and left a congregation there, appointing Charles Lowe as the pastor. In later years several small denominations claimed this congregation as foundation for their organization, citing Seymour as founder.[129] He continued to travel and speak at Pentecostal gatherings throughout the country when asked, but the invitations grew increasingly fewer. By the end of his life, he often attended Pentecostal meetings as a regular member of the

---

[129]These include the Apostolic Faith Churches of God, headquartered in Franklin, Virginia.

congregation, without any recognition by leaders. Especially within white circles, the elder statesman was often left sitting in the congregation while others who would have been without a platform had it not been for his ministry graced the podium. Some gave a nod of acknowledgment to his presence. Others completely ignored his presence.

One place where Seymour was always welcomed was with his friend Charles Harrison Mason, who had found his Pentecostal experience in Seymour's meetings. Mason considered him a father in the faith and frequently invited him to speak at the Annual Convocation for the Church of God in Christ.[130] John G. Lake, another colleague, had received his Pentecostal experience under the ministry of Parham, who had become Seymour's detractor. Even after Parham's denouncement, Lake remained in fellowship with Seymour and invited him to address a congregation of ten thousand believers in the Pacific Northwest. Seymour received a rousing reception from the crowd, who still revered him and listened intently to what he had to say.[131]

By 1922, fifty-two-year-old Seymour was tired and discouraged. Though he had been at the forefront of a movement whose global reach would extend beyond anything he could have imagined, his congregation had dwindled to little more than a handful. His efforts to bring unity to the movement had apparently failed, and his personal influence had largely evaporated. By September of that year, he had succumbed, dying of what some have called a broken heart. At the end of his life, Seymour exemplified the same humility with spiritual power that had been the hallmark of his ministry at Azusa Street. As one woman who encountered him on what was perhaps his last preaching campaigned described him: "The glow would be on that man's face. . . . He was no man to exalt himself, but a humble man. When you'd meet him at the door you could just feel . . . he was a real man of God."[132]

The widely read newspaper the *Pentecostal Herald* carried Seymour's obituary. It simply and correctly said of him that "his parish was the world."[133]

---

[130]Larry Martin, *The Life and Ministry of William J. Seymour,* The Complete Azusa Street Library 1 (Joplin, Mo.: Christian Life Books, 1999), pp. 313-14.

[131]John G. Lake, *John G. Lake: His Life, His Sermons, His Boldness of Faith* (Ft. Worth: Kenneth Copeland Publications, 1994), p. 25.

[132]Nelson, *For Such a Time as This,* p. 269.

[133]"Brother Seymour Goes Home," *Pentecostal Herald*, October 1, 1922, p. 1.

FINAL TAKEOVER ATTEMPT

Before Seymour died he placed the ministry in his wife's hands, and at his death, she became pastor of the small congregation. With her at its head, the already faltering ministry would take several blows that ultimately proved fatal. The first seven years after Seymour's death were relatively uneventful, though seemingly unproductive. Then in 1930, Ruthford Griffith, a white man who claimed to be a Coptic priest, attempted to wrest leadership of the congregation away from Jennie Seymour. At first, without consent of the mission's leaders, who still included Richard Asberry, Griffith started making repairs to the dilapidated building. Eventually, he began to insist on taking leadership of the congregation and tried to have members declare him so. When they resisted, a court battle ensued; Griffith initially prevailed and was awarded rights to the property. Eventually on appeal, the court found in Seymour's favor, and Griffith and his supporters were found to have attempted to defraud the congregation.[134]

Though Jennie retained the pastorate, the later intervention was too late, and the legal proceedings were costly for the small congregation. Many of the few remaining whites sided with Griffith and left, and the small group of black congregants could not bear the resulting financial strain.[135] In 1931, after having lived in the upstairs apartment since her marriage to William, Jennie vacated the termite-infested building that had been condemned as a fire hazard and moved the last beleaguered faithful to her Bonnie Brae Street home—near where the revival began—holding services there until her health failed in 1933. At one point Jennie had attempted to save the mission by mortgaging her home. She later sold the mortgages on the mission and her home to a Los Angeles bank, but when she could no longer make payments, the bank foreclosed on the mission and the building was razed. In 1936, three years after relinquishing leadership of the church, Jennie died at the age of sixty-two, having served as pastor over an increasingly dwindling congregation for fourteen years.

---

[134]"Mrs. Seymour's Rights Upheld," *Los Angeles Times*, Jun 13, 1932, p. 12. See also Robeck, *Azusa Street*, p. 320.
[135]Martin, *Life and Ministry of William Seymour*, p. 331.

CONCLUSION

Seymour's suspicion of the motivation of the whites that surrounded him was not totally unfounded. Parham derided him and the revival he led and hurled racial epithets. Crawford separated from him, accusing him of compromising on holiness and sanctification. Lum left the revival, taking the expertise and mailing list needed to publish the newspaper. Durham attempted to split and control his congregation. Bartleman accused him of worldliness, setting up a rival congregation only several blocks from the mission. So it is not surprising that, several years after the mission was founded, Seymour wrote limitation into its doctrine and polity on who could lead the congregation. Disenchanted by the attitudes of some entrusted whites, Seymour later incorporated into the formal structure of the mission's governing documents directions that the directors of the Apostolic Faith Mission—the bishop, vice bishop and trustees—should be people of color.[136]

With Jennie's death the ministry of the Azusa Street Mission ended, and for the next half-century the work of William Seymour would be largely ignored by those who would take the reins of the Pentecostal movement. For those fifty years a seeming conspiracy of silence by white religionists relegated Seymour to a footnote in the already small volume of research on Pentecostalism. As a result, even many black Pentecostal congregations knew—and still know—little of his significant contribution. It would not be until the 1970s, when two unlikely scholars—one a black political scientist and the other a white historian—would attempt to reinsert him into the history of the movement.[137]

Yet, while contemporary scholars of African American Pentecostalism point out the early racist tendencies in the movement that precluded Seymour from being credited for his contribution, blame for the oversight cannot be solely placed on white religionists. Petty sectarian attitudes in early African American Pentecostalism played a role in Seymour's marginalization within its history. While his colleague Charles Mason honored Seymour during his lifetime, black denominational founders and leaders in

---

[136]"Constitution of the Apostolic Faith Mission: Article C," in *Doctrine and Disciplines*, p. 49.

[137]See James S. Tinney, "William J. Seymour: Father Of Modern-Day Pentecostalism," in *Black Apostles*, ed. Randall K. Burkett and Richard Newman (Boston: G. K. Hall, 1978), and Nelson, *For Such a Time as This*.

general paid little attention to the role of Seymour or the revival in their own histories. Particularly, before the last quarter of the twentieth century, when black consciousness took on greater importance, these histories short-sightedly played up the role of their respective sectarian founders.

At the centennial of the movement, phenomenal growth has brought new interest in Seymour from unlikely sectors. Though he never rose to the stature of a Luther, Calvin or Wesley, and his name is unknown even among many evangelical Christians, Yale University has recognized him as "one of the ten most influential leaders in American religious history."[138] In 1999, the Religion Newswriters Association named the Azusa Street Revival as one of the top ten events of the past millennium.[139] And in 2000, *Life* magazine named the birth of the Pentecostal movement one of the top one hundred events of the twentieth century, placing it at position sixty-eight.[140] Seymour's slow but phenomenal rise from obscurity in the past few decades serves to focus attention on the important contribution of the "one-eyed Negro preacher" that his own movement once tried to forget.

---

[138]Yale University historian Sidney Ahlstrom said that Seymour personified a black piety "which exerted its greatest direct influence on American religious history," quoted in Vinson Synan, "Pentecostalism: William Seymour," *Christian History* 65 (2000): 17-19.

[139]Religion Newswriters Association, Results of 1999 Survey of Top Ten Religious Stories of the Millennium and of the Decade, www.azusastreetriders.com/our-name.

[140]Azusa Street Riders website, www.azusastreetriders.com/images/stories/life20mag20232068 .pdf.

5

WHAT HATH GOD WROUGHT

THE RISE OF AFRICAN AMERICAN TRINITARIAN PENTECOSTAL DENOMINATIONS

And the Lord added to the church daily those who were being saved.

ACTS 2:47 NKJV

THE FAILURE OF THE AZUSA STREET MISSION to flower into a denomination was, at least in part, a failure of the vision of its founder, William Seymour, who saw God's people united in love under the power of the Holy Spirit, without regard to gender, race, culture or class. Moreover, it signaled the beginning of the demise of his personal influence on the direction of the Pentecostal movement but did not mean an end of the influence of black leadership within that movement. Rather, instead of being solidified in the hands of one charismatic leader, that influence would be diffused throughout a network of charismatic men and women whose unique gifts and personalities would create denominations of every kind in every area of the country and modern world that would broadcast the Pentecostal message. Many of these would be African Americans who would spread the movement among a growing, recently emancipated but still largely disenfranchised black population.

Though all major black Pentecostal denominations owe some allegiance to Azusa Street, not all have been directly tied to it. The sometimes circuitous route from Los Angeles usually came through one of three avenues. First, some black Holiness groups, such as the United Holy Church, had populated the American South and saturated it with the message of sanctification, baptism with fire and race pride at least a generation before the revival began. They simply moved into the Pentecostal camp. They incorporated the language and understanding that tongues were initial evidence of Holy Spirit baptism into existing doctrinal understandings. Second, some groups, such as the Fire Baptized Holiness Church, splintered away from existing white Pentecostal bodies that had held their allegiance until racial realities forced a cleavage in the movement. Last, some existing black Holiness groups split over the issue of initial evidence to form two groups, falling into either the Holiness or Pentecostal, as with the Church of God in Christ and the Church of Christ Holiness. Later differentiation would further split the existing camps into more than one hundred denominations based on understandings of the Godhead, the role of women in ministry and leadership, power struggles based only on the personalities of key players within these organizations, and myriad other seemingly miniscule issues that took on ever-increasing importance over the one-hundred-year history of the movement.

Except for those who had been heavily involved in the interracial Holiness camp meetings, whites who came to the Azusa Street Revival generally came from homogeneous settings with little exposure to black styles of worship. Their personal testimonies show that it was, at first, difficult to divest themselves of racial prejudice and become fully involved in the revival. Though many were finally able to do so, at least long enough to receive their Pentecostal experience and imbibe the spirituality of the time, ultimately some, like Parham, could not.

Whites began to slowly drift away from Azusa Street and return to, or form, their own congregations. Ostensibly, these departures were never over race, but the resulting structures represented the racial politics of early twentieth-century America. Though some Azusa Street attendees would be changed forever in their openness to other races, others would leave the revival's heady racial climate to return to existing patterns of racial segregation so much a part of their personal history. Over the next hundred years, the revival's racial openness would dissipate, and the denominations that trace their roots in one way or another back to that phenomenal event would form patterns of racial retrenchment, seldom engaging with each other but borrowing heavily from each other's belief systems, rituals and spirituality.

MAJOR BLACK TRINITARIAN DENOMINATIONAL FAMILIES

United Holy Church of America. Among the most prominent existing black Holiness bodies to be swept into the new tide of Pentecostalism was the United Holy Church (UHC) of America. As one of the earliest black Holiness denominations in the United States, the UHC contends with the Church of God (Cleveland, Tennessee) as the oldest Pentecostal body in the nation while singularly reserving its distinction as the oldest African American Pentecostal body.[1]

The UHC came into existence when a number of men and women met to forge a series of alliances that eventually led to its formation. The initial impetus was a succession of revival meetings conducted throughout North Carolina in the late nineteenth century. The first of these was led by Isaac Cheshier in 1886 in Method, North Carolina, a small town near the capital, Raleigh. Little is known of the content of his message or the social or spiritual atmosphere of the revival, but it served as the catalyst for a fellowship of Holiness adherents that would become the nucleus of black Holiness revivalism in that area. The congregation that grew out of the Method revival would become the first congregation formed under the aegis of this fellowship, but Cheshier did not take leadership of the group. Instead, on the heels of his successful meeting, he joined several other men, including L. M. Mason, G. A. Mials, H. C. Snipes, William L. Fulford and Henry L. Fisher, in forming a fellowship of believers from several black independent Holiness congregations throughout North Carolina who would simply refer to themselves as the Holy People. By the end of that year, these congregations regularly worshiped and fellowshiped and had become known as the Holy Churches in North Carolina.

In 1892, another revival would take place that would be significant for this group. Elijah Lowney of Cleveland, Ohio, preached to overwhelming crowds in a Baptist church in Wilmington, North Carolina, and sev-

---

[1]Both the United Holy Church and the Church of God trace their beginnings to May 1886.

eral new Holiness congregations were formed in the wake of these of meetings. More importantly, during these meetings, Henry Fisher, one of the earliest UHC leaders, embraced the message and experience of sanctification. Sometime later, William Fulford, a former African Methodist Episcopal pastor who had later affiliated with the Fire Baptized Holiness Church and who had been involved in the 1886 meeting, established a large congregation in Wilmington that grew quickly to more than fifteen hundred members.

For the next year, the loosely affiliated Holiness congregations continued to fellowship freely with each other but did not form an organization. In 1894, when the first convocation was held in Durham, North Carolina, several congregations in Virginia had joined the group, which now went by the name the Holy Churches of North Carolina and Virginia. But even at that time no formal organization was established. That move did not come until 1900, when Charles and Emma Craig, who had been instrumental in establishing one of the oldest congregations in the denomination, called the leaders who had been loosely scattered throughout the area to meet to organize an independent association of black Holiness congregations. In that same year, a separate group led by C. J. Wilcox, Joseph Silver and John Scott convened the Union Holiness Convention. It was there that Fisher was ordained. At that meeting, L. M. Mason, who had been serving as informal president of the loose affiliation since 1894,[2] was chosen as the first president of the body, and P. M. Marable as vice president. This team served for only one year. Later that year, the two groups merged, taking on the name Holiness Church of North Carolina. At the next annual meeting, Fulford was chosen as president and W. C. Carlton as vice president. This pair served for fifteen years, from 1901 to 1916. During this period, the United Holy Church embraced the tenets of Pentecostalism so that, after existing for two decades as a Holiness group, this body was swept into the Pentecostal movement.

During Fulford's tenure, a number of small congregations joined the original group, so by 1902 it was ready to formally organize. It was also during this period that the denomination embraced the Pentecostal doctrine of initial evidence. In an article sent to Azusa Street's *Apostolic Faith*

---

[2]"History of the United Holy Church of America," The United Holy Church of America, www.uhcoa.org/aboutus.html.

in March 1907, simply titled "In Durham, N.C.," Fisher reported that

> some of the Lord's people here have received their Pentecost and spoken in
> tongues. Glory! A red hot meeting is now going on. Bro. Fulford, who has
> the gift of tongues, is leading it under the direction of the Holy Ghost. The
> saints are being baptized with the Spirit. I too have received Him and have
> spoken in some kind of a language, I know not what. It is glory here now.
> What we are now praying for is to have the nine gifts of the Spirit here in
> full operation. This city has been mightily stirred on account of the tongues.
> Nearly the whole of North Carolina is being stirred among the Holiness
> people, white and colored.[3]

But though many of its leaders and members embraced and experienced
the Pentecostal Holy Spirit baptism with speaking in tongues—which was
not new to members of the denomination and had been experienced by
some within its ranks during a number of earlier revival meetings[4]—UHC
leaders never embraced classical Pentecostalism's insistence on the language of *the* initial evidence or the doctrine that the experience was normative for all Spirit-filled believers. Instead, the denomination adopted a
via media, which held the Holiness understanding of sanctification as a
foundational necessity for every true believer and speaking in tongues as
one of gifts of the Spirit available to those who had been sanctified. Its
statement of faith simply declares,

> We believe the Holy Ghost is given upon the sanctified life in fulfillment
> of the promises of Jesus. . . . This includes: Baptism by Jesus in the Holy
> Spirit providing purging, initial filling, being brought under complete con-
> trol of the Spirit in an and act and recurring acts of refilling, providing
> power for the believer and boldness to witness. . . .
>
> The Holy Ghost . . . convicts and converts sinners, dwells in the be-
> liever, keeps the believer from the power of sin and leads him to the father,
> through His Son, Jesus Christ.[5]

By 1912, though he was still pastoring his sizable Goldsboro congregation, Fulford's influence on the United Holy Church was compromised by

---

[3]"In Durham, N.C.," *Apostolic Faith* 1, no. 7 (1907): 1.
[4]William C. Turner alludes to this in "An East Coast Celebration of Azusa: Theological Implications," *Journal of Pentecostal Theology* 16, no. 1 (2007): 32-45.
[5]Standard Manual and Constitution and By-laws of United Holy Church of America, Article
10.

a theological controversy that arose within the United Holy Church during his tenure, in which he was accused of preaching the doctrine of "everlasting life in the flesh." While little information is given about the exact tenor of his teaching, presumably those who heard him believed that he was proposing the understanding that those who are saved remain on earth eternally and, because they are immune to it, do not see physical death. Fulford remained at the helm of the United Holy Church during this period, but this teaching was considered heresy by other UHC leaders, who held Fulford to be in error.[6] When he would not recant the teaching, which he felt others misunderstood, Fulford was officially reprimanded by the board of elders and presbyters. Little is known of the accomplishments of his continued tenure within the denomination, but presumably he took a less active role in its leadership; and his name is conspicuously absent from extant church records from that early period. Though he continued to serve as president until 1916, he was finally disfellowshiped from the denomination in 1918.[7]

Throughout Fulford's tenure, Henry Fisher had been a prominent, behind-the-scenes leader. He served as editor in chief of the Holiness Union, the organization's newspaper and as chairman of the Foreign Missions Board, and Sunday school superintendent. By 1910, he had headed a team responsible for developing a manual. In it, the name was changed to the United Holy Church of America. Two years later, and four years before he was elected president, the organization was incorporated under that name. In 1916, Fisher was chosen as president, and the group came to be known as the United Holy Church of America.

Fisher proved to be one of the most significant leaders to emerge throughout UHCA history. From the time he assumed office, and during the more than thirty years he served, he was to bring about several important operational changes, including introducing a level of organizational structure that had previously been missing from the denomination. During his entire tenure as president, Fisher was aided by General Johnson (G. J.) Branch, who served as UHC vice president and president of the Northern

---

[6]William C. Turner, *The United Holy Church of America: A Study in Black Holiness-Pentecostalism* (Piscataway, N.J.: Gorgias Press, 2006), p. 25.
[7]*Yearbook of the United Holy Church 1918*, pp. 11-12, cited in Turner, *United Holy Church of America*, p. 64.

District. Branch, who had come into the UHC from the Freewill Baptist Church, was a moderately wealthy real estate owner with exceptional business skills, which helped set the UHC on strong administrative footing.[8]

The missionary endeavors of the UHC began in 1918 with the establishment of a board of missions and sending Isaac and Annie Williams to Liberia as the denomination's first missionaries. Though Annie died in 1922, Isaac remained in Liberia until his death, in 1942. For much of the early 1900s, UHC missionary work was concentrated in that country, and several other missionaries joined Williams, establishing stations throughout the country. Other works were begun in the Caribbean, with churches established in Bermuda, Barbados and Jamaica.

The district structure of the United Holy Church has important implications for its unfolding history. For the first forty-five years, UHC congregations were concentrated in the southern part of the country, primarily in North Carolina, South Carolina and Virginia; and the early headquarters for the church was Durham, North Carolina. The Southern District came into being with the founding of the denomination and is the largest and strongest district in the body. The Northern District was formed in 1920; the Northwestern District followed in 1924. By that year the United Holy Church had spread to the West Coast, and churches had been established in California and, by 1931, this district of the UHCA had congregations in Pennsylvania, Ohio, West Virginia, Kentucky and Michigan. The congregations that had been established in Barbados later affiliated with another Pentecostal body. It was not until twenty-five years later that that United Holy Church again had a presence on that island, when Bishop Henry Gentles founded the Mt. Olive United Holy Church and brought several existing independent congregations into the denomination.[9]

Just before the outbreak of World War I, the UHC purchased land in Dunn, North Carolina—making a triangle connecting Raleigh, Fayetteville and Goldsboro—to build an educational facility but abandoned the project during the war. Nearly twenty years later, in 1936, land was purchased in Greensboro, North Carolina, and plans for a Bible training school

---

[8]For a discussion of Branches contribution to the UHC, see Turner, *United Holy Church of America*, pp. 70-74.

[9]For a discussion of the work of the UHC in Barbados see, *50th Anniversary Journal: Reflecting on the Past with Joy while Facing the Challenges of the New Millenium—Our Golden Anniversary, 1949-1999* (Barbados: United Holy Church of America—Barbados District, 1999).

were developed. When bank funding for the project could not be secured, the funds were raised internally. The building was completed and the first classes of the Bible Training School were held in 1944. Since that time, however, little further effort has been made to develop the educational institution and financial support for such an effort remained minimal.

When Fisher died in 1947, Branch assumed leadership of the denomination, serving only two years, until his death in 1949. He was followed by Henry H. Harrison, 1949-1963, and Walter Strobhar, 1963-1980. Under Strobhar's leadership, separate Virginia and North Carolina districts were organized. Joseph Bowen served from 1980-1992. By that year the denomination had put new polity in place that limited the term of the general president to four years and voted not to return Bowen to the position. Instead, Walter Talley, who had served as the first president of the Virginia District, was the first general president elected to serve under the new rule. He assumed office in 1992 but died in 1996, several months before his term would have expired. Odell McCullom was elected to complete his term and, since no limitation was placed on how often a person could run for the office, was reelected to a new four-year term in 1996 and again in 2000 and 2004. At McCollum's death, in 2005, Elijah Williams assumed the office of General President.

Mt. Sinai Holy Church. In 1924, Ida Robinson, pastor of a Philadelphia UHC congregation, had gained considerable exposure within the denomination and throughout the small community of black Pentecostal congregations along the East Coast for her dynamic preaching and singing. Her fiery preaching delivery and dynamic singing made her so popular that Fisher and Branch regularly invited her to travel and minister with them in revival meetings throughout the area. But Robinson's ministry did more than help UHC leaders grow churches. It piqued the interest of other women who, often for the first time, saw a woman minister with the same power and charisma as the men they were used to hearing. The notoriety of her ministry spurred many other UHC women to seek ordination and a more public ministry.

Though the body had been open to the ministry of women since its founding, the surge in interest in pastoral ministry among them proved to be more than leaders were willing to accept. In response, Fisher, Branch and other leaders made a proclamation to the General Assembly that they would no longer "publicly ordain women" and would restrict previously ordained women to serve only in lower levels of ordained ministry. Unwilling to settle for that arrangement, Robinson used her Philadelphia congregation as the "mother church" and headquarters of an organization that would explicitly promote the ministry and leadership of women.

Such a decision was to prove to have consequences far beyond those Fisher and Branch had intended. For Robinson, whose exceptional gifting secured her future in the UHC, saw their move as unfair to other women. When Robinson withdrew from the denomination, several supporters, including many women rejected for ordination as well as other female and male pastors sympathetic to her stand, accompanied her; and several congregations from the parent body realigned themselves with Robinson. At the new denomination's first convocation, in September 1924, one year after its founding, the seventeen congregations included several that had come from the United Holy Church.[10]

At least one schism occurred during Mt. Sinai's early years. A dissenting group, dissatisfied with the decision of Robinson and the church leadership to relax the ban on men wearing neckties, left to form Glorious Mt. Sinai Holy Church. Generally, however, though individual congregations left from time to time, additional congregations were slowly added. In the 22 years that Robinson was at its helm, the denomination grew to 84 churches, stretching from New England to Florida.[11] At its height, in 1988, the organization had grown to 154 congregations,[12] yet in the 42 years since then, the growth that Mt. Sinai experienced under Robinson has never again been realized.

By the time Robinson died, in 1946, a pattern of women's leadership had been established that would stand for half a century. The next three presiding bishops were women whom Robinson had personally groomed to assume leadership. As a young woman, Elmira Jeffries, a charter member of Mt. Sinai from the UHC, started leading Tuesday noonday tarry service at Robinson's Mt. Olive congregation. She subsequently pastored several congregations, holding increasingly important positions, including

---

[10]Ibid., p. 36.

[11]Mt. Sinai Holy Church of America, *Celebrating Our Legacy: Mt. Sinai Holy Church of America, Inc.*, vol. 1 (Philadelphia: Mt. Sinai Holy Church of America, n.d.), p. 140.

[12]Felton Best, "Loosing the Women" (paper presented to the Society for Pentecostal Studies, Twenty-Fourth Annual Meeting, Wheaton, Ill., November 1994), p. 11.

vice president under Robinson.[13] She was elected as presiding bishop directly after Robinson's death and served until her own death in 1964. Eighty-eight-year-old Mary Jackson, another charter member who had taught the preacher's class at Mt. Sinai and assisted Robinson with finances, succeeded Jeffries, serving until her death at age 102.[14] Amy Stevens, who like the others had previously served in a number of capacities including usher and Sunday school teacher, was elected presiding bishop at age 71, serving until her death in 2000 at age 88.[15]

Since Robinson's death, a pattern of preference for male leadership at the higher levels of authority has clearly developed within Mt. Sinai. As early as 1980, less than one-half of Mt. Sinai's bishops were women; and by 2000, only one-third of Mt. Sinai bishops were women. Interestingly, however, the actual rate of participation of women in all levels of leadership has continued to decline from the time of Robinson's death until the present. Though there are large numbers of women in ministry, the proportion of women pastors and the proportion of women with governing and oversight responsibilities continue to slowly but steadily fall. Of the 160 ordained ministers[16] who were part of the organization in 1996, 125 (more than three-fourths) were women.[17] However, in that same year, most of these women served in secondary roles as evangelists, assistant pastors or support staff; only 45 of the 102 pastors were women.[18] Only 8 of the 19 bishops were women.

Along with the decline of women in top positions, the steady decline in

---

[13]Mt. Sinai Holy Church of America, *Celebrating Our Legacy*, pp. 142-43. The succeeding presiding bishop is elected by the board of bishops at the time of the death of the existing presiding bishop.

[14]Ibid., p. 148.

[15]Ibid., pp. 5-6. According to Larry E. Williams, "The Way God Led Them: A Historical Study of the Mt. Sinai Holy Church of America, Inc." (Ph.D. diss., Howard University, 1998), p. 95, Stevens's husband, Charles, was first nominated as president at age of ninety-one but declined due to his age, in favor of his wife who was subsequently elected to the position.

[16]Again, the issue of ordination is that of "full clergy rights." Even within Mount Sinai, the right to serve institutional positions of governance is reserved for ordained clergy. While the pastorate is not, one is more likely to be assigned to a pastorate if fully ordained. Bishops are also selected from the ordained clergy.

[17]Best, "Loosing the Women," p. 10.

[18]Within Mount Sinai, as with some other Pentecostal bodies, ordination and ministerial placement are not linked. An individual might be ordained a minister, an elder, and not serve in pastoral ministry. The person would most likely serve as an itinerant evangelist or in some other supportive position such as assistant pastor.

proportion of women in pastoral leadership has accelerated. Within the first 26 years (nearly one generation) there was only a 9 percent fall. However, with the succeeding 24 years the rate of decline almost doubled to 16 percent. Moreover, most of the women currently serving as bishops are older women who entered the denomination and rose through the ranks during Robinson's lifetime or shortly thereafter. Though highly revered for their early contributions, most are no longer able to play a viable role in Mt. Sinai's governance. The younger, male bishops who have more recently been elected are now the decision makers—and the real leadership of the Mt. Sinai organization.

Mt. Sinai Holy Church remains a relatively small denomination, largely unknown outside of the African American Pentecostal community. At its height, the denomination had less than 200 congregations, primarily along the East Coast. By 1996, that number was down to 102 with approximately 10,000 members, including 1 congregation in Cuba, 7 house churches in India and 2 congregations in Guyana, South America.[19] And, as with the denomination, Robinson remains largely unknown except among a small circle of dedicated admirers and scholars of black women's history.

Mt. Calvary Holy Church of America. Four years after Robinson left the UHC, another one of its prominent pastors, Brumfield Johnson, preached a revival in Winston-Salem, North Carolina, in which 249 people experienced conversions. Many of these new converts expressed a desire for Johnson to serve as their pastor, so a new congregation was started under the official name Mt. Calvary Holy Church of America, Inc. A year later, Johnson had chartered a new denomination under that name.

Like Robinson in Mt. Sinai, it was principally Johnson's own efforts that built the nucleus of Mt. Calvary. He would organize evangelistic teams and take them wherever he was invited to preach, organizing the new converts from his campaigns into the nucleus of a new congregation, and then he would appoint a pastor to care for them. The evangelistic teams that worked with Johnson served two purposes: First, they were the advance and support teams for the revival, setting up and tearing the necessary facilities for each meeting and ensuring that logistical needs

---

[19]Mt. Sinai Holy Church of America, *Celebrating Our Legacy,* p. 204.

were met. Second, they also formed the core of new congregations established in the wake of these meetings. By the time of his death, there were
eighty churches in thirteen states. Many of them had been established in
this manner.

Like its parent body, the UHC, Mt. Calvary has never insisted on initial evidence of tongues as a necessary sign of Holy Spirit baptism. Instead,
without denying the reality or importance of the experience, the denomination insists that no single gift is evidence of the Holy Spirit's presence
and, without rejecting its designation among Pentecostal bodies, holds
that the entire church was baptized in the Spirit on the day of Pentecost.

The first denominational headquarters was established in Baltimore,
Maryland, but by 1942 it had been relocated to Buffalo, New York. A
Bible School was opened in Littleton, North Carolina, to train ministers
and Christian workers, but it was short lived as a stand-alone institution.
In 1956, it affiliated with the Teamer Religious and Educational Enter-
prises of Charlotte, North Carolina, to offer correspondences courses.

When Johnson died in 1972, he was succeeded by Bishop Harold Ivory
Williams of Durham, North Carolina, who served until 2008, when failing health required him to step down. He was succeeded by Bishop Alfred
Owens of Washington, D.C. By 2006, Mt. Calvary had grown to fifty-
eight congregations in the United States, primarily along the East Coast,
along with several mission congregations in Europe, Asia and Africa.

One reason for Johnson's departure from the United Holy Church was
the parent denomination's more open stance on women in ministry. As a
result, although Mt. Calvary permitted women to serve as pastors from its
inception and began ordaining women as bishops in 1991, the earlier limitation on women may have been instrument in a split that occurred in
1972, when two women, Ardell Tucker and Dorothy Austin, left to form
the National Tabernacles of Deliverance. Tucker had formerly been a
member of the oneness Apostolic Faith Church of God but had accepted
the trinitarian understanding of the Godhead and had left that body to
join Mt. Calvary.

The new denomination began with a revival at Mt. Calvary Deliverance Tabernacle, a congregation the two women had established under
Johnson's direction in August 1964 in New Haven, Connecticut. By 1966,
they had organized additional congregations in Bridgeport, Connecticut,

and Danbury, Connecticut. The two women served together at its helm until 1980, when Austin died. Tucker continued to lead the denomination until 2006, when Austin's grandson, Robert L. Smith IV, took leadership. By that time, the denomination had fourteen churches.[20]

Original United Holy Church of America. Since these breaks with the UHC were not because of any fissure over polity or doctrine, both Robinson and Johnson retained much of the parent body's polity for their new organizations. Robinson also maintained ties with the UHC. But while these two relatively early schisms resulted in the founding of entirely new denominations, in 1972 a schism began to unfold that caused an internal rift in the UHC that would take several years to heal.

The United Holy Church originated in the South, and from the beginning its strength lay there. The Southern District had been the largest and strongest district within the denomination, and not only did it have the largest number of congregations; but also the denomination's international headquarters were located in Greensboro, North Carolina. The district was home to numerous strong churches that were led by strong and charismatic pastors whose influence was felt throughout the denomination, and many of the prominent UHC lay leaders hailed from its congregations. One of the stronger and most prominent leaders in the district was Bishop James A. Forbes Sr., and he would be instrumental in driving the issues that ultimately led to schism.

One of the issues driving the split was the sheer size and influence of the Southern District. In an attempt to diffuse some of that influence, UHCA leaders had suggested that the district be subdivided by state. In 1972, the officers of the Southern District, under Forbes's leadership, responded to this suggestion by taking the unauthorized action of dissolving the United Holy Church of America and drawing up a new charter as the Southern District of the United Holy Church.

Some suggest much of the schism may have resulted from a personality clash between two leaders, Bishop Forbes and Bishop Joseph Bowen, vice president of the parent body, who presumably was interested in acquiring Forbes's position as president of the Southern District.[21] At any rate, rela-

---

[20]"Tabernacle History," Mount Calvary Deliverance Chapel website, www.mtcdtchurch.org/History.html.
[21]For a discussion of the relationships between the two men and the various factions, see Carla L.

tionships between the Southern District and the leadership of the United Holy Church continued to deteriorate until the dramatic departure of the southern group occurred during the 1977 General Convocation after Bishop Forbes delivered a speech in which he adamantly declared to the gathered assembly, "Brothers and sisters . . . we thank you for the fellowship through the years. Permit the Southern District to go its sundry ways as the bishop's message indicated today. Whether you vote, or whether you don't vote, we're gone. God bless you."[22]

Following his speech, most members of the Southern District walked out of the convocation and formed a new body, the Original United Holy Church of the World, Inc., claiming to be entitled to represent the assets of the original group since many of the churches found within it were congregations that had been part of the denomination from its earliest years. That name was later shortened to Original United Holy Church International.

The loss of the Southern District would prove to be significant for the small body, whose strength was mainly in the South, the Northeast, and the Midwest. One hundred congregations left with the Southern District. Though overtures were made by the parent body to allow any Southern District congregations to remain with the body, only seven congregations agreed to do so, continuing to represent themselves as the Southern District of the United Holy Church.[23]

The schism resulted in a lengthy trial, which pitted Forbes and the Southern District against the mother denomination and its leaders over ownership of the properties of individual congregations. During the period, Forbes approached the leadership of the International Pentecostal Holiness Church (IPHC) about seeking a possible affiliation with that group, and an agreement was drawn up and approved by IPHC General Conference in 1977.[24]

The split lasted for twenty-three years. During that time, other smaller

Bowens, "The Division and Reunification of an African American Non-Secular Organization: Factors That Caused the Split and Merger of a Religious Organization" (Ed.D. diss., George Washington University, 2003), pp. 124-25.

[22]Ibid., p. 109.

[23]Ibid., p. 82.

[24]Thad M. White, "A Brighter Future," *Pentecostal Holiness Advocate* 63, no. 10 (1979): 4-5. See also Vinson Synan, "Pentecostal Holiness Church," in *Encyclopedia of Religion in the South*, ed. Samuel S. Hill (Macon, Ga.: Mercer University Press, 1984), p. 583.

bodies split from the parent group. But in 2000, the two major factions joined with these smaller factions to officially reunite. By that time, most of the leaders who had been involved in the original schism were in leadership, and many of the local congregations and individual pastors within these bodies had continued to be in fellowship with each other. By 2006, there were more than five hundred congregations within the United Holy Church. Most of these were in the United States; twenty-three were in the Caribbean. Almost two-thirds of the U.S. congregations remain in the South.

The Church of God in Christ. In 1895 two young former Baptist preachers—Charles Price Jones and Charles Harrison Mason—forged an alliance that would ultimately lead to the founding of what would become one of the most prominent African American Christian denominations in the world. By that time, both men had publicly embraced the Holiness movement and the experience of sanctification and had subsequently been disfellowshiped from their Baptist congregations and conventions. Beginning with a revival the two held in a cotton gin in Lexington, Mississippi, in 1896, they were to work closely together for the next decade, organizing the Church of God in Christ (COGIC) as a Holiness denomination that would grow to encompass congregations throughout the Tennessee River valley and serve as the foundation for what was to become by the end of the twentieth century the largest African American Pentecostal denomination in the world.

Once ousted from his Baptist congregation, Mason received permission to use an abandoned gin house in Lexington, Mississippi, 160 miles northeast of Jackson for a new sanctuary. His ministry there became a resounding success, with several converted and sanctified, and laid the groundwork for one of the leading congregations within the new body. The next ten years saw new congregations spring up throughout the valley and existing congregations affiliate with them to solidify a Holiness organization under leadership of the two friends, who preached a message of the necessity for sanctification and the empowerment of the Holy Ghost. But events of 1907 were about to touch the Church of God in Christ and split it into two denominations—one Holiness, the other Pentecostal.

Several months after the Azusa Street Revival began, the two leaders got wind of the spiritual fervor it was causing on the West Coast. They decided to send a contingent consisting of Mason, along with two trusted colleagues,

J. A. Jeter and D. J. Young, to Los Angeles to ascertain the spiritual authenticity and direction of the new movement. Reportedly, this was not Mason's first acquaintance with William Seymour, whom he had met when the latter made a trip to Arkansas near the turn of the century to see either one or both of the two leaders.[25] And apparently this was not Mason's first encounter with the experience of speaking in tongues, for several years before going to Azusa Street, Mason had had experiences of God speaking to him in an unknown tongue and had wrestled with what these visitations might have meant and whether they were authentic. Mason's first reaction to what he saw and heard at Azusa Street was not without qualification, as he would later testify, "The first day . . . I sat to myself. I saw and heard some things that did not seem scriptural."[26] But within a short time, he was convinced, noting that "when I heard some speak in tongues I knew it was right." Once he determined that the experience was authentic, however, both Mason and Young received their Pentecostal experience at Azusa Street. After this encounter, at least with Mason, the issue was settled.[27]

On route back to Tennessee, Mason stopped in Portsmouth, Virginia, to conduct revival meetings. During this time, more than six thousand conversions were reported. But the delay meant that he was not the first to reach his congregation and colleagues with the news of what he had found in Los Angeles. While Mason was traveling, Seymour's associate and traveling evangelist Glenn Cook had visited his congregation, preached his own experiences and reported favorably on the Los Angeles meetings. By the time Mason reached Mississippi, many in the congregation had embraced the teaching and experience of tongues. Delighted to see the work Cook had accomplished, Mason later reported that, "the fire had fallen before my arrival. Brother Cook . . . was telling the story and the Lord was sending rain."[28]

Not everyone who heard the men's report was convinced of the validity of the experience. Jones had initially supported speaking in tongues as a

[25]Charles Shumway, "A Critical History of Glossolalia" (Ph.D. diss., Boston University, 1919), p. 173.

[26]Charles H. Mason, "Elder Mason Tells of Receiving the Holy Ghost," in *The History and Life Work of Elder C. H. Mason, Chief Apostle, and His Co-laborers*, ed. Mary Mason (s.l.: s.n., 1924), p. 26.

[27]Ibid., p. 30; Ithiel Clemmons, *Bishop Charles Harrison Mason and the Roots of the Church of God in Christ* (Bakersfield, Calif.: Pneuma Life, 1996), p. 62.

[28]Ibid., p. 64.

spiritual gift given to the sanctified, Spirit-filled believer. However, he and several others within the fledgling denomination chafed at the idea that it was the only valid evidence of Holy Spirit baptism, insisting that Mason and the others refrain from making that claim. When they would not, matters came to a head. At the annual convocation in 1907, debate over initial evidence waged for three days. In the end, Jones's group prevailed and the General Assembly withdrew fellowship from Mason. With the split, Jones's group maintained the larger number of the more than one hundred congregations that had aligned themselves with the fellowship. Only about ten congregations left with Mason.[29]

Once the schism occurred, Mason wrote to ministers who had embraced the new understanding, inviting them to Memphis to discuss the possibility of organizing. In September of 1907, delegates from eight congregations in Tennessee, Mississippi, Oklahoma and Arkansas met with Mason and twelve individual ministers to form the Pentecostal Church of God in Christ. The first convocation of the new body was held in November.

Mason was aided in his efforts by D. J. Young, a former school teacher and presiding elder in the African Methodist Episcopal Church who had been affiliated with the Burning Bush Association after accepting the doctrine of sanctification and came in contact with Mason after moving from Chicago to Memphis. Around the turn of the century, Young was traveling throughout the South as an evangelist and then established a church in Pine Bluff, Arkansas.[30] Young worked intimately with Mason during the formative years of the COGIC, and in 1912, Mason appointed him overseer of Texas. After resigning that position to return to the evangelistic circuit, he was appointed overseer of Kansas in 1917 and served in that position until his death in 1927.[31] During the early years, Young served as publisher of the denominational periodical, *Whole Truth,* as well as the COGIC's Sunday school literature. He founded the D. J. Young publishing company, which continued to publish the Sunday school literature for fifty years.[32]

[29]Lewis F. Morgan, "The Flame Still Burns," *Charisma and Christian Life*, November 2007, p. 47.
[30]Charles H. Pleas, *A Period in History of the Church of God in Christ* (Memphis: s.n., 1991), pp. 64-65.
[31]Ibid., p. 65.
[32]Lemuel Thuston, "Restoring the Way of Holiness: Celebrating the Ministries of Pioneer D. J.

Between 1907 and 1926, Jones and Mason's bodies remained locked in a legal battle over the right to use the name Church of God in Christ. Mason asserted that God had specifically revealed that name to him in a vision and that he had convinced Jones to adopt the identification. Reasoning, therefore, that the name rightfully belonged to his group, Mason prevailed and was awarded ownership of the designation in 1909. Over the next sixteen years, Jones filed a series of appeals, and though Mason's group officially changed its name in 1922, the appeals continued until 1926, when Mason's group was given exclusive right to its use.

While on the surface the split between the two leaders was simply over whether speaking in tongues was the initial evidence of Holy Spirit Baptism, in reality, it signaled a deeper fissure between the two that was as much about a difference in spiritual temperament as any specific issue. Jones sought to promote a style of worship that was more constrained and less emotive, a preference clearly on display of his characterization of the Pentecostal movement:

> The tongues cult . . . [by which] many good and earnest people were deceived . . . has apparently a gift of tongues, but it never proved a Pentecost like the second chapter of Acts and never will, for the simple reason that it is a spiritual fake supported by false interpretations and false applications of Scripture, nor has the supposed gift of tongues proven real.[33]

Though not denying the authenticity of the experience, Jones saw the experience of tongues as only one possible evidences of Holy Spirit baptism. Mason, on the other hand, viewed his Azusa Street experience as essential to his personal quest to preserve elements of slave religion in African American worship and make its presence felt within the COGIC worship experience.

But not only did Jones reject Mason's contentions; but also, mainline pastors ridiculed Mason's prayer and healing rituals, especially his display of misshaped roots as "magic" and pure superstition. He in turn rejected what he saw as accommodationist tendencies in mainline black Christianity that played down more emotive elements such as dancing, drumming and Spirit possession. Mason, however, sought to give both a biblical and

Young," *Advocate* 6, no. 3 (2008): 4.
[33]Charles Price Jones, *The Gift of the Holy Spirit in the Book of Acts* (1903; reprint, Chicago: National Publishing Board, Church of Christ [Holiness] U.S.A., 1996), p. 42.

cultural interpretation to elements of Pentecostal worship, and the more his detractors protested, the more tenaciously he held on to these practices and his interpretation of them as rooted in African spirituality.

White ministers in the COGIC. From 1907 until 1914, the Church of God in Christ was in a unique position as the only body within the new movement registered with the federal government to grant recognized ministerial credentials. Because of this, Mason provided the critical service of signing credentials for both black and white Pentecostal ministers who had been disfellowshiped from their mainline congregations and denominations. With these in hand, they were not only able to function as pastors and evangelists but also to take advantage of discounted clergy railroad fairs and register as conscientious objectors during World War I.

Though Mason credentialed nearly 350 white ministers in the seven years following the COGIC's rebirth as a Pentecostal denomination, this arrangement proved to be untenable for the majority of them. A growing breach culminated in a meeting in Hot Springs, Arkansas, signaling the end of formal ties with Mason and the beginning of a new fellowship, the Assemblies of God, in which he was, apparently, not invited to participate as a leader, though the group reportedly entered into a "brotherly" agreement with Mason that they would divide the work of evangelizing along racial lines.[34]

Like Seymour, who became his close friend and associate, Mason nevertheless worked hard to maintain racial unity within his young movement. Moreover, he maintained close alliances with other sympathetic white leaders, counting A. J. Tomlinson, leader of the Church of God (Cleveland, Tennessee), and J. H. King of the Pentecostal Holiness Church among his friends. Even with the 1914 exodus to form the Assemblies of God, a number of white ministers remained with Mason. Among those who remained loyal was the "Kentucky Cyclone Evangelist" James Logan Delk, who met Mason in 1904 in Conway, Arkansas.[35] Delk was one of few early white Pentecostals to publicly and soundly renounce racism. He did so in statements such as:

---

[34]See the more detailed discussion of the formation of the Assemblies of God and its roots in the COGIC in chap. 7.

[35]James Logan Delk, *He Made Millions Happy* (Lexington: James Delk, 1945), quoted in Lewis Morgan, "The Flame Still Burns," *Charisma and Christian Life*, October 2007, p. 58.

I hope that the reader, especially the Colored race, will realize the signifi-cance of a white man writing about a colored man. Neither Brother Mason nor myself believe in segregation or Jim Crow, but all people, either white or colored, do not see this in the same light. I have a little daughter . . . and she is the pride of our life. But if I did not believe that God loved the black-est Negro girl as much as He loves my own daughter, I would stop writing books, throw my Bible aside, and never preach another sermon.[36]

Not only did a number of white ministers remain in COGIC, but whites continued to participate in COGIC worship services, and several COGIC congregations continued to have white members. But white participation in the denomination continued to erode as new white Pentecostal congre-gations and denominations sprang up. For example, in Los Angeles, E. R. Driver had planted and pastored the city's first Church of God in Christ congregation in 1914. It existed as a multiracial congregation, but the con-stituency declined dramatically once Aimee Semple McPherson estab-lished her massive Angelus Temple congregation

Even as the number of white ministers in the COGIC continued to decline, Delk maintained his affiliation, becoming Mason's close confi-dante; and that association often proved costly for him within the white community. Because of it, for example, he was beaten twice by members of the Ku Klux Klan.[37] Yet Delk was a strong leader in his own right. His broad interests included running revivals throughout the country and hosting a radio broadcast. His political aspiration led him to maintain friendships with local and national political leaders and to run for governor of Missouri in 1932. During World War II, when most available steel was being directed to the war effort, Delk drew on his friendships with Sena-tors Alben Barkley, who later became vice president, and Happy Chandler, twice governor of Kentucky, and then U.S. Senator Harry S. Truman of Missouri and Tom Stewart from Tennessee to help COGIC secure enough of the precious commodity to complete Mason Temple in Memphis. But he also counted among his associates Elizabeth "Lizzie" Woods Robinson who, after Delk introduced her to Mason, was to become the first leader of the COGIC Women's Department.[38] Delk stayed with the organiza-

[36]Ibid.
[37]Clemmons, *Bishop Charles Harrison Mason*, p. 24.
[38]Morgan, "Flame Still Burns," p. 45.

tion until death in 1963, two years after Mason.

William B. Holt, a blond-haired German COGIC pastor who served as the national field secretary before becoming the COGIC's first general secretary, from 1910-1920, was another trusted confidant who traveled regularly with Mason, serving as Mason's aide and secretary and as superintendent of COGIC Spanish missions in California. Their relationship appeared even closer than that maintained by Mason and Delk; presiding bishop Louis Ford noted that the pair were like blood brothers.[39] Their close friendship drew suspicion from the FBI, who monitored them during World War I, believing that Mason might incite blacks to align with Germany. Church of God in Christ churchman and historian Donald Weeks recounted that "the secretary of war could not reason why a white man would be connected with an almost all-Negro church."[40] When Mason was arrested by federal agents and thrown into a Lexington, Mississippi, jail for violating the Sedition Act, Holt raised the two thousand dollars to bail him out. After his release, Mason continued to fellowship with whites, while also condemning segregation.

Leonard P. Adams, a lawyer and pastor of Grace and Truth Church of God in Christ in Memphis, had been part of the Cumberland Presbyterian Church, was one of the first white ministers to unite with Mason in Memphis and led a Holiness congregation near Mason's church. After experiencing Pentecostal Spirit baptism in 1908, Adams joined the Church of God (Cleveland, Tennessee). But in 1910, following a disagreement with General Overseer A. J. Tomlinson, Adams left the denomination and his congregation affiliated with the COGIC. Though Adams was present at the 1914 Assemblies of God organizing meeting, he did not join the new organization, deciding instead to continue to work with Mason.[41]

Another white, August Feick, had worked with famed evangelist Maria Woodworth-Etter in the first quarter of the twentieth century and later served as pastor of the Woodworth-Etter Tabernacle in Indianapolis, Indiana. Reportedly, after Mason asked him to organize the white COGIC churches, he

---

[39]Joe Maxwell, "Building the Church of God in Christ," *Christianity Today*, April 8, 1996, p. 26.
[40]Ibid.
[41]Ibid. See also Morgan, "Flame Still Burns," p. 48.

withdrew from the Assemblies of God to work with the black leader.[42]

Like Seymour, Mason could not sustain his effort to promote racial unity within his denomination. By 1924, despite his efforts to maintain an open policy on race within the COGIC, he capitulated to growing pressure for a degree of separation between blacks and whites. The denomination established a minority conference for white congregations and ministers from across the country, which remained in existence until the mid 1930s. By 1933, however, Holt found himself at odds with the COGIC's majority black leadership, who dismissed him from the fellowship, at the same time setting off debate about whether whites and blacks could practically work and worship together. With his departure, the COGIC experiment in interracialism effectively came to an end.[43]

By the end of the twentieth century, white congregations in the COGIC had all but disappeared, though some individual white members continued to frequent COGIC worship services. Further, some more prominent COGIC congregations, particularly megachurches such as West Angeles COGIC in Los Angeles, continued to attract a fairly larger number of whites to their congregations.

Consolidations and schisms. Like the rest of Pentecostalism, the COGIC, which had been born out of schism, did not escape further schism within its own ranks. Indeed, both during and after Mason's lifetime, the denomination would see a number of schisms, each of which would bring a number of spinoff groups into existence.

Elias Dempsey Smith, founder of Triumph the Church and Kingdom of God in Christ, joined forces with Mason shortly after his group was founded in 1904. But while Mason was open to interracial cooperation and fellowship, Smith made a distinction between the "church militant of whites and the peace loving church of blacks. Further, Smith rejected Mason's emphasis on speaking in tongues. Smith pulled out of the COGIC in

---

[42]Cecil M. Robeck Jr., "The Past: Historical Roots of Racial Unity and Division in American Pentecostalism," *Cyberjournal For Pentecostal-Charismatic Research,* www.pctii.org/cyberj /cyberj14/robeck.html#N_72_.

[43]For discussion of this period, see David Daniels, "Charles Harrison Mason: The Interracial Impulse of Early Pentecostalism," in *Portrait of a Generation: Early Pentecostal Leaders,* ed. Grant Wacker and James R. Goff (Fayetteville: University of Arkansas Press, 2002), pp. 255-70; and Craig Scandrett-Leatherman, "Can't Nobody Do Me Like Jesus: The Embodiment of Aesthetics in Afro-Pentecostal Rituals" (Ph.D. dissertation, University of Kansas, 2005), pp. 340-41.

1912 and resumed leadership of his original body.[44]

In 1915, after members of the National Baptist Convention congregation led by J. H. Morris experienced Pentecostal Spirit baptism, they broke away to form a separate body, which they also called the Church of God in Christ. In 1921 this group, made up largely of Morris's own family, brought their congregations into fellowship with Mason. In 1925, however, members of the original smaller group withdrew from the larger body to form the Free Church of God in Christ. By 1935 there were 19 congregations and 874 members in the denomination, and by the late 1940s there was only one additional congregation.[45] Since that time, little additional information has surfaced about the group.

In 1927, Bishop S. E. Looper of Ohio pulled out of the COGIC to form the Free Unity Church of God in Christ. Looper concentrated his efforts within that state and by 1949 had established branches of the body in Cincinnati, Columbus, Akron, Chillicothe and Barberton.[46] By 2006, however, no information was available regarding these congregations.

In 1932, Bishop Justus Bowe broke with Mason to establish the Church of God in Christ, Congregational, after the COGIC rejected a proposal to adopt a congregational polity, voting instead to retain an episcopal form. Bowe, who served as overseer of Arkansas, had been among the first ministers to respond to Mason's call to reorganize after his split from Jones. But almost from the beginning, Bowe exhibited an independent attitude that other COGIC clergy resented. In one instance, for example, his refusal to heed a warning to forego holding a reorganization convocation in Arkansas before Mason's suit with Jones was settled caused the denomination to lose its property in that state.

In 1934 another COGIC schismatic, George Stack, who had been disfellowshiped because he challenged the COGIC tithing system, joined with Bowe, and for the next ten years the two served at the head of the denomination. But Bowe returned to the COGIC in 1945, leaving the smaller body intact under Stack's leadership. By 1971 the Church of

---

[44]"Triumph the Church and Kingdom of God," in *Encyclopedia of African American Religion*, ed. Larry Murphy, J. Gordon Melton and Gary Ward (New York: Garland, 1993), p. 761.

[45]"Free Church of God in Christ," in *The Encyclopedia of American Religions*, ed. J. Gordon Melton (Tarrytown, N.Y.: Triumph, 1991), pp. 1174-75.

[46]James Edward Blackwell, "A Comparative Study of Five Negro Storefront Churches in Cleveland" (M.A. thesis, Case Western University, 1949), p. 208.

God in Christ, Congregational, reportedly had forty-three congregations, including six in Mexico and four in England. Except on the issues
of tithing and governmental structure, its polity is similar to that of the
parent body.

One consistent motivation for the formation of new denominations
out of the COGIC has been the denominational stand regarding the
ordination of women and their involvement in pastoral leadership. Mozella Cook pulled out from the parent body in 1947 to form the Sought
Out Church of God in Christ. Two years later, the denomination had
only four congregations and sixty members,[47] and probably grew no
larger than that figure. Despite these small numbers, however, Cook is
significant because she was one of the first women to pull out of the
COGIC specifically to move into a position of full denominational leadership. Later, in 1968, Ernestine Cleveland Reems, daughter of COGIC
bishop E. E. Cleveland, would leave to found her own independent congregation, Center of Hope Community Church in Oakland, California.
In 2000, Reems was consecrated bishop of Monument of Faith, International Assembly.[48]

In 2004, the issue of women's involvement in leadership was, arguably,
part of the catalyst for the formation of another new denomination, when
David Grayson, former COGIC pastor, bishop and district superintendent, was consecrated as presiding bishop of the Church of God in Christ
(New Day). Grayson had been formerly consecrated as a bishop within the
COGIC by Gilbert Patterson in 1987 and had been a part of the denomination for several decades. The group that left with him included thirty-
two COGIC congregations and, in all, about two thousand members from
forty congregations, primarily in Tennessee, Alabama, Mississippi and
New York. The new denomination is almost identical to the parent body
in structure and belief, except that it welcomes the ordination of women as
both elders and bishops. After fighting with the COGIC in court over the
use if the parent denomination's name, the new group was forced to change

[47]"Sought Out Church of God in Christ," in *The Encyclopedia of American Religions*, ed. J. Gordon Melton (Tarrytown, N.Y.: Triumph, 1991), p. 1175.
[48]Frank A. Jones, "The Season of the Woman: Pastor Ernestine Cleveland Reems Is Chosen
Bishop," *Gibbs*, January 22-29, 2007, www.gibbsmagazine.com/Bishop%20Reems.htm. That
organization, founded by Richard Henton, became Monument International Church Assemblies.

its name to New Day Church International.[49]

Defections such as those by Cook, Reems, Day and others did not have a large impact on the COGIC, and during Mason's lifetime, these schisms left the COGIC largely unscathed. The vast majority of members remained loyal to the parent body, whose growth has geometrically eclipsed the combined total of all the schismatic groups.

Growth and development. During its first two and a half decades, the COGIC's growth was steady, yet relatively slow. By 1934, there were approximately 25,000 members in 345 congregations throughout 21 states and the District of Columbia. That year, Mason appointed five bishops, I. S. Stafford, a medical doctor from Detroit; Emmett M. Page of Dallas; William M. Roberts of Chicago; Ozro T. Jones of Philadelphia; and Robert E. Williams. Mason also set ten state supervisors in place.

All of the five bishops were extraordinarily gifted leaders. All but Jones preceded Mason in death. Less is known of Williams than the other four. Page had been with Mason since his initial split with Jones over the issue of tongues and had been subsequently appointed by Mason as overseer of Texas. Roberts had been a member of Mason's Memphis congregation, serving at one time as assistant pastor. He left that city to establish the first COGIC congregation in Illinois. As a political activist, Roberts participated in a group of clergy and other leaders who came to Washington, D.C., in 1941 to protest for fair employment for blacks, and he served as chairman of the board of education of the Council of Negro Churches.

Jones, who was the first of the five consecrated by Mason, had been overseer of Pennsylvania. Shortly after being converted as a young man, he served with his brother and sister to launch an evangelistic campaign that resulted in eight new COGIC churches being formed. Like Mason, Jones supported racial inclusion where possible, and many of his early preaching campaigns attracted interracial audiences. From 1916, he had been the editor of the *Young People's Willing Workers Quarterly,* which during the early years of the movement was one of the largest Christian education publications available.

---

[49]See Janel Davis "A New Day? COGIC Split Puts Church at Odds," *Memphis Flyer* 1, no. 779 (2004): www.memphisflyer.com/memphis/a-new-day/Content?oid=1113295; Wiley Henry, "COGIC Church Did Not Split; Grayson Said It's a 'New Day,'" *Tri-State Defender* 53, no. 4 (January 28, 2004): 1A.

Within the next three decades, spurred by the movement of blacks into urban areas in the Great Migration, denominational growth increased more than tenfold so that, by the time of Mason's death in 1961, its membership was nearly 383,000. Twenty years later, by 1981, it had increased tenfold again, to more than 3.7 million. The late phenomenal growth of COGIC has made it arguably the largest Pentecostal body in the United States and among the fastest-growing Christian denominations in the world.[50] It is also the second largest African American denomination in the United States, second only to the National Baptist Convention, USA. Further, the COGIC has increasingly distinguished itself among African American Pentecostal denominations by the degree of institutional structure that has developed within it. From 10 churches in 1907, the COGIC has become a global religious organization, with more than 6 million members spread across 59 countries.

The big schism. The seven years following Mason's death is referred to by some COGIC historians as "the dark period." During that time the denomination was wracked by a much larger and potentially devastating schism than any it had previously experienced. In 1926, thirty-five years before his death, Mason had framed the constitution to stipulate that upon his demise, leadership would revert to a board of bishops, who would supervise the election of two or more bishops who would have oversight of the denomination.[51] But during his later years, Mason had designated a successor, Ozro T. Jones of Philadelphia, the surviving member of the original five bishops he had appointed. After Mason's death, Jones assumed leadership and held the position of senior bishop until his death in 1968. His major contribution to the denomination was holding it together during the turbulent period of uncertainty following Mason's death. Under his administration, the first official manual of the denomination was published. When Jones died, the position of senior bishop was abolished, and a much contested process of electing a presiding bishop was begun.

With Jones's death, the COGIC again found itself in litigation, remaining in court for six years while three groups vied for the denomina-

---

[50]Though the Assemblies of God, with an estimated fifty-five million worldwide constituents, is the largest global Pentecostal body.

[51]*Official Manual with the Doctrines and Discipline of the Church of God in Christ, 1973* (Memphis: Board of Publication of the Church of God in Christ, 1991), p. xxxi.

tion's name and property. In 1968, the court ordered COGIC leaders to convene a constitutional convention to restructure the denomination along more democratic lines. By its end, the denomination was ready to hold its first general election. Finally, a group led by Bishop James Oglethorpe Patterson, Mason's son-in-law, prevailed, and he was elected presiding bishop. Eventually many of the schismatics returned to fellowship with the parent body. Not everyone, however, was pleased with the outcome of the convention, and this was not the last of the schisms.

Patterson, who had been consecrated bishop in 1955, served as senior pastor of Pentecostal Temple Church of God In Christ for forty-eight years. Before his death, Mason appointed Patterson to the Executive Committee created to assist with the denomination's administrative affairs. When, after Mason's death, the committee became the executive board, Patterson served as its secretary as well as the denomination's general, a member of the board of directors and manager of the publishing house.

During the twenty-one years he served as presiding bishop, COGIC emerged from its position as a relatively small, Holiness-Pentecostal sect to become one of the major black religious bodies in the nation. Part of emerging from its sectarian posture was aligning itself with major national Christian organizations, including the National Association of Evangelicals, the Congress of National Black Churches, the Pentecostal World Fellowship and the North American Congress on the Holy Spirit. Under Patterson's leadership, the COGIC took steps to establish the Charles Harrison Mason Seminary in Atlanta, Georgia, as the first Pentecostal seminary accredited by the Association of Theological Schools. He also worked to establish and the C. H. Mason system of Bible colleges, the Church Of God in Christ bookstore and the publishing house. As founding president of the World Fellowship of Black Pentecostal Churches, Patterson used his influence to attempt to bring a degree of unity within a movement that was clearly prone to schism.

Not everyone, however, was completely satisfied with the choice of Patterson as presiding bishop, or the direction the COGIC had taken. In 1969, fourteen bishops, led by Bishop Illie L. Jefferson and David Charles Williams Sr., objected to the shift from a single senior bishop to the twelve-man board to whom the presiding bishop was accountable. This group invited those who wanted to return to what they saw as the "only constitutional system of government of our church" with a senior bishop vested with the power to govern the denomination as directed by God to join with them in forming the Church of God in Christ, International. They elected Williams as senior bishop. In 1982, COGIC, International, reported two hundred thousand members, three hundred congregations and sixteen hundred ministers. Today the denomination, whose headquarters was moved to Jonesboro, Arkansas, has congregations in Africa as well.

Progress continues. In 1990, seventy-six-year-old Bishop Louis H. Ford, a prominent pastor and political leader in Chicago, succeeded Patterson as interim and then presiding bishop. Ford had used the pastorate of the burgeoning St. Paul Church of God in Christ congregation in Chicago to not only gain denominational prominence but also to involve himself in local political life. As presiding bishop, Ford exhibited what Ithiel Clemmons has referred to as "a restorationist vision" for the COGIC, attempting to return the denomination to its pristine glory days while improving and expanded physical as well as spiritual structures. He spearheaded refurbishing the mother church, Mason Temple, and Saints Junior College. Sociologist Robert Franklin contends that Ford's political savvy helped raise the political profile of the Church of God in Christ. For example, Ford invited then Arkansas governor and presidential candidate Bill Clinton to address the 1991 Holy Convocation. Once Clinton was elected, Ford maintained a political friendship with him and drew on it to support community projects for his constituents.

When Ford died suddenly in March 1995, Atlanta pastor and Ford's first assistant bishop Chandler Owens was tapped as interim bishop. Four months later, he was elected to the office. Many COGIC leaders and rank-and-file laity considered Owens's style heavy handed. He attempted to wrest power out of the hands of the board of bishops and centralize it within his position as presiding bishop. At one point he asserted, "I have the authority to make all of the decisions within the church without any disruption or confirmation. I have a board—a general board—that approves my decisions, but they're still my decisions. Same as the Catholic Church—same identical deal."[52]

---

[52]"COGIC Presiding Bishop Ousted," *Christianity Today,* January 4, 2001, p. 22.

But such an assertion led to repeated challenges to Owens's leadership. In 1998 three members of the twelve-member board of bishops—including later presiding bishop Charles Blake—called for a special election to unseat him and replace him with Ozro T. Jones Jr., of Philadelphia. Their bid was unsuccessful when assembly delegates voted to postpone the election until the following year, when the regular general elections were to be held. In that election, the General Assembly voted not to return Owens to his position. Instead, they elected Gilbert Earl Patterson, pastor of Memphis's Temple of Deliverance COGIC. Patterson was a grandson of COGIC's founder. Patterson was reelected in 2003. Under his leadership, the denomination reportedly grew to several million members in fifty-eight countries.[53]

Church of the Living God Pillar and Ground of the Truth. In 1908, Mary Magdalena Lewis Tate held a series of revival meetings in Greenville, Alabama, in which some one hundred people experienced Holy Spirit baptism with tongues and which would serve as the catalyst for a new congregation and the nucleus for a new denomination. Later that year, Tate was ordained bishop and first chief overseer of the Church of the Living God Pillar and Ground of the Truth and within a short period had established congregations throughout the rural East Coast, as dedicated followers moved into communities, promoting among family members and others her doctrine of "true holiness." The little sect that was forming adamantly insisted that their movement arose without any tie to the earlier Holiness movement and without knowledge of the Pentecostal revival breaking out around them. Still, there is evidence that Tate might have been an early member of William Christian's Holiness group, the Church of the Living God (Christian Workers for Fellowship).[54] But such an assertion was necessary, however, since Tate saw herself as primarily called to revive the New Testament church. Yet

---

[53]Estimates of COGIC membership range from a low of three million to a high of more than six million. At any rate, it has the largest constituency of any predominantly African American Pentecostal denomination.

[54]E.g., her name appears on at least one CWFF church roll and several elements of Tate's theological emphasis and CLGPGT polity mirror those found in the CWFF. In some cases, work in Tate's documents can be found almost verbatim in CWFF founder William Christian's work, *Poor Pilgrim's Work, in the Name of the Father, Son, and Holy Ghost*, no. 3, published in 1896. It may be, however, that rather than having been a member of the group, Tate discovered and read Christian's work and finding agreement with his beliefs, incorporated them into her own theology.

her vision went beyond purely spiritual concerns to incorporate a strong social consciousness that was specifically directed at attempting to develop "institutions and . . . educational facilities for the Church, Bible training schools and business colleges, general and local orphanages and rescue homes, academies, local schools and . . . facilities along educational lines necessary for the church."[55]

The episcopal structure Tate put in place included boards of bishops and elders and a General Assembly, ostensibly with authority to conduct the denomination's business. In actuality, though, the majority of power was vested in Tate's hands, where most decision-making rested. She took for herself "complete authority to approve, disapprove, or annul any rule or decree made by any person . . . in . . . or out of the Church if such rule or decree [wa]s . . . and intended for the Church of the Living God, the Pillar and Ground of the Truth."[56] Additionally, the chief overseer's name was to appear on "each and every" deed entered into by local congregations.[57] She also developed guidelines for establishing, administering and supporting the educational institutions she envisioned; and for several years, while residing in Orlando, Florida, she ran an elementary school. Tate demanded that individual congregations collect two annual offerings to fund this school, as well as a proposed Saint Mary Magdalene College, and to fund other schools and colleges that she envisioned establishing throughout the country,[58] though these other institutions never materialized.

Despite protestations of separation from other Pentecostal bodies, the schism that had become the hallmark of early Pentecostalism would also find its way into the Church of the Living God Pillar and Ground of the Truth (CLGPGT). One of the earliest groups to split from Tate's denomination was the First Born Church of the Living God, established in 1913 by four men, Bishop C. H. Bass, Quincy Crooms, Simon Crooms, and Clarence Blakely, in part because they objected to what they considered as the CLGPGT's liberal stance in allowing women to be preachers.[59] The

[55]*The Constitution, Government and General Decree Book of the Church of the Living God, the Pillar and Ground of the Truth (Incorporated)* (Chattanooga, Tenn.: New and Living Way, 1924), pp. 23, 29 and 50.

[56]Ibid., p. 9.

[57]Ibid., p. 25.

[58]Ibid., p. 66.

[59]Beth Wolk, "Women and the Church—North America" (unpublished manuscript, http://dickinsg.intrasun.tcnj.edu/diaspora/women.html).

constitution and bylaws were drawn up in 1921. Its headquarters are in Waycross, Georgia. During the early 1920s the denomination had at one time been home to George Baker, later known as Father Divine, the quasi-Pentecostal cult leader, who presided over an international following[60] and made claims of his own deity.

The pattern of schism within the CLGPGT continued when a further split occurred in the new body in 1939. Clarence Blakely broke away to form The First Born Church of Christ Written In Heaven. In the mid-1990s there was a second split in the national organization of the First Born Church, and twelve of the congregations under the leadership of Bishop Alfred Howard, started a new affiliation called Worldwide Abundant Life Fellowship.[61] Its headquarters are in Mt. Lebanon, Tennessee.

By 1914, Tate's organization had established congregations in Georgia, Illinois, Alabama, Kentucky, Florida and Tennessee; but the schismatic tendency continued when second break occurred, in which Bishop R. A. R. Johnson left to form the House of God, Holy Church of God, the Pillar and Ground of the Truth House of Prayer for All People (Hebrew Pentecostal). The new body kept the Holiness roots inherited from CLGPGT, strengthening its Judaic emphasis and adding a number of more rigid Jewish strictures, including keeping the literal Saturday Sabbath and several of the Jewish festivals and observing Jewish dietary laws.[62]

By 1916, Tate's organization had spread to nineteen states, Washington, D.C., and several foreign countries. In that year, a third schism occurred, when Bishop Archie White led his growing Philadelphia congregation into the House of God, Pillar and Ground of the Truth, Inc. This schism in particular was partly over the issue of women's leadership. White—who like Mason of the Church of God in Christ—had been initially ordained in the Baptist Church, held a conservative position regarding women's leadership and did not approve of women as bishops.[63]

[60]Bob Queen, "Over 2000 at First Born Church of the Living God Assembly," *Washington Afro-American,* October 21, 1975, p. 18.
[61]Richard Ripani, "Music of the Garden of Prayer Tabernacle," *Tennessee Historical Society Bulletin* 60, no. 2 (2002): 58.
[62]*Constitution, Government and General Decree Book,* p. 49.
[63]Felton Best, "Breaking the Gender Barrier," in *Black Religious Leadership from the Slave Community to the Million Man March: Flames of Fire,* Black Studies 3 (Lewiston, N.Y.: Edwin Mellen Press, 1998), p. 163.

While the CLGPGT shares core beliefs with other Pentecostal bodies, Tate's primitive scriptural exegesis and claims to exclusively divine revelation produced distinctive theological understandings that separate her body from other Pentecostal denominations. First, she insisted that the organization's name was the divinely unique, true name for "God's latter day house."[64] Other denominations, she insisted, had assumed dangerous "nick names"[65] not sanctioned by God. Her followers, and even those who later broke with her, took that assertion seriously, and each faction that broke from the original body retained the phrase "Church of the Living God." Most also retained "Pillar and Ground of the Truth" as part of their name.

Tate further modified existing Pentecostal understandings of Communion, terming the ritual as Passover and using water rather than grape juice or wine, and only unleavened bread. She and her followers understood that water, not wine, was a part of Christ's blood that flowed from his pierced body on the cross. The restriction on leaven comes from Old Testament Passover, and the CLGPGT Communion observance is always followed by foot washing, a symbolic ritual in which every member is expected to participate. While not adopting the literal Saturday Sabbath of the breakaway group, the denomination holds a Sabbath understanding of Sunday, declaring it a day of rest when members are expected to abstain from hard work and involve themselves entirely in the worship services.

Tate's Church of the Living God expanded generally rigid Pentecostal piety to cover almost every area of a person's life.[66] There is a strong prohibition against partaking of any kind of alcoholic products, including medicines that contain alcohol. But there are also restrictions on eating pork, swearing or taking oaths, gambling, dancing, participating in or attending sports events, and attending movies or reading fiction. Members are also expected to tithe. Moreover, CLGPGT membership is limited to those who have received the baptism of the Holy Spirit with evidence of tongues.[67] To maintain the standard of "true holiness" within the body,

---

[64]See *Constitution, Government and General Decree Book.*

[65]Ibid., p. 10.

[66]*Constitution, Government and General Decree Book*, p. 49. Upholding Old Testament legal and feast customs was an element that was unique to Tate's organization.

[67]Ibid., p. 37. This membership requirement goes beyond that of most Pentecostal denominations, which strongly encourage their members to seek Holy Spirit Baptism but do not withhold membership on the basis that one has not received it.

fellowship with other churches is prohibited. Access to the pulpit is limited only to ministers who are members of the denomination.

Her followers saw a special significance in Tate's ministry, even among the already special significance Pentecostals generally ascribed to themselves. Their belief that her endeavor was "the beginning of true holiness in the last days" is reflected in declarations that the denomination was "established in these last days by Saint Mary Magdalena, who is also an apostle Elder of Jesus Christ, by the will of God and chiefly an Elder of the Church, a mother, a light to the nations of the earth. Saint Mary Magdalena, the First chief Overseer and true Mother in True Holiness."[68]

These followers, who informally addressed their leader as "Mother Tate" and publicly ascribed more formal titles such as "Reviver" and "Chief Overseer," "Senior Bishop" and "Apostle Elder"[69] were convinced of her, and their, unique role in reviving the New Testament church. For them, the CLGPGT was not simply another Pentecostal denomination but an attempt to "reestablish" the New Testament church in such a way as to restore a purity and holiness that others—even her Pentecostal brothers and sisters—had missed. They were convinced that the elements God had uniquely revealed to her—the name of the church, Sabbath rest, water for Communion and regular washing of the saints' feet—were essential to such restoration.

Like so many other early Pentecostals, Tate's attraction to divine healing led her to regularly pray for the sick and to prod her followers to forego conventional medicine. Tate believed, moreover, that Christians who exercised genuinely strong faith could live entirely without doctors and medicine, to which only weaker Christians resorted. Several testimonies from CLGPGT members highlight this belief, recounting "miraculous" healings that allegedly came about because of her prayers.

During her lifetime, Tate's body grew to little more than one hundred congregations—most with constituencies of less than one hundred members. The total constituency never grew to more than several thousand persons, most of whom personally sat under Tate's ministry at one time or another. Before her death in 1930, Tate established procedures for orderly

---

[68]Ibid., p. 83.
[69]All of these titles are used in various sections of *The Constitution, Government and General Decree Book.*

succession within the denomination. They called for an executive council of bishops and elders to determine who should be installed as chief overseer. Though this procedure was followed, no consensus could be reached on a single successor. Instead, the council initiated a "temporary" arrangement in which three people who had worked closely with Tate were selected to run the organization. The office of chief overseer was divided into leadership of three geographical regions, called dominions, each encompassing sixteen of the then forty-eight states.[70]

Once the arrangement was in place, however, repeated attempts to resolve the stalemate proved fruitless, and a permanent three-way separation occurred. Each body pays allegiance to the legacy of Tate's work and doctrine. Each retains some part of the original title of the founding body, and each dominion has its own independent governing structure and headquarters. Over the ensuing years, the respective dominions have been involved, from time to time, in litigation among themselves concerning the disposition of the assets of the mother church.[71]

Tate's daughter-in-law, Mary Frances Lewis Keith, took over the Keith Dominion, headquartered in Nashville, Tennessee. The widow of Tate's son, Walter, led the organization until her death in 1962. It uses the name the House of God Which is the Church of the Living God the Pillar and Ground of the Truth, without Controversy, Inc. The body has more than two hundred congregations throughout the country as well as Haiti and Jamaica. More than half of these congregations are in three states: Florida, Georgia and South Carolina. The rest are clustered primarily in the South and the East Coast.

The McLeod dominion, the Church of the Living God, the Pillar and Ground of the Truth, Which He Purchased with His Own Blood, was headed by Bruce McLeod, who was related to Tate by marriage. When

---

[70] *Seventy-Fifth Anniversary Yearbook*, p. 23. At that time, however, the denomination was still primarily relegated to the East Coast. This partitioning, in fact, gave each chief overseer specific jurisdiction over any further growth within his or her respective dominion.

[71] See a discussion of these issues in *The House of God which is the Church of the Living God, the Pillar and Ground of the Truth, Without Controversy, Inc., The Constitution, Government, and General Decree Book*, 3rd rev. ed. (Philadelphia, 1936), pp. 93-107. Even here, there is controversy with the Keith Dominion later contending that its name, the House of God Which is the Church of the Living God, the Pillar and Ground of the Truth Without Controversy, is the initial name that Tate chose for her organization but that other factions obliterated any records that bore witness to that fact.

McLeod died in 1936, his wife, Mattie Lou McLeod, moved into the leadership of the denomination. Since she later remarried, the denomination, which has headquarters in Indianapolis, has also come to be known as the Jewell Dominion. Its forty-seven congregations are located primarily in Florida, Michigan and Ohio.

The original name, the Church of the Living God the Pillar and Ground of the Truth, was maintained by the Lewis dominion, under the leadership of Tate's son Felix, who served as chief overseer until his death in 1968. Its congregations are concentrated in the South—primarily in Florida and Mississippi. Headquarters for this dominion are in Nashville, where it maintains the New and Living Way Publishing Company. Yet the dominion has remained comparably small in relation to its sister bodies, with only approximately twenty congregations and two thousand members.

Fire Baptized Holiness Church of God of the Americas. Though the body known as the Fire Baptized Holiness Church of God of the Americas (FBHCA) was never itself part of the Holiness movement, it had deep roots in a multiracial Holiness body that originally carried the name and that eventually evolved into the largely white Pentecostal Holiness Church. The Fire Baptized Holiness Church, founded in 1898 by J. H. Irwin, included blacks and whites from its inception, and held interracial conventions and supported integrated congregations throughout the South.

In 1908 the parent body had moved into the Pentecostal camp through the evangelistic efforts of G. B. Cashwell and had, on the surface at least, continued the interracial ethos that had characterized much of both the Holiness and early Pentecostal movements. In that year, a group of five hundred blacks, under the leadership of William Edward Fuller Sr., separated from the parent body to form an independent denomination. Since the parent body was a predominantly southern organization, the blacks were largely concerned about the disparity between accommodations for them and whites at denominational conventions, as well as about the criticism the integrated worship services that these meetings received. The new group held its first General Council in Greer, South Carolina, in November of that year and decided that it should be called the Colored Fire Baptized Holiness Church, and Fuller was elected general overseer.

Reportedly, the decision to break from the parent body was mutual, and the move had been largely congenial. While the black group had been associated with the larger organization, it had accumulated twenty-five thousand dollars in property and assets, which they were allowed to retain. Yet, following their departure, though fellowship continued between individual members and congregations, there was little official contact between the two groups. Indeed, after the separation, the parent group made no attempt to retain any record of the earlier involvement of black members. For example, the memoirs of J. H. King, who worked with Fuller under B. H. Irwin and led the parent group church for more almost a decade, between 1900 and 1909, makes no mention of the early black faction or of Fuller's contribution.[72]

When the first General Council of the new black denomination was convened, there were twenty-seven churches with 925 members and sixty-six ministers. A year later, the first edition of the denomination's periodical, *True Witness*, published. The Fuller Normal and Industrial Institute was organized in 1912 in Atlanta, Georgia. It opened with one instructor and two students. In 1913, it moved to an eighteen-acre campus in Toccoa, Georgia, and then, in 1923, to its location in Greenville, South Carolina, where it consolidated with the Fuller Normal Junior School. The institution currently operates as a small private Christian school. Its campus also houses the denominational headquarters.

From 1908 to 1922 the church was called the Fire Baptized Holiness Church of God. During the 1922 General Council, the decision was made to change the name to the Fire Baptized Church of God. In 1926, the name was permanently changed to Fire Baptized Holiness Church of the Americas.

In 1922 Fuller was elevated to the position of presiding bishop. In all, he served at the helm of the denomination for fifty years, until his death in 1958. By that time, there were more than eight hundred congregations in the United States and the West Indies. On his deathbed, Fuller was approached by a small white segment of the Fire Baptized Holiness church that had separated from the parent body with the proposal that the two groups reunite. But when the whites refused to yield the chair of presiding bishop to the larger, black denomination, no union occurred.[73]

---

[72]J. H. King and Blanche L. King, *Yet Speaketh: Memoirs of the Late Bishop Joseph H. King* (Franklin Springs, Ga.: Publishing House of the Pentecostal Holiness Church, 1949).
[73]Andy Lewter, "Re-Imagining Pentecostalism" (paper presented to the conference on African

At his death, the Seventeenth Quadrennial Session of the General Council met in Greenville, South Carolina, and elevated five men to the bishopric: Charles Calvin C. Chiles, who had previously served as secretary and treasurer; Gustavus Guyhart Gary; Cleve A. Mills; Ezell Z. Bowman; and William E. Fuller Jr., the founder's son, who was elevated to presiding bishop. The younger Fuller also remains as bishop of the First Episcopal Diocese and chairman of the bishop board. In 1996, the denomination, which had grown to 24,000 members served by 2,500 ministers in 1,003 churches in the United States, Canada, England, Jamaica and the Virgin Islands, relocated its headquarters to Greenville, South Carolina.

The FBHCA is perhaps one of the last classical Pentecostal bodies to hold to a rigid, defined standard of personal piety governing almost all aspects of its members' lives. Adherents continue to refer to the denomination's Book of Discipline for guidance on appropriate apparel as well as engagement in social activities and other practical decisions. Inspiration for this rigid stance stems from the denomination's self-understanding as a Holiness body, for as the discipline in part declares,

> We believe that it is just as important to have Fire as the Holy Ghost. Hebrews 12:29 says, "For our God is a consuming fire." Fire is un-compromising. Fire Baptized Saints will not compromise with the wrong in themselves. Fire will do four things: First, light up; Second, warm up; Third, purge; and Fourth, purify. Fire Baptized folk are lit up, warmed up, purged, and purified. When we use "Fire" in our name we use it as a symbol of the uncompromising God.[74]

The discipline is explicitly detailed regarding issues that even many other classical Pentecostal Christians have come to see as a matter of personal conscience, insisting, for example, that

> women should not wear short skirts nor short-sleeved dresses, but are to dress in modest apparel. The wearing of pants in any form (long, short, or in-between) is prohibited unless employment requires this manner of attire for protection. A change in attire must take place before leaving the employment area. . . .

American Pentecostalism, "All the World: Black Pentecostalism in Global Contexts," Harvard University Divinity School, Cambridge, Mass., March 2005).
[74]Patrick L. Frazier Jr., *Introducing the Fire Baptized Holiness Church of God of the Americas: A Study Manual* (Wilmington, N.C.: Greater Eastern North Carolina District, 1990), p. 8.

Saints of God must never enter gambling casinos, dancing halls, movies, nor houses of ill repute. No member of the Fire Baptized Holiness Church of God is permitted to attend any kind of sports activity on the Lord's Day. We must refrain from following after anything that is calculated to destroy our spirituality. Mothers, Deacons, Pastors, and Elders are to be held responsible for the enforcing of the rules.[75]

Further, the polity of the discipline also soundly rejects other theological understandings regarding the nature of salvation, and of sanctification, insisting that

there are those who contend that sanctification is a progressive work. To them we say, "If Paul says for the preservation of the saints' spirits, souls, and bodies, they could not be preserved blameless in the process. That would negate our 'blameless' standing. If we are preserved blameless, we must be blameless before preservation. We do not speak in terms of sinless perfection for this is a quality that can only be associated with God Himself. We must attain Christian perfection."[76]

This type of rigid polity has ensured that the denomination has not kept up with the growth exhibited in older classical sister bodies such as the COGIC and UHC. Instead of major schisms within the denomination, however, the FBHC has generally seen its numbers decline through individuals' leaving to align themselves with more progressive bodies. One exception was the defection of a group led by Bishops Nathaniel Simmons and Charles Williams, who left with several key congregations to establish Sounds of Praise Pentecostal Fellowship Ministries, in 1994. Simmons led the denomination for four and half years. At his death in early 1999, his brother, Allen Simmons, was elevated to the office of presiding bishop. While upholding a commitment to "conduct ourselves as becoming Holy people of God and refrain from participating in anything that would dishonor God or bring a reproach upon the Church," such rigid stances as restrictions on women' apparel are modified.[77] The new openness facilitated comparably rapid growth in the Sounds of Praise Pentecostal Fel-

[75]Ibid., pp. 74-75.
[76]Ibid., p. 80.
[77]"Belief Statement," Sounds of Praise Pentecostal Fellowship Ministries website, http://sop pfm.org/silver/testtemp7/ADDEDPAGE.asp?sregid=862003102639&linktype=2&linkorder=7&DOCUMENTID=22&hmid=7.

lowship. The denomination currently has more than sixty congregations with seven districts, primarily along the east coast of the United States but also in the Caribbean and Africa and is poised to overshadow the growth of the parent body.

The House of the Lord and Church on the Mount. Despite circumstances that would have signaled another son who was disqualified to succeed his father, the House of the Lord provides an example of a prodigal son who returned home to find a place of leadership within his father's organization.

House of the Lord sprang up from a schism within a group that many contemporary classical Pentecostals would come to denounce as a heretical cult. When Bishop Emmanuel Grace began the denomination the United House of Prayer for All People, it was a solid Holiness body. Slowly, Grace began to move his denomination away from its Holiness roots and doctrine, and his followers began to exalt him as being equal with Christ through such attestations as, "Salvation is by Grace only. Grace has given God a vacation, and since He is on vacation, don't worry about Him. If you sin against God, Grace can save you, but if you sin against Grace, God cannot save you."[78]

Among the many within the ranks who found a home in other sanctified settings was Bishop Alonzo Austin Daughtry. As a third-generation minister whose grandfather was a slave preacher, Daughtry had been reared in a Methodist family of some local prestige and prominence. In 1926, however, much to the family's dismay, Daughtry came under the influence of "Sweet Daddy" Grace at the Savannah House of Prayer for All People, where he experienced salvation and the Pentecostal Holy Spirit baptism. Soon after becoming a member of that congregation, Daughtry was called to the ministry and shortly after was ordained.[79]

In 1927, Daughtry traveled to Augusta, Georgia, to establish a congregation and spread Grace's message. But soon becoming disillusioned with the degree of reverence he sensed other followers giving to Grace, he attempted to temper it through his preaching. But a sermon he preached in

---

[78]Arthur H. Fauset, *Black Gods of the Metropolis: Negro Religious Cults of the Urban North* (Philadelphia: University of Pennsylvania Press, 1970), p. 26.

[79]Jonathan Grossman and Natan Lipton-Lubet, "Oberlin's House of the Lord: A History of Oberlin's Youngest Church," Oberlin College and Conservatory website, www.oberlin.edu/external/EOG/AfAmChurches/HouseoftheLord.htm.

1929 that compared what praise Grace was receiving from followers with the undue adulation Paul received from the inhabitants of Malta led to a showdown with Grace, and Daughtry was forced to leave Grace's movement. Some of Grace's followers joined him to form a new church, which would become the House of the Lord.[80]

Soon Daughtry founded a number of churches from Georgia and South Carolina. Along with the churches, Daughtry always made pains to ensure the economic well-being of his congregants, purchasing burial plots and opening stores to ensure the solvency of his creation. He unsuccessfully stood up to local insurers, who battled him for control over selling burial plots and the like. Although he lost the case, his battle ensured the further popularity of his church.

In 1942, branches were founded in Harlem and Brooklyn, New York. Again, this was accompanied with the opening of church stores to ensure its profitability, among these a candy store and land-buying initiatives. For the next ten years, the church grew in its new northern urban environment, adding converts and working to ensure the good of its parishioners' lives.

From the beginning Daughtry pushed a progressive social agenda. His congregations were interracial, even in the heart of the South. Within his congregations, he promoted economic development programs that challenged his constituents to be concerned not only about the spiritual welfare of themselves and their families but also the social welfare of their communities.

Alonzo Daughtry had prophesied that his son, Herbert, would take over leadership of the church. However, the younger Daughtry at first rejected both his father's prophecy and religion, and eventually landed himself in prison. When the elder Daughtry fell ill in 1952, he could not call on his son to lead the church and so turned over the reins to Elder Inez Conry. Though she was not ordained a bishop, Daughtry had ordained her an elder. She served as presiding minister of the House of the Lord for eight years without ever taking the title of bishop. Her major contribution was to keep the organization stable until Daughtry's fourth son, Herbert, could take over the reins.

Alonzo Daughtry's prodigal son was converted to Pentecostalism while in prison and after his release was ordained and installed as the pastor of the Brooklyn church. Within a year, he rose to be the church's third na-

---

[80]Ibid.

tional presiding minister, in fulfillment of his father's earlier prophecy. Throughout his leadership, Daughtry has extended the national prominence of the House of the Lord Pentecostal Church by involving his congregation and the denomination in major local and national social issues. Among his many accomplishments, Daughtry founded the Coalition of Concerned Leaders and Citizens to Save Our Youth. During the height of the civil rights movement, this body was integral in developing the coalition that led to formation of the Black United Front, a political activist organization. Daughtry served as its first chairman from 1980-1985.

The House of the Lords represents a unique hybrid within classical Pentecostalism. The denomination uses a baptismal formula incorporating language that attempts to satisfy objections from either camp: "I baptize you in the name of the Father, the Son and the Holy Ghost, in Jesus' name."[81] Even the understanding of the Godhead differs from that of either classical trinitarian oneness Pentecostals: "We believe that Jesus Christ and God the Father are one . . . in substance. They are of the same divine substance; one in attribute—making their names interchangeable; one in purpose, in goals, etc., but they are separate beings."[82]

One of the most distinguishing aspects of the House of the Lord is the level of its social engagement. Daughtry is an active and outspoken civil rights leader who encourages his members to be engage in the variety of causes that affect the African American community. He was integral in founding the National Black United Front in response to a need to address economic, political and educational disparity for blacks.[83] His activism has not always been understood or accepted by other black Pentecostal leaders, who tend to promote more accommodationist or reform approaches to social issues. The least acceptable tenet to many believers may be the denomination's assertion in its statement of faith that "Jesus Christ was essentially African in orgin."[84]

---

[81]Herbert D. Daughtry Sr., Albert G. Miller, Francine C. Pearce and Renaldo Watkis, eds., "Baptism," *The House of the Lord Churches: Official Orientation Material* (s.l.: The House of the Lord and Church on the Mount, 2001), p. 2.

[82]*The Articles of Faith* (Brooklyn: The House of the Lord and Church on the Mount, 2003), p. 5.

[83]"Daughtry, Herbert Daniel," in *Biographical Dictionary of African-American, Holiness Pentecostals, 1880-1990*, ed. Sherry S. DuPree (Washington, D.C.: Middle Atlantic Regional Press, 1989), p. 71.

[84]"What We Believe," The House of the Lord Fellowship, Bergin County, New Jersey, www .holnj.org/whatwebelieve.html.

DELIVERANCE CHURCHES

A variety of healing rituals, including anointing with oil, laying on of hands, and sending prayer clothes or handkerchiefs as a point of contact for heightening one's faith, were integrated the larger fabric of Pentecostal worship. They stood alongside speaking in tongues, interpretation of glossolalic messages, prophetic utterances and the like as signs of God's inbreaking presence. The pages of the *Apostolic Faith* were filled with story after story of miraculous healing. One such article said,

> A brother living in the east had been down sick for quite a while and sent a handkerchief to be blessed as in Bible times. His sister brought it to the Mission, praying for the Lord to show her to whom she was to give it, and the Lord showed her to give it to Sister Sallie Trainor. She immediately took it upstairs and as she knelt before the Lord, the Spirit came upon her in great power and she prayed in tongues, and kissed the handkerchief three times, as the Spirit seemed to lead her. It was sent with a prayer and the brother was immediately healed.[85]

An article in a later volume of the newspaper spoke of the astounding result such faith might bring about.

> The Lord has wonderfully healed me from cataracts of nine years standing. Glory! glory! glory! glory be to my dear Redeemer's name! Soon as I received the handkerchief, or as soon as I opened the letter, such power went through my whole being as I have never felt before, and I praise Him, I feel the healing balm just now go through soul and body. . . . So she pitched her medicine out once for all and took Jesus for her only Doctor.[86]

Even in the earliest days, some evangelists made the practice of ministering healing to the sick their specialty. Those who claimed this gift and whose ministry bore the greatest fruit were in demand throughout the country, and congregations held healing revivals, regularly scheduled healing services and incorporated healing ritual into worship services. But there were also those who saw healing as a more central theme of Pentecostal spirituality, building congregations and, in some instances, entire denominations centered on ministering healing for physical, emotional, mental, material and spiritual distress. These bodies came to be known as

---

[85]Untitled Article, *Apostolic Faith* 1, no. 2 (1906): 1.
[86]E. W. Johnson, "Healed By The Lord," *Apostolic Faith* 1, no. 9 (1907): 4.

deliverance churches, and their leaders understood and preached that almost every instance of human discomfort—illness, mental distress, poverty and the like—was due to some form of demonic oppression and was therefore a candidate for deliverance.

These churches put strong emphasis on the practical use of spiritual gifts, especially divine healing, miracles and exorcism to bring about "deliverance"—the expulsion of evil spirits—in order to overcome physical, psychological and emotional problems.[87] This tradition of evangelistic faith healers sees the root of all human problems as spiritual, and sees release from ailments as coming through traditional Pentecostal such practices as anointing with oil, laying on of hands, use of blessed prayer clothes or other objects and through practices often reminiscent of spiritualist congregations. Over the years a number of bodies of various sizes have carried the designation "deliverance." Yet the emphasis of these groups runs along a fairly long continuum. While some focus on physical or psychic healing, others promote a more holistic approach that aggressively seeks to cure the ills of surrounding communities.

Arturo Skinner's Deliverance Evangelistic Center in Newark, New Jersey, is a notable example of this tradition. In his early life, Skinner had been a member of Rosa Horne's Brooklyn congregation but as a young man left the church to work as a Broadway dancer and got caught up in the Harlem social scene, including heavy drinking and drug use. By age twenty-eight, he was contemplating suicide, when he experienced what he claimed was a miraculous conversion and a call to the ministry. Within a short period, Skinner was holding tent meetings and within three years had established a church in his apartment that emphasized the kind of deliverance and healing ministry that had saved his own life. Reminiscent of Aimee Semple McPherson in Los Angeles in the 1920s and 1930s and Lucy Smith in Chicago in the 1930s and 1940s, the walls of the sanctuary were filled with wheelchairs, crutches, canes and other prosthetic devices hung as a testimony to the many reported healings that occurred—some of them instantaneous.

The weekly deliverance services from the Newark church and a second location in Harlem were augmented, first, by Skinner's "Hour of Deliver-

[87]Stephen Hunt, "Managing the Demonic: Some Aspects of the Neo-Pentecostal Deliverance Ministry," *Journal of Contemporary Religion* 13, no. 2 (1998): 215-30.

ance" radio broadcast that not only reached people in the United States but also Mexico, Canada and the Caribbean and, second, by supernatural deliverance crusades, which regularly filled auditoriums across the United States with crowds of thousands. In 1957 he created the Deliverance Evangelistic Centers, Inc., Worldwide, and a number of congregations aligned themselves with Skinner's ministry, which eventually included between forty and fifty affiliated churches around the globe.

When Skinner died suddenly of a stroke in 1975, at age sixty-one, thirty-five-year-old Ralph Nichol assumed the pastorate of his church; but no leader was chosen to head the association of churches that had affiliated with Skinner, who is still revered as the founder of the organization.

Tabernacle of Prayer for All People, founded by Apostle Johnnie Washington in Brooklyn, New York, is another example of the deliverance tradition. Washington started out as a gospel singer, became a minister in the Christian Church (Disciple of Christ) and went on to affiliate with the Church of God in Christ in his native New Orleans but rejoined a Disciples of Christ congregation after moving to New York.

Washington started his ministry as a street evangelist and in 1976 started a tent ministry in Brooklyn. Within a short time, Washington had started the Tabernacle of Prayer church as a storefront congregation. A year later, the Lowes Valencia Corporation donated a thirty-five-hundred-seat theater to the Tabernacle of Prayer church. Though he suffered from a number medical problems, including a bout with cancer, Washington preached a resolute message that denounced traditional medical means, and he refused to seek medical care. He apparently suffered a stroke near the end of his life. Insisting to those that counseled him that God would heal him if he saw fit, Washington continued to refuse medical treatment. He died in 1986, at the age of fifty-six. By the time of his death, there were thirty-six congregations within the Tabernacle Fellowship primarily reaching along the East Coast as far north as Massachusetts.

The Deliverance Evangelistic Church, founded by Benjamin Smith in Philadelphia in 1961, claims eighty-three thousand members in thirty-two congregations and eighty-one affiliated ministries.[88] From the outset, Smith involved his congregation in providing food, clothing and shelter

---

[88]Harold Dean Trulear, "Deliverance Evangelistic Church: Transforming Lives and Communities," *Impact* 10, no. 3 (1997): 10.

for the impoverished in the neighborhood and is currently home to several dozen outreach programs, including community patrols, special education and a Bible school.

One of those who benefited from the church's ministry and who sees Smith as a spiritual father was a sixteen-year-old gang member named Eugene Rivers, who was saved under Smith's ministry. After attending Harvard University, Rivers went on to become a prominent pastor in Boston who emulated Smith's example of commitment to the urban black community through his Four Points program. Smith died in 2002 at age eighty-seven.

Henry L. Porter Evangelistic Association (HLPEA), Inc., or Westcoast Centers, in Sarasota, Florida, was founded in 1971 by its namesake. In 1980, the Westcoast Center for Human Development and the Westcoast Center for World Evangelism were birthed under the umbrella of the HLPEA, Inc. Porter earned a doctor of mathematics degree from Yale university and shortly after returned to his undergraduate alma mater, Florida A&M, as one of the youngest faculty members at the university. While there, he established Spiritual Growth and Enlightenment Prayer Groups, which rapidly expanded to the University of Florida, Florida State University, University of South Florida and New College. Porter has a national television broadcast, *Henry Porter and the Love Campaign*, which began airing locally in 1986 and moved into the national market in 2004.

CONCLUSION

Among the black trinitarian groups, only the Church of God in Christ has garnered a substantial national presence. In terms of the sheer size of its constituency, it has surpassed all other black trinitarian bodies by at least tenfold, rivaling the Assemblies of God for the position of largest Pentecostal body in the nation. The numerous schisms within trinitarian bodies have ensured that no other denominations could garner enough momentum or members to grow to any significant size. The impact of these bodies on African American Pentecostal spirituality, however, far exceeds their numeric growth. A survey of the typical African American neighborhood reveals a myriad of these small Pentecostal groups sprinkled throughout the community. Their collective influence far exceeds their individual impact on the spiritual landscape of the African American community.

Table 5.1. Characteristics of Representative Black Trinitarian Pentecostal Denominations

Denomination	Year Est.	Founder	Parent Body	Constituency
Church of God in Christ	1877	Charles Harrison Mason		6,000,000
United Holy Church	1886			29,000
Church of the Living God Pillar and Ground of the Truth (Lewis Dominion)	1903	Mary Magdalena Lewis Tate	CLG (CWFF)	50,000
Fire Baptized Holiness Church of America (FBHC)	1908	William Fuller	Pentecostal Holiness Church	9,800
First Born Church of the Living God	1910	Joseph Echols	CLGPGT	
Holy Church of the Living God, the Pillar and Ground of the Truth House of Prayer for All People	1918	R. A. R Johnson	CLGPGT	
House of God which is the Church of the Living God, the Pillar and Ground of the Truth, Inc.	1919	Archibald White	CLGPGT	26,900
United Pentecostal Council of the Assemblies of God	1919	George Phillips/ Alexander Howard		25,900
Mt. Sinai Holy Church of America	1925	Ida Robinson	UHC	
Free Church of God in Christ	1925	Justus Bowe		75,000
Free Unity Church of God in Christ	1927	S. E. Looper	COGIC	
King's Apostle Holy Church	1929	Carrie Gurry		
Mt. Calvary Holy Church	1930	Brumfield Johnson	UHC	

Table 5.1. Continued

Denomination	Year Est.	Founder	Parent Body	Constituency
Church of the Living God the Pillar and Ground of the Truth which He Purchased with His Own Blood, Inc. (McLeod Dominion)	1931	Bruce L. McLeod	CLGPGT	
House of God Which is the Church of the Living God, the Pillar and Ground of the Truth Without Controversy (Keith Dominion)	1931	Mary Lewis Keith	CLGPGT	
Church of God in Christ Congregational	1932	Charles Williams/ Illie Jefferson	COGIC	
Soul Saving Station for Every Nation	1940	Billy Roberts		
General Assembly Church of the Living God Pillar and Ground of the Truth				
Sought Out Church of God in Christ	1944	Mozella Cook	COGIC	
The Alpha and Omega Pentecostal Church of God of America, Inc	1945	Madeline Mabe Phillips		400
Mount Calvary Pentecostal Faith Church, Inc.	1932	Rosa Artimus Horne		20,000
Church of God in Christ, International	1969	Illie Jefferson/ David Williams	COGIC	200,000
National Tabernacles of Deliverance	1972	Ardell Tucker/ Dorothy Austin	MCHCA	200,000
New Day Church International	2000	David Grayson	COGIC	

6

GOD AND CHRIST ARE ONE

THE RISE AND DEVELOPMENT OF BLACK ONENESS PENTECOSTALISM

Go ye therefore, and teach all nations, baptizing them in the name of the Father, and of the Son, and of the Holy Ghost.

MATTHEW 28:19 KJV

Repent, and be baptized every one of you in the name of Jesus Christ for the remission of sins, and ye shall receive the gift of the Holy Ghost.

ACTS 2:38 KJV

IN THE SPRING OF **1913,** FAMED HEALING evangelist Maria Woodworth-Etter preached at the Apostolic Faith Worldwide Camp Meeting in Arroyo Seco, California. Rivaling the excitement of the early Azusa Street meetings, the meeting drew more than two hundred Pentecostal faithful, who gathered for a month-long revival celebration of teaching, preaching and prayer. By 1907 meetings of this type were common among Pentecostal believers who wanted to spread the fire as long and as far as possible. They arose as an attempt to maintain the fervor of the early Azusa Street meetings, and, by most accounts, this year's meeting was a rousing success. Several future Pentecostal leaders were present, and many received salvation, Holy Spirit baptism or healing. But this meeting would become most known as the birthplace of one of the major fissures within the infant movement that would break it into two opposing camps with lines of theological demarcation that have endured until the present.

In that same meeting, Canadian evangelist Robert McAlister, an Azusa Street attendee who had been instrumental in spreading the Pentecostal message into Canada, administered baptism to new converts. Before undertaking this responsibility, he preached a short baptismal homily in which he briefly pointed out that the New Testament apostles never used the actual baptismal formula "in the name of the Father and of the Son and of the Holy Spirit," outlined in the Matthew 28:19 passage. Rather, he insisted, they invoked "the name of Jesus" in all of their recorded baptismal ritual, seeing this as a faithful response to Jesus' command.[1] Although McAlister would concede when pressed that the trinitarian formula was not necessarily wrong, he insisted that the shorter formula was preferable.[2]

Though oneness views were circulating prior to the Arroyo Seco meeting,[3] McAlister's seemingly simple suggestion would be the catalyst that would change the face of the infant Pentecostal movement, setting off a chain of controversy that would leave it with a deep fissure. Though this schism did not revolve around race, racial concerns colored the theological argument that came to be essentially over the nature of the Godhead. Within two years of McAlister's proclamation, the entire Pentecostal movement had been turned upside down and the first black oneness denomination had been planted.

On the evening of McAlister's message, John Scheppe was one of the more than two hundred ministers in attendance. After the service, while other campers slept, he spent the night praying about what he had heard and by morning was claiming that God had revealed to him what he later described as "a glimpse of the power of the name of Jesus."[4] As the sun rose, Scheppe ran through the camp shouting at the top of his voice the

---

[1]Frank J. Ewart. *The Phenomenon of Pentecost* (Hazelwood, Mo.: World Aflame, 1947), pp. 104-6.

[2]Ibid., pp. 93-94. MacAlister later refuted the oneness baptismal formula and fully embraced the trinitarian understanding.

[3]See, e.g., Douglas Jacobsen, *Thinking in the Spirit* (Bloomington: Indiana University Press, 2003), p. 194.

[4]Vinson Synan, *The Holiness-Pentecostal Movement in the United States* (Grand Rapids: Eerdmans, 1997), p. 156.

perceived revelation that was to change the understanding of many Pentecostal believers, first about the correct method of administering baptism
but ultimately about the nature of the Godhead.[5]

Another of the ministers in attendance was Australian-born Canadian
Frank J. Ewart, a former pastor from Portland, Oregon, who had been
expelled from his Baptist congregation for accepting Pentecostal Spirit
baptism in 1908. Subsequently he had worked for a time with Florence
Crawford's Apostolic Faith Mission in Portland and then moved on to Los
Angeles to join William Durham at his mission there. Ewart took over the
congregation after Durham's untimely death but within a short time left to
start his own congregation.[6]

After listening to McAlister and Scheppe, Ewart was convinced that
"Jehovah of the Old Testament was Jesus of the New Testament" and that
Jesus was the proper, redemptive name of God. Many who heard this new
teaching began to search the Scriptures for a biblical foundation for the
appropriate baptismal formula. For almost a solid year after the Arroyo
Seco meeting, Ewart extensively explored the Scripture regarding the
matter. At the end of that search, he was convinced that McAlister and
Scheppe's understanding was correct. By the end of 1913, McAlister had
begun rebaptizing converts in Canada.[7] In April 1914, two weeks after the
organizational meeting of the Assemblies of God (AG) in Hot Springs,
Arkansas, Ewart preached his first message on baptism in the name of
Jesus at a tent meeting in Belvedere, California. He set out from there to
convince as many of his colleagues as possible of the truth that Pentecostal
believers should be baptized in the "name of Jesus" and if they were already
baptized should be rebaptized using the new formula. Over the next few
years, he used his periodical, *Meat in Due Season*, to promulgate this new
doctrine, drawing hundreds to the oneness understanding. Ewart's students came away convinced that "the Apostles always baptized in the name
of Jesus." They understood Jesus' command as requiring baptism in his
name and saw that "there is no biblical record of any one person ever being
baptized, as some believers are today, using the formula 'in the name of the

[5]Carl Brumbeck, *Suddenly from Heaven: A History of the Assemblies of God* (Springfield, Mo.: Gospel Publishing, 1961), p. 191.
[6]Ewart, *Phenomenon of Pentecost*, p. 91.
[7]James L. Tyson, *The Early Pentecostal Revival: History of the Twentieth Century Pentecostals and the Pentecostal Assemblies of the World* (Hazelwood, Mo.: Word Aflame, 1992), p. 170.

Father, and of the Son, and of the Holy Ghost.'"[8]

Most of the earliest converts to the new understanding were found among the finished-work camp, especially within the loosely organized Assemblies of God. Indeed, Ewart was one among several of its own leaders, including Glenn Cook, Eudorous Bell and Howard Goss, who adopted the new teaching. Goss and Bell had been the chief organizers of the 1914 meeting that led to the forming of the Assemblies of God.

Cook, who had received his Holy Spirit baptism at Azusa Street and worked on the mission staff taking the Pentecostal message to Indiana and Tennessee, was one of the first leaders Ewart convinced of the "new issue." After Cook and Ewart rebaptized each other and the two set off again to spread the teaching through their speaking and writing. Cook had been instrumental in taking the message of Azusa Street to Mason's Tennessee congregation. In 1915, he left Los Angeles again to take the new revelation to the Midwest, stopping in St. Louis to hold a weeklong revival and baptizing his converts in the Mississippi River.

Little more than one year after being formed, the Assemblies of God found itself embroiled in a bitter controversy regarding the new baptismal formula, which several of its leading ministers had adopted, among them Eudorous N. Bell, a general presbyter and editor of two periodicals— *Weekly Evangel* and *Word and Witness*. Bell had first been vehemently opposed to the teaching, publishing several articles in *Word and Witness* (which later became the official AG periodical).[9] But passionate and persuasive proponents of the new "truth" won Bell over.[10] He and another AG leader, H. G. Rodgers, one of G. B. Cashwell's converts, later accepted the new issue and were rebaptized in a camp meeting hosted by Rodgers in Jackson, Mississippi.

Other AG leaders, including Howard Goss, adopted the new teaching. Goss, who had been converted under Charles Parham's ministry and attended his Bible school for a short while and had been elected to serve on the first General Presbytery of the AG, was rebaptized by Bell in 1915. He

[8]For an eyewitness reminiscence of this period, see Ewart, *Phenomenon of Pentecost*, p. 95-105.
[9]See, e.g., E. N. Bell, "The 'Acts' on Baptism in Christ Name Only," *Word and Witness*, July 1915, p. 1; and "The Sad New Issue: Over the Baptism Formula in the Name of Christ Only," June 1, 1915, p. 2.
[10]J. Roswell Flower, "Brother Bell Has Been Rebaptized in the Name of Jesus Christ," *Word and Witness*, August 1, 1915, p. 2.

went on to become a leader in the Pentecostal Assemblies of the World
(PAW) and, in 1945, became the first general superintendent of the United
Pentecostal Church, which came into being after the predominantly white
group broke from the PAW and merged with smaller oneness groups.

D. C. O. Opperman, a former member of Dowie's Zion City[11] who had
known Parham while the latter was evangelizing in Texas, soon followed
suit. Indeed, all the members of the Assemblies of God executive board,
except executive secretary J. Roswell Flowers, a former Baptist minister
converted to Pentecostalism under the ministry of Durham, were won to
the new teaching and were rebaptized. Flowers had heard Cook's teaching, but deciding that it was unbiblical, attempted to head off Cook and
Ewart's contact with fellow ministers and forewarn them of the heretical
doctrine. Among those to whom Flowers wrote was Garfield T. Haywood, a prominent black pastor of a large Indianapolis congregation. Haywood regularly fellowshipped with Assembly of God leaders, among
whom were many who also accepted Cook's understanding of the issue. By
the time he received Flowers's warning, he and many members of his congregation had already accepted the teaching and had been rebaptized by
Cook.

The controversy that ensued was a central focus of the AG's Third
General Council, and both sides sent strong delegations to protect their
interests. After deliberation, the council proposed a compromise—simply denouncing the practice of rebaptism and allowing congregations to
use either formula and continue teaching their beliefs as long as they did
not impose them on the other. Following the meeting, however, oneness
proponents became more aggressive in attempting to convert those who
remained skeptical. The next year, the General Council was more vola-
tile. Prior to the meeting, both camps had repeatedly hurled accusations
of heresy at the other through sermons and articles in periodicals. Char-
acterizations of the meetings highlight their contentiousness nature,
specifically the racial undertones that colored it. Reportedly, for example, AG leader T. K. Leonard specifically singled out Haywood for at-

---

[11]Dowie, a Scottish evangelist and faith healer branded himself "Elijah" and saw himself as the
embodiment of Old Testament prophecies. His Zion Christian community, founded in Illinois in 1896, emphasized theocratic rule, communal living and divine healing. His Christian
Catholic Apostolic Church, which grew to several thousand members, preshadowed the Pentecostal movement, drawing several who would become Pentacostal leaders.

tack, calling his new understanding "hay, wood, and stubble," and allud-
ing to Haywood's publication, *A Voice Crying in the Wilderness*, said that
those who followed were "all in the wilderness, and . . . have a voice in
the wilderness."[12]

Oneness adherents opposed efforts by Assemblies of God leadership to
craft a statement of faith that included a trinitarian baptismal formula. The
trinitarian party, however, struck a decisive blow when it was able to rewin
Bell, who wielded great influence in the denomination and the council.
Because of him, the trinitarians were able to hold on to control. Bell was
not the only trinitarian who briefly considered adopting the new baptismal
formula. Reportedly, Church of God in Christ founder, C. H. Mason, was
privately baptized in Jesus' name in Chicago in 1930 but stopped short of
promoting the new teaching when many of the leaders under him refused
to accept it as valid. He was, however, among the many black trinitarian
Pentecostals who continued to have some fellowship with Apostolic believers.[13] Aimee Semple McPherson, founder of the International Church of
the Foursquare Gospel, and Maria Woodworth-Etter, who preached the
pivotal camp meeting in which the teaching was first aired, are also believed to have been baptized in Jesus' name; and Frank Bartleman, the
earliest historian of the Azusa Street Revival, never joined any Pentecostal
denomination but continued to fellowship with both oneness and trinitarian believers. Though none of the three promoted the teaching, which they
came to see as divisive, they tolerated those who did.

But the intensity of the controversy within the Assemblies of God
forced it to depart from its former noncreedal stance to formulate a "Statement of Fundamental Truths." Prominent among these articles was language declaring that the Godhead was "one Being of three persons."[14]

With this move, 156 ministers and over 100 congregations pulled out
of the recently formed fellowship, aligning themselves squarely with the
Apostolic camp, as it came to be known. At the end of 1916, many of those

---

[12]Robert Mapes Anderson, *Vision of the Disinherited: The Making of American Pentecostalism*
(Peabody, Mass.: Hendrickson Publishers, 1992), pp. 189-90. Leonard was a former minister
in the Christian and Missionary Alliance and founder of the Gospel School in Finley, Ohio,
and worked secretly with Flowers to draft the resolution that became the basis for organization
of the Assemblies of God.

[13]David K. Bernard, *A History of Christian Doctrine, Volume 3—The Twentieth Century A.D.
1900-2000* (Hazelwood, Mo.: n.p., 1999), p. 75.

[14]"Statement of Fundamental Truth" (Springfield, Mo.: Assemblies of God).

ministers met in Eureka Springs, Arkansas—some 228 miles from the site of the Hot Springs meeting that established the AG, to establish a new organization, the General Assembly of Apostolic Churches.

From the beginning, the new organization incurred several problems that were to hamper its growth and ensure an extremely short life. Most importantly, it failed to gain federal government recognition as a religious body, which was necessary for its ministers to receive exemption from military service or obtain discounted clergy fares on the trains. This obstacle would prove to be insurmountable, for without these the fledgling organization was unable to attract new ministers and congregations. To solve these problems, leaders merged with a sister denomination, the Pentecostal Assemblies of the World, which by now had also become a oneness denomination.

The use of the shorter baptismal formula was not entirely new. A number of people, including Charles Parham, had used it for several years without insisting on a definition of the Godhead, which would become an integral component of the later theology.[15] The early Pentecostal movement exploded in a period in which believers were open to prophetic pronouncement and understood God as doing a "new thing" in directing the church back to its primitive roots. In such an atmosphere, they expected that the Holy Spirit would directly intervene through tongues, interpretation, and prophecy and with a word of revelation. In this heady spiritual climate, many did not want to miss any work God might be doing. Oneness Pentecostals saw their movement arising from a supernatural impartation of revelation to build on the doctrinal distinctive of initial evidence.

What began, however, as a simple disagreement over baptismal formulas ended as a full-blown argument over the nature of the Godhead, with those in the oneness camp rejecting the historical formulations of the doctrine of the Trinity. Their detractors castigated them as heretics and without the theological sophistication to name it as such came to equate the new formulation with earlier modalistic heresies such as Sabellianism.[16] Eventually other elements insisted that baptism was a necessary step in

---

[15]See Brumbeck, *Suddenly from Heaven*, p. 192; and Anderson, *Vision of the Disinherited*, p. 176.

[16]Sabellianism is the third-century theological understanding that held to the Godhead existing as a divine monad that by process of expansion projected itself successively in revelation as Father, Son and Holy Spirit. As Father it revealed itself as Creator and lawgiver. As Son it revealed itself as Redeemer. As Spirit it revealed itself as the giver of grace.

being "born of water"—and therefore was requisite for salvation rather than merely an outward sign of an inward grace.[17]

This period also saw the capitulation of a prophetic, racially unified movement that once stood as a witness to the unifying power of the Holy Spirit and its fracture into homogeneous white, black, Latino and other cultural factions. These groups continued to claim and share an experience of Pentecostal baptism in the Spirit and to evidence such gifts as glossolalia, prophecy and divine healing. But the color line that Bartleman had declared had been "washed away in the blood" had been redrawn. And God's healing power did not appear to be strong enough to cure the disease of racial division. Further, a schismatic spirit had been planted in the very fabric of Pentecostalism that continued to plague every segment of the movement, leading to the denominational proliferation in evidence today.

THE RISE OF BLACK APOSTOLIC DENOMINATIONS

Within ten years of the explosion of this new theology onto the landscape, several denominations had come into being that would maintain and spread its message throughout the African American Pentecostal community. By 1979, there were no less than thirty such denominations. Several others groups had come into existence and disappeared either because of amalgamation with other bodies or because of schism and decline. The earliest of these bodies were clustered in the East and Midwest, and though historian Vinson Synan contends that southern states are largely untouched by the movement, African American oneness congregations now dot the entire U.S. landscape. Some estimate that 70 percent of all U.S. Apostolic Pentecostals are African American and that 40 percent of black Pentecostals are Apostolic.[18]

The Church of God (Apostolic). The oldest of the black Apostolic bodies was founded in Danville, Kentucky, in 1897 and incorporated as a trinitarian Holiness denomination, the Christian Faith Band, by Thomas Cox's organization in 1901. It is uncertain when the body adopted a Pentecostal

---

[17]Brumbeck, *Suddenly from Heaven*, p. 192.

[18]"Global Statistics," in *The New International Dictionary of Pentecostal and Charismatic Movements*, ed. Stanley Burgess, Eduard M. van der Maas and Patrick Alexander (Grand Rapids: Zondervan, 2002), p. 286.

doctrine; but sometime after 1913, Cox was converted to the oneness movement through his association with Robert Lawson, who would later found the Church of our Lord Jesus Christ of the Apostolic Faith. In 1915, the name of the church was changed to what leaders considered the more biblical designation of Church of God (Apostolic). Cox led the denomination for forty years, until poor health forced him to relinquish leadership of the church to Eli Neal. When Cox died in 1943, Neal and Bishop M. Gravely assumed positions as copresiding bishops because neither man was willing to submit to the other's leadership. After two years, Gravely was dismissed because he initiated divorce proceedings against his wife. The denomination did not consider the grounds for the divorce to have biblical support, and though the denomination was prepared to allow Gravely to remain in his pastoral position, a lengthy litigation ensued. When Gravely lost the court case, he was removed from his pastoral position and disfellowshiped from the denomination. That same year, the organization was incorporated and Neal assumed leadership. The denomination reached it height numerically in 1938, when it had more than thirty thousand members in forty-nine congregations. But the schismatic pattern would repeat itself several times over the next decades.[19]

The Pentecostal Assemblies of the World. When the first meeting of the Pentecostal Assemblies of the World convened in Los Angeles in 1907, it was simply a loose fellowship of congregations that embraced the Pentecostal message; it was neither black nor oneness. The next year, Jacob J. (J. J.) Frazee, who had been part of Florence Crawford's Apostolic Faith Mission and had worked at Frank Bartleman's Eighth and Maple Street congregation after receiving the Pentecostal Spirit baptism at Azusa Street, was elected secretary pro tem, and elected as its first general superintendent in 1912, serving at least until 1917. After the PAW merged with the General Assemblies of the Apostolic Assemblies, Frazee would again be elected to serve as general secretary of the new body, serving in that position for one year when he was replaced by E.W. Doak.[20] By 1925, Frazee was among the white leaders who had left the PAW.[21]

Garfield Thomas Haywood obtained PAW credentials in 1908, while

---

[19]See further discussion of the Church of God (Apostolic) below.
[20]Tyson, *Early Pentecostal Revival*, p. 89.
[21]Ibid., p. 201.

it was still a trinitarian body, and later brought his congregation into the denomination. Earlier that year, Haywood had received the Pentecostal Spirit baptism[22] and had begun worshiping at a small PAW storefront church in Indianapolis pastored by Henry Prentiss, who had received his Pentecostal Spirit baptism at the Azusa Street Revival.[23] Within a year of Haywood joining the fellowship of thirteen members, Prentiss had moved to New York City and turned the pastorate over to his young protégé. After a short period, Haywood had built the fledgling group into a racially mixed congregation of between four and five hundred. At the time that the "new issue" came into eminence, Haywood's Indianapolis church was gaining prominence among local Pentecostals. By that time, it was the largest and most racially integrated Pentecostal congregation in Indiana during a period when the Ku Klux Klan was at the point of its greatest influence in that state. Many resources record that Haywood had been a founding member of the Assemblies of God and had achieved some prominence in that organization. Though such an accomplishment would have been significant for a black man, Haywood never held AG credentials. He did, however, maintain associations with prominent AG leaders and frequently spoke in their congregations and meetings.[24]

When Cook first approached him with the new doctrine, Haywood was skeptical. After praying about it and seeing its validity, he had a change of heart, was rebaptized and subsequently rebaptized his entire congregation. His influence drew large numbers of northern blacks into the movement and the PAW, and he joined Howard Goss, Frazee, Opperman and Ewart in reforming as a oneness denomination. Since the majority of the PAW's earliest constituents were white, all the earliest leaders except Haywood were white. At the new body's first general meeting, three white men were elected as leaders: Frazee as general superintendent and chair-

---

[22]His conversion was Spirit baptism and subsequent ministry in winning other to the movement was briefly reported in a short untitled article of the May 1908 volume of the *Apostolic Faith* 1, no. 13 (1908): 1.

[23]Larry Martin, *The Life and Ministry of William J. Seymour*, the Complete Azusa Street Library 1 (Joplin, Mo.: Christian Life Books, 1999), pp. 252-54, 311.

[24]According to his biographer, Morris Golder, Haywood emphatically stated , "[I] have never been connected with the Assemblies of God as a movement since its organization . . . in 1914. I carried PAW credentials since 1911. It would be impossible to 'go back' to a place you have never been." Golder quotes Haywood directly in *History of the Pentecostal Assemblies of the World* (Indianapolis: s.n., 1973), p. 36.

man, former AG leader Opperman as secretary and Goss, another former
AG leader, as treasurer. Haywood and Ewart were tapped to sign ministe-
rial credentials. Four blacks—Haywood, Robert Lawson, Alexander R.
Schooler and F. I. Douglas—were elected as field superintendents.[25]

PAW leaders decided to consolidate Haywood's newsletter, *The Voice
Crying in the Wilderness*, published between 1910 and 1922, and two other
independently published periodicals into *The Christian Outlook*, with
Haywood as editor.[26] It, along with numerous tracts and pamphlets Haywood produced, promulgated oneness theology among the faithful while
attempting to convince others of its truth. His writing was instrumental
in spreading the oneness message throughout the African American Pentecostal community and was instrumental in formulating oneness theological conceptions that have served as the foundation for much of contemporary oneness theology, particularly among African Americans.
Also as a prolific hymn writer, several of the dozens of hymns that he
penned in the first quarter of the nineteenth century are still sung not
only in oneness Pentecostal circles but also throughout the Holiness-
Pentecostal community.[27]

When the PAW was formally incorporated in 1919, it moved its headquarters to Indianapolis and put a board of elders in place to assist the
general secretary with the growing denomination's business. Nearly three-
fourths of the PAW's initial membership was white. The move of the
headquarters, however, changed "the complexion of the organization . . .
significantly from one that was predominantly white to one where blacks
represented the majority of its membership."[28] But Haywood's popularity,
along with the organization's commitment to racial equality, ensured that
the number of blacks drawn to PAW would rapidly increase. From that
point on, many of the denomination's officers and a majority of its committee members were black.

---

[25]Ibid., p. 48.
[26]Along with Haywood's *Voice Crying in the Wilderness*, these included Opperman's *Blessed Truth*
and Ewart's *Meat in Due Season*. *The Christian Outlook* continued to be the official publication.
[27]Notable among his works are, "I See a Crimson Stream," "Jesus the Son of God," "Thank God
for the Blood," "The Day of Redemption" and "We Will Walk through the Streets of the
City."
[28]Paul D. Dugas, *Life and Writings of Elder G. T. Haywood* (Stockton, Ga.: Apostolic Press,
1968), p. 646.

During the 1919 general conference, Haywood was elected as general secretary—at the time a one-year appointment. For the next several years, as the denomination grew, he held a number of positions of increasing influence. Stepping down from his original one-year tenure as general superintendent, he was elected as secretary in 1920, as executive vice chairman and then as general secretary, both in 1922.

While whites still held a number of important positions, and the board reflected the racial diversity of the body, several members of the board including Schooler, Lawson and Joseph M. Turpin were black. The growing proportions of blacks made some whites uncomfortable, and the apparent racial harmony of the PAW began to show signs of serious fissure. By the early 1920s several moves by white PAW ministers signaled a weakening of what had proven to be the longest running interracial experiment within American Pentecostalism.

The motivations for their initial objections were practical. Pentecostal believers regularly held regional Bible conferences at which they searched the Scripture for truth regarding their faith, fellowshiped with one another, and aired whatever concerns and issues had surfaced within their ranks. The 1922 Southern Bible Conference, which took place the same year that Haywood was made general secretary, was different. Some Southern whites felt this arrangement posed undue economic hardship on them by requiring them to travel more extensively than the northern brethren. They contended that having a racially mixed organization hampered the movement's growth among other southern whites who were less open to racial mixing. Further, some whites began to object to having their credentials signed by a black man because they felt that those credentials would not be accepted in the segregated South.

The invitation letter declared its purpose to be "to work for greater unity," noting that "the South has long looked . . . and hoped for true fellowship and unity," and contending that "this is not to be the beginning of a new movement." Nonetheless, the meeting signaled the end of the tenuous unencumbered fellowship that existed between the two races.[29] Until this time, the organization's assemblies had been held in the north so that both races could participate freely and blacks could have access to adequate

---

[29]Tyson, *Early Pentecostal Revival*, pp. 245-46.

lodging unavailable to them in the South. In 1923, the assembly adopted "Resolution No. 4," stating that

> because of conditions now existing in many parts of the country through no fault of the brethren but rather those opposed to the work of the Lord it is deemed advisable that two white presbyters sign the credentials for the white brethren [especially in the South] and two colored presbyters sign the papers for the colored brethren.[30]

Some whites felt that even the signature of a black man on their credentials would hamper efforts to reach other whites. Though black leaders questioned how anyone would know the signer's race, a compromise was struck, and Haywood appointed Howard Goss to signed credentials for whites who demanded it and T. C. Howard to sign the credentials of blacks.

The following year, in a move that signaled increased discomfort, several whites suggested that two separated administrative structures be established within the PAW—one for whites and another for blacks. Each would exist under a unified covering, but each would also maintain their own places of worship, boards, ministers and printed materials. The two branches were to be titled "Eastern" and "Western," obscuring the racial distinction while at the same time upholding the real racial division, since they were not to be aligned along geographic boundaries but would simply be populated by race. The blacks rejected this suggestion.

In that same year, whites in the Texas District changed the name of the district to Pentecostal Assemblies of Jesus Christ and established two administrative structures within that state. When blacks in the national body rejected such a structure for the general church, the majority of the white constituents pulled out to align themselves with the new organization. Still, several whites remained within the denomination, leaving it with the most interracial presence in the Pentecostal movement. After a number of other schisms and amalgamations within white Pentecostal ranks, the newly formed body went on to become the United Pentecostal Church International, eventually becoming the largest oneness denomination in the United States.

[30]"Resolution 4," Minutes of the General Assembly of the Pentecostal Assemblies of the World, October 4-6, 1923, cited in Morris Golder, *History of the Pentecostal Assemblies of the World* (Indianapolis: Morris E. Golder, 1973), p. 79.

A year after the split, there were twelve hundred ministers in the PAW; the denomination adopted an episcopal governmental structure and elected Haywood presiding bishop. Whites who cherished the interracial fellowship of the PAW stayed with the organization, and its leadership continued to reflect a commitment to racial unity. The assembly elected an interracial board with two white men, G. B. Rowe of Indiana and A. F. Varnell of Illinois, and three black men, Haywood, Schooler and Turpin, at the head. By that year, another contingent of white ministers left the PAW to join the Pentecostal Ministerial Alliance (PMA), a body that had formed in Tennessee in 1925. The relatively few whites who remained with the PAW faced several challenges, including being in a minority position and at the same time being ridiculed by white colleagues for their loyalty to the PAW.

When Haywood died suddenly that year at the age of fifty, no plan was in place for his successor. After his death, white PAW bishops attempted to initiate a merger with the new Pentecostal Ministerial Alliance to reconstitute an interracial PAW. When the whites suggested, however, that any reconstitution be under two administrations separated by race, black PAW leaders balked. As a result, no merger occurred, but several blacks were offended by this move, left the organization and joined the Apostolic Churches of Jesus Christ. The remaining black members called a reorganization meeting.

Samuel Grimes, an early black PAW missionary to Liberia, succeeded Haywood as presiding bishop. Though Grimes was to remain in office for thirty-five years, until his death in 1967, his administration did not go unchallenged. Bishop Samuel Hancock had been one of the original seven presiding PAW bishops and one of the blacks who supported the PMA merger. When it did not materialize, he left the PAW to help form the Pentecostal Assemblies of Jesus Christ. After a short while, he returned to the PAW and was reelected to the bishopric.[31] Hancock felt he was Haywood's legitimate heir and challenged Grimes for the presiding position. When a forced runoff vote failed to unseat Grimes, Hancock, who had married Haywood's widow, left the PAW, again. This time, he founded the Pentecostal Churches of the Apostolic Faith (PCAF), serving as pre-

---

[31]"Pentecostal Assemblies of Jesus Christ," in *The Encyclopedia of American Religions*, ed. J. Gordon Melton (Tarrytown, N.Y.: Triumph Books, 1991), 1:376.

siding bishop of that denomination until his death in 1963.[32] (See the discussion on the PCAF below.)

Though whites continually constituted a decreasing proportion of PAW membership, throughout the civil rights era the denomination maintained its commitment to interracial fellowship and leadership, deliberately structuring biracial partnerships at the head of the denomination, to ensure it was met. As presiding bishop, for example, Grimes was assisted by Ross Paddock, a white pastor from Michigan. When Paddock assumed the head position in 1967, Frank Bowdan, a black pastor from Flint, Michigan, served as his assistant presiding bishop. That team was followed in 1974 by Francis Smith and Lawrence Brisbin, a black presiding bishop and a white assistant presiding bishop. After that time, as white participation in PAW continued to decline, it became increasingly difficult to continue this pattern. Currently the presiding bishop, Horace Smith, and his assistant are a black team, and very few whites remain in the denomination.

At the end of the twentieth century, the Pentecostal Assemblies of the World had succumbed to the dominant racial patterns in the nation and had become a predominantly African American denomination. However, it remained the most racially integrated of all oneness or other Pentecostal bodies. In 1997, PAW reported one million members in forty-two hundred churches worldwide. Eighteen hundred of those congregations are in the United States. More importantly, between 1920 and 1935, the denomination served as the mother to a number of smaller black oneness bodies, and truthfully, almost every existing oneness body—whether black or white—can somehow trace its heritage back to the PAW.

Apostolic Overcoming Holy Church of God. In 1915, nine years after the Azusa Street Revival and at a time when the oneness controversy was at it height on the West Coast, William Thomas Phillips, a largely unknown Holiness minister, son of a Mobile, Alabama, Methodist Episcopal pastor, founded the Ethiopian Overcoming Holy Church of God as a trinitarian body. Reportedly Phillips's interest in the life of holiness spurred him to undertake an independent study of Scripture, from which he gained, without contact with existing Apostolic groups, a revelation of the Godhead. Within the next twelve years, it too would join the ranks of those who

---

[32]James C. Richardson Jr., *With Water and Spirit: A History of Black Apostolics* (Washington, D.C.: Spirit Press, 1980).

embraced oneness Pentecostal doctrine. At age nineteen, Phillips was converted in a tent revival conducted by Azusa Street veteran Frank Williams. He was ordained by Williams in 1913 and became an evangelist in 1916. For a short time he was a member of the Apostolic Faith Mission Church of God before branching out into his own organization.

The term *Ethiopian* denoted Phillips's emphasis on a religion that would meet the spiritual needs of black folks in the segregated South. But he grew to desire to lead a church aligned more closely with what he felt was a biblical picture of the church. By 1927, that desire demanded a name change; the word *Apostolic* replaced *Ethiopian* in 1927, as an expression of Phillips's expanded vision of a racially inclusive church that would be clearly identified as an Apostolic (or oneness) denomination.

During its earliest period, worship within the Apostolic Overcoming Holy Church of God (AOHC) was among the most emotional within black Pentecostal bodies, with some outside observers describing the free form ritual as chaotic. Indeed, it was noted even among other Pentecostals as a denomination of extremes. But Phillips made no excuses for the highly emotive character of his congregations and encouraged his members to express themselves freely.

Phillips led the church for fifty-nine years, until his death in 1974. He traveled extensively, holding revivals and planting new congregations throughout the South. By the time of his death the denomination had grown to three hundred churches in the United States, India, West Africa and the Caribbean, with a constituency of more than one hundred thousand, including a small number of white congregants. Within the United States, congregations are concentrated in Alabama, Kentucky, Illinois, Oklahoma and Texas, but a few are found in other states.

The AOHC maintains an interesting posture in relationship to other Christian bodies, separating themselves in spiritual matters—its members do not fellowship with other Pentecostal bodies in worship—but joining together to promote the practical benefit of the black community—Phillips regularly associated with secular leaders on practical matters. For instance, he was so active in supporting the civil rights struggle that his home was bombed in 1965. Ironically, denominational changes have not resulted in an influx of other races, and it remains to this day a predominantly African American body.

The founder was succeeded by Jasper Roby, who moved the denominational headquarters to his home church, AOH Cathedral in Birmingham, Alabama. Roby served from 1973 until his death, in 2000, when George W. Ayers assumed the position of presiding bishop.

The Church of Our Lord Jesus Christ of the Apostolic Faith. One of the first splits within the PAW that had no racial motivation was orchestrated by Robert Lawson, who had been converted under Haywood's ministry and would become one of the most prominent black Pentecostal leaders in the country, a champion of progressive social causes among oneness thinkers as well as the spiritual father of many who were to make a mark on the movement. A mutual acquaintance who had become a member of Haywood's church introduced Lawson to his pastor. After having been diagnosed with tuberculosis (then considered a fatal disease), Lawson began attending worship services at Christ Temple. During one of these times, Haywood prayed with him and he received healing. Shortly after that, he was converted, baptized in Jesus' name and received the Pentecostal Spirit baptism. A natural leader, Lawson's preaching gift became apparent, and Haywood tapped him to plant churches in St. Louis and San Antonio before he assumed a pastorate in Columbus, Ohio. He was also either elected or appointed to a number of administrative positions within the denomination.

During Lawson's three-year stay in Columbus, he and Haywood began to disagree over three practical issues. First, Lawson specifically objected to the PAW's openness to the ministry and ordination of women. While women had served as pastors and leaders in the PAW since its founding, Lawson felt that Scripture constrained women from taking on such public roles; he was disturbed that Haywood allowed women a degree of freedom in the leadership of the church. Second, the two men also disagreed on appropriate dress for women since Lawson wanted stricter control over their attire. He was adamant that women should not attend worship without having a covering of some sort on their heads. He was also concerned that women refrain from wearing immodest clothing, including skirts that terminated above the knees, sleeveless dresses and blouses, cut-out shoes, jewelry, and makeup.

Finally, Lawson was unhappy with what he considered the PAW's unscriptural divorce-and-remarriage stance, holding that divorce should not be allowed for any reason; and if one was divorced before becoming a Christian, even on the grounds of adultery, he or she should not remarry as long as their former spouse was living. Haywood, too, initially held the conviction that the remarriage of a divorced person while a former spouse was alive constituted adultery. But when a divorced family member joined his church and received the Pentecostal Spirit baptism, Haywood had a change of heart, concluding that "our former views on the subject were wrong." Further, he insisted that those who were divorced and remarried before being filled with the Spirit were forgiven for their past sin, while divorce and remarriage among saints who were already a part of the church was still prohibited.[33] Even this concession was too lax for Lawson.

At the 1918 PAW Convocation, Lawson attempted to present his views to the gathered body. When refused the opportunity, he resigned, and by 1919 he had moved to New York City, where he first preached on the street corners and held tent revivals and then moved on to hold services in two Harlem homes. Within a short time, Lawson had built a storefront congregation that quickly grew to approximately two hundred members, and larger quarters had to be sought. His success began attracting other oneness ministers, and Lawson began building the Church of Our Lord Jesus Christ of the Apostolic Faith (COOLJC), sending preachers, missionaries and teachers to establish churches throughout the United States as well Africa and the Caribbean. As an entrepreneur, Lawson established at his Harlem congregation a daycare center and school, opened several stores, and owned a small publishing company that produced the denomination's official publication, *The Defense of the Gospel.* As a prolific music and prose writer, he penned a number of hymns that have become standards within the African American Pentecostal movement and developed a number of tracts that found wide circulation within the movement. More importantly, Lawson, an political activist and outspoken race critic, developed works such as *Anthropology of Jesus Christ Our Kinsman Redeemer,* written in 1925, and *An Open Letter to a Southern White Minister on Prejudice,* written approximately twenty-four years later, in which he challenged the theological ground on which racial discrimination was founded.

In 1926, Lawson's interest in education led him to establish the Church

---

[33]Garfield T. Haywood, *The Marriage and Divorce Question in the Church* (Indianapolis: Christ Temple, n.d.).

of Christ Bible Institute. The move made him one of the first black Pentecostals to promote a trained clergy. By 1950 that school was fully accredited by the New York State Board of Regents. But his interest in education was not limited to the postsecondary level. In 1945, he started the R. C. Lawson Institute in Southern Pines, North Carolina, which provided a private education for hundreds of inner-city children.[34]

At Lawson's death in 1961, William Bonner became pastor of the then three-thousand-member mother church, Greater Refuge Temple, in Harlem, and the convocation acted on his recommendation to select a three-man Apostles' board, with Bonner, Bishop Hubert J. Spencer and Bishop Maurice H. Hutner as the first three members, with Spencer unanimously elected to preside over the denomination. A year later the board expanded to five Apostles, and Bishop John W. Pernell[35] and Bishop Henry Jones were added.

Spencer's seven-year tenure was most memorable for bringing stability to the denomination, holding it together during a tumultuous period of recovery from the loss of the only presiding bishop it had known. Bonner, who had been ordained by Lawson in 1947 and subsequently served as a pastor in Brooklyn and Detroit and as assistant pastor at Lawson's Harlem congregation, followed Spencer. By 2006, he was still at the helm of the denomination. By the end of the twentieth century, COOLJC had approximately 30,000 members in 450 churches in the United States. There are also congregations in Africa, the British West Indies, the Dominican Republic, England, Haiti and the Philippines. The major importance of the Church of Our Lord Jesus Christ can partly be seen in the number of spinoff denominations that owe their beginnings directly to this body.

Church of the Lord Jesus Christ of the Apostolic Faith. The first major schism with COOLJC came in 1933, when Sherrod C. Johnson founded the Church of *the* Lord Jesus Christ of the Apostolic Faith. Johnson had served as a minister within Lawson's Harlem congregation and had risen

---

[34]Cited on website of Christ Temple Church, Clinton, Maryland, "Keeping a Dream and Name Alive," *Contender for the Faith*, Fall 1992, http://christtemple.tripod.com/about_wlf.html.

[35]Pernell was pastor of a Richmond congregation and was a respected and influential Bible scholar within the denomination. However, convinced that the Lord had shown him a new revelation, he began to teach that "Yahweh," the Old Testament name for God, was the appropriate title for God in the church age. The COOLJC governing board charged him with being in error, and when he would not recant, he was disfellowshiped.

to prominence as a state overseer within the COOLJC organization. Though he agreed with Lawson on major doctrinal issues, including divorce and remarriage and refusing women the right to preach, he challenged his mentor's stand on more practical issues such as the appropriate dress of a saint. Johnson's disagreement with what he saw as Lawson's more liberal stance was reminiscent of the latter's conflict with Haywood. Johnson insisted that women should dress as modestly as possible, "pertaining to holiness."[36]

Johnson also held extreme positions against observing traditional holidays such as Christmas, Palm Sunday, Easter and Lent, which he considered to be pagan observances, not endorsed by Scripture.[37] Because of such restrictions, he was considered ultraconservative, even by other black oneness believers, and his doctrinal stances distanced his group from those who did not hold the same rigid strictures. Johnson used the radio to regularly debate with other Pentecostal and church leaders. For several years, for example, he used his radio broadcast to fight with Lawson on a number of biblical and doctrinal issues.

Johnson's seemingly primitive theological understanding belied a man of sharp intellect. He received a Ph.D. from Rutgers University. After forty-two years of leading the denomination, Johnson died in 1961, and Samuel McDowell Shelton became secretary general, leading the denomination for the next thirty years and maintaining the rigid strictures put into place by Johnson. With Shelton at its head, the denomination's radio broadcast, *The Whole Truth,* expanded its reach into the Caribbean, Europe, Africa and India. Carrying on the tradition of contentious confrontation, Johnson's successor, S. McDowell Shelton, was often heard to defiantly proclaim on his broadcast, "Everybody can't be right."

By 1980, the church had grown to more than one hundred congregations in the United States, England, Africa, Jamaica and the Bahamas. Throughout his tenure Shelton remained unmarried but adopted six sons. At Shelton's death two sons—Roddy J. Shelton (or Elder Shelton Nehemiah) and Kenneth Shelton (Elder Shelton Omega) claimed the legal

---

[36]See further on women in Johnson's denomination in chap. 8.
[37]See Bishop S. C. Johnson, *False Lent and Pagan Festivals,* ed. and rev. Bishop S. McDowell Shelton, www.apostolic-ministries.net/false_lent.htm; and *The Christmas Spirit Is a False Spirit,* www.apostolic-ministries.net/xmas.htm.

right to control the church and its corporate assets.[38] Their dispute set off a string of schisms, characterized in court documents as "a bitter and prolonged dispute" that would splinter the denomination into four smaller bodies. Extended court cases have continued to tie up the final disposition of the assets of the mother denomination.

At present, the denomination founded by Sherrod C. Johnson is today known as the Whole Truth Church of the Lord Jesus Christ of the Apostolic Faith. By 1997, this faction had 25,000 members in 140 congregations—80 of these in the United States and another 60 in the Caribbean, Central America, West African and the United Kingdom. The remainder of the denomination has splintered and reemerged as three bodies: the Holy Temple Church of the Lord Jesus Christ of the Apostolic Faith, the Apostolic Ministries of America and the First Church of Our Lord Jesus Christ of the Apostles' Faith.

Way of the Cross Church of Christ. Bishop Henry Chauncey Brooks had come to Washington, D.C., to plant a congregation in 1917. The congregation had enjoyed a degree of success as an affiliate of Lawson's Church of our Lord Jesus Christ. But in 1927, after Lawson approached Brooks about relinquishing his fledgling congregation to Smallwood Williams on the assumption that one strong congregation would better serve the denomination than two smaller churches, Brooks broke away. He simply wanted to lead his own congregation independent of existing organizational structure that would limit his control. Brooks's leadership of the local congregation spanned a forty-year period, from 1927 until his death in 1967. Under his lead, that congregation grew to nearly three thousand members and congregations were planted and added throughout the eastern United States; Brooks and his followers incorporated the organization as Way of the Cross Church of Christ.

After Brooks's death, his brother Bishop John L. Brooks served as presiding bishop until 1981. During his administration seven churches were added in Ghana, West Africa, and a national foreign missions effort was begun. At the time of the younger brother's death, the Way of the Cross had grown to forty-eight congregations with more than fifty thousand members. The younger Brooks was succeeded by Bishop LeRoy Cannady, who introduced

---

[38]Philadelphia Court of Common Pleas, Orphans' Court Division, S. McDowell Shelton, Deceased, O. C. No. 1569 DE of 1994.

organizational structure into the denomination with the formation of several executive and auxiliary organizations to carry out the denomination's business at the local, national and international levels. Under his leadership, the denomination grew to nearly one hundred congregations.[39]

Bible Way Church of Our Lord Jesus Christ World-Wide. In 1927, when Lawson approached Brooks to relinquish his Washington pastorate, it was so that he could consolidate the COOLJC effort in that city under another young pastor whom he had sent to the area, Smallwood E. Williams. For the next twenty-five years, Williams, also the denomination's general secretary and Lawson's heir apparent, built that local congregation and a reputation for himself as a charismatic preacher and social activist. Near the end of that period, Williams began to question what he saw as Lawson's authoritative style. For Williams, one of the most egregious concerns was Lawson's opposition to consecrating other bishops, though many COOLJC pastors led sizeable congregations. In the early days of COOLJC, Lawson had consecrated several bishops, appointing them over specific territories. Later, he changed the designation to "state overseer" to eliminate what he saw as "the pride and wrong impression people were taking as bishop."[40]

In 1957, Williams and several other prominent COOLJC pastors convened a National Pentecostal Ministerial Conference to air their concerns. From this conference, a group led by Williams broke from COOLJC to form the Bible Way Church of Our Lord Jesus Christ. Williams was consecrated as presiding bishop; and John S. Beane, McKinley Williams, Winfield A. Showell, and Joseph Moore were also consecrated bishops. In all, approximately seventy churches withdrew from the Church of Our Lord Jesus Christ of the Apostolic Faith to form the new organization.

The split was not over doctrinal issues, and Bible Way continued to hold doctrinal distinctives similar to its mother body. Though the two men had enjoyed a generally cordial working relationship, Lawson reportedly saw Williams's actions as a "conspiracy to take over the church and supplant him."[41] Further, Williams took what was considered a moderate

---

[39]"History," National Youth for Christ of the Way of the Cross Church of Christ International, http://wotccyfc.org/content/view/32/49/.
[40]Richardson, *With Water and Spirit*, p. 81.
[41]Ibid.

doctrinal stance for oneness Pentecostals and was considerably more flexible and progressive than many other oneness leaders.

Just as Lawson had done, Williams positioned himself as one of the few oneness leaders to consistently engage the larger context of social injustice; Bible Way was among the first Apostolic churches to show interest in political issues. Williams used the political system to the advantage of his congregation as well as other Washington blacks. Under his leadership, Bible Way built a moderate-income apartment complex for members of his congregation and the surrounding community and opened a grocery store in a neighborhood that had been shunned by the larger chains. He was also able to use his political clout to forestall the wholesale demolition of a major portion of the community surrounding his church for the construction I-95, a major interstate in the eastern United States. Today, travelers from the southern coast of the country to New England are forced to go around rather than through the nation's capital because of efforts in which Williams played a major part.

In 1995 the denomination Williams built had approximately 300,000 members in 350 congregations worldwide. No major schism occurred in the Bible Way organization during Williams's lifetime. After his death, denominational leaders adopted an "Order of Succession and Constitution" calling for its two highest-ranking bishops, Lawrence Campbell and Huie Rogers, to each serve a three-year trial term as presiding bishop before the body would vote on Williams's official successor. The two men agreed that Campbell would hold the office of presiding bishop from 1991-1994; then Rogers would serve for three years. At the end of his term, however, Rogers called for a sabbath year of no voting, effectively attempting to delay the vote for a year. When the majority of bishops refused to accept the resolution, the denomination split. Both factions, however, continued to represent themselves as the original church.

Most bishops, pastors and churches stayed with Campbell, and this branch remains the largest entity of the two, with approximately five hundred churches worldwide. This group became the International Bible Way Church of Jesus Christ, Inc. Though the two organizations are similar in structure and doctrine, Campbell, whose church's headquarters were in Danville, Virginia, began to make progressive changes to the organization under his leadership, including ordaining women to the office of elder.

When Campbell retired in 2006, Cornelius Showell was elected to preside over the body, whose headquarters were moved to his four-thousand-member home congregation, First Apostolic Faith Church, in Baltimore. Rogers's group, Bible Way Church of our Lord Jesus Christ World-Wide, Inc., has its headquarters in Columbia, South Carolina, and has approximately 250 churches throughout the world. It also retains ownership of the mother church, Bible Way Temple in Washington, D.C.

The schism in Bible Way may have been circumvented altogether had Smallwood Williams's original intentions been carried through. Williams had been grooming his son Wallace as heir to the denomination's leadership. The younger Williams was a graduate of Howard University, and with his musical talent he was instrumental in forming the Howard University Gospel Choir. That talent, coupled with a dynamic preaching style, had been instrumental for drawing and retaining young Pentecostals in the organization. Wallace had served on his father's pastoral staff and was considered a rising star in the organization. When he was allegedly was found to be in an adulterous relationship, however, the senior Williams removed him from his staff and from future consideration as his successor.[42] Wallace went on to found a small independent congregation, which he still leads, but his ministry never reached the stature of that of his father.

PROLIFERATION OF BLACK ONENESS DENOMINATIONS

In his book *With Water and Spirit*, James Richardson lists seventeen black oneness denominations that came into existence between 1906 and 1979.[43] In the relatively short period between that time and the beginning of the twenty-first century (only 21 years), at least an equal number have come into existence either through schism or by the efforts of a single charismatic individual. While all of these bodies maintain the insistence in the need for following the oneness baptismal formula, they

---

[42]Traditionally, prominent black Pentecostal pastors and bishops are succeeded by their sons. For example, Monroe Saunders Jr. succeeded his father at First United Church of Jesus Christ; William Fuller Jr. followed his father within the Fire Baptized Holiness Church; and James Richardson Jr. took over the Apostle Church of Christ in God from his father. After the death of his father, the now bishop of Bible Way World Wide, Cornelius Showell, took over the pastorate of the prominent First Apostolic Church in Baltimore, Maryland.

[43]Richardson, *With Water and Spirit*, pp. 39-100.

each add a distinctive spin on some area of doctrine that separates it from the others.

Original Glorious Church of God in Christ Apostolic Faith. Among those bodies identified by Richardson is the Original Glorious Church of God in Christ Apostolic Faith, Inc., which has roots in the 1921 founding of the Glorious Church of God in Christ by C. H. Stokes. In 1928, Stokes was succeeded as founding bishop by S. C. Bass, but in 1952, when Bass married a divorced woman after the death of his first wife, approximately half of the fifty congregations defected to form a new organization under the leadership of W. O. Howard. The organization never grew to more than a few dozen congregations in the United States, while there are more than one hundred congregations overseas. The group, whose headquarters is in Elyria, Ohio, had two hundred ministers and over twenty-five thousand members worldwide.[44]

Highway Christian Church of Christ. Highway Christian Church of Christ was founded in 1929 in Washington, D.C., and chartered in 1936 by James H. Morris, who had been part of the PAW. Though Morris remained on friendly terms with his PAW colleagues, the major distinguishing mark of the Highway Christian Church is a rigid, conservative piety. Its leaders maintain that the "saints" should dress predominantly in black and white and eschew worldly colored apparel, which many within the PAW preferred. Bright colors and even pastels were considered "loud, flashy, [and] ostentatious." Further, the denomination does not ordain women, though it will accept a woman into fellowship who is already ordained but requires those coming into the denomination as pastors to relinquish their pastorate to a man.[45] Rigid positions such as these have precluded further growth of the small denomination. In 2002 there were nineteen congregations and about two thousand members.

Spinoff Denominations from the Church of God (Apostolic). Numerous small oneness bodies were formed in the last half the twentieth century. In 1940, after founding bishop Thomas Cox of the Church of God (Apostolic) became ill, several pastors became dissatisfied with the public lead-

---

[44]"Original Glorious Church of God in Christ Apostolic Faith," in *Melton's Encyclopedia of American Religions,* 8th ed., ed. J. Gordon Melton (Detroit: Gale Research, 2009), p. 375.
[45]Richardson, *With Water and Spirit,* p. 70.

ership and personal lifestyle of his eventual successor, Bishop Eli Neal.[46] Questions concerning Neal's autocratic style and personal morality caused the first split, when in the 1940s, five elders—J. W. Aubrey, James C. Richardson, Jerome Jenkins, W. R. Bryant and J. M. Williams—left to form the Apostle Church of Christ in God in Winston-Salem, North Carolina. In 1948, the headquarters of the mother denomination moved to its present location in Winston-Salem. Within a year the denomination had added congregations in New York and Pennsylvania. However, in 1952, Robert Doub, the overseer of Pennsylvania, challenged Audrey's position as presiding bishop. When the majority of the denomination backed Audrey, Doub left to found Shiloh Apostolic Temple, with his Pennsylvania congregations serving as its headquarters. A year later, Audrey was replaced by Richardson as presiding bishop.

In 1956, after his petition to be consecrated as a bishop was refused, George Wiley left the denomination to found Mt. Hebron Apostolic Temple of Our Lord Jesus Christ, which would incorporate in 1963 in Yonkers, New York. Since his wife had worked with the youth department for many years, the couple had developed a following among this group. As a result, many of the younger members of the denomination left with them into the new organization.[47] These groups have generally remained small, with largely regional constituencies, but the fissure has led to a steady decline in the Church of God (Apostolic), which by the last quarter of the twentieth century had fifteen thousand members in forty-three congregations primarily along the East Coast.[48]

Within the three-year period beginning in 1971, two more splits would occur. In that year, Bishop Audrey would lead a splinter group out of the organization. In 1974, a second group would leave under the leadership of John Wiley. Presumably these two groups remained largely independent congregations since no record can be found of denominations formed under the leadership of either man, but several larger groups would be formed over the next two decades.

Pentecostal Churches of the Apostolic Faith. In 1957, Samuel N. Han-

---

[46]See the discussion of Neal above.

[47]Sherry Sherrod DuPree, *African-American Holiness Pentecostalism: An Annotated Bibliography* (New York: Garland, 1996), p. 262.

[48]"Church of God Apostolic," in *Melton's Encyclopedia of American Religion*, p. 370.

cock and Willie Lee pulled out of the Pentecostal Assemblies of the World to found the Pentecostal Churches of Apostolic Faith.[49] Hancock began teaching a doctrine that deviated from the traditional oneness understanding by suggesting that Jesus was only the Son of God, not actually God himself. Although the PAW leaders issued a clarifying statement and tolerated Hancock's teachings, they declined to elect him to the position of presiding bishop, a post Hancock felt he deserved. Disappointed over that development, Hancock left with three other bishops to form the new denomination.

Once Hancock founded Pentecostal Churches of the Apostolic Faith, he continued the deviant teaching, and though a faction within the denomination objected to this deviation, as long as he lived they tolerated that teaching and remained loyal to him. On Hancock's death, Willie Lee, who at the time was pastor of Christ Temple Church, the congregation Haywood had led, succeeded Hancock. But when Lee persisted in that teaching, a schism occurred when the majority of the churches returned to the "orthodox" oneness doctrine. Lee was disfellowshiped. Elzie Young move into the position of presiding bishop, and the church returned to the traditional Apostolic doctrine. By 1980, the denomination had grown to approximately 25,000 members with 380 ministers serving 115 churches in the United States, Haiti and Liberia.

True Vine Pentecostal Churches of Jesus. In 1961, after twenty-five years of affiliation with the trinitarian Pentecostal movement, and being affiliated with several trinitarian denominations, Robert Hairston felt a growing dissatisfaction that would lead to his departure to align himself with oneness Pentecostalism and to found the True Vine Pentecostal Churches of Jesus. His growing dissatisfaction centered largely on three concerns. First, Hairston was generally dissatisfied with several polity issues with his organization. Second, he had earlier accepted baptism in Jesus' name as the biblically correct formulation. But since Hairston rejected some other tenets of the Apostolic movement, including necessity of baptism in Jesus' name for salvation and with it regenerational baptism, he might have been content to remain a minority voice in a denomination that had tolerated his deviation in doctrine. But, third, Hairston's departure was also prod-

---

[49]See the more detailed discussion of Hancock's role in, and departure from, the PAW above.

ded by his own personal situation, since the fact that he had divorced and subsequently remarried while his former wife was alive proved to be problematic for several of his colleagues.

Church of God in Christ Jesus (Apostolic). In the mid-1930s Randolph Adolphus Carr established a congregation known as Rehoboth Church of God in Christ within the trinitarian COGIC organization,[50] in Baltimore, Maryland. Carr severed ties with COGIC in 1946, when he adopted a oneness doctrine. The body, which came to be the Church of God in Christ Jesus (Apostolic) (COGICJA) in 1947, is headquartered in Baltimore, Maryland. Carr presided over this organization from 1945 until his death in 1970. The COGICJA, Inc., has more than fifty churches throughout the United States, Canada, Jamaica, Bermuda and the West Indies.

The Holy Temple Church of Christ. When Way of the Cross founder Henry Brooks died in 1968, Elder Joseph Weathers, who had served as a chief assistant to Brooks, appeared to be the most likely person to succeed him. When this did not happen and instead Brooks's brother was elevated to the position of presiding bishop, Weathers broke away with approximately one hundred members of the Washington congregation to form the Holy Temple Church of Christ.

The Church of God and True Holiness. The Churches of God and True Holiness organization was established by the late Bishop John Wesley Garlington Sr., in December 1927 in Buffalo, New York. Soon churches were added in Virginia, New York, North Carolina, Ohio (Cleveland and Cincinnati), Florida, Delaware and South Carolina. Bishop Garlington led this organization until his death in 1943, when Bishop Thomas Benton of Norfolk, Virginia, became the presiding bishop. After Bishop Benton's death in 1958, Bishop Frank Jackson became presiding bishop, serving until 1961, when Joseph Peeler of Buffalo, New York, was appointed the presiding bishop. After Peeler's death three years later, John Kennon was appointed to the office of presiding bishop. He was followed in 1968, by John W. Garlington Jr., son of the founder. After fire damaged the headquarters church in Buffalo, the national headquarters were relocated to Cleveland, Ohio. Bishop Albert E. Dixon Sr. was appointed the presid-

---

[50]"History," The Church Of God In Christ Greater Maryland First Ecclesiastical Jurisdiction, http://gmdfirst.org/index.php?option=com_content&view=article&id=62&Itemid=75.

ing bishop and served for more than thirty years in that position.

At one point, the denomination was accused of placing members in involuntary solitude, and its leaders were under surveillance by the FBI.[51] Today, this organization has churches in six states and two countries.

ONENESS PENTECOSTAL PRACTICE AND DOCTRINE

After McAlister preached his Arroyo Seco camp meeting message followed by John Scheppe's midnight revelation, the concern of the "new issue" was primarily that the correct, biblical formula for baptism be followed in the nascent Pentecostal movement. Within a few years a number of followers were rebaptized "in the name of Jesus" as a perceived obedient response to this new truth. Soon entire congregations submitted themselves to this new truth, as people who had experienced the dynamic outpouring of the Holy Spirit were hungry for a continued, visible move of God and were willing to do whatever was required bring it about.

From that simple proclamation, however, an elaborate, but not always consistent, theology developed that grew to encompass conceptions of the nature of the Godhead, the character of Christ's deity and the mode of salvation. According to black oneness historian James Richardson, two common themes ran (and continue to run) through oneness Pentecostal theology: the necessity of repentance for one's sinful past and turning toward God. Within the abundance of oneness Pentecostal bodies that emerged over nearly one hundred years, however, adherents have forged distinctive understandings that are at odds with evangelical understandings. Many oneness groups insist, for example, that in order to be saved, all believers must be baptized by immersion in water in the name of the Lord Jesus Christ. They also insist that these believers must receive the baptism of the Holy Ghost, which must be accompanied with the initial evidence of speaking in tongues. A third theme that runs throughout the center of oneness theology is the refutation of the orthodoxy of the historical doctrine of the Godhead. In this reformulation they deny the trinitarian conception as essentially tri-theistic. In its place they propose that there is one person in the Godhead who appears throughout periods of salvation history successively as Father, Son and Holy Spirit; and that person is Jesus Christ.

---

[51]DuPree, *African-American Holiness Pentecostalism*, pp. 254-55.

Regenerational baptism. The belief in the necessity of water baptism by immersion as an essential ritual act to obtain salvation is a hallmark of oneness Pentecostalism. For all Pentecostals, the act of baptism is an essential ordinance—an obedient response to the command of Jesus to baptize in the name of the Father and of the Son and of the Holy Spirit. But while trinitarian Pentecostals believe it to be a simple act of obedience, for oneness Pentecostals, the Matthew 28:19 passage represents a specific command by Jesus. They see depictions of baptism in the book of Acts in which the apostles used the Jesus formula as obediently fulfilling this command.[52] Oneness leaders make the exegetical point that Jesus commanded the disciples to baptize in the name—not the names—of the Father, Son and Holy Spirit. For them, therefore, water baptism in the name of Jesus is more than a ritual act. It is required for salvation and according to this understanding, "Unless you are baptized in Jesus' name, you don't have it right," and "you are not saved"; and "You do not have the New Birth Jesus spoke of."[53]

As with other early Pentecostals, oneness believers sought to restore authentic biblical doctrine, which they felt had been compromised or misunderstood for hundreds of years. Indeed, their self-identification as "Apostolic" speaks of the attempt to follow what they saw as the apostles' example of obedience to biblical commands. For them, "[Baptism] in the name of Jesus . . . is Apostolic in origin and practice. . . . No other mode of baptism is to be found in the New Testament. For more than one hundred years after Pentecost, the believers were baptized in the Name, Jesus Christ."[54]

The formula invoked during baptism certainly sets the baptism ritual of oneness Pentecostals apart from that of other Pentecostals. But importantly, baptism is not only essential for salvation; baptism itself is salvific. The doctrine of regenerational baptism insists that it is only after a person has repented of his or her sin and been baptized in Jesus' name that the process of salvation begins. Faith in the atoning work of Christ apart from such baptism is not sufficiently salvific. Having expressed faith in Jesus Christ and the desire to be saved, one must be baptized for the re-

---

[52]Acts 2:38; 8:16; 10:48; 19:5.
[53]Sherrod C. Johnson, *The New Birth*, cited in Richardson, *With Water and Spirit*, p. 107.
[54]Monroe Saunders, *Book of Discipline and Order of the United Church of Jesus Christ (Apostolic)* (Washington, D.C., 1965), pp. 21-22.

mission of one's sins; for it is in the act of baptism that regeneration begins, and it is through baptism that justification comes. Invoking the
King James Version of the Acts 22:16 passage, "And now why tarriest
thou? arise, and be baptized, and wash away thy sins, calling on the name
of the Lord," oneness believers would argue that persons who have not
submitted themselves to the act of baptism by immersion in the name of
Jesus are not saved.

The statement of faith of Lawson's body, the Church of Our Lord Jesus
Christ of the Apostolic Faith, reads in part: "We accept God's plan of salvation of baptism by water and spirit . . . [and that] water baptism in the name
of Jesus Christ is essential for forgiveness of sins, and confirms our belief
that Jesus Christ is the Son of God."[55] But perhaps the most rigid exposition of this understanding was expressed by Bishop Sherrod Johnson,
founder of the Church of the Lord Jesus Christ of the Apostolic Faith, who
was insistent that "no one is saved regardless to whom he or she may be
without having the water, spirit, and the blood. These three agree in one. If
you have the spirit, and refuse the water, you are not saved. You cannot have
the blood and refuse water and the spirit. The Bible says: 'One Lord, one
faith, one baptism.'"[56] The doctrinal statement of Johnson's denomination
epitomizes the refutation of those who would use another formula:

> The modern way . . . of converting men and women . . . is unscriptural such
> as: Joining a church; raising the hand and accepting Christ as your personal
> Savior; bowing your head; slipping up a finger; accept Christ right where
> you are; the hour of decision, etc. is man-made doctrine and not according
> to the Word of God. Every man or woman that has not been baptized ac-
> cording to Acts 2:38 and received the Holy Ghost according to Acts 2:4, is
> still in their sins.[57]

The statement of faith of the Apostle Church of Christ in God succinctly affirms this same understanding: "We believe that the *only* means
of being cleansed from sin is through repentance, faith in the precious

---

[55]"Statement of Faith," The Church of Our Lord Jesus Christ of Apostolic Faith, www.cooljc
.org/AboutUs/StatementofFaith/tabid/70/language/en-US/Default.aspx.

[56]S. C. Johnson, "Sirs, What Must I Do To Be Saved?" www.apostolic-faith.org/sirswhat.asp.

[57]Sherrod C. Johnson, "Who Is This That Defies and Challenges the Whole Religious World
on These Subjects?" (Philadelphia: Church of the Lord Jesus Christ of the Apostolic Faith,
1958), p. 5.

blood of Jesus Christ *and* being baptized in water in Jesus' name."[58]

Requisite for Holy Spirit baptism and tongues. While regenerational baptism sets the process of salvation in motion, classical oneness Pentecostals would also argue that it is still not sufficiently salvific. For them, water baptism is a necessity, and baptism of the Holy Spirit with the initial evidence of speaking in tongues is an additional requirement. Neither the baptism of the Holy Spirit nor the initial speaking in tongues that accompanies it are optional for the true believer. Using the passage in Acts 2:4 as a referent, the statement of faith of COOLJC succinctly states, "We believe that rebirth by the Holy Spirit is absolutely essential today as it was in the days of the Apostles."[59] An excerpt from Bible Way's founder provides a clear formulation of the insistence of the necessity of Spirit baptism for salvation. It reads, "THE BAPTISM OF THE HOLY GHOST IS THE BIRTH OF THE SPIRIT . . . ; that spiritual baptism is necessary to put anyone into the kingdom of God . . . and is evidenced by speaking in tongues as the Spirit of God gives utterance."[60] The practical importance of this understanding is demonstrated in the repeated testimony of the saints in black oneness congregations of every sort that "I've been saved, sanctified, and filled with the Holy Ghost, according to Acts 2:4." Oneness saints have come to see the integration of these experiences as the sign of the authenticity of their claim to salvation. Again, in one of the most rigid declarations of this understanding, the Church of the Lord Jesus Christ of the Apostolic Faith simply asserts, "If you have not been . . . filled with the Holy Ghost speaking in tongues . . . you are not saved."[61]

The nature of the Godhead and Christology. Some early groups who practiced baptism in Jesus name still maintained a traditional understanding of the Trinity. For them, the issue was simply over the formula for baptism. Within a fairly short time, however, their theological speculation grew to question the nature of the Godhead itself, as oneness Pentecostals

---

[58]"Statement of Faith," Apostle Church of Christ in God, Inc. (emphasis original), www.apostle churchcg.org/believe.htm.

[59]"Statement of Faith," The Church of Our Lord Jesus Christ of the Apostolic Faith, www .cooljc.org/AboutUs/StatementofFaith/tabid/70/language/en-US/Default.aspx.

[60]Smallwood E. Williams, *Rules and Regulations of the Bible Way Church World Wide, Inc.* (Washington D.C.: Bible Way Church Publishing, 1962), p. 37, cited in Richardson, *With Water and Spirit*, p. 119.

[61]Sherrod C. Johnson, *The New Birth* (s.l.: Church of the Lord Jesus Christ of the Apostolic Faith, s.d.), cited in Richardson, *With Water and Spirit*, p. 107.

began rejecting formulations that had stood for centuries as the bedrock of Christian theology and began asserting that those formulations were essentially tri-theistic. Employing a hermeneutic that rested heavily on literal King James translations as the most authentic representation of God's Word and on a rigid dispensationalist eschatology, they insisted that there is only one God who appears in different dispensations in three distinct modes. For them, this Godhead consists of one Spiritual essence—not three self-conscious persons. This understanding became an essential doctrine of black oneness Pentecostal denominations. As the Church of Our Lord Jesus Christ states, God

> was the Father in creation, the Son in redemption, and today, He is the Holy Ghost in the Church. . . . In Christ all the fullness of the Deity lives in bodily form . . . [and] Jesus Christ is the name of God that was given to this generation as the *only* Name whereby the people of this Grace dispensation of time can be saved.[62]

Accordingly, PAW teachings reject contentions that the doctrine of the Trinity is substantiated by Scripture, insisting instead that it must be "read into the sacred text [since] the Bible is the book of one God who has revealed himself in many ways."[63] Importantly for them, Jesus was the eternal Father made visible, apart from whom there is no God. "We believe that at the final consummation of all things there will be only one God, and that will be our Lord Jesus Christ."[64]

Though some critics call this understanding a "unitarianism of the Son," they often fail to make the important distinction between oneness Pentecostals and mainline Unitarians. Unlike the classical Unitarian understanding of the Godhead (which disregards the Trinity, insisting that Jesus does not share the same level of deity as the Father), oneness Pentecostals see Jesus as God, or more directly that "Jehovah—God of the Old Testament is Jesus Christ of the New Testament."[65] For them, Jesus is not the second person of the Trinity—Jesus is all of God. In the incarnation, the entirety of the Godhead became Jesus in the flesh—without abandon-

[62]"Statement of Faith," Church of Our Lord Jesus Christ of the Apostolic Faith, www.cooljc.org/AboutUs/StatementofFaith/tabid/70/language/en-US/Default.aspx.
[63]Ibid.
[64]"Creed, Discipline and Doctrine," *Minute Book of the Pentecostal Assemblies of the World* (Indianapolis: Pentecostal Assemblies of the World, 1972).
[65]Richardson, *With Water and Spirit*, p. 126.

ing any aspect of his divine nature. The body Jesus inhabited was only a temporary temple. As such, death—or destruction of that body—did not in any way destroy the infinite Spirit that was Jesus. After Jesus' death, we have that same God with us as the Holy Spirit.

At the core of the oneness understanding of the Godhead is the "theology of the name," which contends that in the dispensation of the law, the name for God was Jehovah, but in this dispensation—the dispensation of grace—the name of God, not just that of the Son, is Jesus. In this conception, Jesus is not simply the second person of the Trinity; he is the entire Godhead. Richardson uses Lawson's exposition of the use of Jesus' name to explain this theology,

> Father is not a proper name, nor son, nor Holy Ghost. Father expresses a relationship, also Son, and the Holy Ghost means Holy Spirit, but does not mean His name, but his nature. "Holy" is an adjective meaning more "excellent," "pure in heart," and Spirit is a noun but not a proper name. So they that baptize in the [Trinitarian] formula . . . do not baptize in any name at all. . . . If we have not baptized in the name of Jesus, then we have not baptized in any name at all.[66]

Further, oneness believers insist that the entire Godhead was incarnated in Christ and that the physical body of Jesus was a temporary temple of that Godhead. When Jesus died, the infinite, eternal Spirit of God continued to live and is among us today as the Spirit of Jesus.[67] For them, Jesus is God and all the fullness of the Godhead dwells in him.

Unfortunate turn. Black oneness Pentecostals tend to be among the most fundamentalist of all Pentecostals. Generally, they reject all other modes of baptism that do not involve full immersion, insisting that all other modes of baptism (i.e., sprinkling, pouring or infant baptism) are without biblical merit. Indeed, they declare that these modes are the "inventions or traditions of men" without apostolic approval or sanction.[68] In the most severe cases, especially in the earliest days of the movement, some oneness Pentecostals even refused to fellowship with other Pentecostals who did not concur on what they saw as a vital issue of faith.[69] The most

[66]Ibid., p. 125.
[67]Ibid., p. 129.
[68]Ibid., p. 124.
[69]Ibid., p. 121.

rigid black oneness believers are closed to fellowship with all other believers. Sanctions for breaching this boundary include not allowing anyone who does not affirm their specific theological understandings into their pulpits as well as banning other believers from the Communion table and forbidding members of their congregations from attending worship at trinitarian churches.

Notably, some leaders, especially younger, seminary-trained leaders, tend to take a more moderate stand, not denouncing fellow believers who hold broader soteriological understandings. The tenet on the church in the statement of belief of the Way of the Cross Church of Christ, for example, makes room for such a broader understanding. While insisting that there is a biblical standard for "full salvation" that includes "repentance, baptism in water by immersion in the name of Jesus for the remission of sins, and the baptism of the Holy Ghost with the initial sign of speaking with other tongues as the Spirit gives utterance," it allows that "salvation comes by grace through faith based on the atoning sacrifice of Jesus Christ."[70]

Ultimately, one may question why black Pentecostals are so heavily represented in the oneness camp. In response, Roswith Gerloff contends that what has made oneness theology so attractive to African Americans as well as "the African Diaspora [who are] descendants of slaves is its radicality."[71] Gerloff challenges that the theology of the movement "grafted itself into the cultures of their disadvantaged urban poor [who were] a people less inclined than others to follow established authority and more open to 'new revelation.'"[72]

Trinitarian Pentecostal critiques of oneness Pentecostalism. One of the earliest criticisms of the "new issue" was lodged by Azusa leader William Seymour, who specifically, yet tersely, addressed the new baptismal formula. In his *Doctrines and Disciplines of the Azusa Street Mission*, published in 1915, at the height of the controversy within the still very young Pente-

---

[70]"What We Believe," Way of the Cross Church International, http://wotcc.net/content /view/16/35/.

[71]Roswith Gerloff, "Blackness and Oneness (Apostolic) Theology: Crosscultural Aspects of a Movement" (paper presented at the First Occasional Symposium on Aspects of the Oneness Pentecostal Movement, Harvard University Divinity School, Cambridge, Mass., July 4-7, 1984).

[72]Ibid., 87.

costal movement, Seymour inferred that the practice was unbiblical, insisting instead that "we do not believe in being baptized in the name of Jesus only. We believe in baptizing in the name of the Father and of the Son and of the Holy Ghost as Jesus taught his disciples."[73]

In a letter written in 1925, ten years after this new theology came to the forefront, Mary Magdalena Tate, founder of the Church of the Living God, was adamant that oneness teachings constituted a "false belief," explaining that the apostles only used the formula including Jesus' name among the Jews who had formerly rejected him as Messiah.[74] In 1945, Charles Mason was invited by his personal friend Robert Lawson to St. Louis to address a convention of the Church of God in Christ. During his message, Lawson explained that though he believed in the Sonship of God, the Fatherhood of God and the Holy Ghost, after Jesus was put to death in the flesh, he was no longer the Son of God but was the Spirit of the Lord. Mason replied,

> I listened to hear the brother say that he had made a mistake in his saying after he heard the scripture read which showed that he was wrong. . . . The one in the Godhead People are undertaking to show God this wrong saying. The three that agree in earth say that there are three in heaven. Who can say that God and His Son and the Holy Ghost did not know how to count? . . . They said that "Three in Heaven," but some the wise today say they see it better. "God saw Three and said Three." But the "One in the Godhead People" say they only see "One" and could not be "three." God said three and could make them one. But we may see one and cannot make them three.[75]

But though Seymour, Mason and other early trinitarian leaders were quick to refute oneness doctrinal understandings, they did not break fellowship with oneness believers, and African American oneness and trinitarian Pentecostals have historically been more comfortable with each other than is true in the white arena. Certainly there is not the level of denounce-

---

[73]William Seymour, *Doctrines and Disciplines of the Azusa Street Mission of Los Angeles California* (Los Angeles, 1916), p. 8.

[74]Mary Magdalena Tate, "A Letter from Mother Tate Concerning Baptism in the Name of 'Jesus Only,' " May 1925, in Meharry H. Lewis, ed., *Mary Lena Lewis Tate: Collected Letters and Manuscripts* (Nashville: New and Living Way Publishing, 2003), pp. 34-35.

[75]Lillian Brooks Coffey, ed., *Yearbook of the Church of God in Christ* (Memphis: The Church, 1926).

ment of oneness theology among black trinitarians as one would find in the
Assemblies of God or the Church of God. Perhaps the strongest criticism
of black oneness theology, however, has come from white trinitarian Pentecostal bodies. The Assemblies of God, in which the original controversy
was centered, went as far as moving away from its earliest noncreedal stance
to respond to the perceived threat to orthodox Christian doctrine posed by
this new formulation. It specifically rejects any notion that the name of
Jesus is an appropriate appellation for the Godhead, insisting that "the appellation, 'Lord Jesus Christ,' is a proper name. According to them, it is
never applied in the New Testament, either to the Father or to the Holy
Spirit. It therefore belongs exclusively to the Son of God."[76]

The Church of God (Cleveland, Tennessee) roundly refutes oneness
theological formulations, openly questioning whether oneness believers
should even be considered authentic believers. Further, though the denomination will allow those who have been baptized using the oneness
formula to become members, some pastors urge them to be rebaptized
with what they consider the more biblical, trinitarian formula. Additionally anyone who seeks to enter ministry within the denomination must
declare they have been baptized "in the name of the Father and of the Son
and of the Holy Spirit," or present themselves for rebaptism.

Some detractors contend that the roots of oneness belief can be found
in early modalistic conceptions of the Godhead formed during the patris-
tic period. Oneness Pentecostals, careful to point to historic ties with first-
century baptismal practices,[77] reject that characterization. At the same
time, they insist that, while all three of the modes of the Godhead are one
God, God carries the name Jesus such that Jesus is the Father, Jesus is the
Son and Jesus is the Holy Spirit.

Response from other Pentecostals generally excluded Apostolics from
some Pentecostal ecumenical efforts (especially those that reach outside of
African American Pentecostalism). The most visible exclusion has been
from the re-formed multiracial umbrella organization, Pentecostal and
charismatic Churches of North America (PCCNA) that was constituted to

---

[76]The General Council of the Assemblies of God, *Statement Of Fundamental Truths Approved by
the General Council of the Assemblies of God, Oct. 2 To 7, 1916*, http://ag.org/top/beliefs/state
ment_of_fundamental_truths/sft.pdf.

[77]Richardson, *With Water and Spirit*, p. 123.

replace the all-white Pentecostal Fellowship of North America. The PC-CNA's statement of faith specifically affirms, "We believe there is one God, eternally existing in three persons: Father, Son, and Holy Ghost." With this succinct statement, it precludes involvement of oneness denominations.[78]

Nonetheless, more general openness of black oneness and trinitarian Pentecostals in all but the most rigid oneness proponents (such as Johnson and Shelton) means they are more likely to engage in collaborative efforts based on shared concerns and less likely to push the theological envelope. Many may not go as far as Smallwood Williams in deliberating attempts to found an ecumenical community among black oneness and trinitarian Pentecostals. Yet, while white trinitarian and oneness bodies have tended to pronounce anathemas against each other, black Pentecostals have achieved a degree of tolerance, and as Roswith Gerloff contends, black oneness Pentecostals

> emphasized the baptismal formula of the early church rather than specula-
> tive considerations about the inner nature of the Godhead articulated by
> the white [oneness Pentecostals]. Blacks called themselves "Apostolic," not
> Oneness, in devotion to the "power of the Name of Jesus" and the fight
> against discrimination and injustice. . . . They overcame the separation
> within Pentecostalism by a biblical triadic emphasis and the surrender to
> Jesus as the sole savior and reconciler.[79]

More importantly, many of the average black Pentecostal believers are unaware of the distinction in the understandings. At the grass roots, black oneness and trinitarian Pentecostals regularly fellowship with each other in revivals, conferences and numerous other worship events. Most sermons that come across these pulpits stay away from divisive issues, concentrating instead on common themes on which black Pentecostals agree.

CONTEMPORARY EXPRESSIONS OF BLACK ONENESS PENTECOSTALISM

Notwithstanding explicit theological differences, the fluid nature of the African American Pentecostal community and the opportunities forged

---

[78]"Pentecostal/Charismatic Churches of North America, Constitution and Bylaws," adopted by the Board of Administration, Colorado Springs, Colo., October 2005.

[79]Roswith Gerloff, "Encyclopedia of Pentecostal and Charismatic Christianity" *Pneuma* 29, no. 2 (2007): 319.

by the burgeoning charismatic and neo-Pentecostal movements have opened doors for a number of oneness Pentecostal personalities to develop thriving ministries extending beyond the confines of the Apostolic tradition. While holding private convictions regarding the validity of oneness doctrine, some black oneness leaders have downplayed sectarian issues for a more engaging message and have adopted cross-generational and cross-cultural styles that are more attractive within charismatic and evangelical churches. Several have become the superstars of the Pentecostal and neo-Pentecostal movements, with ministries that are recognizable and even venerated around the globe.

At the turn of the twenty-first century T. D. (Thomas Dexter) Jakes had become one of the most recognizable names in both popular American religious and secular culture. Forestalling most criticism of his oneness ties without refuting its essential elements, the founding pastor of the thirty-thousand-member Potter's House draws a multiracial following that is largely unaware of his black oneness roots. Within that congregation, the rites of baptism are celebrated by immersion in the name of Jesus Christ.

The doctrinal statement of Jakes's Pater Alliance describes the three persons in the Godhead as "manifestations." This definition has been adequate for those within his congregation and for thousands of followers from various Christian traditions. These include pastors who, though soundly trinitarian, regularly join in his events, listen to his sermons and read his material. Many parishioners and leaders who are engaged by his Christian pragmatism find the issue of his oneness position inconsequential.

Another oneness proponent, Noel Jones, has had no trouble drawing followers from the broader movement. Jones, the pastor of the seventeen-thousand-member City of Refuge in Los Angeles, served for several years as PAW diocesan bishop of California. In contrast to the denomination's clearly oneness doctrinal position on the Godhead, Jones's statement does not address the issue. His influence in broader Pentecostal-charismatic circles is evident through a column in *Gospel Today* magazine, frequent appearances on Trinity Broadcasting Network (TBN) and appearances as a panelist on both the C-SPAN cable network and National Public Radio (NPR) programs. The broader reach of his messages allows him to draw such diverse followers as former Crips and

Bloods gang members, entertainment superstars such as talk show host Tavis Smiley, and wealthy business people and other professionals to his congregation. Attracted by his upscale and highly demonstrative yet often intellectually stimulating sermons, they pay little attention to what they would consider an insignificant theology that has little practical application.

Jackie McCollough's ties to oneness Pentecostalism have not precluded her from becoming one of the most visible women preachers in the African American community or from gracing some of the most prominent trinitarian pulpits in the United States or throughout the world. Since the 1980s McCollough has been in demand as a speaker, traveling nationally and internationally. Indeed, few Pentecostal men or women could match the attention the Jamaican-born evangelist gained during that period. But McCollough brings something else to her ministry that few oneness Pentecostals leaders share—a keen and highly educated intellect. She has not only received a master of arts degree in Philosophy from New York University and a doctor of ministry degree from the Drew Theological Seminary but also went on to pursue postgraduate study at Jewish Theological Seminary.

Joseph Garlington, son of Bishop John Garlington, a founder of the Church of God of True Holiness, has emerged as one of the most recognized black preachers on the evangelical circuit. The noted musician is also a stalwart in the charismatic music industry and regular keynote speaker for events for Promise Keepers, the international evangelical men's movement. The statement of faith of his Reconciliation Ministries International nuances its position on the Godhead, asserting that "we believe in the one true God who has revealed Himself as existing in three persons: Father, Son, and Holy Spirit; distinguishable but indivisible."[80]

CONCLUSION

Oneness Pentecostals characterize themselves by several theologically significant labels. While the term *oneness* refers to a refutation of the trinitarian understanding of the Godhead, "Jesus only" identifies the movement as only administering the rite of water baptism exclusively "in the name of

---

[80]"Doctrinal Statement," Reconciliation Ministries International.

Jesus." Related, and most importantly, the Apostolic characterization of themselves speaks of an understanding of being faithful to the New Testament witness that saw the apostles invoking Jesus' name in their baptism ritual and therefore carrying out Jesus' command in the spirit rather than the letter of the law.

As a group, black oneness Pentecostals represent the second largest communion within African American Pentecostalism and are only surpassed in numbers by the Church of God in Christ. The initially interracial Pentecostal Assemblies of the World would remain its flagship denomination, but like its trinitarian brothers, oneness Pentecostalism would be fractured by schism. The result would be a proliferation of black oneness bodies, each of them centered on a charismatic leader who diverged in some seemingly minute element of doctrine. Again, like their trinitarian brothers, most of the denominations would be clustered around specific geographical areas and, outside of the PAW, few would have a truly national presence or show dynamic growth.

Table 6.1. Characteristics of Representative Black Oneness Denominations

Denomination	Year Est.	Founder	Parent Body	Constituency
Church of God, Apostolic (COGA)	1877	Thomas Cox		15,000
Pentecostal Assemblies of the World (PAW)	1906	J. J. Frazee		1,500,000 (2006)
Apostolic Overcoming Holy Church of God	1915	William T. Phillips		10,714 (2000)
Apostolic Faith Mission Church of God	1906	F. W. Williams		10,730
Emmanuel Tabernacle Baptist Church Apostolic Faith	1916	Martin Gregory		
Church of Our Lord Jesus Christ of the Apostolic Faith (COOLJC)	1918	Robert C. Lawson	PAW	45,000 (1992)
Glorious Church of God in Christ (Apostolic Faith), Inc.	1921	C. H. Stokes		

Table 6.1. Continued

Denomination	Year Est.	Founder	Parent Body	Constituency
New Bethel Church of God in Christ (Pentecostal)	1925	A.D. Bradley, Lonnie Bates	COGIC	
House of the Lord	1925	W. H. Johnson		
Way of the Cross Church of Christ (WCCC)	1927	Henry C. Brooks	COOLJC	50,000
The Churches of God and True Holiness	1927	John W. Garlington		
Highway Christian Church of Christ	1929	James Morris	PAW	3,000
Church of the Lord Jesus Christ of the Apostolic Faith	1933	Sherrod C. Johnson	COOLJC	
Apostle Church of Christ in God	1940	J W Audrey, J. C. Richardson, Jerome Jenkins, W R Bryant, J. M. Williams	COGA	2,150
Progressive Church of Our Lord Jesus Christ, Inc.	1944	Joseph D. Williams Sr.	COOLJC	
Church of God in Christ Jesus (Apostolic)	1946	Randolph A Carr	PAW	
Original Glorious Church of God in Christ (Apostolic Faith), Inc.	1952	W. O. Howard	GCGCAF	25,000
Shiloh Apostolic Temple, Inc.	1953	Robert Doub	ACCG	
Pentecostal Churches of Apostolic Faith	1957	S. N. Hancock	PAW	25,000
Bible Way Church of Our Lord Jesus Christ World-Wide (BWWW)	1957	Smallwood Williams	COOLJC	250,000
Bible Way Pentecostal Apostolic Church	1960	Curtis Jones		
United Church of Jesus Christ Apostolic, Inc.	1961	James Thorton		2,000

Table 6.1. Continued

Denomination	Year Est.	Founder	Parent Body	Constituency
True Vine Pentecostal Churches of Jesus	1961	Robert Hairston		900
Free Gospel Church of the Apostles Doctrine	1962	Ralph Greene		
Mt. Hebron Apostolic Temple of the Lord Jesus of the Apostolic Faith, Inc.	1963	George Wiley	AGGC	3,000
Holy Temple Church of Christ, Inc.	1969	Joseph Weathers	WCCC	
The United Churches of Jesus Christ (Apostolic)	1969	Monroe R. Saunders	CGCJA	100,000
Apostolic Church of Christ, Inc.	1969	Johnnie Draft, Wallace Snow		
Apostolic Assemblies of Christ	1970	G. N. Boone	PCAF	3,500
Apostolic Church of Christ Jesus, Inc.	1970			
Universal Church of Christ	1972	Robert Jiggets, Jr.		
The House of the Lord and Church on the Mount	1930	Alonzo Daughtry	House of Prayer for All People	
United Way of the Cross Churches of Christ of the Apostolic Faith	1974	Joseph Adams	WCCC	1,100
Evangelistic Churches of Jesus Christ	1974	Lymus Johnson	COOLJC	
United Churches of Jesus Apostolic	1970	J. W. Audrey	ACCG	2,000
Redeemed Assembly of Jesus Christ Apostolic	1979	Douglas Williams, Frank Harris	GCCC	2,000
Living Witness of the Apostolic Faith		Charles Poole		
Greater Emmanuel Apostolic Church, Inc.		Quander Wilson		

7

SINGING THE LORD'S SONG IN A STRANGE LAND

BLACKS IN WHITE PENTECOSTAL DENOMINATIONS

For . . . those who carried us away captive asked of us a song,

And those who plundered us requested mirth,

Saying, "Sing us one of the songs of Zion!

PSALM 137:3 NKJV

THE AZUSA STREET REVIVAL UNFOLDED during one of the darkest periods in American race relations, when almost every segment of society operated with dual, segregated realities. Lynching was common in the South, and race riots occurred with regularity throughout the country.[1] What is more, most denominations and congregations were divided along the same rigid racial boundaries. Ten years earlier, the 1896 *Plessy v. Ferguson* Supreme Court ruling upheld racial segregation, declaring separate facilities for the races satisfied the Fourteenth Amendment so long as

---

[1]In the ten years surrounding the Azusa Street Revival (1901-1911), 932 lynchings of African Americans took place in the United States. During that same period, two of the most serious race riots in the country's history occurred in Atlanta in 1906 and Springfield, Illinois, in 1908.

they were of equal quality. The proclamation set a precedent for the next sixty years of American race relations. Jim Crow laws in the South and Border States mandated separate public accommodations, and de facto Jim Crow practices were lived out in almost every other area.

Yet Frank Bartleman depicted extraordinary racial harmony in early Pentecostalism, in which people of every race and culture gathered to experience God's presence.[2] They sang, prayed and danced in the Spirit; laid hands on each other to impart Holy Spirit baptism and healing; exhorted each other in sermons, prophetic pronouncements, messages in tongues and interpretation of those messages. The degree of equality that these Christians exhibited was unprecedented even within the Christian church, for they not only disregarded ethnic or racial heritage but also gender, class or other social qualifications in determining who would be allowed to participate, minister or take a leadership role at the revival.

Within eight years of its beginning, however, race relations had deteriorated to the point that the mission that housed it had become a small, predominantly black congregation, and most ethnic groups within the movement worshiped in separate congregations. Within twenty years of its start, racial, ethnic and often cultural separation within the movement was complete. Of course, racial lines between blacks and whites were most strictly adhered to in the southern states, where Jim Crow laws were strongest.[3] But racial and ethnic separation was also evident in the Midwest and West. With few exceptions, regular interaction between black and white Pentecostals had all but ceased.[4] Further, by the end of the same period, the Pentecostal movement would see a proliferation of new denominations, fueled in part by schisms rooted in doctrinal, social and personal concerns but none of them without the taint of racial politics.

Whatever the source of initial demarcation, most factions, and the denominations that sprang from them, would continue to follow the early pattern of racial segregation that began near the end of the revival. Several de-

---

[2]Frank Bartleman, *How Pentecost Came to Los Angeles: As It Was in the Beginning* (Los Angeles: Frank Bartleman, 1925), p. 54.
[3]This was also the area of the country where the Holiness Pentecostals had their strongest following and many of the Holiness Pentecostal groups had their denominational headquarters.
[4]The Oneness denomination, Pentecostal Assemblies of the World, maintained an interracial posture throughout most of the early history of the movement. Even presently, a small number of whites remain in the denomination.

nominations, including the Fire Baptized Holiness Church of the Americas and the Church of God in Christ, had earlier shown a degree of racial integration. But even these capitulated to the reigning cultural mores and divided along racial lines, leaving one major Pentecostal denomination—the Pentecostal Assemblies of the World—to extend its interracial witness beyond the movement's earliest years. Out of these factions would come a new alignment into two camps—one essentially white, the other predominately black.[5]

As denominational formation progressed, racial lines were never so tightly drawn that there was no slippage. Some whites eschewed racist tendencies to pursue unity with their black brothers and sisters, leaving Holiness and, later, Pentecostal churches still generally the most integrated religious bodies in the country. In the succeeding one hundred years, the majority of black classical Pentecostals have worshiped in solidly black congregations in predominantly black denominations headed by black leadership, with the vast majority in one body, the Church of God in Christ, and another large segment in the numerous oneness bodies, the largest being the Pentecostal Assemblies of the World.

Though they continued to find limited acceptance and experienced social and spiritual isolation from their white brothers and sisters, a number of blacks remained in or joined predominantly white Pentecostal denominations. Their presence within these groups has often been almost imperceptible, and generally they have suffered internal segregation and patriarchal attitudes. In *White Sects and Black Men in the Recent South*, historian David Harrell estimates that by 1958 approximately a half million blacks were affiliated with white denominations of some type, almost all in segregated congregations and only eight thousand in predominantly white congregations. He further estimated that twenty years later, in 1971, the situation remained largely unchanged.[6] David Michel estimates that by 1990 there were only forty thousand African American Pentecostals in predominantly white Pentecostal denominations.[7] While no newer num-

---

[5]Certainly there were other cultural and racial divisions within the nascent movement such as Latino and Russian, and other congregations began to emerge within a few years of the end of the Azusa Street Revival.

[6]David Edwin Harrell Jr., *White Sects and Black Men in the Recent South* (Nashville: Vanderbilt University Press, 1971), p. 41.

[7]David Michel, *Telling the Story: Black Pentecostals in the Church of God* (Cleveland, Tenn.: Pathway, 2000), p. 20.

bers are available, this represented less than 1 percent of the estimated seven million black Pentecostals and an infinitesimally small percentage of the African American population of thirty million in the United States at that time.

Few among this small yet significant number have risen to prominent positions. Still, within those denominations blacks have striven to make their presence known, keep their heritage as being both black and Pentecostal intact, and address the spiritual and material concerns of their communities with the limited denominational resources allotted them. Within these bodies, blacks are found in one of three patterns. Most often, as Harrell indicated, they lead or are members of predominantly black congregations. In some instances, they are members of largely white or multiracial congregations usually pastored and largely led by whites. Least often, they are members of predominantly black congregation pastored by whites. In the latter two instances, blacks have almost invisibly been subsumed by the broader ethos of white Pentecostalism their leaders purvey. Often these leaders shelter their congregations from denominational structures so that black members never come face-to-face with denominational racial politics.

Throughout the first half of the twentieth century, rigid segregation laws made it difficult for interracial bodies to provide adequate accommodations for blacks at national meetings convened below the Mason-Dixon Line. Since many of these groups were rooted in the southern Holiness movement, whites generally felt at home in the South and were often reluctant to accommodate their black brothers and sisters. As a result, black participation in national meetings was limited. And where denominational leadership was determined by electoral systems, opportunities for blacks were limited since smaller numbers ensured they seldom garnered enough votes to gain office. Where leadership was by appointment, officials of these bodies rarely appointed blacks to the most visible positions if they were not directly related to their own black churches and issues.

Further, those blacks who sought ministerial appointment in these bodies have historically found it difficult to obtain pastoral appointments with the same level of support as their white peers. Related, black pastors have been more likely to be bivocational and serve smaller congregations. Denominational media have rarely given black individuals or congregations the same level of coverage as whites, and contributions from black writers are conspicuously absent unless they specifically deal with evangelism within the urban context or depict some form of dysfunction within the black community.

Prior to the Supreme Court ruling in *Brown v. Board of Education,* Christian schools and institutions of higher education were no less likely than their secular counterparts to uphold racial restrictions. Educational opportunities at white Pentecostal institutions were generally closed to black students. Some larger, more established mainline denominations attempted to compensate by creating separate but certainly not equal educational programs for blacks. Less materially endowed Pentecostal institutions were unable to do this, leaving black constituents who desired education opportunities with no choice but to attend secular institutions or those supported by other faith traditions.

The pre–civil rights attitudes and behavior of white Pentecostal leaders toward black constituents can best be described as condescending and paternalistic and at worst outright patronizing. Yet, following the lead of secular society, the civil rights movement caused white Pentecostal bodies to gradually remove most vestiges of de jure segregation, while elements of de facto segregation remained—especially in the areas of leadership and allocation of resources. With the coming of the twenty-first century, Pentecostal bodies again followed the lead of secular society by putting into place a number of initiatives aimed at removing remaining barriers to racial cooperation so that a more conciliatory attitude has begun to emerge. Still, within classical white Pentecostalism, as with much of evangelical Christianity, African American enfranchisement still lags behind mainline churches, and blacks are still locked out of full participation and marginalized to varying degrees.

EXPERIENCES OF BLACKS WITHIN THE DENOMINATIONS

These generalizations are helpful for establishing a picture of the overall presence of blacks in white Pentecostal denominations. A more precise picture can be obtained, however, by looking more closely at the outworking of racial politics within particular Pentecostal denominations in the United States over the last one hundred years.

The Church of God (Cleveland, Tennessee). Harrell has asserted that of all the large (white) Pentecostal bodies, the Church of God (Cleveland,

Tennessee)[8] is the only one with a black membership.[9] While this assertion may be exaggerated, the denomination is the largest white Holiness-
Pentecostal denomination with the largest number of African American
constituents. Even so, the proportion of African Americans is relatively
small, accounting for less than 10 percent at the beginning of the twenty-
first century. More importantly, among Church of God blacks within
the United States, the majority are Afro-Caribbean or second- or third-
generation Afro-Caribbean descendents who are clustered in a small
number of geographic areas, including New England and the Southeast,
with the largest contingent in one state—Florida.

Several reasons could be suggested for a larger proportion of blacks in
the Church of God than in other white Pentecostal bodies. First, though
all white Pentecostal bodies practiced a degree of racism prior to the civil
rights movement, as one of the most solidly southern white Pentecostal
bodies, the denomination's congregations were concentrated in areas where
blacks clustered prior to the Great Migration. Such proximity often made
uneasy bedfellows, but it also led to cross-exposure in camp-meeting style
revivals generally open to racial interaction. Here people who had very
little daily social intercourse and who attended racially segregated churches
met in the most spiritually intimate setting to sing, pray, tarry, testify and
shout together. For a few short hours they shared a common experience of
the outpouring of the Holy Spirit. Much like slave masters a century earlier, white Church of God leaders had to concede that the blacks who
shared this encounter were brothers and sisters in Christ.

Second, since the majority of its early black Caribbean constituency had
united with the denomination while in their homeland, where their congregations flourished, they had not experienced the racial politics of the
denomination within the United States. It was only when large numbers
began to immigrate to the continent and attempted to set up separate congregations that they faced the reality of limitations. By then, however, a
degree of denominational loyalty had been established.

From its founding in 1886 as a Holiness denomination (the Christian
Union) until 1909, the denomination remained entirely white. By that

---

[8]The postscript is included with the name to distinguish the body with the Holiness denomination that shares the same name but is headquartered in Anderson, Indiana.
[9]Harrell, *White Sects and Black Men*, p. 42.

year, when Bahamians Edmond and Rebecca Barr were filled with the Holy Spirit at a camp meeting in Durant, Florida, joined the denomination and received ministerial credentials, the denomination had accepted the Pentecostal doctrine of Holy Spirit. At the time, there were about three hundred members in eight churches, and the Barrs' efforts led to the establishment of the first black Church of God congregation. Within three years, there were three additional black congregations in Miami, Coconut Grove and Webster, Florida, and the Barrs returned to their homeland to found its first missionary outreach.

Church of God historians have been reluctant to credit the Barrs with being the first denominational missionaries, instead giving that distinction to a white couple, R. M. Evans and his wife,[10] who joined the Barrs in the Bahamas in early 1910. Blacks within the denomination, however, maintain that this honor goes to the Barrs, whose work in the Bahamas, along with that of black leaders throughout the Caribbean, was to bear fruit for the denomination in two ways. First, it prompted the phenomenal growth of the Church of God, not only in the Caribbean but also wherever indigenous and foreign missions took root. Second, these congregations served as a recruiting station for other Caribbeans who would later immigrate to the United States as well as the United Kingdom to establish new congregations or swell the ranks of existing ones.

As the denomination's black constituency grew, so did concerns about how to handle the "race issue."[11] In 1912, Edmond Barr was appointed overseer of black churches in Florida, the state with the largest black representation. This move was both progressive and regressive. It was progressive in that it elevated a black man to an unprecedented position of denominational leadership but regressive in that it signaled the beginning of solidification of racial segregation in the denomination. During Barr's tenure, several blacks joined the denomination: in 1913, the first official ministers roster included 11 blacks out of 107 clergy.[12] Only 3 of the 45 ordained ministers—Edmond Barr, Samuel Rice and D. O. Will—were black. At year's end, five more blacks were on the roster. One of these was

---

[10]Early evangelical historians often reported spouses without identifying their first names.

[11]See, e.g., David Michel's discussion of the Haitian and Jamaican constituency of the Church of God (Cleveland, Tennessee) in *Telling the Story*, pp. 75-85.

[12]Charles Conn, *Like a Mighty Army: A History of the Church of God, 1886-1995*, rev. ed. (Cleveland, Tenn.: Pathway, 1994), pp. 132-33.

also ordained. Two years later, however, the denomination enacted a measure that erased any progress that had been made with Barr's appointment. It appointed a white man, Sam Perry, to oversee Florida's black churches, while retaining a separate overseer for Florida's white churches.

Between 1915 and 1922, race relations between the Church of God and its black constituency experienced a period of flux that generally followed the ebb and flow of the racial climate and black progress within American society. By 1915, nine black congregations had been established in Florida, and Barr was again appointed overseer of the state's black churches, essentially making him overseer of the entire "colored work" because, though at least one congregation had been established in Tennessee, the majority of black congregations were in Florida. Barr held the position for only two years, and in 1917, Perry was named overseer of the entire state, with oversight of both black and white churches.

Though blacks could attend the denomination's General Assembly, from the first years of their involvement, the largely southern denomination followed existing racial mores in assembly logistics. In most areas, separate seating was set aside for blacks; when the assembly was held in the South, the reality of segregated lodging and eating facilities ensured that blacks did not have access to the same caliber of accommodations as their white brethren. Further, the small number of blacks in attendance assured that no black person would be elected to any leadership positions not directly related to their own work, and black leadership was never showcased in either the spiritual or administrative sessions of these assemblies. So by the end of the second decade of the twentieth century, blacks, who were still concentrated in Florida and a few other southern states, requested and were granted the right to hold their own assembly while still attending the General Assembly.

Ambrose J. Tomlinson, the first general overseer of the Church of God, was aware that the denomination's blacks needed an outlet for their gifts and abilities unavailable within the existing assembly structure. In 1919, he created a separate worship service within the assembly for blacks to have an opportunity to lead, sing and preach under the watchful eye of church hierarchy. This token inclusion did not completely satisfy blacks, who continued to hold their separate assemblies. Yet even this was not enough for some. So in 1920, several black congregations left the denomination to join the Church of God in Christ.[13] For the next four years, though a number of blacks remained in the denomination, the major contact between the two races was sending representatives to each other's events.

As general overseer, Tomlinson tried to introduce progressive measures into denominational polity and to integrate African Americans more fully into the church. He repeatedly spoke to the general assemblies of the desirability of full relationships between all Christians regardless of race. Further, he openly lamented the limitation placed on interracial relationships south of the Mason-Dixon Line. His efforts generally met with resistance from other leaders or fell on deaf ears. In his 1913 work, *The Last Great Conflict,* Tomlinson was among the first white Pentecostal leaders to acknowledge William Seymour's influence on the Pentecostal movement.[14] Further, he was among a number of whites who began an early affiliation with Charles H. Mason.[15] As early as the 1920s, he appointed black ministers to key positions in the general church, including appointing five—J. H. Curry, W. V. Eneas, William Franks, David La Fleur and Thomas Smith—to serve as overseers of states with some white constituents. Several blacks also served on General Assembly subcommittees. Smith and John Shaw served on the Home Missions Committee, Thomas Richardson served on the Education Committee and C. F. Bright served on the Questions and Answers Committee.[16]

Despite Tomlinson's efforts, however, in 1922 another large exodus of black ministers occurred. This loss further seized Tomlinson's attention. Subsequently, when a delegation of blacks approached him to request that a black person again be appointed to oversee their work, he granted that request, noting that while he did not like separation between the races, "it [was] not always convenient, [nor] best, for different races to meet together regularly for worship."[17]

To stem the out flux, Tomlinson and the Committee on Better Gov-

[13]"Pentecostalism," in *Encyclopedia of African American Religions*, ed. Larry G. Murphy, J. Gordon Melton and Gary L. Ward (New York: Routledge, 1993), p. 590.

[14]Ambrose J. Tomlinson, *The Last Great Conflict* (1913; reprint, New York: Garland, 1985).

[15]Harold Hunter, "A. J. Tomlinson's Journey Toward Racial Reconciliation," *Church of God History and Heritage* (Winter-Spring 2003), http://faculty.leeu.edu/~drc/BlackMinistryExhibit/tomlinsonarticle.htm.

[16]Michel, *Telling the Story*, p. 38.

[17]Minutes of the Seventeenth General Assembly of the Church of God (Cleveland, Tenn.: Church of God Publishing House, 1922), pp. 25-26.

ernment created an autonomous black judicatory, appointing Thomas Richardson as overseer. White Church of God historians generally contend that pressure for racial segregation came equally from both races.[18] It cannot be ignored, however, that blacks were at least in part reacting to the lack of acceptance extended them by the general church. They did not want separation for separation's sake, because of prejudice against whites or the belief that they were inferior to whites. They sought an opportunity for full participation in the denomination's ecclesial structure of the general church and were aware that such opportunity was not forthcoming. Rather, they felt that that level of participation could only be experienced in a separate enclave.

Yet Richardson's appointment was to be short-lived; he served only one year. In 1923 Tomlinson, who had been under fire from other church leaders, ostensibly because of his autocratic governing style, was ousted as general overseer. There is some indication, however, that this move was due in part to his more progressive ideas regarding race, which offended some white colleagues.[19] With his departure, even limited openness to black leadership further declined. Richardson was loyal to Tomlinson and moved with him to his newly formed organization, the Church of God of Prophecy.[20]

On Richardson's departure, another black, David La Fleur was tapped to oversee the black work. By then, that constituency had grown to include several northern congregations. In 1925, La Fleur called the first black national assembly, with these northern blacks invited to attend. A year later, in 1926, a representative group of blacks again approached the General Assembly to request that they not only be allowed to hold their own assembly but also to elect their own leadership rather than serve under an appointed overseer. The General Assembly ratified both requests, though blacks who chose to do so could still attend the General Assembly. Further, overseer F. J. Lee instructed La Fleur that if "at any time, [he] de-

---

[18]See, e.g., H. Paul Thompson Jr., "On Account of Conditions that Seem Unalterable: A Proposal about Race Relations in the Church of God (Cleveland, TN)," *Pnuema* 25, no. 2 (2003): 240-64.

[19]See Harold Hunter, "A. J. Tomlinson's Journey," for a short discussion of how Tomlinson's views differed from that other Church of God leaders.

[20]From its inception, Tomlinson's new body, the Church of God of Prophecy, has shown a degree of racial inclusiveness that is absent from any other Pentecostal body except the Pentecostal Assemblies of the World. Blacks and other minorities have served in most levels of leadership throughout its eighty-year history.

cided that blacks had made a mistake, they could pass a resolution stating that they chose to remain with the Assembly as they were before."[21] In the short term, no such resolution was forthcoming and annual national assemblies continued for forty years.

Not all Church of God blacks felt separation was the solution. Some northern blacks, who presumably had not experienced the same level of discrimination as their southern brothers, were against it and approached the general overseer separately. They asked, and were granted, exclusion from the black judicatory and retention of General Assembly voting privileges. The overwhelming number of black congregations, however, remained in the South—the largest number in Florida. As a result, each black congregation was allowed to determine whether they would participate in the white assembly, the black assembly or both.

Despite the desire of most blacks to maintain a separate organizational structure, no leader emerged to direct black ministers and congregations into forming a separate black denomination. Indeed, internal problems among black ministers kept them from making the progress they had expected would be possible as a separate judicatory. Though no reason can be found in the records for the request, within two years, black leaders asked the General Assembly to rescind their power to select an overseer and reclaim appointive responsibility for itself, while blacks would retain power to ratify such an appointment.

When La Fleur resigned in 1928, he was succeeded by Bahamian John Curry, who served from 1928 to 1938. During his tenure a major structural change occurred in black church governance. Up until that time, the unofficial overseer of the black work had actually been the overseer of Florida's black churches.[22] The few other black churches throughout the country had been informally and voluntarily tied to this structure. Curry became official overseer of the entire black work, including the northern congregations who had earlier protested the arrangement. Yet blacks could still elect to attend either the general or national assembly or both.

In spite of little material support from the general church throughout

---

[21]F. J. Lee, Cleveland, Tenn., to Zephaniah Ambrose, Miami, December 23, 1926, cited in Thompson, "On Account of Conditions that Seem Unalterable," p. 259.

[22]To date, Florida remains the only state divided into to two jurisdictions, largely along racial lines. The Cocoa State Office serves the black pastors and congregations. The Tampa State Office serves a largely white constituency.

this period, black leaders were determined to meet the material needs of their constituency. In 1930, they began acquiring resources to build an auditorium in Jacksonville, Florida, to serve as the home for the local congregation, headquarters for the black work and facilities for the national assembly. This project progressed slowly because responsibility for its funding was left entirely to the blacks, with no assistance from the general church. As such, it became a major project for its women's auxiliary. Though partially constructed by 1932, final completion took more than twenty years, and the facility was not completed until 1954. A second project at first appeared to fare much better. Recognizing the need to care for less fortunate members of their communities, leaders proposed construction of an industrial home and school in Eustis, Florida. The first stage of the project was completed in 1934, again supported primarily by the fundraising efforts of the women's auxiliaries. With no substantial material support from the general church, the debt for the facility was not retired until 1948.

Norbert S. Marcell took the office of the overseer of the black work in 1938 and served until 1946. As his tenure began, the black work was heavily in debt because of the Jacksonville facility. Under his administration, however, the debt was retired, improvements were made in the facility and the boy's dormitory of the orphanage was completed. In 1944 blacks again sought and received permission to elect their own overseer, but little else changed for the next twenty years. The first overseer to be elected under this system was Willie L. Ford. During his first term, from 1946 to 1949, the debt for the orphanage was paid off and a national missions program was established among the black churches. George Wallace served from 1949-1954, the year that the Jacksonville auditorium was finally completed.[23]

Ford again served from 1954 to 1958. During this second tenure, blacks made slow, unsteady progress in expanding their congregations but failed to keep pace with the growth in white congregations. White leaders wanted more tangible growth among the black constituency, so following Ford's second tenure, they again rescinded the authority of blacks to elect their overseer, and the first white overseer of the entire "colored work," J. T. Roberts, was appointed. Though his appointment was controversial

---

[23]"Church of God Auditorium Completed," *The Church of God Gospel Herald* 13, no. 8 (1954): 3.

among blacks, he proved to be a sympathetic advocate of their needs and, ironically, in the seven years that he served as overseer, black churches achieved several important milestones. The number of congregations grew from 102 in nineteen states to 214 in twenty-four states, and membership more than doubled from little more than 2,900 to more than 7,600. Additionally he was able to negotiate favorable terms with lending institutions, which allowed the black judicatory to construct or improve several edifices.[24] In 1959 and again in 1960, he enlisted instructors from the still segregated Lee College to conduct summer Bible institutes for black ministers. The southern institute was held in Jacksonville, Florida, and the northern in Philadelphia. Most importantly, at the end of his tenure, Roberts presented a motion to the General Assembly to end segregation of the churches once and for all.[25]

The last overseer of the black work was David Lemons, son of an early Church of God pioneer. Lemons, who was white, took office in 1965, at the height of the civil rights movement and just as the racial strictures within the church had begun to give way. He served for only one year because, in 1966, the General Assembly voted to disband the colored work and dissolve the position of overseer of the black work. In its place, the General Assembly established the office of black liaison at its international headquarters and tapped H. G. Poitier, a black pastor who had been the secretary-treasurer of the colored work from 1949 to 1964, to serve as its head.[26]

Throughout the period of separation, black clergy and churches remained officially part of the General Assembly. Tithes and other finances from black congregations were still handled by the general secretary treasurer, though these were reserved for use by black congregations. Additionally, beginning around the 1950s, the denomination's national periodical, the *Evangel*, regularly reserved a space to promote news of the black work.[27]

---

[24]Presumably due partly to economic discrimination and partly to limited financial resources, black congregations had often been unable to secure favorable lending terms or finances for projects on their own.

[25]For a discussion of Roberts's tenure, see Michel, *Telling the Story*, pp. 33-34, and Crews, *The Church of God: A Social History* (Knoxville: University of Tennessee Press, 1990), pp. 168-70.

[26]Michel, *Telling the Story*, pp. 34-35.

[27]Before that period, it was rare to find any articles related to blacks within the denomination that did not center on the white evangelistic or missionary efforts or some perceived dysfunction within the African American community.

It carried stories of new urban outreach and evangelism but paid little attention to the myriad of problems facing black communities or general-interest stories that involved blacks. This task was left to the *Gospel Herald*, a publication first published in 1936. Peter C. Hickson, a pastor who served as the historian of the Church of God Colored Work, also edited the periodical, which continued to be published as a national publication until the early 1970s. After that period, it was published at the state publication for the all-black Cocoa District of Florida.[28]

Prior to the successes of the secular civil rights movement, the most gracious characterization of Church of God white leadership toward its black constituency would be paternalistic and reluctant. Paternalism was evidenced by acceptance of a philosophy that held that the black persons who filled the denomination's pews and supported it with their material resources were Ham's cursed descendants requiring imposition of the social restraints that Jim Crow laws implied. Like their southern neighbors, many Church of God leaders saw attempts to promote integration as coming from efforts by outside agitators with suspect political agendas, most probably with Communist leanings.

A 1946 survey given to an all-white sociology class at Lee College is indicative of the kind of racial prejudice prevalent in the Church of God at that time. It found that only 7.5 percent of the students indicated they would consent to a blood transfusion from a black person without reservation. Thirty-two percent indicated that they would take the transfusion in a life-or-death situation. Sixty-one percent responded that they would not have the transfusion under any condition. A majority of these students expressed concern that such a procedure might affect them negatively or transmit undesirable black characteristics.[29]

The tenuous efforts of obtaining a satisfactory resolution to the race issue is most evident in Florida, the state with the largest concentration of blacks in the denomination and the only state to remain administratively divided along racial lines. The number of blacks within the Church of God in Florida clearly rivals the white constituency in that state. Still, in

---

[28]At that time the subtitle on the masthead was changed from "Published in Interest of the Church of God Colored Work" to read, "Published in the Interest of the Church of God State Headquarters, Jacksonville, Florida."
[29]Charles R. Beach, "Jim Crow or Jesus Christ," (unpublished manuscript [Jan 8, 1947]), pp. 1, 6, cited in Crews, *Church of God*, pp. 165-66.

2007, the Cocoa state office is headed by an overseer with responsibility for black churches. The overseer of the West Palm Beach office leads white congregations within the state.

Election of a black person to a position of national authority did not occur until almost eighty years after blacks first entered the Church of God. In 1986, the General Assembly expanded the council of twelve to form the council of eighteen[30] and mandated that the body have a black member. Though there had previously been no black member of the council, that year, two blacks—prominent pastor Wallace Sibley and Goodwin Smith, then overseer of Bermuda—were elected. Even after this historic election, however, the real governing power of the denomination rests in the hands of the five-member Executive Committee, and by the end of the twentieth century, no African American had been elected to a coveted position as a member of that body. The new initiatives came about because blacks had gained a degree of political savvy where the church was concerned. For example, earlier black ministers who had been eligible for ordination saw no benefit in securing it. They now began to reconsider that ordination would give them voting power and some clout in the assembly. The denomination's black constituency had reached a critical mass such that their sheer numbers, if used astutely, could guarantee them a degree of enfranchisement.

Further, as the twentieth century drew to a close, racial attitudes within the denomination began to reflect the more open attitudes within American society, and denominational leaders wrestled with how to more fully integrate its African American constituency into the fabric of the church. Throughout the 1990s a number of aggressive steps were initiated by denominational leaders to increasingly involve a small number of blacks in more visible positions. While these moves signaled some progress, the resulting efforts have not been completely satisfactory for either blacks or whites. Some black leaders felt this was not enough and became more vocal in demanding a larger place within the denomination. At the same time, some whites within the denomination were still

---

[30]This body is elected from among the ordained male ministers during the biennial General Assembly to serve with the international executive committee (of five overseers) to form the international executive council, the body that establishes polity and directs the ministries of the church.

concerned that things might be moving too fast. The increasing tension sometimes resulted in blacks taking more aggressive steps to ensure that their voice was heard.

In 1995, a year after the all-white Pentecostal Fellowship of North America was restructured as the multiracial Pentecostal and Charismatic Churches of North America, two black pastors, Sam Ellis and Jesse Abbott, invited their colleagues along with several sympathetic white ministers to meet in Atlanta, Georgia, for a racial reconciliation conference. Though the conference was not sanctioned by denominational leaders, who attempted to dissuade individual ministers from attending, approximately thirty people, including some prominent white pastors, met together to explore race relations in the church. A year later, black ministers worked through the denominational structure to convene the Unity of the Spirit Conference at Lee University. This second meeting, which was sanctioned, drew black and white leaders for three days to discuss race relations in the denomination and, again, suggest possible solutions. Along with Church of God constituents, prominent black church scholars Leonard Lovett and Oliver Haney, both of whom were affiliated with the Church of God in Christ and the Interdenominational Theological Seminary, lent support to this effort by delivering papers on racism in the Pentecostal movement. These efforts were to bear some fruit in pushing the denomination to take a more visible stand in support of general equality both within the denomination and the broader society.

It was not until 2000, thirty-six years after the passage of the civil rights amendment, however, that the Sixty-Eighth General Assembly of the Church of God produced a resolution titled "Racism and Ethnic Disparity." This resolution went far beyond the 1964 resolution in using explicit language to refute earlier held presuppositions regarding racial equality.[31] David Harrell asserts that with the action taken in 1966 to eliminate the black judicatory, the Church of God became "perhaps the first southern church to integrate completely,"[32] and Carolyn Dirksen, Lee College vice president and religious scholar, further insists that "the structural change of the Church of God was actually completed before the Methodist Church

---

[31]Minutes of the Sixty-eighth General Assembly, 2000, p. 89.
[32]Harrell, *White Sects and Black Men*, p. 89.

moved on its black 'central jurisdiction.'"[33] Certainly, there were a few courageous white voices that pushed for more equitable treatment of blacks within the denomination. For example, Hollis Gause, celebrated Church of God theologian, has consistently warned that religion should not be used to justify social oppression such as racial prejudice and discrimination. He further admonished that such actions gave a ring of truth to the Marxist accusation that religion is the opiate of the people.[34]

Notwithstanding such assessments, the Church of God remains an essentially white body in structure with blacks primarily engaged in the life of African American congregations and initiatives and having little involvement in the life of the broader church. Despite a more openly espoused policy toward inclusiveness, congregations generally remain segregated—especially outside of large metropolitan areas. Members of black congregations remain largely tied to congregations and meetings promoted by black leaders. Some crosscultural involvement occurs in carefully structured activities. Blacks attend Lee University in record numbers. Youth camps and regional and national youth activities are integrated, but the leadership of these events is still essentially white. In 2006, Wallace Sibley was appointed as the denomination's director of home missions and evangelism, the only top-level position to be filled by a black person outside of the office of black ministries. Regional and national boards remain largely populated by whites, though some African Americans have begun to attain elected and appointed positions at this level. Several blacks serve on a few state boards,[35] including ministerial examining, home missions and evangelism, and youth boards. A number serve as district overseers over largely black districts. Yet the three-man leadership team[36] of the majority of state offices generally remains segregated.[37]

Why Church of God blacks never formed their own organization has

---

[33]Carolyn Dirksen, "A History of Black Churches in the Church of God," *Church of God Evangel*, February 28, 1972, p. 12.

[34]Hollis R. Gause, "The Beginning of Spiritual Decay," *Church of God Evangel* (April 23, 1962), p. 9.

[35]Most notably in states with heavy black participation in the denomination, such as New York, New Jersey and southern New England

[36]This team consists of a state overseer or administrative bishop, the director of evangelism and home missions, and a state youth director.

[37]For the names of these officials, see the Minutes of the General Assembly of the Church of God, published biennially by the denomination.

never fully been answered. One possibility is simply that no strong leader has emerged who could lead their ministers and congregations into a separate body, as W. E. Fuller had done when the Fire Baptized Holiness Church of America emerged from the Pentecostal Holiness Church. Another might be that blacks believed that white support—even patronizing white support—stood them in better stead within a racist society than they could achieve on their own. Presently, there are more than six hundred black congregations, approximately 10 percent of the more than 6,100 U.S. congregations[38] in the Church of God. Many of these still represent congregations whose members are of Afro-Caribbean descent. Indeed, the majority of the denomination's black congregations are still in the Caribbean or Great Britain. Many of these have never been affiliated with any other Pentecostal body through several generations.

The Church of God of Prophecy. When A. J. Tomlinson left the Church of God in 1923, he and his followers founded the Tomlinson Church of God, maintaining their headquarters in Cleveland, Tennessee, home of their parent denomination. Due in part to his Quaker foundations, Tomlinson's attitude on race differed markedly from many of his former colleagues, and from its outset he took steps to include blacks in the new body. Historian Harold Hunter indicates that a year after its founding, Tomlinson's church had black constituents in Florida, North Carolina, Georgia, Alabama, Kentucky, New York, Tennessee and the Bahamas.[39] A year later, the General Assembly passed a resolution against the Ku Klux Klan, becoming one of the few white Pentecostal bodies to do so.

From the outset, Tomlinson's openness allowed the Church of God of Prophecy (COGOP), as it came to be known, to forge a racial polity that differed significantly from its parent and other classical Pentecostal denominations. The denomination never established a separate enclave or steered blacks to other Pentecostal groups. As a result, from its inception, the COGOP has been arguably the most integrated of all predominantly white Pentecostal denominations.[40] The efforts of Tomlinson and his successors did not go unnoticed by the secular society or other white religionists. The denomination suffered persecution for its stand, and its ministers

---

[38]"Master Directory—Local," www.churchofgod.org/directory/churches.cfm.
[39]Hunter, "A. J. Tomlinson's Journey."
[40]Harrell, *White Sects and Black Men,* pp. 94-96.

were regularly imprisoned or subjected to violence for allowing or participating in mixed-race meetings.[41]

Several circumstances in Tomlinson's personal history, besides his Quaker sensitivities, opened him to a more inclusive racial posture. He was raised in an Indiana community with a substantial African American presence and was exposed to black-hosted summer camp meetings that attracted white worshipers as well. As a young man, he was introduced to the views of famous revivalist Charles Finney, who denounced slavery from the pulpit.

Though individual congregations tended to be set up and maintained along racial lines, regional and national assemblies were generally fully integrated. Blacks participated in General Assembly activities, not only as singers but also as preachers, leaders and members of important committees. While other white Pentecostal denominations maintained segregated recreational facilities to ensure that no unseemly racial mixing would occur among their young people, COGOP Bible training camps were integrated and openly used by all the denomination's constituents. Finally, while most white bodies pointed to Charles Fox Parham as founder of the Pentecostal movement or maintained that it was solely a work of the Holy Spirit with no specific human foundation, Tomlinson was among the earliest white Pentecostals to praise "Dr. Seamore" (sic) and give priority to the Azusa Street Revival as a founder.[42] At the 1935 General Assembly, he spoke of the "middle wall of partition" that had been "broken down by the cross" and of the tragedy of the limited increase of black membership. The following year, the General Assembly proposed building an orphanage for children of color because the church is "for all races."[43]

Other white COGOP leaders shared Tomlinson's concern about the denomination's need to increase efforts to reach the black harvest.[44] At one General Assembly, for example, two white state overseers, W. M. Lowman and L. A. Moxley, preached sermons urging attendees to make efforts to reach all races. Tomlinson's 1941 General Assembly address again returned to the theme of breaking down the "middle wall of partition," but

---

[41]Hunter, "A. J. Tomlinson's Journey."
[42]Ibid.
[43]Ibid.
[44]Ibid.

his interest in racial reconciliation was not only targeted to the blacks; he also included Native Americans. And his efforts at reconciliation went beyond impassioned General Assembly sermons. He appointed several persons of color to high-level administrative posts. In some states, the COGOP may have been the first church to defy Jim Crow laws in their worship services. Today African Caribbeans, African Americans and Latin Americans are charged with the leadership of states whose composition includes European Americans as the majority.[45]

At Tomlinson's death in 1943, his son, Milton, continued the policy of full integration, ensuring that the organization's leadership included blacks at every level and that it was the largest racially mixed denomination in the South between the 1940s and 1960s.[46] Though not openly involved in the civil rights movement, the denomination was one of few white Pentecostal groups to consistently maintain that "racial distinction was sinful" and call other Pentecostal church leaders to account on the issue. In 1948, for example, the COGOP declined to join the segregated Pentecostal Fellowship of North America (PFNA) because of its racial polity.[47]

By 1991, African Americans accounted for 16 percent of the denomination's membership—more than any other predominantly white Pentecostal body—and blacks and other minorities have continued to hold leadership positions throughout the denomination. During the 1990s Bishop E. L. Jones served as general field secretary, and Adrian Varlack served as world missions secretary, coordinating all work outside the United States.[48] Currently two of the seven general presbyters are black. Bishop Sherman Allen serves as bishop over Africa, and Bishop Brice Thomson serves over

---

[45]Ibid.

[46]Harrell, *White Sects and Black Men*, p. 94.

[47]Cecil M. Robeck, "The Past: Historical Roots of Racial Unity and Division in American Pentecostalism" *Cyberjournal for Pentecostal-Charismatic Research* 14 (May 2005): www.pctii .org/cyberj/cyberj14/robeck.html. PFNA is a cooperative organization established in Chicago in 1948 by eight Pentecostal denominations for the purpose of "interdenominational Pentecostal cooperation and fellowship." PFNA was formed to help bridge doctrinal divisions. Several Canadian and U.S. Pentecostal bodies were members of the organization including the Assemblies of God, the Church of God (Cleveland, TN), the International Church of the Foursquare Gospel, the Pentecostal Holiness Church, Open Bible Standard Churches and the Pentecostal Assemblies of Canada. What is notable for our discussion, however, is that missing from this group was any representation from black Pentecostal bodies, including the Church of God in Christ, the Fire Baptized Holiness Church or the United Holy Church, who were invited to participate. Additionally, Oneness Pentecostal bodies were also excluded.

[48]Ibid.

the Caribbean and Atlantic islands, leaving the COGOP with the most racially inclusive leadership of any U.S. Pentecostal denomination.[49]

The Assemblies of God. As the largest Pentecostal body in the world, the Assemblies of God (AG) has more than 50 million adherents globally, and it is the face of classical Pentecostalism to much of the outside world, providing a window into the movement's social and spiritual conscience. Yet its racial legacy has been compromised by the very circumstances that brought it into existence, since it owes that existence, in part, to the type of racial schism that would be the hallmark of Pentecostal reality for the next one hundred years.

In 1907, the Church of God in Christ (COGIC), led by its black founder, C. H. Mason, was the only Pentecostal body chartered by the federal government to provide ministerial credentials. These credentials allowed pastors and evangelists to obtain discounted rail fares, and as the threat of World War I loomed, were vital for obtaining conscientious-objector status. So at first white and black Pentecostal ministers sought credentialing with Mason. The nature of the arrangement is unclear. Some contend it was a loose association and that Mason only lent his name to give the credentials legitimacy.[50] Others insist there was a formal association, and white ministers were under Mason's direct oversight. In either case, white ministers soon became dissatisfied with the arrangement, and by 1914 several, including Howard Goss, Eudorous Bell and D. C. O. Opperman, issued a call that invited "all Churches of God in Christ and All Pentecostal or Apostolic Faith Missions who desire truth" to meet in Hot Springs, Arkansas, "to cooperate in love and peace to push the interest of the kingdom of God everywhere."[51] While Pentecostals of all races regularly read the movement's numerous periodicals and presumably were privy to information about the meeting, letters to individual ministers excluded blacks and Latinos. In spite of this oversight, though none appear in the official picture, several blacks were present at the meeting, but they were relegated to segregated seating in the balcony.[52]

---

[49]Hunter, "A. J. Tomlinson's Journey."
[50]Robeck, "The Past."
[51]Eudorus N. Bell, "General Convention of Pentecostal Saints and Churches of God in Christ, Hot Springs, Arkansas, April 2 to 12, 1914," *Word and Witness* 9, no. 12 (1913): 1.
[52]Howard N. Kenyon, "Bishop Mason and the Sisterhood Myth," *AG Heritage*, spring 1987, p. 12.

Reportedly, Mason attended one session, delivered a sermon and gave his blessing to the new organization.[53] Nevertheless, the meeting essentially ended any semblance of the movement's racial unity, for the new body was almost entirely white. Though several white ministers stayed with the COGIC, a reported gentlemen's agreement between the two groups would come to color AG race politics for the next one hundred years. It would repeatedly surface as the "sisterhood myth." It insinuated that in the initial separation of the two bodies there was an understanding that COGIC would evangelize and minister to blacks and the AG would do the same for whites, not infringing on each other's territories and that if inquiries were made, individuals would be referred to either denomination based on race.[54]

Even this "understanding" did not preclude individual blacks from continuing to affiliate with the AG, and in 1915 African American Ellsworth Thomas, a pastor from Binghamton, New York, sought and received AG credentials. Thomas, who served until his death in 1936, was the first, and possibly the only, AG minister to have carried the designation "(colored)" on his credentials.[55] J. Edward Howard was ordained in 1919 and pastored in Newark, New Jersey, until withdrawing in 1926 because he felt "self-conscious about his position in [the] fellowship."[56] Isaac and Martha Neeley were among few blacks at the originating Hot Springs meeting. The two were subsequently appointed as missionaries to Liberia in 1920. Before gathering the necessary finances, however, Isaac was appointed associate pastor at historic Stone Church in Chicago in 1923. He died suddenly that same year, but the next year Martha went to Liberia as a single missionary, serving there until 1930. Though small numbers of individual blacks continued to be credentialed with the AG, it would be forty years later, in 1964, that another black couple, Edward and Ruth Washington, would receive a regular missionary appointment.

The racial makeup of the early AG was influenced by two realities:

---

[53]Willie T. Millsaps, "Willie Millsaps remembers C. H. Mason at Hot Springs," *AG Heritage*, June 6, 1984, p. 8. See also Bell, "General Convention," p. 1.

[54]See Howard N. Kenyon, "Bishop Mason and the Sisterhood Myth," *AG Heritage*, spring 1987, p. 12.

[55]Howard Kenyon, "Black Ministers in the Assemblies of God: Ellsworth F. Thomas First Black Minister Credentialed in 1915," *Heritage*, spring 1987, p. 11.

[56]Ibid.

geography and structure. First, the AG geographic sphere can be characterized as rural, smalltown and midwestern. Though congregations were found in other areas of the country, most were located in suburban areas with higher concentrations of whites rather than urban cores with black concentrations. Related, when the AG was most heavily concentrated in the southern portion of the Midwest and as congregations began to join the fellowship in significant numbers, AG leadership did not want to alienate white southern sensitivities by promoting integration. Second, during its earliest years the AG (which designates itself as a fellowship rather than a denomination) had no established racial polity and generally honored the sovereignty of local congregations, leaving each church to decide how it would handle the race issue. Since many white pastors were uneasy with the race issue, the denomination, essentially, did nothing.

By the late 1930s, however, a small but growing number of African Americans were affiliating with the AG, and some were seeking credentials. Increased interest in credentialing brought the matter of handling such requests to a head. Bruce Gibson, pastor of an interracial congregation in Winlock, Washington, served in ministry several years before being credentialed in 1935. Gibson left the AG when he moved east to pastor a black congregation, but rejoined after returning to the Northwest. In 1939, a brother Elison, pastor of a middle-class church in the Bronx sought credentials on the recommendation of Robert Brown, pastor of Manhattan's prestigious Glad Tidings Tabernacle. In keeping with the sisterhood myth, he was referred to the COGIC after the General Council deliberated on the issue and recommended that, if blacks apply for ministerial recognition, they only be granted license to preach in the district in which they are licensed or, if they desire ordination, be referred to "colored organizations."[57] One of AG's largest and most prominent churches, however, Glad Tidings in New York, not only had black members; but also its pastors, Robert Brown and Marie Burgess Brown, regularly allowed blacks to minister in the pulpit. One of the Brown's protégés, Harold Thompson, was accepted to Eastern Bible Institute,[58] licensed by the Eastern District in 1941 and ordained seven years later.

[57]General Presbytery Minutes, 1939, p. 2, quoted in Kenyon, "An Analysis of Ethical Issues in the History of the Assemblies of God," (Ph.D. dissertation, Baylor University, 1988), p. 84.
[58]Now Valley Forge Christian College.

BLACK FIRE

Though the AG vacillated between promoting and backing away from the sisterhood myth based on the expediency of the moment, it remained the rationale for postponing substantial action on the race issue. The General Presbytery repeatedly went through a series of deliberations that resulted in either tabling the issue or referring it for further study. In 1943, for example, the General Council considered a resolution to "promote missionary activity among our American colored people."[59] In the ensuing discussion, the situation in the South, the need for evangelism among African Americans and the question of whether such activity would be viewed as "competition" with the COGIC were reviewed. The resolution was finally referred to the executive presbytery for further study.[60]

When the General Council met in 1945, Bruce Gibson pled for creation of a colored branch within the AG, informing the council that he had established a Bible school to train black ministers that he hoped would affiliate with the Assemblies of God. In response, a resolution was put forth that resolved, in part, that the denomination "encourage the establishment of Assembly of God churches for the colored race and that when such churches are established they be authorized to display the name, Assembly of God—Colored Branch."[61] While noting that the black-white relationship within the AG was "conforming to American law and society," the resolution made it plain that the "work among blacks would remain 'distinct and separate,' and the Colored Branch would be under the supervision of the Home Missions Department. . . . Further it made it clear that '[no] transfers to or from any District [would] be given or received.'"[62] Gibson was tapped to head the project, but a year later, the General Presbytery reversed its decision, proposing instead the establishment of a "separate colored Pentecostal Church to which the denomination would lend 'assistance, counsel and financial aid,'" and requested that a follow-up report be made,[63] though no action was taken

---

[59]General Council Minutes, 1943, p. 13, cited in Kenyon, "An Analysis of Ethical Issues," p. 85.

[60]Ibid.

[61]General Council Minutes, 1945, p. 31, cited in Kenyon "An Analysis of Ethical Issues," p. 86.

[62]Ibid. This restriction did not exist for any whites in the denomination.

[63]General Council Minutes, 1946.

on that recommendation. Again, in 1947, the Resolutions Committee moved to establish a colored branch because a report conducted two years earlier saw "no testimony comparable to that of the Assemblies of God" being presented among U.S. blacks.[64] The council, again, set up a committee to study the issue and bring recommendations, though there is no record that such a committee was ever formed and the issue failed to materialize on the 1949 council agenda. By that year, deliberation of the council was overshadowed by another, more inflammatory issue—the New Order of the Latter Rain.[65] The AG never established such a branch.

It would be seven years before the council would again seriously consider race relations within the denomination. In 1956, the General Presbytery authorized a study on the questions of segregation and integration. The committee, formed a year later, found that the denomination had been guilty of neglecting the spiritual needs of African Americans while investing heavily in African missions.[66] It suggested that the inequity be redressed by offering assistance to black churches with similar doctrinal stances, establishing a (separate) structure for training leaders of black churches, providing assistance to "young black ministers outside of the AG and treating these black ministers as peers, and as equals."[67] At the same time, the document recommended that integration of AG churches was inadvisable since unresolved issues remained in the larger society. It cautioned that no public statement be made until absolutely necessary and warned that moving too rapidly could result in even "greater mistakes," since full integration would be detrimental to the AG's existing "Negro ministry," because black pastors were "educationally disadvantaged." It further took the position that capable black ministers would be left without employment if they had to compete with whites for pastoral placements since white congregations probably would not call a black pastor.[68]

---

[64]Minutes of the Twenty-Second General Council of the Assemblies of God, Grand Rapids, Michigan (September 4-9, 1945), p. 43.

[65]Richard M. Riss, "Latter Rain Movement," in *The New International Dictionary of Pentecostal and Charismatic Movements,* ed. Stanley Burgess, Eduard M. van der Maas and Patrick Alexander (Grand Rapids: Zondervan, 2002), pp. 830-33.

[66]"Segregation versus Integration," General Presbytery File 1, p. 8.

[67]Ibid., pp. 8-9.

[68]Ibid., p. 9.

Moreover, for the crafters of the report, full integration was problematic on two fronts. First, few African Americans would attend an integrated church where whites were in the majority, and second, "unsaved white people" would not "attend or allow their children to attend Sunday School where large numbers of blacks were in attendance."[69] The report recommended that the AG move slowly. Accommodation of regional differences that would not hinder progress and expansion would become the denomination's position.[70] But the issue was not settled, and in December 1958, the AG named a final committee to study the feasibility of establishing some form of "Colored Fellowship." After a year of deliberation, its report differed little from that made thirteen years earlier and was tabled with no publicity.

In the wings, the number of gifted AG blacks was growing, and they were seeking, but not always finding, viable ministry positions. Still, some of these were having the kind of ministry success the AG could not ignore. Such success, along with mounting pressure for change from the surrounding society, was pushing the AG to reconsider its posture concerning race.

Robert Harrison became one of the most visible symbols of the denomination's racial inequity. Though not the first African American to seek and be denied credentials because of race, the exceptional Bethany Bible College student caught the attention of his professors who, after his 1960 graduation, encouraged him to seek AG credentials. But his request was rejected by the supervisor of the California-Nevada District because it was "not the policy of our denomination to grant credentials to Negroes."[71]

The statement made to Harrison was inaccurate on several counts. First, several districts, including the New York–New Jersey District, had been ordaining blacks for some time. In 1952, seven years after he had addressed the General Council about establishing a colored branch, Gibson had his AG credentials, and during the period in which he was not officially affiliated with the group he had continued to minister at AG meetings throughout the North. But, ironically, four decades before Harrison's request, Cornelia Jones Robertson, a prominent evangelist who had served as Harrison's grandmother, had been ordained with the same district in

---

[69]Ibid.

[70]Ibid., p. 7.

[71]Robert Harrison and James H. Montgomery, *When God Was Black* (Grand Rapids: Zondervan, 1971), p. 29.

1922 and pastored AG congregations in San Francisco and Oakland. Harrison, an experienced musician, pastor and evangelist, went on to join the Billy Graham evangelistic team, gaining national prominence traveling around the United States and to several foreign countries with one of the most visible ministries within evangelical Christianity. Once Harrison's work came to the attention of AG presbyters, they quickly granted him ordination. Nevertheless, he became an outspoken critic of AG racial polity and a proponent of progressive action.

During the 1950s and 1960s, AG leaders and publications were generally silent regarding the country's civil rights struggles, except to insinuate that protest might be coming from Communist agitation.[72] Two articles related to race were the only attention the *Pentecostal Evangel* gave the issue of race during that period. One dealt with witnessing techniques,[73] the other with what it saw as a dearth of a true biblical witness among blacks.[74] This silence was broken only by a number of caricatures depicting blacks in a less than flattering manner.[75]

A major artery for the infusion of blacks into the AG has been Teen Challenge, the ministry to gang members started by David Wilkerson in 1958 in New York City. By the end of the century, the program had grown to more than 170 U.S. centers, and its success proved a mixed blessing to the denomination. While providing a vehicle for thousands of every race to find deliverance from addictions, it introduced many to the AG for the first time. Gaining access they would have never otherwise had, the blacks and Latinos, as well as whites, who traveled and ministered with Wilkerson were hosted by white AG congregations. A number of these were drawn to the denomination, and several—including some African Americans—sought ministerial credentials. Thurman Faison entered the AG through Teen Challenge and worked with former gang leader turned evangelist Nicky Cruz in Brooklyn, New York, before planting successful congregations in Harlem and Chicago. He was thrust into the AG lime-

[72]See discussions of these attitudes in Gerald Sheppard, "Attitude of Pentecostals toward Civil Rights, Civil Liberties and Welfare Efforts" (paper presented to the Society for Pentecostal Studies, Dallas, November 8-10, 1990).

[73]Alma Ware Crosby, "Witnessing to Negroes," *Pentecostal Evangel*, August 6, 1961, p. 7.

[74]"U.S. Negroes Said to Be Without 'Pure Gospel,'" *Pentecostal Evangel*, April 1, 1956, p. 11.

[75]E.g., "U.S. Negroes Said to Be Without 'Pure Gospel,'" p. 11, asserted that "as far as the 'pure gospel' is concerned the vast bulk of (black) U.S. citizens are as ignorant as remote tribes in Africa, to whom no missionary has ever gone."

light when, in 1965, he became the first black minister to address the General Council and was heavily involved in efforts to improve the denomination's response to blacks. His work was the focus of the first article that the *Pentecostal Evangel* published highlighting the positive contribution of African Americans.[76]

In 1970, AG leaders met with a group of black pastors to hear recommendations on effectively ministering in the black community without competing with the COGIC. By this time, the body had begun to publicly condemn racism while acknowledging its presence within the church, and for the first time the General Council issued a statement asserting that racism and prejudice were "sins against God, who has created all humankind in His image." The statement called for repentance from those who had "sinned against God" by participating in racism through thought or action, involvement in church and social structures that upheld it, or by failure to address it. The statement ended with a definitive stand against racism, which said,

> We pray for God to give us the courage to confront the sin of racism where it may be found in our lives, in our churches, in our society structure, and in our world. We must cooperate with the Holy Spirit in actively rooting out racism at home and abroad and seeking the reconciliation of men and women to God and to each other.[77]

But that statement failed to put forth any concrete steps for bridging the gap that had developed between the AG and the black community, so none were initiated at that time.

Two years later, Spencer Jones entered AG ministry through another route, becoming one of the first black students to attend Central Bible College in Springfield, Missouri. Graduating in 1972, he has gained a degree of visibility that is rare for blacks within the AG, pioneering churches in Indianapolis, Minneapolis, Tampa, Orlando, Fort Lauderdale, Houston, Dallas, Gary and Charlotte before serving as pastor of Southside Worship Center Assembly of God in Chicago. He is one of only few blacks to have served as an executive presbyter and was a featured speaker at the denomination's 1993 General Council.

---

[76]Statement of the General Presbytery of the Assemblies of God Regarding Social Concern (Springfield, Mo.: General Presbytery of the Assemblies of God, 1968).
[77]Ibid.

Some of the more material attempts to rectify the long-standing breach between the AG and its black "sister denomination" came from grass-roots efforts by AG pastors and congregations rather than the leadership. In 1992, for example, New Orleans minister George Neau founded the first School of Urban Missions as an independent institution to provide ministerial training to low-income inner-city students. Once the school showed some success, the AG lent its name and support. In 2004, it entered into an agreement with the COGIC to operate the school. The 2005 devastation of Hurricane Katrina displaced several students, forcing them to move to a second campus, launched in 1999 in Oakland, California. By 2006, approximately 130 students, 65 percent of them African American, were working toward an associate of arts degree in biblical studies.

In 1998 the National Black Fellowship (NBF) was created as "a representative voice for blacks within the AG" to aid evangelizing the black community while providing renewal, fellowship, training and other assistance to black pastors and congregations. Zollie Smith, a highly visible black person in the AG who had previously been assistant superintendent and later executive secretary of the New Jersey District was tapped to serve as president. By 2006, the NBF was being called on to help formulate new strategies for including minorities.[78]

As the Assemblies of God has moved into the twenty-first century, a new willingness to engage ethnic diversity and racial reconciliation has emerged among its leadership. AG leaders were at the center of those calling for the disbanding of the all-white Pentecostal Fellowship of North America and the forming of interracial Pentecostal and Charismatic Churches of North America. AG expenditures for urban outreach into communities largely populated by African Americans have been expanded, and as a result the denomination has seen substantial growth in the number of African American and multiracial congregations. Between 2003 and 2006, the percentage of blacks in the AG reportedly grew from 6.7 to 8 percent.[79]

The Pentecostal Holiness Church. The Fire Baptized Holiness Church

---

[78]In 2007, Smith became the director of U.S. mission, the first black member of the AG executive presbytery.

[79]"District Summary for Number of Adherents by Race, 2006," Assemblies of God Vital Statistics Report, 2003 and 2006, http://ag.org/top/About/Statistics/Statistical_Report_2 and http://ag.org/top/About/Statistics/Statistical_Report_2006.pdf.

(FBHC), founded in 1898 by J. H. Irwin, had been interracial from its
inception, not only holding interracial conventions but also supporting integrated congregations. Within its ranks was William E. Fuller, a prolific
African American church planter who was one of four members of its executive board during its earliest years. Besides Fuller, who had previously
served as ruling elder of South Carolina, several blacks held important
positions, including Alice M. McNeil from Fayetteville, North Carolina,
who served as a ruling elder; Isaac Gamble from Kingstree, South Carolina; and Uncle Powell Woodbury from Marion, South Carolina.[80] And
Irwin held meetings in cooperation with the African Methodist Episcopal
Church in his hometown of Lincoln, Nebraska.[81]

Still, the attitude of Pentecostal Holiness Church affiliate G. B. Cashwell, who almost single-handedly introduced Pentecostal spirituality to
Holiness groups in the Southeast, exemplifies the benevolent paternalism
or ambivalence held by many white Holiness and Pentecostals. On the one
hand, Cashwell's 1903 report to church leaders mentioned that the black
churchgoers he encountered in his evangelistic travels "seemed to be filled
with the Spirit, and the white people of the community say they live it. . . . I
expect to meet many of them in the kingdom of Jesus."[82] Yet Cashwell
exhibited some of the same concerns about blacks as many of his white
southern brethren. Though drawn to the Azusa Street Revival by reports
of the Spirit's outpouring, Cashwell was disquieted by the thought of sitting under Seymour's ministry and even more disconcerted about having
blacks lay hands on him to pray for Holy Spirit baptism. Vinson Synan
asserts, however, that after five days of seeking, he discarded racial feelings and invited Seymour and several others to lay hands on him, so that
finally in early December, 1906, he received the Pentecostal experience.[83]

In 1908, the same year that Cashwell's ministry was instrumental in the

---

[80]"Official List of Ordained Evangelists," *Live Coals of Fire* (Lincoln, Nebraska) 1, December 1,
    1899, p. 8, and "Official List of The Fire-Baptized Holiness Church," *Live Coals* (Royston,
    Georgia) 3, January 11, 1905, p. 3.
[81]Craig Charles Fankhauser, "The Heritage of Faith: An Historical Evaluation of the Holiness
    Movement in America" (M.A. thesis, Pittsburg State University, Pittsburg, Kans., July 1983),
    p. 121.
[82]G. B. Cashwell, *Holiness Advocate*, Oct 15, 1903, quoted in Paul Harvey, *Freedom's Coming:
    Religious Culture and the Shaping of the South from the Civil War Through the Civil Rights Era*
    (Chapel Hill: University of North Carolina Press, 2005), p. 134.
[83]Vinson Synan, *Old Time Power* (Franklin Springs, Ga.: Advocate Press, 1973), pp. 107-8.

denomination's adopting the doctrine of initial evidence, Fuller approached the other board members requesting that black congregations (many of which he was instrumental in founding) be allowed to form a separate body, in part because segregation laws made it impossible to secure adequate facilities for interracial meetings. When he left, he took the one-third of the denomination with him to form the Fire Baptized Holiness Church of America, an entirely black denomination, leaving an entirely white denomination, the Fire Baptized Holiness Church, behind.

Three years later, in 1911, the white Fire Baptized Holiness Church joined the predominantly white Pentecostal Holiness Church (PHC) of North Carolina, founded in 1900 by A. B. Crumpler, and took the designation of the latter group as its new name. Prior to the merger, the PHC was only loosely affiliated with black congregations or infrequently held interracial revival meetings. Sometime before the merger, a separate "colored convention" was formed among the blacks who had remained within the FBHC. This convention was adopted into the new church, and since by 1911 there were a number of African Americans still in the denomination, the assembly set aside one of the eight existing regional conventions as a separate "colored convention."

The PHC maintained that the partitioning of blacks within the parent body was by mutual consent, with the initiative for the action coming from blacks. In reality, both whites and blacks were cognizant of the criticism their interracial meetings engendered from outside whites, and blacks often saw the treatment they received from their PHC leaders as patronizing and condescending. Rather than suffer the indignity of being partitioned, the black convention subsequently withdrew. In 1913, the general conference voted to drop this colored conference from its rolls and expel the black congregations.[84] But instead of joining the existing black Fire Baptized Holiness Church that had been formed under Fuller, they formed the autonomous Black Pentecostal Holiness Church.[85]

Within two years, the two Pentecostal Holiness Church bodies had no official contact with each other. Neither did the white Pentecostal Holiness Church have official contact with the black Fire Baptized Holiness Church. After that time, most instances of interracial worship occurred

---

[84]Ibid., p. 147.
[85]Ibid.

either when whites visited black churches to hear white ministers like G. F. Taylor or Cashwell preach or, more frequently, in the less structured environment of revivals and camp meetings. Indeed, almost all evidence of earlier black involvement in the Pentecostal Holiness Church is absent from both the official records and popular accounts of denominational history for several years following the last split.

Interestingly, though Fuller had been a prominent member of the Fire Baptized Holiness Church and was actively involved in leadership within the body, J. H. King made no reference to his involvement when he wrote its history in 1921; and the only contact this black leader had with his parent organization was when he attended the funeral of his former mentor in 1946. Throughout the intervening years, individual blacks were still attracted to specific white PHC congregations, but for a number of reasons, black participation in the Pentecostal Holiness Church has been minimal. Though in 1922, the General Board overturned its earlier stand and agreed that "anyone, regardless of race, should be accepted into the denomination,"[86] the overture was complicated by several restrictions. Among these were the insistence that "the colored element shall always be confined to the Conference, or Conferences, north of the Mason-Dixon line"; "no colored person shall ever hold office in an Annual Conference"; and "no colored person shall ever be a delegate to a General Conference."[87]

PHC leaders agreed with other white Pentecostals that Holy Spirit baptism was available to all without regard to social category, but that this shared spiritual experience did not lead to a change in one's social situation or elevate blacks from their God-ordained lower station. For example, to answer the question, "Where did the negro come from?" the editor of the *Pentecostal Herald* responded, "The colored man comes from Ham. . . . His descendents were a consequence of the curse pronounced on him . . . to be inferior and servant-like people."[88] In the years immediately following World War II, the PHC determined that "the most practical way of reaching the South's colored people" was to "work through established colored churches."[89] It was certainly not prepared to consider a strategy promoting

---

[86]Ibid., p. 329.
[87]Minutes of the General Conference of the Pentecostal Holiness Church, January 4, 1922.
[88]Paul F. Beacham, "Light on the Subject," *Pentecostal Holiness Advocate* 49 (1960): 10.
[89]Harrell, *White Sects and Black Men*, p. 41.

integration of blacks into its structure, contending that "opening the doors of our church to colored people generally has never been either practical or necessary."[90]

Eventually, even such entrenched attitudes had to give way to social pragmatism. As the civil rights movement moved into full swing at the end of the 1950s and communities and congregations were facing the race question head on, the general executive board appointed a committee to investigate avenues of communication between the Pentecostal Holiness Church and black Pentecostals. By 1965, as Pentecostal bodies were still wrestling with finding more moderate language to articulate a racial posture, the Pentecostal Holiness Church's General Executive Board was directed to "seek to establish communication with sincere religious leaders among American Negroes . . . form Negro Associate Conferences and . . . constructively assist our Negro friends with the moral and spiritual problems . . . so prevalent and so pressing."[91] The 1969 General Conference adopted a resolution affirming the church's commitment to "not discriminate against any person due to race, color or economic status." Eight years later, in 1977, PHC leaders appointed Thadeus White as liaison to black congregations within and outside the denomination. In 1979, the denomination signed an agreement with the United Holy Church in which the two bodies agreed to recognize each other as sister Pentecostal churches.[92] By 1980, the PHC was taking a more progressive posture—establishing and strengthening relations with predominantly black denominations and making specific advances to the Fire Baptized Holiness Church, its daughter denomination, which it had ignored for decades. In 1998, for example, when the FBHC celebrated its centennial, PHC leaders were on hand for the first time, with PHC presiding bishop James Leggett joining Bishop W. E. Fuller Jr., son of the FBHCA founder, on the podium.

In 1991, presiding Bishop B. E. Underwood, who was president of the all-white Pentecostal Fellowship of North America, joined in initiating steps that would lead to one of the defining moments in late-twentieth-

[90]Ibid.

[91]Minutes of the Fifteenth General Conference of the Pentecostal Holiness Church, 1965, 72, cited in Vinson Synan, *The Holiness-Pentecostal Tradition: Charismatic Movements in the Twentieth Century,* 2nd ed. (Grand Rapids: Eerdmans, 1997), p. 185.

[92]Synan, *Holiness-Pentecostal Tradition,* p. 185.

century American Pentecostalism when that body would be dismantled and rebirthed as the multiracial Pentecostal and Charismatic Churches of North America. During "The Memphis Miracle" (as it came to be known), Underwood led pastors in a time of repentance and reconciliation that, presumably, would open a door for change throughout the movement. Two years later, in 1996, Underwood again led the denomination, which had by now taken the designation of International Pentecostal Holiness Church (IPHC), in convening a solemn assembly in which racism was among seven sins for which it repented, along with sexism, spiritual pride, judgmentalism, controlling spirit, male domination, elder brother syndrome and greed. This assembly is only one indication that white Pentecostals had finally come to see racism in spiritual rather than pragmatic terms and that white leaders had begun to own their part in perpetuating this sin. In regard to the "sin of racism," the missive from the IPHC confessed, "We weep for this dark blot on the pages of our history."[93]

In January 2004, Macon Wilson became the first director of African American ministries in an attempt to link black IPHC congregations with training and resources in church planting, church growth and pastoral ministry. After decades as a primarily southern, rural denomination, and despite what the denomination characterizes as a new urban thrust of church planting in major American cities, the presence of blacks within the IPHC can at best be described as insignificant. In 2005, while there were only 27 African American congregations in the IPHC (in comparison to 381 Latino congregations), the denomination held its first National African American Conference in Houston, Texas. In that same year, another 100 congregations were characterized as multicultural. Presumably these are majority white or mixed congregations that have some black

[93]"Sin of Racism," Liturgy from the Solemn Assembly of the International Pentecostal Holiness Church, August 23-24, 1996, Fayetteville, N.C., http://arc.iphc.org/solemn/racism.html. Specifically the missive declares "We confess that racism, with its hatred, bigotry and exclusion, is a sin which has brought division to the body of Christ. We have excluded a part of our Pentecostal heritage. By doing so, we have lost blessings of life and growth that could have been ours. We confess that we have overtly and covertly participated in our racist culture. We failed to support our Black brothers and sisters in their long struggle for equal rights. We now renounce and turn from our racist views and actions and celebrate our unity and equality in the body of Christ."

membership.[94] One of the most prominent blacks in the Pentecostal Holiness Church is E. V. Hill II, pastor of Calvary Temple Pentecostal Holiness Church in North Hollywood, California, and son of renowned Missionary Baptist pastor and preacher E. V. Hill Sr.

The International Church of the Foursquare Gospel. According to historian James Tinney, the International Church of the Foursquare Gospel is the only Pentecostal body in which thoroughly integrated congregations are more than minimal.[95] Yet, possibly because blacks are so well integrated into existing congregations, they are the least visible community of African American Pentecostal believers. The flamboyant early Pentecostal leader Aimee Semple McPherson openly challenged many early Pentecostal and societal mores. Not the least aspect of this defiance was her refusal to uphold racial conventions that had solidly reemerged within the Pentecostal movement.

McPherson also ignored legal race restrictions, openly allowing people of all races to attend her meetings across the country, even when preaching in the South. Where law or custom made it impossible, McPherson held separate meetings—one for whites and one for blacks. Several blacks served in leadership roles in these meetings, working in the music ministry, as prayer counselors or as altar workers. Worship at McPherson's church, Angelus Temple, regularly featured singing of Negro spirituals, and McPherson encouraged the forming of quartets to perform that music.[96] McPherson's regard for prolific African American hymn writer Thoro Harris led her to work with him to composed at least two hymnals for Angelus Temple.[97]

Three months after building Angelus Temple, McPherson opened the Lighthouse Institute for Foursquare Evangelism (LIFE) Bible College. Immediately blacks were admitted, and black Angelus Temple members

---

[94]International Pentecostal Holiness Church, "Ethnicity Non-Anglo U.S. Churches & Members 2005," *2007 Statistical Report for Year Ending December 2006*, http://info.iphc.org/globaldesk/2007/Ethnicity.jpg.

[95]James S. Tinney, "Black Origins of the Pentecostal Movement," *Christianity Today*, October 8, 1971, p. 6.

[96]Doretha A. O'Quinn, *Silent Voices, Powerful Messages: The Historical Influence and Contribution of the African-American Experience in the Foursquare Gospel Movement* (Los Angeles: International Church of the Foursquare Gospel, 2002), p. 35.

[97]Thoro Harris and Aimee Semple McPherson, *Pentecostal Revivalist* (Los Angeles: Aimee Semple McPherson, 1920); Aimee Semple McPherson and Thoro Harris, *Foursquare Favorites* (Los Angeles: Echo Park Evangelistic Association, 1929-1935).

were encouraged to attend. There were four black students in the first class, with thirty-six blacks graduated from the college in the 1920s and 1930s.[98] Curiously, most of these found places to minister at Angelus Temple, while others went out to start congregations outside of the Four-square movement, because unlike their white classmates, the earliest black graduates of the college did not receive Foursquare pastoral appointments. Such an appointment would not come until 1942, when Wardell and Pearl Oliver were appointed to plant a new congregation, Hooper Avenue Zion Foursquare Church in Los Angeles.[99] That work began with ten members in a renovated rooming hotel but grew to be a significant work among the black Foursquare constituency. It was not until twenty-five years later, in 1967, however, that the first black man, Paul Hackett, professor of Old Testament, was asked to join the LIFE Bible College faculty—though even this late date presumably made him the first African American to be appointed to the faculty of a predominantly white Pentecostal academic institution.

McPherson was noted for her association with secular personalities, including such stars and politicians as Anthony Quinn, who played saxophone in the church band as a teenager; Charlie Chaplin, who designed sets for her illustrated gospel messages; and journalist and social critic H. L. Mencken. But she also associated with Christian leaders of all varieties, including African Americans pastors Emma and Henry Cotton. McPherson highly esteemed the Cottons, and on several occasions they shared what had become, by that time, one of the most visible pulpits in the Pentecostal movement. In 1936, the Cottons spearheaded a six-month-long thirtieth Azusa Street anniversary celebration at Angelus Temple that boosted McPherson's then declining congregation and helped bring it back into prominence. During that time, the Cottons joined other notable Pentecostal speakers to minister daily in multiracial worship services reminiscent of old Azusa Street meetings that drew thousands to experience preaching, prayer, shouting, dancing in the spirit and divine healing. McPherson credited these meetings with being the launching pad that

---

[98]O'Quinn, "Appendix A: African American Students of Life Bible College, Los Angeles California, 1920-2000," in *Silent Voices, Powerful Messages: The Historical Influence and Contribution of the African-American Experience in the Foursquare Gospel Movement* (Los Angeles: International Church of the Foursquare Gospel, 2002), pp. 206-13.
[99]O'Quinn, *Silent Voices*, pp. 39-42.

attracted renewed worldwide attention to the Pentecostal movement.[100]

Despite her seeming progressiveness, McPherson's racial politics were puzzling. Openness to active participation of blacks in the Foursquare Church did not preclude her maintaining a long-standing relationship with the Ku Klux Klan. She accepted their money and preached in secluded meetings. Reportedly, however, her association with the extremist group did not stem from common race notions, since she openly challenged their racist beliefs and secretiveness on several occasion. What she held in common with the Klan was a fundamentalist interpretation of religion and old fashioned moral ideals that supported prohibition and stood against socialism and Communism.[101]

Following McPherson's death, the racial openness in the Foursquare Church abated somewhat, and her successors were less receptive to its African American constituency. Blacks felt less welcomed in local congregations as well as regional and national denominational meetings. Though no separate black enclave was formed, a single designation, "Zion," was coded into the names of all black churches. Further, district superintendents often showed a degree of racial insensitivity when dealing with black congregations, creating a climate of distrust and aggravation for their pastors. Still, while Foursquare leaders publicly asserted a desire to increase minority participation in missions, going as far as placing an ad in the *Foursquare Advance* and asking blacks to apply to go to the mission field, they often found reasons to restrict blacks from such missions appointments. When Marie Johnson applied for a missionary appointment to Brazil in the 1940s, for example, her application was denied due to "concern for the health of an African American to deal with the climate differences of foreign countries."[102] She was later to make the trip on her own.

Yet, within this less attractive climate, a small number of black Foursquare congregations began to form, and a small number of black individuals and families who joined predominantly white Foursquare congregations continued to grow. In neither case was a critical mass of blacks ever formed, nor did blacks ever formally break with the denomination, as did

---

[100]Aimee Semple McPherson, *This Is That: Personal Experiences, Sermons and Writings of Aimee Semple McPherson* (Los Angeles: Echo Park Evangelistic Association, 1923), pp. 245-47.
[101]Edith L. Blumhofer, *Aimee Semple McPherson: Everybody's Sister* (Grand Rapids: Eerdmans, 1993), pp. 179-83, 235-45.
[102]O'Quinn, *Silent Voices*, p. 113.

those in the Fire Baptized Holiness, or set up a separate enclave, as did those in the Church of God. But as hostile treatment from leaders continued, members of black Foursquare congregations simply refused to participate in denominational events, choosing rather to attend meetings with other black denominations. When black women, for example, felt ostracized at their own women's conferences, they decided to attend those given by the Church of God in Christ.[103]

As of 2002, seventy-three of nineteen hundred U.S. Foursquare congregations had black pastors.[104] The majority of these, like most Foursquare congregations, are located along the West Coast in areas that have historically had smaller concentrations of blacks. In recent years, however, Foursquare leaders have sought to increase African American representation. In 2004, the denomination established a Department of Urban and Multicultural Ministries to "assist and support urban leaders serving serve minority congregations" by focusing on church planting and outreach and tapping Art Gray, who had been appointed two years earlier to the highly visible position as corporate secretary, to serve as executive director.[105]

United Pentecostal Church. While oneness Pentecostals are quick to point out that they were able to maintain an interracial posture longer than any trinitarian Pentecostal body, the largest oneness body in the United States—the predominantly white United Pentecostal Church—began as a splinter group from the multiracial Pentecostal Assemblies of the World (PAW), reflecting the same stormy racial history, and currently exhibits a racial pattern that mirrors its trinitarian siblings. The United Pentecostal Church resulted from an amalgamation of the whites who left the PAW in 1924 to form the Apostolic Churches of Jesus Christ with another predominantly white denomination that would come to be known as the Apostolic Church of Jesus Christ.

In 1931, the group's leaders proposed a merger with the PAW that would allow the two bodies to again form a multiracial denomination with the stipulation that the two groups would essentially maintain separate governing structures. With that possibility rejected, the white groups came

[103]Ibid., p. 42.
[104]Ibid., pp. 214-18.
[105]"Rev. Arthur Gray, Director of Urban and Multicultural Ministries," www.foursquare.org
/news/article/five_highly_significant_announcements_regarding_people.

together to form the Pentecostal Assemblies of Jesus Christ. Despite its beginnings, the new organization took steps to ensure that racial disparity within its ranks would be minimized. Early on, its leaders determined that the governing presbyter board would consist of twelve members—six white and six black. Four of the first five general assemblies had to be held in the North because black members could not secure adequate accommodations in the South. Yet this caused a hardship for southern white pastors who could not afford the cost associated with traveling north.

In 1936, the General Assembly made the policy that presbyter board representation should reflect the denomination's racial composition, which at that time was 80 percent white and 20 percent black. Yet apparently such overtures offended many of the blacks who remained in the organization, and at the 1937 General Assembly, several resigned and returned to the PAW. Presumably, this included all of the blacks on the presbyter board since after their departure this board was for the first time made up entirely of whites. Between 1938 and 1945, several more blacks left the organization to return to the PAW. In the latter year, the Pentecostal Assemblies of Jesus Christ and the Pentecostal Churches merged and formed the United Pentecostal Church (UPC). Though a small number of blacks have historically been affiliated with the UPC since its founding, initially African American ministers were not listed in the regular section of the ministerial directory. Instead, they were listed in the back of the directory in a section titled "the colored branch."[106]

Throughout much of the civil rights era, the United Pentecostal Church maintained the same relatively silent posture as its trinitarian siblings. Still, the denomination has generally characterized itself as interracial. When the Pentecostal Fellowship of North America was formed in 1948 as an Anglo-American organization, the UPC declined to join on two points: while it rejected the trinitarian doctrinal stance of the group, it also refused to relinquish its own interracial policy.

Today, UPC evangelistic efforts targeting blacks are centered on a national black evangelism conference that annually addresses the community's special needs and trains UPC ministers and laity to reach that community. Several thousand persons attend these events, which elects a

---

[106]"The Colored Branch," *Manual, United Pentecostal Church*, 1945.

director and board, which operates as part of the home missions division. While the denomination does keep racial statistics, the majority of the UPC's black constituency is Caribbean, with most of these coming from Jamaica.[107] The largest black congregation in North American, Faith Sanctuary in Toronto, Ontario, has over one thousand members. Granville McKenzie, the pastor of that largely Jamaican congregation, is the highest-ranking black in the UPC, serving as the executive superintendent of Canada. His church is one of the UPC's most successful congregations. It operates Faith Academy with classes for children up to sixth grade; a Bible college, Faith Institute; and a 150-unit nonprofit seniors' residence, located on-site.

Interestingly, while there are a number of majority black or integrated UPC congregations throughout the United States, African American blacks have been reluctant to attach themselves to the denomination, and black oneness denominations have been reluctant to associate with white oneness colleagues. Caribbean blacks have been less so, presumably because they do not attach the same racial history to its beginnings and unfolding. Within the United States, the largest black UPC congregations are located in large metropolitan areas along the East Coast. Additionally, there are a number of multiracial congregations scattered throughout the country.

The Apostolic Faith Church. The smaller bodies that developed over the life of the Pentecostal movement exhibit a variety of attitudes and practices regarding their black constituencies. Since these bodies generally operate under more authoritarian leadership than larger groups, they often reflect the racial attitudes of their leaders. Like Tomlinson's Church of God of Prophecy, Florence Crawford was socially progressive in many ways. Two influences within her life possibly gave Crawford a more liberal attitude concerning race and the inclusion of blacks within the Apostolic Faith Church. First, Crawford was raised by parents who, along with their colleagues, were free thinkers, many of whom were abolitionist. Second, in her secular rescue and social service work, Crawford had come into contact with people from many cultures and economic classes. Her background suited her to be integrally involved in the racially inclusive atmosphere of

[107]Interview with Robin Johnston, curator of the archives of the United Pentecostal Church International, September 19, 2007.

the Azusa Street Revival, where she worked closely with its African American founder, William Seymour, in strategic positions of leadership. During the revival, she had led interracial evangelistic teams throughout the Northwest in promoting the message of the revival. As a result, her organization was considered a model of interracial fellowship. She also regularly led interracial evangelistic teams throughout the Northwest.

As a result, Crawford's Apostolic Faith Church exhibited an open attitude toward blacks and racial mixing.[108] According to Ernest Williams, an early AG leader, even after the initial period of racial harmony had ended for much of the movement, there were still a few pockets that refused to bend to the racial pressures of the day. He noted that Crawford's Apostolic Faith movement was among them and that it "made no distinction [in race]. There was great freedom . . . to testify . . . speak . . . praise the Lord. And God's blessing was upon them irrespective of their color."[109]

Though some might see Crawford's reluctance to continue serving under the leadership of a black man as contributing to her abandoning Seymour's Azusa Street Mission, there is no support for such a charge. Indeed, the denomination she established has consistently shown the strongest record of racial equality of all predominantly white Pentecostal groups, and the interracialism of the Apostolic Faith Mission permeated every aspect of the ministry. The literature of the organization reflected its multiracial commitment. *Higher Way*, the official magazine of the denomination, continues to regularly carry stories of ministry to and by blacks in a number of cities, and Sunday school literature continually reflects the awareness of issues within the black community. Further, the region where the Apostolic Faith has had its greatest impact is in Sub-Saharan Africa, where there are several hundred churches. More important, and unlike the Foursquare Church, the interracial witness of the Apostolic Faith Church outlived its founder. Even today the denomination is noted for its multiracial congregations and openness to people of color at every level of leadership: in local congregations as well as denominational responsibility.

---

[108]Klaude Kendrick, *The Promise Fulfilled: A History of the Modern Pentecostal Movement* (Springfield, Mo.: Gospel Publishing House, 1961), p. 58.
[109]Ibid., p. 43.

CONTEMPORARY PATTERNS OF INTERRACIALISM

Though Pentecostal denominations appear more integrated than mainline churches, the figures within classical Pentecostalism may be skewed by a small number of highly visible, integrated megachurch congregations.[110] In reality, the number of blacks worshiping in white congregations or in predominantly black congregations under white leaders is significantly less than those in black congregations. As secular attitudes toward racial openness are changing, however, these former numbers are growing. The shift began almost immediately at the end of the 1960s civil rights push, when changing housing and school patterns brought members of the races into increased personal interaction for the first time, and the congregations that have resulted from this openness take a variety of configurations. Except in the megachurches, it is still rare to find large numbers of white congregants worshiping under black leadership; blacks worshiping under the leadership of a white pastor and pastoral staff are more common.

In the earlier days of this period, the introduction of more than a small number of black families into an established white congregation almost ensured that it would eventually become predominantly black. Within many contexts, the leadership of the congregation would remain exclusively white or make room for a small number of blacks as long as the balance of the congregation had a larger representation of whites. Often, as families reached the point where children reached dating age, they were reluctant to remain in mixed congregations and expose their children to the opportunity for interracial dating.

Increasingly, some leaders, especially younger, white theologically trained pastors who do not carry the earlier generations' racial baggage, have deliberately reconfigured existing congregations or built new multiracial congregations. Worship in these congregations blends elements from both cultures; music, preaching styles, outreach efforts and related ministries reflect the sensitivities of the various cultures represented in the congregation. Black gospel music is sung beside country gospel, shouters sit side-by-side with those who only raise their hands. The most progressive of these develop multiracial staffs, placing blacks and other people of color in highly visible positions. As interracialism has become a fact of

---

[110]"Race and Religion in Indianapolis," *Religion and Community* 4, no. 2 (1999): www.polis .iupui.edu/RUC/Newsletters/Religion/vol4no2.htm.

American life, mixed-race congregations derive significant capital from this identity and often advertise themselves as such. In the highly segregated religious reality that has characterized modern American Pentecostal history, these multiracial congregations provide a powerful witness for prodding that segment of the movement that lags behind.[111]

CONCLUSION

Early white Pentecostals leaders' racial attitudes can best be summed up in sentiments espoused by Pentecostal Holiness leader J. A. Synan, that "people can be saved without becoming crusaders for segregation or integration."[112] While these whites defended the pragmatic expediency of such separation and saw no moral or ethical implications, African Americans saw it as sin. As Harold Hunter relates about the PHC, as Pentecostal groups became more centralized, formal, and structured and less flexible, the movement's interracial character declined.[113]

Despite receiving unequal treatment, some African Americans remained within largely white denominations. In these bodies, not only were they precluded from holding denominational leadership positions, but they were also barred from availing themselves of the normal privileges of membership. Even after the civil rights movement, progress toward their full involvement remained generally slow and the deliberations many. Often, only within the last quarter of the twentieth century was any real progress toward inclusion made.

The proportion of blacks in classical white Pentecostal bodies remains relatively small. For example, in 2006, there were only 304 black Assemblies of God churches out of a total of 12,311 (only about 2.5 percent) congregations in the United States. In comparison, there were 2,217 Latino congregations.[114] In 2005, there were 219,000 blacks out of nearly 3 million U.S. adherents. In the same year, in the Pentecostal Holiness Church, there were only 27 African American congregations out of a total of nearly 2,000.

---

[111]Scott Thumma, "What God Makes Free Is Free Indeed: Nondenominational Church Identity and Its Networks of Support" (paper presented to the annual meeting of the Religious Research Association, October 1999).

[112]J. A. Synan, "Meeting in Chicago," *Pentecostal Holiness Advocate* 48 (May 9, 1964): 8.

[113]Harold D. Hunter, "International Pentecostal Holiness Church" (paper presented to the Pentecostal World Conference, Han Young Theological University, Seoul, Korea, 1998).

[114]"Statistics of the Assemblies of God (USA)," Assemblies of God USA, http://ag.org/top/About/Statistics/Statistical_Report_Summary.pdf.

Early in the history of modern Pentecostalism, whites approached the race issue in the same way Charles Barfoot and Gerald Sheppard have contended they handled the issue of women's leadership—relinquishing their prophetic role for respectability.[115] What Klaude Kendrick has said about the Assemblies of God can be applied to racial ethics of much of white Pentecostalism:

> [Its] approach to ethics with regard to racial discrimination has been reactionary. It has determined its course by what the status quo of society and particularly [its] expression . . . in evangelicalism have directed. Its major concern has been with what white America would find acceptable and it has acted only when forced to do so by circumstances beyond its control or when imitation of associate organizations has appeared safe. . . . [It] has proven willing to accept black Americans only when such actions involves little or no risk to its palatability among its white constituency.[116]

Whether the denominations practiced exclusion or separation, racial attitudes were given biblical and theological warrant that had social implications for blacks. Such attitudes precluded the possibility of attempts at genuine racial integration while providing spiritual rationale and support, which exonerated leaders from any charge of personal racism. They were simply following biblical principles for maintaining the God-designed social order.

But such attitudes could not remain sheltered from the realities of American pluralism and wider opportunities for blacks in secular society that the civil rights movement brought about. White Pentecostal denominational leaders eventually had to admit that the blacks who attended their churches were capable of leading or providing input to the same congregations. Yet, whatever degree of multiracialism has found its way into Pentecostal congregations, again, it has often been driven more by secular pragmatism than by the prophetic witness of a movement with roots lying in a deep appreciation of the full humanity of all people empowered by the Spirit of God.

---

[115]Charles H. Barfoot and Gerald T. Sheppard, "Priestly vs. Prophetic Religion: The Changing Roles of Women Clergy in Classical Pentecostal Churches," *Review of Religious Resources* 22, no. 1 (1980): 2-17.
[116]Kendrick, *Promise Fulfilled*, p. 176.

8

IF IT WASN'T FOR
THE WOMEN

And your sons and your daughters shall prophesy.

JOEL 2:28

In 1945 Sinclair Drake and Horace Cayton pointed out that "the ban on women pastors in regular [African Amrerican] churches has increased the popularity of Pentecostal, Holiness churches . . . where ambitious women may rise to the top."[1] This observation points to one of the least appreciated aspects of African American Pentecostal history—women's role in the development of the movement. As Cheryl Townsend Gilkes's title, *If It Wasn't for the Women,* highlights, black Pentecostalism would be considerably poorer without their contribution.[2] Despite generally being locked out of higher levels of denominational leadership, women not only filled the pews but also established and pastored congregations, served as missionaries and developed the numerous auxiliaries that helped fuel the Pentecostalism's phenomenal growth. Their in-

---

[1]Sinclair Drake and Horace R. Cayton, *Black Metropolis: A Study of Negro Life in a Northern City* (New York: Harcourt, Brace, 1945), p. 165.
[2]Cheryl Townsend Gilkes, *If It Wasn't for the Women: Black Women's Experience and Womanist Culture in Church and Community* (Maryknoll, N.Y.: Orbis, 2001).

volvement helped move a marginalized movement into the center of the contemporary American and global religious scenes. However, as Jane Sims astutely contends, "The absence of women's stories and particularly those of women of color, from official historiographies . . . creates the perception that women's role was minimal or non-existent."[3]

Historically, with the exceptions of smaller, more cultlike groups, few black Pentecostal denominations granted women what Mark Chaves defines as "full clergy rights"—ordination and all the rights and privileges inherent with it.[4] Although at the outset Pentecostal women outnumbered men and were accorded a place in ministry and leadership rarely available within the American religious context, as the movement spread, the freedom granted women vacillated widely among factions, with no single discernable pattern, except that as institutionalization occurred, women's leadership was increasingly restricted.

Black Pentecostal women's role models had been women abolitionists and black Holiness women healers and evangelists. These women's autobiographies are some of the most poignant, insightful writings of the nineteenth-century black church.[5] Women were prominent from the earliest days of that movement, and despite efforts that proscribe their participation in its leadership, Holiness women have continued to play a vital role in the congregations and denominations of Pentecostalism's older sister.

BLACK PENTECOSTAL WOMEN LEADERS AT AZUSA STREET

The import of women's roles in Pentecostalism was evident in William

---

[3]Jane A. Sims, "Telling Our Story: The Role and Contribution of Women, Particularly Women of Color, in the Formation of the Pentecostal/Holiness Movement and the Pentecostal Assemblies of the World" (master's thesis, Christian Theological Seminary, Indianapolis, 2002), p. 106.

[4]Mark Chaves, *Ordaining Women: Culture and Conflict in Religious Organizations* (Cambridge, Mass.: Harvard University Press, 1997). According to Chaves, denominations that grant full clergy rights are those in which there is "formally open access [to women] to all religious positions within a denomination." He distinguishes these from denominations that grant women limited ordination or license them for ministry but bar them from holding institutional leadership roles (see pp. 2-3).

[5]See, e.g., William Andrews, *Sisters in the Spirit: Three Black Women's Autobiographies of the Nineteenth Century* (Bloomington: Indiana University Press, 1986), or Amanda Berry Smith's *An Autobiography: The Story of the Lord's Dealings with Mrs. Amanda Smith, the Colored Evangelist: Containing an Account of Her Life Work of Faith, and Her Travels in America, England, Ireland, Scotland, India, and Africa as an Independent Missionary* (Chicago: Meyer & Brother, 1893).

Seymour's nascent congregation, which was initially composed largely of black women house servants, a few white women and men of both races who met daily to pray for revival. In April 1906 these black women were among the first to experience the Pentecostal Spirit baptism. They followed Seymour to the Azusa Street location, where they were joined by women and men of every nationality, taking on a variety of roles that thrust the revival into national and international attention. Every aspect of the revival bore the touch of a woman's hand, and many of these hands were black. As the revival moved to Azusa Street, these women with no formal biblical training joined white women from various walks of life to exercise ministry and leaderships gifts. They could be found leading worship, preaching, giving messages in tongues or interpreting those same messages, prophesying, or praying at the altar with new converts and seekers for Holy Spirit baptism and healing. In fact, one element of the revival that drew public attention—and a degree of derision—from the secular press was the regular sight of white men, several of them prominent members of the clergy or community, kneeling before black women who prayed with them to receive Holy Spirit baptism.

Perhaps the greatest evidence of Seymour's early prophetic understanding of women's roles in the revival and the movement it birthed is reflected in a statement he made:

> Before Jesus ascended to heaven, holy anointing oil had never been poured on a woman's head; but before He organized His church, he called them all into the upper room, both men and women, and anointed them with the oil of the Holy Ghost, thus qualifying them all to minister in this Gospel. On the day of Pentecost they all preached through the power of the Holy Ghost. In Christ Jesus there is neither male nor female, all are one.[6]

Although Seymour was indebted to several women for making him aware of the Pentecostal experience, getting him to Los Angeles and supporting his ministry, his growing reluctance to grant women complete equality was evident in two ways as the mission developed. First, in formalizing its doctrinal statement, Seymour made a distinction between the roles men and women would have in worship and ministry. In *Doctrines and Disciplines of the Azusa Street Mission of Los Angeles California*, Seymour

---

[6]Untitled article, *Apostolic Faith* 1, no. 10 (1907): 4.

insisted that "all ordination must be done by men not women. Women may be ministers but not . . . baptize or ordain in this work." Further, the liturgy that Seymour developed for the ordination service clearly indicates that all laying on of hands and prayer within such services was to be done by "elders."[7] This suggests that already the levels of ministry women might aspire to were somewhat restricted. Perhaps the rank of elder, and then bishop, was restricted to men, with women relegated to lower ranks with less ministerial privilege.

Women served on the loosely organized administrative board in the earliest days of the mission. Increasingly, however, tighter structure excluded women from positions of authority. Four of the five people who served on the board of trustees that finally had legal responsibility for governance of the mission were men. The only woman granted a position on that board was Seymour's wife, Jennie Evans Seymour. But Seymour never entirely excluded the possibility of women's leadership. After having been disenchanted by the racial attitudes of some trusted whites, the incorporated formal structure of the Azusa Street Mission stipulated that his successor be a *person of color*, not specifically a *man* of color,[8] leaving room for the possibility that the person could be a woman.

By the time of this turn in Seymour's thinking, women of every race had substantially contributed to the revival's success. White women such as Florence Crawford, who served as overseer for California and the Northwest, and Clara Lum, who helped Seymour publish the *Apostolic Faith*, were joined by Latino women such as Susie Valdez and Rosa de Lopez, who separately evangelized their communities in Los Angeles and throughout California. Several women, such as Ivy Campbell, traveled alone; some, such as Lillian Garr, May Evans and Ardella Meade, worked alongside their husbands and took the Pentecostal message to mission fields across the country and the world. Along with this group, at least four black women made substantial contributions to the mission's and the revival's success.

Neely Terry. Neely Terry was the catalyst for Seymour's move to Los

---

[7] William Seymour, *Doctrines and Disciplines of the Azusa Street Mission of Los Angeles California* (Los Angeles, 1916), pp. 91, 64.

[8] Ibid., p. 50. Though the very next paragraph does call for the vice bishop to be a "colored man."

Angeles. Terry belonged to the small Holiness church pastored by Julia Hutchins[9] and first encountered Seymour while visiting family in Houston and attending Lucy Farrow's church at a time when he was serving as interim pastor. On returning to Los Angeles, Terry spoke to Hutchins about inviting Seymour to serve as associate pastor. Hutchins trusted Terry's initial assessment of Seymour as a man of integrity and an anointed preacher.

Once rejected by Hutchins's congregation and locked out of the church that called him to Los Angeles, Seymour found himself without a place to live or preach and with little resources to sustain him. Since Terry probably felt some responsibility for his situation and was a cousin to the Asberry Family, in whose home Seymour conducted his initial Bible studies, it may have been her intervention with them that was instrumental in finding him a place to carry out his ministry. It is not known, however, what role if any Terry actually played in the revival.[10]

Lucy Farrow. Lucy Farrow heard Charles Fox Parham when she was visiting Houston and left her pastorate for a time to work as governess for his family as they traveled throughout Kansas holding revivals. While she was serving them, she received the baptism of the Holy Spirit. She pastored the Houston church Seymour attended before coming to Los Angeles and introduced him to the doctrine and phenomenon of Holy Spirit baptism with tongues. During her absence from Houston, Seymour filled in as pastor. When she returned to resume the pastorate, she shared with him about her experience and explained what she had learned of Parham's doctrine of Spirit baptism with evidence of speaking in tongues. Subsequently, she introduced Seymour to Parham,[11] thus setting up the chain of events that ultimately led to the beginning of the Azusa Street meeting.

It is uncertain who arrived in Los Angeles first, Seymour or Farrow. Nonetheless, after the two reunited at Azusa Street, Farrow took on an important role in the meetings. Though she does not appear to have taken on an official position, she stayed for several months, serving as one of the ministers in the congregation and possibly serving as a mentor to Sey-

---

[9]Several sources erroneously place Terry as the pastor of the congregation.
[10]See further discussion of Terry in chap. 4.
[11]Farrow and Seymour's early relationship is detailed in Susan Hyatt, "Spirit Filled Women" in *The Century of the Holy Spirit: 100 Years of Pentecostal and charismatic Renewal*, ed. Vinson Synan (Nashville: Thomas Nelson, 2001), pp. 245-46.

mour. Those who encountered her at Azusa Street considered her a powerful woman of God, and several future Pentecostal leaders experienced their Pentecostal Spirit baptism at her hands. On leaving Los Angeles in August 1906, she conducted revivals in Virginia, New York, North Carolina, Texas, Louisiana and England on her way to Liberia. While in Virginia, she held services in Portsmouth and Norfolk, in which two hundred were saved and baptized with the Holy Spirit, and planted new congregations in both cities. Farrow stayed in Johnsonville, Liberia, for seven months. Reportedly, while there, she was able to minister in the Kru dialect.[12] Returning to Los Angeles, she continued to minister from a "small faith cottage" in the back of the Azusa Street Mission where people came for prayer.

Julia Hutchins. After a short period of prayer and consideration, Julia Hutchins invited Seymour to come to California to help with the work. Though their preaching of the need for the initial evidence of tongues precluded him from taking on that role, the invitation had brought Seymour to that city and set the stage for the unfolding of the revival. Hutchins's initial rejection of Seymour's message of Holy Spirit baptism accompanied by the evidence of tongues was overshadowed when she was later won to his understanding and became a regular Azusa Street Revival participant and a solid supporter of his ministry. Hutchins reportedly "received the gift of the Uganda [*sic*] language,"[13] and with her husband and niece, Leila McKinney, she accompanied Farrow to Liberia. During her stay there, she detailed the group's activities and God's miraculous workings in their midst in reports carried in *Apostolic Faith*.[14] Once Hutchins returned from Africa, she encouraged other groups of missionaries to go to that country, but little is known of her further involvement at Azusa Street.

Jennie Moore Seymour. Jennie Evans Moore was the first woman to receive the Pentecostal experience at the Bonnie Brae prayer meetings.[15] She

[12]"Pentecostal Missionary Reports," *Apostolic Faith* 1, no. 4 (1906): 1.

[13]"Testimonies of Outgoing Missionaries," *Apostolic Faith* 1, no. 2 (1906): 14.

[14]Ibid., p. 1; "Sister Hutchins Testimony," *Apostolic Faith* 1, no. 2 (1906): 1; "A Girl's Consecration for Africa," *Apostolic Faith* 1, no. 2 (1906): 1; "Speeding to Foreign Lands," *Apostolic Faith* 1, no. 5 (1907): 3; and "In Africa," *Apostolic Faith* 1, no. 7 (1907): 1.

[15]Some report her to be the first person to speak in tongues in the Bonnie Brae Street prayer meeting, before the group moved to Azusa Street. See Cecil M. Robeck Jr., "Jennie Evans Moore," in *The New International Dictionary of Pentecostal and Charismatic Movements*, ed.

later recounted this experience, in which she fell to the floor while speaking six distinctive languages. As she spoke each language, the message was accompanied by an interpretation in English. During this episode, she recalled an earlier vision and was given the revelation of its meaning:

> When the power came on me I was reminded of the three cards which had passed me in the vision months ago. As I thought thereon and looked to God, it seemed as if a vessel broke within me and water surged up through my being, which when it reached my mouth came out in a torrent of speech in the languages which God had given me. I remembered the names of the cards: French, Spanish, Latin, Greek, Hebrew, Hindustani, and as the message came with power, so quick that but few words would have been recognized, interpretation of each message followed in English, the name of the language would come to me.[16]

After beginning to speak and prophesy in Hebrew, Moore then went to the piano and began playing, singing and praying in tongues. Miraculously, prior to that evening she had never had a piano lesson or played the piano. In her own words,

> I sang under the power of the Spirit in many languages, the interpretation both words and music which I had never before heard, and in the home where the meeting was being held, the Spirit led me to the piano, where I played and sang under inspiration, although I had not learned to play.[17]

In another dramatic episode several days later, Moore was working as a household maid, assisting her employer in serving a dinner party. After serving the meal, Moore and her employer were discussing a household issue, when Moore spontaneously began to fluently speak in tongues, frightening her employer, who thought Moore might be suffering from a mental collapse and insisted she take time off to rest.[18] The group moved to Azusa Street, and from the beginning Moore took an increasingly active leadership role in the mission, serving on the administrative board and being appointed as a city missionary, along with Phoebe Sargeant.[19]

Stanley Burgess, Eduard M. van der Maas and Patrick Alexander (Grand Rapids: Zondervan, 2002), pp. 906-7.

[16]Jennie Evans Moore, "Music From Heaven," *Apostolic Faith* 8 (May 1907): 3.

[17]Ted Olsen, "American Pentecost: The Story Behind the Azusa Street Revival, the Most Phenomenal Event of Twentieth-Century Christianity," *Christian History* 17, no. 2 (1998): 14.

[18]Alexander Boddy, "At Los Angeles, California," *Confidence*, October 1912, pp. 233-34.

[19]There is no detailed description of the responsibilities this position entailed.

Moore's marriage to Seymour was later to be a catalyst for one of the major schisms that would challenge the existence of the mission. After their marriage Jennie worked alongside her husband in leading the mission. When he died, she pastored the then-dwindling mission until her health failed.[20]

BLACK PENTECOSTAL WOMEN LEADERS
SINCE AZUSA STREET

Once black Pentecostal denominations began to formalize, the shape of women's roles tended to take on the particular bent of each organization's respective leaders. Those leaders with Baptists foundations were less likely to be egalitarian. Women in these groups had to content themselves with working in secondary roles alongside, and in the shadow of, men who became prominent leaders. They were no less gifted nor worked less stridently in defense of the gospel, but they bowed to social and denominational conventions regarding the role of women in society and the church. They were given titles such as "evangelist" or "missionary," though the titles carried different meanings than conventionally understood. Instead of preaching at revivals and evangelistic services within their communities or spreading the gospel throughout the country or around the world, like their male colleagues, these women were often confined to teaching and preaching to women and youth within their local churches or throughout the fellowship of congregations in a single denomination—often under the direct oversight of a man.

Denominations with Wesleyan Holiness roots tended to be egalitarian. Women in these groups joined the sea of Spirit-empowered believers who understood Holy Spirit empowerment as a call to minister the gospel to a lost world. Women became the foot soldiers, often serving in places men did not want to go. They dug out new churches in unbroken ground where no Pentecostal congregation had previously stood. They brought those congregations to viability; then a male pastor moved in and built up the "church." They served on mission fields for lower pay and fewer benefits than men would accept. A few women took seriously the vision of radical equality that

---

[20]Larry Martin, *The Life and Ministry of William J. Seymour*, Complete Azusa Street Library 1 (Joplin, Mo.: Christian Life Books, 1999), p. 231. See also the account of Moore's involvement at Azusa Street in chap. 4, pp. 143-58.

Holy Spirit baptism promised and refused to be limited in ministry. They saw themselves as equally anointed or qualified and compelled by God to carry out their destinies as leaders of congregations and bodies of congregations. Several of these bodies fared equally well as those founded by their male colleagues. Some of them continued to draw a small number of adherents over the span of their history. Others enjoyed a brief stay.

Mary Magdalena Tate. As the Azusa Street Revival moved into full swing in the West, a considerably smaller, localized Pentecostal outpouring was unfolding among African Americans on the opposite coast. Its founder, a self-educated black woman, began her ministry in 1903—two years after Parham's initial formulation and three years before the Azusa Street outpouring—as a Holiness minister, carrying out "missionary journeys" throughout the Ohio Valley and the South. Reportedly unaware of the Pentecostal revival springing from these two leaders, her followers characterize her meetings as "the first great Pentecostal revival," insisting that she came to the revelation of initial evidence on her own and that "God had not moved upon religious leaders of their day to teach Holy Ghost Baptism" and that she "had never seen [such] manifestation of the power of God in such manner upon anyone except herself."[21]

In 1908, Tate's miraculous healing from a near-fatal illness was accompanied by a spontaneous episode of speaking in tongues, prompting her to add the doctrine of initial evidence to her message of sanctification. That year she organized Holiness bands that had formed under her leadership into the first congregations of the Church of the Living God the Pillar and Ground of the Truth,[22] and took the title of bishop, becoming the first woman to receive that rank in a nationally recognized religious body and hold the rank of presiding bishop of a Protestant Christian denomination.[23]

Tate's primitive, restorationist exegesis insisted that her organization's name was divinely unique, and the only God-given name for the present-day church. For her, other denominational names were "dangerous nick names" not sanctioned by God.[24] Tate's exclusivist self-understanding saw

---

[21] *Seventy-Fifth Anniversary Yearbook*, p. 8.
[22] Ibid.
[23] Wardell Payne, ed., *Directory of African American Religious Bodies: A Compendium by the Howard University School of Divinity*, 2nd ed. (Washington, D.C.: Howard University Press, 1995), p. 95.
[24] Ibid., p. 10.

her call as "reestablishing" the New Testament church, restoring a purity other Pentecostals missed[25] and orchestrating the beginning of last days of true holiness. The practical outworking of this ecclesiology led to unique sacramental understandings. She used water, rather than juice or wine, and only unleavened bread for Communion, which she referred to as Passover and which was always followed by footwashing. Sunday was a Sabbath, requiring abstinence from work and total involvement in worship services. Tate's rigid personal piety demanded tithing and proscribed eating pork, swearing or taking oaths, and partaking of any alcoholic products, including medicines containing the substance.[26] Church membership was limited to those who evidenced Holy Spirit baptism with speaking in tongues;[27] fellowship with other churches was prohibited; and access to the pulpit was limited to ministers within the denomination.[28]

Though she suffered from chronic diabetes, Tate promoted divine healing and regularly prayed for the sick. Testimonies recount "miraculous" healings that came about because of her prayers,[29] and she urged followers to forgo doctors and conventional medicine, insisting that strong Christians could live entirely without these aids. Many followers subscribed to these teachings and lived relatively healthy lives. Yet both she and her older son succumbed prematurely from conditions that might have benefited from medical care. Tate died in 1930 at age fifty-nine from complications of diabetes and gangrene. On her deathbed, she reportedly chided, "If the saints had the same faith for me that I have had for them, I would be healed."[30]

After her death, the denomination she led for twenty-one years was

---

[25]Helen M. Lewis and Meharry Lewis, ed., *The Beauty of Holiness: A Small Catechism of the Holiness Faith and Doctrine*, 2nd ed. (Nashville: New and Living Way Publishing House, 1990), p. ix.

[26]*Constitution, Government and General Decree Book of the Church of the Living God, the Pillar and Ground of the Truth (Incorporated)* (Chattanooga, Tenn.: New and Living Way Publishing House, 1924), p. 49. This upholding of Old Testament legal and feast custom was an element that was unique with Tate's organization.

[27]Ibid., p. 37. This membership requirement goes beyond that of most Pentecostal denominations that strongly encourage their members to seek Holy Spirit Baptism but do not withhold membership on the basis that one has not received it.

[28]Ibid.

[29]*The Seventy-Fifth Anniversary Yearbook* contains testimonies of those who were healed through Tate's ministry of laying on of hands. See, e.g., p. 9.

[30]Interview with Meharry Lewis.

geographically divided into three sixteen-state dominions encompassing the then forty-eight United States.[31] Each of these, along with at least three smaller groups that came into being because of early schisms, pay direct allegiance to Tate. Each retains part of the original title, "Church of the Living God" and credits Tate as founder while maintaining many of the distinctive elements she established in the original denomination.[32]

Carrie Gurry. Through the men and women she nurtured and mentored to become leaders of larger, more highly regarded, congregations and denominations, Carrie Virginia Gurry's influence reached far beyond the small King's Apostle Holiness Church (KAHC) denomination she founded. In 1911 Gurry founded and incorporated the first Holiness Pentecostal congregation in Maryland, with a small group meeting in her Baltimore home. Raised in the African Methodist Episcopal Church, Gurry was exposed to the Pentecostal experience through the testimony of her daughter-in-law and received the baptism of the Holy Spirit with tongues in 1903, three years before the Azusa Street Revival. While she never visited Azusa Street, it is likely she had the occasion to meet its founder, William Seymour, and his close colleague Charles Mason as they conducted a revival tour throughout her region in 1914.

Gurry's denomination grew slowly as she traveled through Maryland and Pennsylvania, preaching and teaching. In her lifetime, it never reached to more than ten congregations located primarily along the Delmarva Peninsula. It played a significant role, however, in the development of a number of black Pentecostal bodies within both the trinitarian and oneness traditions, and the development of leaders (several of them women) who spent their formative years within the King's Apostle Holiness Church. Among the women, Amy Stevens, who was reared in the KAHC, later served as presiding bishop of the Mt. Sinai Holy Church, founded by

[31]At that time, however, the denomination was still primarily relegated to the East Coast. This partitioning, in fact, gave each chief overseer specific jurisdiction over any further growth within his or her respective dominion.

[32]See more detailed discussion of Tate, and the denomination(s) she founded, in chap. 5. See also a discussion of these issues in "The House of God which is the Church of the Living God, the Pillar and Ground of the Truth, Without Controversy, Inc.," in *The Constitution, Government, and General Decree Book*, 3rd ed. (Philadelphia, 1936), pp. 93-107. Even here, there is controversy, with one of the dominions later contending that its name, the House of God Which is the Church of the Living God, the Pillar and Ground of the Truth Without Controversy, is the initial name that Tate chose for her organization but that other factions obliterated any records that bear witness to that fact.

Gurry's personal friend Bishop Ida Robinson. Violet Fisher, one of a small number of black women to have been elected to the bishopric within the United Methodist Church by the end of the twentieth century, also emerged from the KAHC.[33]

Interestingly, Gurry never took the title of bishop, but appointed a man, Walter E. Campher, as national overseer of the organization, while reserving for herself the title of general overseer. In this way, she maintained leadership of the denomination while circumventing some of the criticism of female authority over men. Even this solution, however, was problematic for some male leaders who served with her, and a number of them defected to found their own organizations rather than continue to serve under a woman. Curry died in 1942 at the age of seventy-seven. After her death, the denomination continued a pattern of slow expansion. Today, there are nearly thirty King's Apostle Holiness Church of God congregations.

Lucy Smith. Lucy Madden Smith typifies many who came to the urban North during the Great Migration. She was born on a plantation in rural Georgia. By 1910, Lucy, her husband, William, and their nine children moved to Athens, Georgia. After William abandoned the family, Lucy moved with her children first to Atlanta and then to Chicago. Like many other new immigrants, Smith found the subdued worship of the large black congregations she first attended sterile and uninviting and continued to search for a more welcoming place. By 1914 Smith had found an at least temporary spiritual home at Stone Church, the predominantly white congregation founded in 1906 by John Alexander Dowie's associate William Piper. Here Smith experienced the baptism of the Holy Spirit and her call to the "work of the Lord."

In 1916, Smith began All Nations Pentecostal Church by holding prayer and faith-healing services in her one-room apartment with a small group of women. During the Depression, the largely uneducated and self-taught Smith formed alliances with prominent local businessmen, allowing her to carry out a substantial outreach ministry throughout Chicago's South Side. While many Chicagoans were out of work or working for meager wages, Smith used these alliances and the assistance of the "saints"—women noted throughout her congregation for personal piety

---

[33]Personal interview with Violet Fisher, June 10, 2006.

and spiritual giftedness—to become the first African American pastor in Chicago to regularly distribute food and clothing without regard to race. Though the majority of the congregation was formed by the poor and blacks, as it grew it became, for many years, the only multiracial congregation on Chicago's South Side, with a sprinkling of poor whites and immigrants from several countries.[34] It became noted for a musical program that eventually included several choirs, a four-piece "orchestra" and "refilling services," where Smith gave special prayer and attention to those seeking Holy Spirit baptism.

In 1925, when she began to broadcast her Sunday night services over local radio station WSBC, Smith became the first black religious leader to broadcast services. In 1933 she added her Wednesday evening program, "The Glorious Church of the Air," which broadcasted a unique mix of gospel programming and appeals for the poor. During thirty-six years of ministry, Smith claimed to have been used in the healing of more than two hundred thousand people, maintaining a "trophy room" in the basement of All Nation's Church to display the medical paraphernalia discarded by those who had been healed. At the time of Smith's death in 1952, All Nation's Church had grown to nearly five thousand members. Her funeral was one of the largest held in Chicago up to that time. Sixty thousand people viewed her body and fifty thousand lined the streets for the processional.

Bishop Ida Robinson. Ida Robinson founded the Mt. Sinai Holy Church of America—the largest African American Pentecostal denomination established by a woman, continually headed by women, and promoting the equality and leadership of women in ministry.[35] Another product of the early years of the Great Migration, Robinson's ministry began in Philadelphia in the early 1920s, first with the Church of God and then the United Holy Church (UHC), where she was ordained and appointed pastor of a small congregation.[36] At that time, though UHC women outnumbered men two to one,

---

[34]A good depiction of the ministry of Lucy Smith can be found in Wallace Best, *Passionately Human, No Less Divine: Religion and Culture in Black Chicago, 1915-1952* (Princeton, N.J.: Princeton University Press, 2005), pp. 147-80.

[35]"Ida Robinson," in *African American Women: A Biographical Dictionary*, ed. Dorothy Salem (New York: Garland, 1993). Following the death of Bishop Amy Stevens in 2000, for the first time, the leadership of Mt. Sinai Holy Church of America was assumed by a man—Bishop Joseph Bell.

[36]The United Holy Church is currently the second-largest African American Pentecostal body in the United States.

Robinson was one of few women preachers. By 1924, however, her reputation as a revivalist had spread among African American Pentecostal congregations along the East Coast, and she traveled and ministered from New York to North Carolina.[37] People regularly filled her church to hear her sing and preach, and many stayed to become members, fueling the congregation's rapid expansion and causing it to move three times to larger locations.[38]

Despite little formal education, Robinson's sharp intellect, excellent leadership skills, giftedness as a preacher and singer, and biblical knowledge did not escape the attention of United Holy Church leadership, who frequently called on her for ministry.[39] Her success and prominence prodded other United Holy Church women to vigorously demand a more public presence. The male leadership responded by finally announcing that they would no longer "publicly" ordain women and would restrict those already ordained to lower levels of ordained ministry.[40] Though her position was secure, Robinson felt God leading her to start a new denomination in which women could freely participate in all levels of ministry.[41] When church leaders attempted to change her mind, she responded that God had instructed her to "come out on Mt. Sinai and loose the women."[42] Perceiving this summons as a direct command, she asked, "If Mary the mother of Jesus could carry the Word of God in her womb, why can't women carry the word of God in their mouth?"[43] Robinson's first steps as denominational head reflected this commitment, as she immediately

---

[37]According to the *Manual of the Mount Sinai Holy Church of America, Inc.*, rev. ed. (Philadelphia: Mt Sinai Holy Church of America, 1984), p. 11, she was especially noted for two songs, "What a Beautiful City" and "O I Want to See Him."

[38]Mt. Sinai Holy Church of America, *Celebrating our Legacy*, p. 110.

[39]Arthur H. Fauset, *Black Gods of the Metropolis* (Philadelphia: University of Pennsylvania Press, 1944), p. 14.

[40]Best, "Loosing the Women" (paper presented to the Society for Pentecostal Studies, Twenty-fourth Annual Meeting, Wheaton, Ill., November 1994). Whether the word *publicly* has any special import is uncertain, for it is not known whether they continued to ordain women privately or what such "private" ordination would have meant.

[41]One of her first acts was to seek legal counsel to set up a charter to create the Mt. Sinai Holy Church of America, Inc. See Owens, *Out on Mt. Sinai: How Bishop Ida Bell Robinson Loosed the Women—An Examination of her Leadership Style.* (Doctor of Strategic Leadership dissertation, Regent University, 2001), p. 36; or Minerva Bell, "Significant Female Leaders and Factors Leading to their Success" (M.A. thesis, Farleigh Dickerson University, 1974), 50.

[42]Best, "Loosing the Woman," p. 9.

[43]Ibid. Also see the Sixtieth Annual Convocation Bulletin of the Mt. Sinai Holy Church of America, Inc., 1984, p. 33.

began to train women and place them in positions of authority. Yet, rather than being exclusivist, she employed both men and women in the organization's ministry and leadership.[44] From 1924 to 1936 Robinson was involved in setting up almost every new local congregation within the organization. She traveled throughout the East Coast to small towns and larger cities conducting revival services, making new converts and establishing local congregations over which she would place a minister as pastor. Many of these placements were women.[45]

After leading Mt. Sinai for 22 years, Robinson died in 1946, at the age of fifty-four. In that time she had built a denomination of eighty-four churches, stretching from New England to Florida.[46] At its height, in 1988, the organization had grown to 154 congregations.[47] Though the denomination had slowly grown by seventy congregations, in the 42 years since her death, the growth that Mt. Sinai experienced under Robinson was never again realized.

Rosa Horn. Though her early upbringing would have seemed to prepare her for a life very different than she ultimately pursued, Rosa Artimus Horn became one of the most controversial black Pentecostal women leaders of the first half of the twentieth century. The granddaughter of a slave, and one of ten children, Horn received a private-school education. By the early 1920s she was widowed and had moved from Augusta, Georgia, where she worked as a dressmaker, to Illinois. Though she had earlier been a member of the Methodist Church, she was ordained by famed evangelist and faith healer Maria Woodworth-Etter. After marrying William Horn, she moved first to Evanston, Indiana, then to Brooklyn, New York. Like many others who found their way to the urban North, Horn was unhappy with the coldness of larger congregations and empathized with others who had been pulled away from their social and spiritual moorings. So in 1926 she established a storefront congregation, Mt. Calvary Pentecostal Faith Church.[48] The church was noted for its exten-

[44]Robinson enlisted along with Bishop James Bell, who served as her first assistant pastor with the New York congregation.

[45]For a region-by-region and church-by-church historical accounting of pastoral deployment, see *Celebrating Our Legacy*, pp. 24-135.

[46]*Celebrating Our Legacy*, p. 140. See also the discussion of Mt. Sinai Holy Church of America in chap. 5, pp. 166-69.

[47]Best, "Loosing the Women," p. 11.

[48]Horn's denomination is variably labeled Mt. Calvary Pentecostal Faith Church, Emmanuel

sive prayer ministry, and Horn became known within the community as the "pray for me priestess."[49]

By 1933, her congregation and personal popularity had grown so much that Horn was invited to begin a radio broadcast on station WHN, making Mt. Calvary the first church in Upper Manhattan wired for broadcasting. The station launched an aggressive advertising campaign promoting a rivalry between Horn and famed Holiness preacher Lightfoot Michaux. By 1936, the often controversial broadcast was already reaching numerous cities along the East Coast. It remained on the air thirty years, and after Michaux's death, Horn became embroiled in a second battle when the station filed a lawsuit against charismatic religious leader Father Divine for trying to intimidate Horn and run her church and her broadcast out of Harlem. The publicity from these squabbles quadrupled the station's audience. Horn's aggressive tactics led her to open confrontations with owners of cabarets, pool rooms, dance halls and other such enterprises. She unsuccessfully engaged the court system in trying to extricate these "dens of iniquity" from her Harlem neighborhood.[50]

By 1934, Horn's church had branches in five cities along the East Coast. In 1959, she moved to Baltimore, where she remained until her death in 1976 at the age of ninety-five. The most famous member of Horn's congregation was author James Baldwin, who belonged to the church as a teenager, served as a minister for several years and used the congregation as a model for some of his writings. His play *The Amen Corner* featured Pastor Margaret, a main character inspired by Horn. His autobiographical novel, *Go Tell It on the Mountain*, depicts the type of Pentecostal worship that would have been so much a part of Horn's congregation.

Charleszetta Waddles. As a young girl Charleszetta Campbell Waddles had dropped out of school to help support her six brothers and sisters, and by fourteen she was married. By 1937, as a twice-married, single mother of ten young children, Campbell was receiving public assistance and reading voraciously to educate herself. She moved to Detroit from St. Louis, where she met her third husband, Payton Waddles, while selling barbeque at a

---

Temple Pentecostal Faith Church, Inc., and Mount Assembly Hall of the Pentecostal Faith of All Nations, Inc.

[49]Bettye Collier-Thomas, *Daughters of Thunder: Black Women Preachers and Their Sermons, 1850-1979* (New York: Oxford University Press, 2005), p. 175.

[50]Ibid., p. 176.

church fundraiser. One day in the late 1940s, Waddles had a vision in which "the Lord told me to feed the hungry and clothe the naked." Armed with this dream, Waddles began holding prayer meetings at her house for small groups of local ladies whom she rallied for involvement in practical, charitable work.

In 1957, several years after receiving the vision and twenty years after moving to Detroit, sixty-year-old Waddles founded the Perpetual Mission for Saving Souls of All Nations. At its height the congregation housed a mission that sheltered the homeless each evening and was used to serve between ninety and one hundred thousand meals annually for thirty-five cents per person. The ministry drew on more than two hundred volunteers to provide emergency financial assistance to families and individuals, job training, a graphic arts program and a culinary education to unwed mothers, prostitutes, abused children, the handicapped, the elderly and the poor, all without government funding. A federal study of emergency assistance in Detroit found that Waddles's operation was the most frequent source for referral services in the city. Waddles worked twelve-hour days as the head of the ministry until she was eighty-two years old. Her extensive operations drew accolades from the secular press, city officials and even the president of the United States.[51] *Life* magazine described her as a "one-woman war on poverty."[52] At one point, Detroiters who called a city-hall hotline at night or on weekends heard a recorded voice telling them, "Detroit city offices are closed at the present time, but will be open tomorrow during regular working hours. In the event of an emergency, call Mother Waddles."[53] In recognition of her efforts, she received an invitation to President Richard M. Nixon's 1968 inauguration. Three years later, the president honored her with a special commendation She died in 2001 at the age of eighty-eight.

WOMEN LEADERS OF SMALL DENOMINATIONS

Mother Mozella Cook, as she was called by her followers, was raised Baptist and converted under the ministry of her mother, who was also a preacher. She subsequently came into the Pentecostal movement through

[51]See "The New American Samaritans," *Time*, Dec. 27, 1971, www.time.com/time/magazine/article/0,9171,905589,00.htm.
[52]James K. Davis, "Mother Waddles: The Gentle Warrior," *Life*, March 22, 1969, p. 87.
[53]"The New American Samaritans."

the Church of God in Christ, but in 1944 she left that denomination to found the Sought Out Church of God in Christ and Spiritual House of Prayer in a garage in Brunswick, Georgia. By 1949 the denomination had four congregations and sixty members and never grew to more than a few hundred members, with congregations in Georgia and Florida.[54]

Beulah Counts had been part of Robinson's Mt. Sinai organization. But Phillips had left that body to join with a Baptist congregation while at the same time holding Sunday school in her home and undertaking a ministry of feeding those in need. In 1944 she moved out from that body to found the Greater Mt. Zion Pentecostal Church in Brooklyn, New York, in 1944. Counts incorporated many of the restrictions of Mt. Sinai into her new organization, including a strict dress code for women who were to shun wearing clothes of worldly color and are limited to blue, gray, black or white.

In 1944, twenty years after Ida Robinson founded Mt. Sinai Holy Church, a former Mt. Sinai member, Madeline Mabe Phillips, founded the Alpha and Omega Church of God Tabernacles in Baltimore, Maryland. Later the name was changed to Alpha and Omega Pentecostal Church of God of America, Inc. There is no clear indication why Phillips left Mt. Sinai; however, it could not have been over the leadership of women, since women had continually been at the head of the Mt. Sinai organization as presiding bishop and occupied many of the top organizational positions. Unlike Robinson, however, Phillips's group never had a large measure of success or garnered the momentum of the parent organization.

Phillips was succeeded by Charles Waters, who left the denomination to form True Fellowship Pentecostal Church of America. John Mabe, brother of the founder, succeeded him as overseer. It is uncertain how many congregations followed Waters, but by 1970, there were only three in Baltimore, one in St. Augustine, Florida, and one in Philadelphia. By 1991, that number had grown to five congregations in Baltimore, a second one in St. Augustine and a mission in Kingston, Jamaica. In the intervening twenty years the membership had slowly grown from four hundred to eight hundred.[55]

---

[54]"Sought Out Church of God in Christ," in *The Encyclopedia of American Religions*, ed. J. Gordon Melton (Tarrytown, N.Y.: Triumph, 1991), p. 1175.

[55]Payne, *Directory of African American Religious Bodies*, p. 153; and Sherry Sherrod DuPree, *African-American Holiness Pentecostalism: An Annotated Bibliography* (New York: Garland, 1996), pp. 137-38.

Inez Conry assumed the pastorate of Alonzo Daughtry's Brooklyn House of the Lord congregation after he became unable to lead, giving the reigns of the church to her on his deathbed, though he felt that one of his own sons would eventually take over the national leadership.[56] She subsequently assumed the role of national president in 1952 and served in both offices for eight years, giving her denomination the distinction of being the only Pentecostal body founded by a man that subsequently elected a woman as presiding bishop. In 1960, Herbert Daniel Daughtry became the church's third national presiding minister.

THE CHURCH OF GOD IN CHRIST

More than half of African American Pentecostals are Church of God in Christ (COGIC) members, and more than half of COGIC members are women. In 2007, COGIC presiding bishop Charles Blake underscored the point by estimating that women made up 60 to 70 percent of the denomination's constituency.[57] Indeed, as the largest African American Pentecostal body, COGIC possibly has more black women members than any other Christian denomination other than the total number who are Baptist. From inception, its prominence within African American Pentecostalism and its unique position on women highlight black Pentecostalism's dilemma in attempting to craft patterns for gender relationships that balance an avowed commitment to the priesthood of all believers and a perceived biblical response to the issues.

Within the COGIC the leadership and ministry of women takes on a distinctive character that was specifically fashioned to allow them a degree of empowerment while maintaining strategic male ecclesial authority. COGIC founder Charles Harrison Mason drew on his Baptist roots[58] to structure a "vital" yet distinctive role for women, allowing them to serve as

---

[56]Jonathan Grossman and Natan Lipton-Lubet, "Oberlin House of the Lord: A History of Oberlin's Youngest Church," Oberlin College and Conservatory, www.oberlin.edu/external/EOG/AfAmChurches/HouseoftheLord.htm.

[57]Valerie G. Lowe, "He Has Seen the Promised Land," *Charisma*, November 2007, p. 60.

[58]The typical historic Baptist attitude toward women in leadership is similar to that put forth by Southern Baptists today. Women were expected to serve in support positions, not in ministerial or pastoral leadership. For an excellent discussion of the attitudes of Baptists toward women in leadership and the struggle women have historically had in the African American Baptist context, see Evelyn Brooks Higginbotham, *Righteous Discontent: The Women's Movement in the Black Baptist Church, 1880-1920* (Cambridge, Mass.: Harvard University Press, 1993).

congregational leaders while reserving the office of pastor and title of preacher for men. They could not be ordained as elder or consecrated bishop but could be licensed as "evangelists" or "missionaries."[59] In this role, they could teach and preach to other women and work to financially support local congregations and the national denomination; direct local, regional and national women's programs; and provide support to pastors and their families. Left out of the normal pastoral track, women who desired to lead congregations were encouraged to "dig out" new works in untested fields and nurture them to viability until a man could take over. According to Ithiel Clemmons, COGIC bishop, church historian, social commentator and Mason biographer, this arrangement

> harnessed the spiritual fervor, mental acumen, physical energy and economic potential of its female members while maintaining male authority.
> . . . The church cultivated female leadership without alienating the men, took advantage of women's abilities to "plant" new congregations without authorizing them to preach or pastor, and established an auxiliary structure that sustained basic Pentecostal-Holiness church doctrine through periods of strife among the church's male leaders.[60]

As Clemmons interpreted these limitations, COGIC women "function[ed] in the ambivalent position of shared, but *secondary* authority . . . preserv[ing] the male dominance that conformed the denomination to biblical imperatives."[61] In the COGIC's one-hundred-year history, women have worked within that structure to make viable contributions that do not infringe on male sensitivities.[62] They served as copastors under their husbands and on pastoral staffs; they served as chaplains and on the foreign mission fields; and they took on other unrestricted institutional roles. They have also involved themselves in the COGIC's ex-

---

[59]These terms do not carry the usual connotation of one who goes out to different locations to win others to Christ. These women worked inside a local church to support its ministry and that of its pastor.

[60]Ibid., pp. 101-2.

[61]Ibid., p. 109. Emphasis added.

[62]Cheryl J. Sanders identifies the model of dual leadership tracks within COGIC as embodying a dialectic of both protest and cooperation. As she sees it, COGIC women are driven, on the one hand, by their struggle against structures and patterns of subordination based on gender. On the other hand, however, she discerns that they are determined to maintain unity with black men in the face of racism and discrimination in the larger society and internal power struggles within the denomination. See Cheryl J. Sanders, "The History of Women in the Pentecostal Movement," *Reconciliation* 1 (Summer 1998): 11.

tensive local and national outreach program, developing a plethora of auxiliaries to address a range of social and spiritual concerns within their churches and communities.[63]

The Women's Department. In the early years of the COGIC, Mason conceived of the Women's Department as an auxiliary of a loose cluster of local prayer and Bible bands, whose structure would mirror the hierarchical system in place for men and in which women could take increasingly important, yet circumscribed, places of service. Within this system, individual women fill significant roles in the local, regional and national church that develop the specific attitudes and skills the denomination values, and women gain an increasing degree of visibility and prominence. The structure affords specially gifted women opportunities to rise to national prominence and exert a level of authority and influence that, at times, rivals, or even surpasses, that given to some men.

The office of the national church mother is the denomination's highest-ranking position for women. The holder of this office appoints women supervisors in each state, who assist her in overseeing the work of women at every level. She ensures that the denomination has a cadre of women organized into various auxiliaries that support local congregations, regional jurisdictions and the national church. At each level women are given a degree of recognition that positions those who serve well for increasing responsibility. This arrangement provides highly qualified women opportunities to attain a level of leadership that would not be available to them were they competing with male colleagues. Yet it does not give them autonomy, for COGIC women operate under men's leadership at three levels. At the congregational level, church mothers direct the women's ministry under the pastor's authority. At the state or jurisdictional level, state mothers operate under the direction of the state or jurisdictional bishop. At the national level, the national mother serves under the presiding bishop.

Women's Department auxiliaries are structured to involve even the young girls in the life of the church. At the earliest ages, boys and girls are grouped together in the Sunshine Band under the direction of women

---

[63] An excellent and thorough discussion of the Women Department and the women who have served at its head is found in Anthea Butler, *Women in the Church of God in Christ: Making of a Sanctified World* (Chapel Hill: University of North Carolina Press, 2007).

teachers. From adolescence, gender stratification begins to take shape. Purity class trains adolescent girls in propriety and etiquette, as well as spiritual development. The Young Women's Council gives further instruction and direction for those between nineteen and forty, involving them in the broader life of the church. The COGIC Women's Council involves women over forty in the church's life.

The national mothers. Starting with Mason, COGIC leaders have taken great care to select women for the national mother's position who exemplify both the godly piety expected of Pentecostal women and the worldly sophistication to extend their influence beyond the denomination. As a result, the six women who would be tapped demonstrate the significant role women have continued to play in the denomination. Throughout its life, these women have repeatedly navigated an essential place for COGIC women's collective energy, vocational hopes and spiritual aspirations. At the same time, each has balanced a strong spiritual influence with a leadership style that does not threaten the existing male privileged power base.

Mason's first choice to head the Women's Department was Lillian Coffey, a young woman of only twenty-one whom Mason and his wife had personally mentored. But Coffey was reticent to accept the position, thinking she might be too young and inexperienced to handle such heady responsibility. Instead, she suggested, and Mason agreed to call on, Elizabeth Isabelle Robinson. Mason met Robinson in 1911 while she was serving as a matron in the Baptist Academy in Dermott, Arkansas. That same year, she converted to Pentecostalism under his ministry and at the November 1912 convocation was appointed to head the newly conceived department. Under her leadership, COGIC women established new congregations, started Bible studies and prayer groups within existing congregations, and engaged in home and foreign missions work. Her crowning accomplishment was organizing what had been a fledgling amalgamation of scattered and often competing prayer and Bible bands into a national effort to raise funds for building a national headquarters for the denomination.

At Robinson's death in 1943, Coffey assumed full leadership of the Women's Department, serving as its head for twenty-one years, until her death in 1964. Though the two worked closely together for a number of years, Robinson and Coffey differed greatly in style and focus. Robinson adhered to a strict holiness code of morality and personal piety, and her austere approach centered on developing the spirituality of COGIC women. In sharp contrast, Coffey's more contemporary style involved her in a breadth of issues and causes beyond those specifically beneficial to the denomination. Her close association with prominent women, including Mary McLeod Bethune and Arenia Mallory, involved her in the broader struggle for "racial uplift" and women's rights that was waged outside of denominational confines. But her influence within the church was undeniable. Coffey, an exceptional preacher and prolific church founder, established congregations in Wisconsin, Ohio, Michigan and Illinois. She initiated several innovations, including founding the Lillian Brooks Coffey Rest Home in Detroit. Yet Coffey is perhaps most noted within the denomination for establishing the National Women's Convention. Conceived in 1950 this annual event has over its nearly sixty-year history grown consistently, now regularly drawing between twenty to twenty-five thousand women and serving as a central focus of the Women's Department annual slate of regional, state and local women's conventions, which draw thousands more.

Annie Bailey served as national mother from 1964 to 1975, after serving as the department's financial secretary under Robinson, then assistant international supervisor and vice president of the Women's International Convention under Coffey. She, like Coffey, had a close relationship with the Mason family, having served as the children's governess. Her husband, Bishop J. S. Bailey, later became a member of the General Board. Besides presiding over eleven women's conventions, Bailey added several auxiliaries to the Women's Department, including the Business and Professional Women's Rescue Squad, the Sunday School Representatives Unit, the United Sisters of Charity, the National Secretaries Unit, and the Junior Missionaries. She also relaunched the magazine the *COGIC Woman* and appointed the first national president of the Sewing Circle-Artistic Fingers.

Mattie McGlothen assumed the position of national mother after having served as supervisor of California and the Northwest for almost half a century. McGlothen founded several new units, including the Education and Scholarship Fund, the Bishops' Wives Scholarship Fund, the Screening Committee for Jurisdictional Supervisors and the Business and Professional Women's Federation. Under her leadership, the Women's Department built a home for missionaries in the Bahamas, furnished a guest house on Saints Junior College campus, and built senior citizens and unwed mothers compounds in Haiti. Between 1985 and 1991, she purchased three homes in Memphis, known as the McGlothen Complex, which now house the administrative offices of the International Women's Department.

The fifth national mother was Emma Crouch, who served from 1994 to 1997. Crouch was married to B. J. Crouch, a prominent preacher who later became a bishop. Like other prominent women, she worked her way through the local, state, jurisdictional and national ranks of the Women's Department, beginning as chairlady of the Young People's Willing Workers after serving as supervisor of women for Texas for twenty years. In 1976, she was appointed as first assistant general supervisor. By the time Crouch was elevated to the higher position, the Women's Department was a highly effective operation; there was no need to organize or reorganize a host of auxiliaries. Instead, Crouch turned her attention to developing a women's council to train COGIC women who were over forty and engage them more in the life of the church.

Unlike her predecessors, as a child, Willie Mae Rivers was not a member of the COGIC but of the African Methodist Episcopal Zion Church. Neither did she have a prominent husband or a close relationship with the founder to pave a path to her appointment. At age nineteen she attended a revival at a COGIC congregation and received the Pentecostal Holy Spirit baptism. Because of her exemplary piety, by the age of twenty, she was appointed "mother" of that congregation.[64] After marrying, Rivers, a mother of twelve, was able to forge a successful ministry that includes a radio broadcast that airs on five stations in the southeastern United States. Her COGIC career includes serving as a district missionary, assistant state supervisor and state supervisor before moving into the top position. She demonstrates the potential paths to leadership within the COGIC women's structure.

Other COGIC women. Though many women found a place for their gifts within the Women's Department, others made places for themselves

---

[64]An honorary distinction usually reserved for an older woman who has served the congregation faithfully for several years.

that went beyond these conventionally circumscribed opportunities. These women had exceptional giftings that could be could not be denied by the hierarchy of the Church of God in Christ. Without challenging the existing gender-stratified structure within the denomination, they carved out significant places for themselves that would affect the ministry and direction of the denomination—not just its women.

One of the most visible examples is Arenia Mallory, who took over leadership of Saints Industrial and Literary School in C. H. Mason's hometown of Lexington, Mississippi, in 1926 and served as its first president until 1975. Under her leadership, the first black high school in Holmes County, Mississippi, became a junior college by 1945 and a four-year institution by 1974. In her fifty years at its helm, the institution trained many men and women whom she personally mentored or inspired to become prominent denominational leaders. Intimately involved in the life of the college, Mallory's intellect and wealth of interest took her far beyond the realm of most Pentecostal women of her day. She frequently traveled with the Jubilee Harmonizers, the college's women's choir, raising money and collecting books and clothing for students and county residents. Early in the 1930s, she worked to bring health and welfare services to Holmes County sharecroppers by convincing former Mississippi resident Ida Jackson, president of the Alpha Kappa Alpha sorority, to set up a summer school for rural teachers. In 1935 the sorority changed its summer educational program into a summer public health program, the Alpha Kappa Alpha Mississippi Health Project, which it also operated out of the Saints school.

Mallory's interest in local and national civil and women's rights issues led her to serve as a member of the National and International Councils of Negro Women, the umbrella organization of black women's groups. Mallory served as vice president from 1953 to 1957. She was also a member of the Regional Council of Negro Leadership, an organization founded in 1951 to promote civil rights, self-help and business ownership in Mississippi—serving on its board from 1952 to 1955. In 1968, despite the fact that Holmes County was predominantly black, Mallory became the first woman and African American to serve on the board of education.

Another example of the broader involvement of women is Sylvia Law, who in 1979, made COGIC history by becoming the first female chief financial officer, establishing national accounting department and budget procedures that are still in use today. Twenty-five years later, in 2004, she was among four women elected to the national board of trustees, along with Mildred Linzy, Cari Barnes and Georgia Lowe. Law garnered more votes than any other delegate vying for a board position. As a professional who has risen to a top management position in her secular career, Law is also an evangelist within the denomination and chairs the COGIC Charities Scholarship Committee, which annually distributes more than one hundred thousand dollars to students pursuing higher education.[65]

The ordination issue. The issue of women's ordination has never been completely settled within the COGIC. For while more than half of the graduates of the COGIC's C. H. Mason Seminary are women, and women make up the majority of the delegates to the general and jurisdictional assemblies,[66] the only universally recognized avenues for COGIC women who seek to serve in ordained ministry are military and institutional chaplaincy in colleges and universities, hospitals and hospices, and correctional facilities. In 1993, for example, the chairman of the General Assembly instructed the Doctrinal Review Committee to prepare a report on the denomination's position. The committee of male clergy of various levels as well as females who held credentials as evangelists and missionaries could not reach a consensus, and the status of women remained unchanged.

None of the six national mothers have challenged the church's stand regarding women's ordination or been openly critical of its gendered hierarchy. Rather, they have found ways to redefine ideas of power within the denomination and harness the power that gifted women possess to further its overall vision. But support for women's ordination came from a seemingly surprising corner. During his seven-year tenure from 2000 to 2007, presiding bishop Gilbert Patterson raised the issue to a new level of public attention. Patterson appointed a woman, DeOla Wells-Johnson, as an associate pastor of his congregation, seating her prominently on the podium with male pastors during worship services that were televised around the world. While Wells-Johnson carried out responsibilities usually handled by COGIC women, such as overseeing

---

[65]"COGIC's Emerging Leaders," *Charisma*, November 2007, p. 64.
[66]Carlyle Church, "The Accommodation and Liberation of Women in the Church of God in Christ," *Journal of Religious Thought* (Winter 1995/Spring 1996): 78.

noonday prayer meetings, she also taught midweek Bible studies at the fourteen-thousand-member congregation—a role often reserved for men.[67] At the 2001 women's convention, Patterson attacked the issue of ordination head on. "We will not let women into the pulpit to speak," he said, "but we will allow drunken politicians to come to the podium smelling of last night's liquor."[68] Patterson's somewhat muted stand was controversial among some women who themselves did not favor women's ordination, fearing that it would dilute the power of a strong Women's Department by drawing away the most gifted women. Still, at the same time that he personally favored a larger role for women, Patterson conceded that most COGIC women did not want the rules regarding ordination to change. "If you take a poll of women in ministry in the Church," he said, "they don't want to be ordained and don't want to pastor, and they certainly don't want to think in terms of being bishops."[69]

Even Patterson's movement toward greater involvement for women came too late for discontented women who had been COGIC members during the earlier years. Those women voiced their opposition by leaving the denomination and have either founded independent ministries or aligned themselves with bodies that are more supportive of women in pastoral and ordained leadership. A number of prominent Pentecostal or charismatic women preachers, including Ernestine Reems, Bishop Barbara Amos, Renita Weems, Claudette Copeland and Yvette Flunder, could not find the freedom they desired within the COGIC and embarked on a path much different than the thousands they left behind.

In 2004, the issue of women's leadership was arguably part of the catalyst for the formation of a new denomination. After thirty-five years as a COGIC pastor, bishop and district superintendent, David Grayson, pastor of Christian Cathedral in Memphis, was consecrated as presiding bishop of the Church of God in Christ (New Day). At its founding, the group included about two thousand members from forty COGIC congregations, primarily in Tennessee, Alabama, Mississippi and New York. It is almost identical to the parent body in structure and belief, except that it welcomes the ordination of women as both elders and bishops. After fight-

---

[67]Valerie G. Lowe, "Leading the Way for Women," *Charisma*, September 2001, p. 46.
[68]Valerie G. Lowe, "God's Man in Memphis," *Charisma*, September 2001, p. 43.
[69]Ibid., p. 46.

ing with COGIC in court, however, Grayson's group was forced to change
its name to New Day Church International.

COGIC women pastors. Though the loose, quasi-episcopal jurisdictional structure discourages women from seeking pastoral ministry,[70] the system does not entirely lock women out of such leadership and provides a loophole for progressive, sympathetic bishops to grant women "regional" or jurisdictional ordination and place them in pastorates. Men such as George McKinney of San Diego, California; O. T. Jones Jr. of Pennsylvania; Levi Willis of Norfolk, Virginia; and Harvey Lewis of Washington, D.C., have used this loophole to ordain women, giving them full rights to function as pastors within their respective jurisdictions. Nevertheless, these women have no standing as ordained clergy in the General Assembly, where they are forced to represent their churches as lay delegates.

Several male leaders have crafted creative ways to involve women in pastoral leadership. In the 1950s, F. D. Washington, a prominent Brooklyn New York bishop, appointed a woman, Emily Bram Bibby, as his assistant pastor. From there Bibby, a renowned gospel singer, moved to Texas and then to Louisiana, serving in several leadership positions, including national evangelist and member of the National Advisory Board of the Women's Department. In many cases, women found their strongest allies in husbands who were willing to take on the system on behalf of their wives. In some instances, women serve alongside their husbands as copastors. In other cases, sympathetic husbands turn over pastoral leadership of their congregations to their wives, involving themselves in the other ministry or vocational pursuits while serving as a "covering" for their wives, deflecting criticism while at the same time protecting them from denominational politics, and often allowing these women complete freedom in ecclesial and administrative oversight of these congregations. While more than one hundred women currently use these mechanisms to serve as COGIC senior pastors, the designation "pastor" is still often withheld, and they are referred to as "shepherdess" by the denominational hierarchy.

Prominent GOGIC women pastors. Azusa Street Revival eyewitness

---

[70]According to a 1990 study conducted by C. Eric Lincoln and Lawrence Mamiya for their seminal work on the black church, COGIC clergy, along with Baptists, were the least likely to support women in the pastorate. C. Eric Lincoln and Lawrence Mamiya, *The Black Church in the African American Experience* (Durham: Duke University Press, 1990), pp. 292-93.

Emma Cotton was one of the earliest examples of women in pastoral leadership on the COGIC fringe. Though she held COGIC credentials, her congregation was never affiliated with the denomination. Having attended the revival as a young woman,[71] for the following thirty years, she and her husband, Henry, evangelized in Louisiana and preached throughout California, planting congregations in Fresno, Bakersfield and Oakland before settling in Los Angeles to pastor Azusa Pentecostal Temple. Cotton was considered a more prominent minister than her husband and did the bulk of the preaching. Since the denomination's ban would not allow her to officially serve as senior pastor, the church remained an independent congregation while she was alive. After her death, Henry aligned it with the COGIC.[72] Eventually this large congregation became one of the most important local COGIC bodies for much of the late twentieth century.

By the time she became pastor of Rescue Temple Church of God in Christ in Greensboro, North Carolina, under the "covering of her husband," Mabel Smith had served as COGIC district missionary and state supervisor of women. Smith "preached out" seven North Carolina congregations before taking on Rescue Temple's pastorate. She used the pulpit and her state position to challenge the COGIC's limitations on women. At the 1981 North Carolina State Convention, for example, Smith asserted,

> I was not called to be a missionary. God told me that I was a prophetess. Yes a prophetess! . . . I was not called to fry fish and chicken. . . . God sent me forth to establish churches. In fact, he has used me to establish seven. . . . I don't have a title of pastor but I'm doing the work. I don't have the title of district superintendent, but I assist my husband . . . supervising the churches I personally hewed out. My ministry has not been certified by man, but . . . sanctioned by God [who] has used me to pray for the sick and see them recover, and I have conducted numerous revivals . . . with hundreds of people in attendance. . . . God places no restrictions on women, only men do. After God has removed the yokes from our necks men have tried to put them back on us. Which is better, to be appointed by man to do a work or to be anointed by God?[73]

---

[71]Emma Cotton, "The Inside Story of the Outpouring of the Holy Spirit—Azusa Street—April 1906," *Message of the Apostolic Faith* 1, no. 1 (1936): 1.

[72]For a discussion of Cotton's life and ministry, see Estrelda Alexander, "Emma Cotton," in *The Women of Azusa Street* (Cleveland: Pilgrim, 2005).

[73]First Jurisdiction, Greater North Carolina Church of God in Christ, State Convention, Au-

On his deathbed, her husband requested that she not attempt to take over the sole pastorate of the congregation without having the requisite male as a covering. So Smith brought in her brother as her covering but continued to function in her highly visible role as pastor.

The practice of a woman assuming the pastorate at the death of her husband has historically been one of the major avenues for women's pastoral leadership.[74] Elizabeth Dabney was a pastor's wife and powerful intercessor in the early 1900s. In 1925 Dabney took over the pastorate of Philadelphia's Garden of Prayer COGIC and led it until her death in 1967. Dabney's work, *What it Means to Pray Through*, was first published by the COGIC publishing board in 1945 and republished in 1987. When the *Pentecostal Evangel* published excerpts from this testimony, Dabney received more than three million letters from all parts of the world from people wanting to utilize or benefit from her prayer technique.[75]

After the death of her husband, B. M. Oakley, in 1974, Irene Oakley sought and received permission to assume the pastorate of Philadelphia's Oakley Memorial Temple, the congregation they had built together. The church flourished under her leadership, and a number of women and men, many who later pastored successful churches, came under her tutelage. One of the most notable of these, Maria Gardner Thomas, assumed the pastorate of Oakley Memorial after her mentor's death. Thomas began speaking at youth services throughout the country while studying law at Laney College in Oakland, California. She soon began traveling as an evangelist and even while serving as senior pastor continued her evangelistic ministry throughout the United States and internationally. Like many COGIC women pastors, Thomas maintains her link with the Women's Department, serving as the chaplain for the steering committee and assistant supervisor for Haiti.

Ailene Gilmore served beside her husband, Clarence, as leader of Faith Tabernacle Church of God in Christ in Paterson, New Jersey, until his death in 1974, when Ailene assumed the pastorate and renamed the church Gilmore Memorial Tabernacle. With her at its helm, the church expanded

---

gust 1981, COGIC State Temple, Washington, North Carolina.

[74]Several women have risen to a level of prominence via this route, including Irene A. Oakley of B. M. Oakley Memorial Temple COGIC in Philadelphia. In an unusual move, another woman, Marie Garden, assumed the pastorate after Oakley's death.

[75]Elizabeth J. Dabney, "Praying Through," *Charisma*, November 2007, p. 18.

its ministry to encompass a preschool and a Christian academy, a twenty-four-hour daycare facility and nursing home, a prison ministry, street outreach, a food pantry, and a mission ministry to Honduras and Haiti as well as mothering several other churches.

WOMEN IN THE UNITED HOLY CHURCH

With Ida Robinson's 1924 departure to found the Mt. Sinai Holy Church of America, a void was created in women's leadership in the United Holy Church (UHC). Robinson did not leave alone; several women and men who were sympathetic to her stance of women's leadership followed her, bringing their congregations with them.[76] Subsequently, the UHC would eventually become the first black Pentecostal church with predominantly male leadership to ordain a woman to be the presiding bishop, adopting a stance on women's leadership that is among the most progressive with the black Pentecostal community. Still, historian William Turner admits that the denomination's history "illustrates problems the Black Church has had in dealing with women who felt the call of God upon their lives."[77]

Women such as Emma Craig, who with her husband, Charles, called the organizational meeting of the UHC, played a major role in the denomination's early years. Between 1900 and 1917, Emma and Charles "preached out" sixteen congregations in North Carolina that became the nucleus of the new denomination. Emma served as general mother of the UHC and was the first president of the Southern District missionary convention, for forty-six years, until her death in 1966.[78] Julia Delk first served as secretary of the board of missions under Henry Fisher, eventually becoming the first woman president of the UHC's missionary department.

Throughout its history, UHC women have pastored congregations that often rivaled those led by males. Women also serve as copastors with their husbands or other male colleagues. By 2006, three women, the late Jestina

---

[76]It is not known whether these congregations had formally joined the Mt. Sinai organization at that time, subsequently joined or were in fellowship with a sister organization, as is a custom among many Pentecostal bodies.

[77]William C. Turner, *History of the United Holy Church: A study in Black Holiness-Pentecostalism* (Piscataway, N.J.: Gorgias Press, 2006), p. 161. While Turner lists several women (Emma Craig, Lucille Light, Julia Delk, Margaret Bennett, A. D. Moore and Gussie Walker), with one exception, he does not specify the contribution these women made to the denomination.

[78]*Centennial Anniversary Journal of the Southern District of The United Holy Church of America* (1894-1994) (s.l.: United Holy Church of America, 1994).

Gentiles in Barbados, Juana Nichols in Panama and Mary Lawrence of Georgia had served at the rank of bishop.

Approximately 140 of nearly 600 UHC congregations are pastored by women. The largest proportion of women pastors are in the Northern District, where more than 30 percent of congregations are pastored by women. But women also pastor nearly one-quarter of the congregations in the three other large districts: Virginia, Southern and Western. Approximately half the churches in the Northeastern and Southeastern districts are pastored by women.

WOMEN IN THE FIRE BAPTIZED HOLINESS CHURCH

The Fire Baptized Holiness Church (FBHC) inherited its egalitarian stance toward women from its parent body, the Pentecostal Holiness Church, which, as most bodies with the nineteenth-century Holiness movement, was open to ordaining women from its inception. From the outset, the FBHC placed no official limitation on the ministry of women, and scholars such as Cheryl Townsend Gilkes contend that the organization was "founded as an egalitarian denomination."[79] However, as with other Holiness-Pentecostal groups, early unofficial attitudes apparently limited women's participation, for a 1916 addition to church polity specifically allowed women to be ordained and sent out as pastors.

When W. E. Fuller organized Fuller's Tabernacle FBHC in Atlanta, Georgia, in 1945, several women, including his wife, Emma, made up the bulk of that congregation. As new congregations were planted, women contributed to their founding and ongoing success, and women continue to be the denomination's mainstay, making up the bulk of the laity in many local congregations. Over time, the FBHC continued to have proportionately more women serving as senior pastors than any other black Pentecostal body, giving women considerably more latitude in these positions than that found elsewhere in the movement. Like other denominations, throughout its history, women have been used to plant congregations, but unlike many other black or white Pentecostals bodies, women have not only been allowed to bring these congregations to viability but also have been allowed to remain as pastors of those viable congregations,

---

[79]Cheryl Townsend Gilkes, "Together and in Harness: Women's Traditions in the Sanctified Church," *Signs* 4 (Summer 1985): 692.

and have been called on to succeed other pastors. Additionally, women hold a number of key jurisdictional posts, serving as education, missions, and youth directors in a number of districts. To date, however, though no official polity prohibits it, no woman has held the highest ranks of jurisdictional leadership, as bishops or ruling elders.

Within the FBHC several auxiliaries channel efforts of women who do not desire pastoral ministry but want to actively work in the church. Since 1916, the Sisters of Charity and Brothers of Love have provided a place for both men and women to work in various enterprises to support the church. Later, the name was shortened to Sisters of Charity, and the organization became an exclusively women's auxiliary. The broader, FBHC Women's Department involves a multitiered operation that advances women through their local congregation to state, regional and national leadership. Within the local church, women serve on ministerial and deacons' boards, as well as on the Mothers Board, assisting in the instruction of younger women, enforcing church rules and assisting with the Lord's Supper.[80]

WOMEN IN ONENESS DENOMINATIONS

The issue of women in church leadership was at the root of numerous schisms that fragmented black oneness Pentecostalism. In the parent black oneness body, the Pentecostal Assemblies of the World (PAW), women initially played a substantial role. They were ordained to serve as pastors, evangelists, missionaries and in other capacities. They were not, however, given access to ecclesial office. The freedom they enjoyed was, in part, responsible for bringing about one of the first splits in black oneness Pentecostalism. Yet no one pattern of women's leadership emerged within its history, and the variety found there mirrors the spectrum found among their trinitarian sister organizations. A small number of oneness groups severely limit women's participation in ministry; but most black oneness groups restrict the ministry of women in some way, while a few allow a high degree of freedom for women in ministerial leadership. Three oneness bodies, the PAW, the Church of Our Lord Jesus Christ of the Apostolic Faith and the Church of the Lord Jesus Christ of the Apostolic Faith, exemplify the variation in responses of oneness denominations to this issue.

---

[80]Patrick L. Frazier Jr., *Introducing the Fire Baptized Holiness Church of God of the Americas—A Study Manual*, www.fbhchurch.org/pf_manual.pdf, pp. 67-69.

Pentecostal Assemblies of the World. Though its early leadership was predominantly male, the majority of PAW members were, and continue to be, women. While early women were ordained and placed into pastorates, they were excluded from the highest positions of denominational leadership (bishop and elder), and even while serving as pastors, they generally carried the title evangelist or missionary. Historically, as with other predominantly black Pentecostal denominations, PAW women have seldom been appointed to viable pastorates. Yet PAW women use the same creative avenues for moving into such leadership roles as COGIC women. Many inherit pastorates from other women who have served as their mentors or from their husbands. Other women plant new congregations.

As the denomination grew, several auxiliaries were put into place to harness women's energies and talents. In 1922, a Board of Women's Work was appointed to coordinate efforts of the organization's women missionaries and evangelists. Presumably, the women who came under the auspices of this group worked within the local congregations.

By the end of the twentieth century, the PAW was affording women higher levels of leadership than most other black Pentecostal bodies. In 1998, for example, four women were elected to executive PAW leadership positions for the first time. Rose Jackson, Ann Storey Pratt and Gwendolyn Weeks were elected to fill three of five lay director positions, and Aletha Cushinberry was elected the first woman general secretary, becoming part of the denomination's executive leadership. These women were nominated from the floor and voted in by lay delegates and women clergy. In 2001, the four were elected to a second term. That convention also passed a resolution allowing women to be appointed as district elders, though they made no decision concerning the capacity in which these elders could serve. Four years later, the convention voted to allow women to serve as district supervisors. At that time, however, there were only 175 women serving in pastorates, out of 2,400 ordained clergy.

As with the COGIC's role among trinitarian bodies, the PAW Women's Department would be a model for women's ministry auxiliaries among oneness bodies. The organization was formally established in 1923. And, like the COGIC, the PAW established a number of peripheral auxiliaries for women who did not find opportunities within the Women's Department. The Federation of Pentecostal Women was formed in 1933 by Gertrude Dickerson as an outreach organization that specifically took on social service projects. Under Dickerson's direction, this group envisioned building a home for the indigent aged within the PAW. That vision never materialized, and the Women's Federation largely came to a halt with Dickerson's death in 1946.[81] However, the auxiliary was able to undertake a number of smaller projects, including providing the financial support to bring young Helen Moore to the United States and help provide for her education. A year after Dickenson formed her group, the Home Missions Department was established to provide financial and spiritual sustenance for women to evangelize new territories and dig out new congregations throughout the United States as well as financial support to women working in overseas fields of duty. Under its sponsorship, a number of women went out to start new congregations and assist struggling ones. The Minister's Wives Alliance was formed in 1952 to provide instruction for and fellowship among pastors' wives. This group also provided scholarships for students at the denomination's Aenon Bible College, donated funds to assist in the purchase of the Pentecostal plaza headquarters in Indianapolis and provided annual support for the Home and Foreign Missions departments. The auxiliary was later renamed the International Ministers' Wives and Ministers' Widows Auxiliary to embrace those women whose husbands were deceased.[82]

In its nearly one-hundred-year history, the stories of a number of great leaders have been told and retold in the several histories that have been written about the PAW. As in much of Pentecostalism, these histories pay little attention to a number of women who played a significant role in its ongoing ministry. Susan Lightford, for example, established King's Assembly in New York around 1909. Though she had previously sensed a call to ministry, it was only two years before starting the congregation that Lightford had heard two missionaries testify of their experience of Holy Spirit baptism with tongues and began to seek the experience. At that time, she was attending a small congregation pastored by William Sturdyvant, who had come from Azusa Street to New York to plant the city's first Pentecostal congregation. After receiving the Pentecostal Spirit baptism, Lightford began preaching on Harlem's street corners. Her efforts gained

[81]Sims, *Telling Our Story*, p. 71.
[82]Ibid., pp. 27-28.

a number of converts who made up the first members of her new congregation. Later, in 1917, Lightford heard the message regarding baptism in Jesus' name from Garfield Haywood's associate Henry Prentiss, who had come to New York from Indianapolis. Determining that this message was true, she was rebaptised and brought her congregation into the Pentecostal Assemblies of the World.[83] By 1919, the church had grown to two hundred members. One of those to be influenced by Lightford's ministry was Robert C. Lawson, who went on to found the Church of Our Lord Jesus Christ of the Apostolic Faith.

Pastor and faith healer Mattie Poole rose from obscurity and a troubled childhood to become one of the leading faith healers within black oneness Pentecostalism. One of eight children of an alcoholic father and an abusive mother, at age thirteen, she was left care for herself. Her situation was so dire that she attempted suicide. A year later, she had a conversion experience and received the Pentecostal baptism of the Holy Spirit under the ministry of Garfield Haywood. By age eighteen, Poole had begun preaching street services. Shortly after her conversion, her future husband, Charles, whom she had already befriended, was converted, and the two started a storefront congregation. That work grew to become Bethlehem Healing Temple, a congregation of several hundred, housing numerous ministries in a multiauditorium facility. Despite her desperate childhood situation, Poole was an accomplished pianist, prolific writer and composer. She authored several books, numerous pamphlets and edited two periodicals, the *Voice of Living Witnesses* and *God Met Us in the Healing Campaigns*. While she worked as assistant pastor alongside her husband, Charles, she carried on a radio program that, at its height, was broadcast on twenty-four stations including major markets throughout the country. But it was her healing ministry, which began simply in the 1930s but grew to include major healing campaigns throughout the country, for which she was most renowned. Hundreds of people crowded churches and halls to hear her preach and have her pray for their healing. Because of the success and notoriety of these campaigns, the Pooles established Bethlehem Healing Temple congregations in Atlanta, Brooklyn and Boston.

---

[83]Ibid., pp. 13-15.

Hilda Reeder, another prominent PAW woman, distinguished herself in missions, serving as the secretary treasurer of the board of bishops. This role was normally reserved for a man, and Reeder was the only woman member of the executive board. Though raised as a Presbyterian, Reeder received her Pentecostal Spirit baptism in 1912 and shortly after joined Haywood's congregation in Indianapolis. Within a short time, Haywood tapped Reeder, a public school teacher, to assist him and his wife with the administration of his congregation's missions work. When the PAW Missions Department was organized in 1919, Reeder assisted Haywood and Andrew Urshan in the effort, but it was not until 1924, after several men had failed to make a go of it, that Reeder was appointed to the position of secretary treasurer. She served in that position until her retirement in 1951. A year earlier she wrote the first history of the PAW Missions Department.

Though Gertrude Dickerson's vision for a substantial missionary effort in Liberia had not materialized by the time of her death, at her insistence, PAW presiding bishop Samuel Grimes sponsored a single missionary woman who would have great impact on that country and the missions work of the PAW. Grimes and his wife, Katherine, sponsored the immigration and education of a young Liberian woman, Ellen Moore Hopkins, who was to have an important role in the PAW's mission efforts in that country. After the couple adopted her she was trained as a nurse, and after receiving two master's degrees, she returned to Liberia as a missionary. She served in that country for thirty-three years, establishing the Samuel K. Grimes Memorial Maternity and Child Welfare Center in a converted warehouse. The work eventually encompassed fourteen buildings, including a 1,000-seat sanctuary, a maternity hospital, two medical clinics and three dormitories. During her tenure, she cared for 700 orphans and poor children, saw 1,300 babies safely delivered and trained 136 nurses who subsequently served not only at the hospital, but throughout Liberia.[84] Moore Hopkins was forced to leave Liberia during the civil war that began in 1989, and the Grimes Center was destroyed during the conflict. She also established the Ralph Bass Junior College.[85]

As a gifted preacher and teacher, the daughter and sister of bishops of

---

[84]Dorothy E. Scott, "Ellen Moore Hopkins," in *Great Women of Pentecost*, ed. Dorothy E. Scott and Ethel Trice (Indianapolis: n.p., 1983), p. 65.
[85]Sims, *Telling Our Story*, pp. 29-31.

Bibleway Churches World-Wide, Carolyn Showell blends deep denominational roots and exposure to black ecumenism and the broader body of
Christ. She typifies the trend of some highly educated Pentecostal women
who maintain ties with the movement through membership in a local congregation but primarily engage in ministry that takes them out of the narrow confines of women's roles within classical Pentecostalism and places
them in mainline denominations. Ordained in the PAW, Showell serves
on the board of presbyters of her brother's First Apostolic Faith Church in
Baltimore, Maryland. As a trained psychologist, she regularly conducts
conferences, workshops and seminars among mixed-gender audiences as
well as women's groups, addressing issues of human development and spiritual growth, and offers a blend of uniquely Pentecostal fervor and intellectual challenge.

One of the most visible and highly educated women in black oneness
Pentecostalism is Pastor Iona Locke. Called to the ministry at eighteen,
Locke's ministry was nurtured under leading PAW bishops, including
F. M. Thomas, Robert McMurray and former presiding bishop Norman L.
Wagner. As a young woman, Locke served as the vice president of the
International Young People's Union and on the pastoral staffs of churches
in California and Ohio. She also traveled as an evangelist, preaching
throughout the United States, Caribbean, Europe and the Middle East. In
1994 she left the PAW and founded Abyssinia Christ Centered Ministries. Locke is one of the most sought-after preachers within the denomination; she regularly draws crowds of thousands. Yet, in order to move into
the highest tiers of black Pentecostal leadership, Locke had to move outside of the PAW denominational bounds when, six years later, she was
consecrated as bishop of Christ Centered Ministries.

Church of Our Lord Jesus Christ of the Apostolic Faith. When Lawson
left the PAW in 1918 to form the Church of Our Lord Jesus Christ of
the Apostolic Faith (COOLJC), it was partly because of his stand against
women's ordination and their freedom to preach and hold pastorates.[86]
Accordingly, COOLJC took a strong stance against women's ordination
and leadership from its inception. Women are not entirely excluded from
ministry; instead, they are allowed to function in tightly circumscribed

---

[86]James C. Richardson Jr., *With Water and Spirit: A History of Black Apostolics* (Washington,
D.C.: Spirit Press, 1980), pp. 54-55.

roles. They can be licensed as social, senior and field missionaries through the organization's Department of Women's Missionary Work. This department operates much like the COGIC's Women's Department. Within its structure, women have an opportunity to take on supportive roles that help ministers and pastors with the responsibilities of the local congregation.

In 1956, Evelyn Lawson, wife of the founder, set up an auxiliary to instruct young ministers' wives to be leaders in their local congregations and help their husbands' work. The Ministers and Deacons' Wives' Guild allows younger women to benefit from the counsel of experienced pastors' and deacons' wives who would set up guilds in their respective congregations. The COOLJC's Women's Council, founded in 1952 by Mother Delphia Perry, focuses on fundraising, pursuing educational endeavors, raising support for foreign missions and promoting social concerns of women within the local congregations. The council provided COOLJC laywomen a voice for their concerns and an arena in which to use their talents. The Missionary Department provides an opportunity for women who feel a call to more public ministry to serve as "missionaries," helping ministers and pastors by visiting widows, orphans and the sick; holding informal biblical counseling sessions; and instructing younger women on family issues. These women also help male leaders evangelize and establish congregations.

The issue that caused the break between the PAW and the COOLJC, however, was about more than just women's roles in the church's leadership. Lawson also held more a much more rigid stance on other issues related to women. He particularly objected to what he perceived as a liberal stance on divorce and remarriage, the more stylish attire that PAW women were adopting in their apparel and the fact that traditions such as requiring women to cover their hair in worship were being abandoned.

Church of the Lord Jesus Christ of the Apostolic Faith. The seemingly rigid stand the COOLJC took on the issue of women paled in comparison to the stand taken by Lawson's protégé, Sherrod Johnson, who left Lawson's organization to form the Church of the Lord Jesus Christ of the Apostolic Faith, in part, because of his even stronger posture on limiting women's leadership. The strength of the new denomination's rigid stand against the ordination of women is reflected in a statement on women preachers, "Can a Woman Preach or Teach the Gospel of Christ," by one of its bishops, Randolph Goodwin:

> It wouldn't be any conflict . . . to ordain women to preach, if I had Bible qualifications for a woman to preach, I would be willing to ordain women. . . . There is no Bible that stands behind a woman teaching or preaching or usurping authority over men or the church. . . . A woman can sing, praise God, clap her hands and dance a praise to God. But, when it comes to preaching and usurping authority over the man . . . she is to keep silent. . . . She can do other works in the church, such as; praying, fasting, ministering to the sick, giving out literature and telling the people where to come and hear the word of God.[87]

Johnson's group not only opposed the leadership of women but also placed even more severe sanctions on women's attire than Lawson's, which allowed women to wear some makeup and jewelry and adorn themselves in modest yet fashionable attire. The more conservative group insisted that women dress as modestly as possible. "Johnson's members," as the women in his denomination came to be known by other Pentecostals, could be recognized by their distinctive attire. Adorned in cotton stockings, long-sleeved, calf-length dresses and a head covering of some type whenever in public, they were also forbidden to straighten their hair with chemical straighteners or hot combs, or to wear makeup or jewelry of any kind, and were specifically forbidden to wear slacks of any kind, calling such action, "women wearing men's apparel" and declaring that to do so constituted "an abomination in the eyesight of God."[88] When several smaller groups broke from the denomination, all of them, to some degree, restricted the ministry and leadership of women.

WOMEN'S AUXILIARIES: STRUCTURES FOR INVOLVEMENT IN THE CHURCH'S LIFE

Obviously, Seymour's model of relative equality did not survive as the predominant model for the burgeoning Pentecostal movement over its one-hundred-year history, but neither did Mason's model of largely confining

---

[87]Randolph Goodwin, "Can a Woman Preach or Teach the Gospel of Christ?" The Holy Temple of the Lord Jesus Christ of the Apostolic Faith, www.theholytemplechurch.org/can_a_woman_preach.aspx.

[88]Bishop S. C. Johnson, *21 Burning Subjects.*

women to a parallel structure that excludes them from the highest levels of denominational leadership. Women who were unwilling to settle for either solution became inventive in forming a number of organizations that gave them a place for authentic involvement in the life and direction of their churches. Deaconess boards allowed women to carry out community service through ministry to the sick, elderly and poor. Pastor's aid clubs gave them opportunities to serve the needs of the pastor and his family. Willing workers groups maintained the sacramental elements of the sanctuary, keeping the altar and the pulpit in order and setting up the table for the Lord's Supper. Prayer bands channeled the spiritual fervor of women who met to intercede for the pastor, the needs of individual members of the congregation or the congregation as a whole. Purity class allowed older women to teach younger women on personal ethics and morality. Other auxiliaries—missionary circles, nurses circles and sewing circles—were established to give the large number of women who make the movements of their home a way to play a substantial role in the life of the church.

These auxiliaries gave women who did not feel called to preach a sense of empowerment. They also offered opportunities to display talents and abilities in ways that left room for visible male authority and leadership without disrupting the gendered power structure. Further, they provided local congregations and jurisdictional, regional and national bodies with the volunteer womanpower required to support their programs. For those who felt called to preach, evangelistic teams provided opportunities outside the regular Sunday pulpit to proclaim the gospel in home Bible studies, on street corners, in jails, nursing homes, women's services, conferences and retreats. The pulpit, however, remained largely the domain of men.

WOMEN'S DAY

In 1907, a year after the Azusa Street Revival began, famed educator and Baptist preacher Nannie Helen Burroughs instituted the annual Women's Day observance "to raise women, not money."[89] The observance quickly gained wide acceptance not only in Baptist congregations but also in black independent and United Methodist congregations as well as other black

---

[89]For a discussion of the origins of Women's Day, see Evelyn Brooks Higginbotham, *Righteous Discontent: The Women's Movement in the Black Baptist Church, 1880-1920* (Cambridge, Mass.: Harvard University Press, 1994).

mainline churches. Despite its conception within more liberal circles, it found wide acceptance in Pentecostal congregations who were introduced to the concept through women such as Bethune's colleagues Mallory and Coffey and became a staple in their liturgical life. As conceived by Burroughs, the purpose of that day was to interest women in local congregations in raising money for overseas missions. Over the years, however, it has increasingly been adapted to other uses, becoming the one Sunday in the church's year when every woman can be involved in some aspect of the worship services and accompanying festivities. They preside, read Scripture, pray and preach. They collect the offering and, more importantly, they generally bring a special offering, for despite Burroughs's intent, the survival politics of many Pentecostal congregations had elevated the fundraising aspect of the ritual. Yet it is their opportunity for women to show strength, since the success of their efforts to raise the necessary resources to sustain their congregation is often singularly most evident at this time.

The Women's Day celebration affords the church the opportunity to recognize women's giftedness and leadership in a way that may not be acceptable throughout the remainder of the church year. It is also an opportunity for women to show their financial strength within the congregation. Numerous fundraising endeavors precede the event, with women engaged in creative strategies to elicit support from friends, family and coworkers to support "the work of the Lord." This work includes augmenting the general or building fund, providing scholarships and other causes felt noteworthy.

EXODUS OF WOMEN FROM CLASSICAL PENTECOSTAL DENOMINATIONS

While many black Pentecostal women have resigned themselves to the limitations of existing systems of participation, which provide them with a level of influence that is never quite explicit and governed by the constraints of male-dominated church politics, other women have been unwilling to settle for these solutions. Many of the most gifted and prepared women find themselves in a system that does not provide the full opportunity to forge the type of ministry they envision for themselves, and it has proven unsatisfactory. It is these women who walk away from the movement that they cherished to seek a more appropriate and accepting place of ministry.

While many of these women have specifically sought out a few progressive evangelical denominations, others have moved entirely away from black conservative religion, affiliating with mainline denominations offering greater opportunities for women's leadership and advancement and more equitable remuneration commensurate with their training and abilities.

One of the most highly visible women to have followed this route is Bishop Violet Fisher. Fisher represents a cadre of women who have been able to successfully navigate between the black Pentecostal movement and the predominantly white mainline church by returning to her roots in the Methodist Episcopal Church. Feeling called to preach at age sixteen and initially not seeing role models within the Methodist Church, she was drawn to the Pentecostal movement, where she found women such as Carrie Gurry willing to mentor her. Ordained an elder in King's Apostle Holiness Church of God in 1965, Fisher was appointed a national evangelist ten years later. But during those years she also taught junior and senior high school because she was unable to make a living in ministry. The denomination, which was founded by a woman, was open to their leadership, but the small organization afforded only a limited opportunity for the kind of ministry that would incorporate her gifts and training.

After completing Vanderbilt University Divinity School in 1988, Fisher returned to the Methodist Church, where she was ordained a deacon and appointed as associate pastor in Chester, Pennsylvania. Two years later, she was appointed a senior pastor in Philadelphia. In 1994, after only six years in United Methodist Church ministry, she was appointed a district superintendent of the Mary McLeod Bethune District.[90] Six years later she was elected bishop of the North, Central and Western New York Annual Conference, becoming the first African American woman to do so in the Northeast Jurisdiction and becoming responsible for eight hundred local churches and fifteen hundred clergy in western and north-central New York. By 2006 Fisher was serving as vice president of the General Board of Global Ministries.

LEADERS OF INDEPENDENT BODIES

Throughout the history of the African American Pentecostal movement,

---

[90]District superintendents were once called presiding elders.

there have always been a number of women who countered classical Pentecostalism's retreat from its early commitment to gender equality by forging a broader place for themselves and other women. While some, like
Showell and Locke, stayed under the covering of parent bodies while conducting their ministries outside its walls, others severed ties with these
denominations, choosing to found independent congregations. Like Mozella Cook's Sought Out Church of God in Christ and Spiritual House of
Prayer, Beulah Counts's Greater Mt. Zion Pentecostal Church or Madeline Phillips's Alpha and Omega Church of God Tabernacles, many
women have found that they still faced the lack of acceptance of women in
the role of senior pastor. Some of these women floundered for years, seeing
only limited growth in their congregations or their organizations remaining fairly small. Nevertheless, they remained unwilling to be tied to denominations that showed little appreciation for their gifts and callings.
Other women developed a substantial following. Some banded with like-
minded women—and men—to establish local, regional, national or international fellowships that maintained Pentecostal doctrinal distinctives
while allowing women greater leadership opportunities. Within these new
bodies, women could insert themselves into roles of ecclesial leadership,
and in a few cases, as the principle leader in the organization.

By 1951, Ernestine Cleveland, daughter of COGIC bishop Elmer Elijah (E. E.) Cleveland, had begun traveling across the country as an evangelist, fully aware of, and dissatisfied with, denominational limits on
women. In 1968, Reems (which is her married name) left the COGIC to
found an independent congregation, Center of Hope Community Church
in a seedy neighborhood in Oakland, California. In the forty years since
its founding with four members, the congregation has grown to more than
two thousand. In 1990, she opened a 56-unit senior housing complex and
in 1992 opened a transitional housing program for homeless mothers and
children. Reems also opened Hope School of Excellence, a charter school
for preschool through eighth grade, and E. C. Reems Gardens, a 150-unit
low-cost housing complex. She also founded Kingdom Builders Ministerial Alliance to mentor urban ministers and support missionary projects in
Haiti and South Africa. She is perhaps most nationally known for the
E. C. Reems Women's International Ministries. The organization, founded
in 1988 to mentor and develop women leaders who found little support

within their denominations, hosts regional conferences and produces and distributes publications and audio and visual instructional materials.

Barbara Amos began preaching at New Community Church of God in Christ in Portsmouth, Virginia, at a young age. Though her pastor was supportive, she was stifled by the COGIC dual-ministry structure. Still, Amos stayed in the denomination, helping a struggling congregation in neighboring Norfolk until 1986, when the pastor stepped down and she took leadership. Within six months, Faith Deliverance Center outgrew its facilities and within ten years had twenty-seven hundred members. Weary of COGIC limitations on women, Amos brought her congregation into Mt. Sinai Holy Church of America, with its heritage of female leadership. She quickly rose to prominence within that denomination, where she was consecrated bishop of North Carolina. She also gained prominence in the broader Pentecostal movement, where in 1994 she was appointed the only woman on the organizing committee of the Pentecostal and Charismatic Churches of North America (PCCNA) and subsequently was the first woman on the board of the newly formed biracial umbrella organization. Even here, however, Amos met gender bias when she "encountered men who refused to remain in prayer and dialogue groups with her present."[91] Undaunted, at one point Amos declared,

> Reconciliation cannot be limited to . . . racial prejudice. . . . Such limitation will be a disappointment to millions of women who comprise the church bodies. It is hypocritical . . . to condone racial equality and . . . gender disparity. . . . The full embrace of the Christian message will make it imperative that we share on all levels. It is not enough to fellowship on "Love the Brethren Day" or have "Annual Women's Week." The Invitation must be extended into decision making positions of responsibility. The welcome mat must be placed not only at the door of the music room, but also at the door of the board room.[92]

By the end of the twentieth century, gender bias had also begun to infiltrate her own denomination, where her more progressive, often controversial leadership style placed her at odds with more conservative leaders. Then, although Amos was heir apparent to the continued legacy of women presiding bishops, having been selected by Bishop Amy Stephens as her

---

[91]Barbara Amos, "Race, Gender, and Justice," *Pneuma* 10, no. 1 (1995): 132-35.
[92]Ibid., pp. 133-34.

successor, the plan never came to fruition. After Stevens's death, Amos was denied the position and subsequently left Mt. Sinai, relinquished the pastorate of her local congregation to another woman, Sharon Reilly, and formed a new association, Faith Deliverance Ministries, in 2000. By 2006, the organization had eleven churches.

Licensed as COGIC evangelist at age eighteen, Claudette Copeland was ordained in 1979 as a chaplain. In 1980 she was commissioned as a first lieutenant in the U.S. Air Force, and she and her husband, David, became the first African American husband and wife chaplain team in the U.S. military. Copeland also served as a missionary to Haiti and several African nations, another area of ministry generally open to COGIC women. However, desiring a broader ministry than generally afforded COGIC women, Copeland earned a doctorate of ministry degree from United Theological Seminary, where she also served for several years as a visiting professor and mentor for doctoral studies. She and her husband serve as copastors of New Creation Christian Fellowship, a nondenominational congregation they founded in San Antonio, Texas, in 1984.

NEW CADRE OF BLACK PENTECOSTAL AND CHARISMATIC WOMEN CLERGY

Advances in black higher education occasioned by victories of the civil rights movement opened new opportunities for African Americans—including African American Pentecostal women—allowing them to pursue higher education and advanced theological degrees in previously unheard of numbers and exposing them to new arenas of the church about which many had been largely unaware. Further, the burgeoning charismatic and neo-Pentecostal movements opened pulpits in denominations that would have formerly been closed to even the most educated Pentecostals. A number of women are as likely to address large Baptist, African Methodist Episcopal and nondenominational megachurch congregations as they were classically Pentecostal small storefronts congregations.

As the pastor of Philadelphia's Sanctuary Church of the Open Door, Audrey Bronson exemplifies this new trend of progressive, seminary-trained, Pentecostal women pastors who are socially and politically savvy. Bronson came from a family of educators and church people. Her father was a school principal and pastor; her mother was a teacher. Her brother,

Oswald, was also a pastor before serving as president of Bethune-Cookman College from 1975 to 2004. She served on the faculty of Cheyney University, a historically black college twenty-five miles west of Philadelphia, for seventeen years and was dean of the Philadelphia Urban Education Institute, a subsidiary of the African American Interdenominational Ministries, and on the Mayor's Transition Team for the city's newly elected mayor. Bronson began evangelistic preaching at age fourteen. In 1975, she founded a congregation of a dozen members in her home. That group has grown to more than two thousand members and houses a Christian academy, Bible institute, apartment complex for the elderly, neighborhood youth basketball program and counseling center. Bronson's broad interests include ecumenical efforts with other evangelicals as well as mainline Christians; promotion of adoption of black children within black churches; and a number of civic, community and educational endeavors including serving on the Executive Committee of the Association of Theological Schools, and as a member of the Black Clergy of Philadelphia.

By the early 1990s, the exposure of a few Pentecostal women on the evangelistic circuit matched that of Jamaican-born evangelist Jackie Mc-Collough. McCollough, a daughter of preachers, taught Sunday school and spoke in church services at a young age, beginning to preach at sixteen. After high school, she first pursued a nursing career, planning to become a pediatrician, before sensing a calling to full-time ministry and pursuing graduate studies in philosophy and religion at Jewish Theological Seminary, where she received a doctorate of ministry degree. Her public ministry began with a home Bible study and ministering in prisons and hospitals. After her 1989 ordination, she served as associate pastor of Elim International Fellowship Church, a oneness congregation in Brooklyn, New York, and traveled as an evangelist, conducting revivals, seminars, workshops and conferences nationally and internationally. Within a short time, McCollough was in demand as a speaker across the United States and North America. Both an academician and a preacher, McCollough is founding pastor of the International Gathering at Beth Rapha; president of Daughters of Rizpah, a nonprofit evangelistic outreach ministry; and teaches hermeneutics at New York Theological Seminary.

The phenomenal explosion of televangelism has been a boon for this new generation of women ministers who eschew contemporary feminist language but tout a message of personal empowerment that is attractive to women from a variety of backgrounds. These women represent the new breed of Pentecostal-charismatic minister who are not satisfied to live by "faith alone" but who draw substantial salaries from their congregations and command substantial honorariums for their appearances at conferences and other venues.

The phenomenon of televangelism has afforded Juanita Bynum a level of visibility and notoriety far beyond anything she once would have hoped to achieve as a COGIC missionary or evangelist. The child of a COGIC minister, she began ministering after graduating from Saint's Academy, where her male classmates were being groomed for positions within the denomination's leadership. By twenty-one, however, she was in a marriage that would shortly end in divorce and had been hospitalized for anorexia nervosa. Bynum left the church for several years, was forced to go on public assistance and then worked as a beautician and flight attendant before returning to the church and the ministry. Within five years T. D. Jakes had invited her to serve as youth minister at his Potter's House congregation. The success of her autobiography, *No More Sheets,* and television exposure with major televangelists such as Jakes and TBN founders Paul and Jan Crouch pushed her into the limelight, and shortly, "prophetess" Juanita Bynum had become one of the most recognizable fixtures of pop Pentecostal culture. In 2001 Bynum married Bishop Thomas W. Weeks III, pastor of the Global Destiny Church in Washington, D.C. A year later the couple staged an elaborate televised wedding on TBN that was viewed by millions. The ceremony capped off a highly visible and controversial marriage that ended with an altercation between the couple in the parking lot of a major Atlanta hotel. Following that incident, Bynum used her visibility to champion the cause of spousal abuse in the secular and religious media; but her persona was somewhat tarnished, and her following, though still large, was also somewhat diminished.

WOMEN LEADERS AT THE END OF THE CENTURY

More than one hundred years after the Azusa Street Revival, the issue of women's leadership in African American Pentecostalism is still unsettled. Undeniably, black women have played a significant role in the unfolding of every era of the modern Pentecostal movement. Gilkes's contention is borne out by the fruit of the extraordinary women who have filled the pews, pulpits and boardrooms of Pentecostal congregations and denominations throughout the country.[93] Yet, at the beginning of the twenty-first century, patterns of Pentecostal women's leadership and subordination remain among the most rigid within the African American Christian church and the variety of patterns of women's leadership and rationales given for maintaining the widely disparate positions continue to be as plentiful as the still growing number of Pentecostal and charismatic denominations. Because of the dilemma, many of the most prominent women in the renewal movement stand outside of classical Pentecostal denominations and are aligned more squarely with the charismatic or neo-Pentecostal movements, overlying existing patterns of women's deployment in those traditions with an understanding of Holy Spirit empowerment that recalls the egalitarian model of earlier Pentecostalism. Those who remain loyal to classical Pentecostalism often find that there is more acceptance for their ministry and leadership outside its narrow confines.

Table 8.1. Characteristics of Representative Black Pentecostal Denominations Founded by Women

Denomination	Year Est.	Founder	Parent Body
Church of the Living God Pillar and Ground of the Truth	1903	Mary Magdalena Tate	
Mt. Sinai Holy Church of America (MSHCA)	1924	Ida Robinson	UHC
Kings Apostle Holiness Church	1929	Currie Gurry	
Sought Out Church of God in Christ and Spiritual House of Prayer	1944	Mozella Cook	COGIC
Alpha and Omega Pentecostal Church of God of America, Inc.	1945	Magdalene Mabe Phillips	
Mount Calvary Pentecostal Faith Church, Inc.	1932	Rosa Artimus Horn	
Greater Mt. Zion Pentecostal Church	1944	Beulah Counts	
Faith Deliverance Christian Fellowship		Barbara Amos	MSHCA

[93]See Cheryl Townsend Gilkes, *If It Wasn't for the Women: Experience and Womanist Culture in Church and Community* (Maryknoll, N.Y.: Orbis, 2001).

9

I WILL DO A NEW THING

AFRICAN AMERICAN NEO-PENTECOSTALS AND CHARISMATIC MOVEMENTS

In the last days . . . I will pour out of my Spirit on all flesh.

ACTS 2:17 NKJV

ONE **S**UNDAY **IN** **A**PRIL **OF** **1960,** Father Dennis Bennett of St. Mark's Episcopal Church in Van Nuys, California, announced to his congregation that he had received the baptism of the Holy Spirit, accompanied by speaking in unknown tongues. His singular confession ignited a chain of events that signaled the beginning of the spread of Pentecostal spirituality within the Episcopal Church, as well as throughout the Roman Catholic Church and much of mainline Protestant Christianity. Originally embraced primarily by students on several college campuses and in small prayer groups in local congregations, denominational hierarchy did not always welcome the movement but often saw its fervor as a throwback to unsophisticated folk religion out of step with enlightened classical Christianity. Within a short time, however, charismatic Christianity, as it came to be known, would take hold of segments of the church that previously had been untouched by Pentecostal spirituality.

By the first half of the 1960s, the classical Pentecostal movement had attained a worldwide membership of nearly eight million. Still, its spirituality was largely practiced by lower- and working-class Americans and marginalized peoples in the two-thirds world. Its emergence in mainline circles positioned it to take off in ways that neither mainline Christians nor Pentecostal believers themselves could have imagined, growing exponentially through two related, and often indistinguishable, movements: charismatic Christianity and neo-Pentecostalism. Through these two streams, old-time Pentecostal religion had influenced approximately 35 percent of American adults, or about 80 million people, by the end of the century. In the intervening years, almost one out of every four Protestant churches in the United States had become a charismatic congregation,[1] and black Christians would find themselves at the very epicenter of this trend. Black mainline Christians were first introduced to charismatic/ neo-Pentecostal spirituality through nondenominational, lay ecumenical efforts such as the Full Gospel Businessmen's Fellowship International and Women Aglow, and through exposure to charismatic leaders such as Kenneth Hagin, Kenneth Copeland, Fred Price and others who burst on the scene with the explosion of the religious broadcasting industry made possible by the proliferation of cable television stations.

To the casual observer, rigid distinctions between Pentecostalism, charismatic Christianity and neo-Pentecostalism may seem superfluous, as if they were simply different labels for one movement. Those who view themselves in this way collectively characterize all three as having emotive worship, high enthusiasm and low theological content. Yet a closer look reveals important differences in their historic antecedents, doctrinal emphases, ecclesiology, theological and practical understandings, and social context. Cross-pollination between the three camps, however, has ensured that by the end of the 1980s the differences between classical and neo-Pentecostalism had become somewhat blurred.

Even when viewed separately from classical Pentecostalism, the two latter movements—charismatic Christianity and neo-Pentecostalism— are often confused, as popular media and scholars often paint them as one phenomenon. Though it is true that distinctions are always unclear, they represent two closely related but different expressions of a new or revised spirituality. Both incorporate elements of classical Pentecostalism into

---

[1]Jennifer Riley, "Charismatic Christianity in US—Myths Exposed," *Christianity Today,* January 8, 2008, www.christiantoday.com/article/charismatic.christianity.in.us.myths.exposed/16054 .htm.

their respective theological understandings, giving them a substantially new form that thrusts them more prominently into mainline Christianity and the public eye. Though they have not entirely welcomed the newcomers, African American religious scholars consider the rise of the charismatic spirituality as one of the black religious context's most significant trends in the past four decades.[2] Even white historian Vinson Synan has ventured the estimate that a third of traditionally mainline black churches—about five million congregants from Baptists, Methodist, Disciples of Christ and other denominations—have embraced charismatic Christianity and/or neo-Pentecostalism.[3]

Charismatic Christianity represents the adoption of Pentecostal spirituality and a growing appreciation of the work of the Holy Spirit in enhancing worship and Christian life without acceptance of Pentecostalism's doctrinal emphasis on tongues as initial evidence. Charismatic Christians overlay this appreciation and personal experience with the Spirit onto liturgical forms and styles of worship within existing ecclesial structures. They form entirely new structures usually as parachurch organizations or subgroups within existing structures. An additional "contemporary" worship service is added to the Sunday schedule, for example, to accommodate those within a congregation who prefer more spirited worship; or an additional Sunday school class, Bible study or prayer meeting is added to the weekly schedule to give vent to charismatic worshipers' desire for more emotive spirituality. Charismatic Christians seek to recover the operation of spiritual gifts evident in the New Testament and apostolic church from Pentecost but are conspicuously absent from the center of subsequent church history. Their worship, prophecy, healing and glossolalia are welcomed, though the latter is understood primarily as a personal devotional gift whereby a believer is drawn into close communion with God.

As charismatic spirituality has grown, emphasis on denominational loyalty has created entirely new organizational structures that defy earlier alignments. Some leaders have eschewed traditional denominational affiliation, preferring to cast themselves as inter- or nondenominational or

[2]See, e.g., Cheryl Townsend Gilkes, "Plenty Good Room: Adaptation in a Changing Black Church," *Annals of the American Academy of Political and Social Science* 558, no. 1 (1998): 101-21.
[3]John Rivera, "A Shift in Their Focus for Black Churches," *The Baltimore Sun*, August 25, 2002, 1A.

to simply identify themselves as charismatic or Christian, preferring to align themselves in loose networks or "fellowships" of like-minded leaders and congregations.

VARIETIES OF BLACK CHARISMATIC CHRISTIANITY

Pentecostal spirituality has, to some degree, successfully recaptured the interracial ethos of earlier Pentecostal forebears. Multiracial congregations—especially within megachurches—have become a highly visible mainstay within the new movement. Still, the emergence of a new black awareness in the latter half of the twentieth century and an interest in recapturing lost elements of African spirituality have allowed highly gifted blacks to emerge as leader both within the multiracial circles and at the head of new black expressions of charismatic spirituality.

Charismatic spirituality, however, could more rightly be designated charismatic spiritualities because the difference in expressions is so strong that, often, all that visibly unites them is belief in the active involvement of the Holy Spirit in the life of the church and believer. Beyond that, the particular outworking of charismatic spirituality often takes on drastically different emphases.

Two expressions of African American charismatic Christianity—the Word-of-Faith movement and black Catholic Charismatic Renewal give some evidence of the breadth of the charismatic movement within the African American community. When viewed separately, they share very little in common, but each speaks to the new attractiveness of Pentecostal spirituality among people who would have earlier considered any tie to such "primitive," emotive religion to be problematic.

Though black worship has historically been more emotive than that of whites, the charismatic movement's start with white, middle-class American evangelicalism did not deter blacks from adopting elements into their own context. To be sure, such elements have been redefined in terms of a rediscovery of ties to deep roots within an African spirituality that never lost its openness to the Spirit.

Blacks in the Word-of-Faith movement. The doctrine goes by several names: "name it and claim it," "health and wealth," the gospel of prosperity, positive confession, the Faith movement, or simply, Word churches. Milmon Harrison identified the four common elements within black Word-of-Faith teaching: (1) promise of the "good life" in this present world as well as in the next; (2) syncretizing of New Thought metaphysical teachings with evangelical, charismatic Christianity and other religious forms; (3) engagement in issues of social injustice, including but not limited to participation in politics; (4) use of marketing products, diversified economic pursuits and utilized mass media in the service of their messages.[4]

Fred Price and Ever Increasing Faith Ministries. Frederick K. C. Price's route to leadership in the movement was circuitous. His parents were nominally Jehovah's Witnesses, but he showed little interest in religion as a young man. He began attending church to attract the attention of his future wife, Betty, and the approval of her parents, all of whom were devout Baptists. Once married, his spiritual interest quickly waned. But shortly into the marriage, Price was converted and called to the ministry. He first served as assistant pastor of a Baptist congregation and then served as an African Methodist Episcopal (AME) minister before moving to a Presbyterian congregation. In 1962, while he was serving that church, his eight-year-old son, Frederick III, was struck by a car while walking home from school and killed.

In 1965 Price moved into the pastorate of a Los Angeles Christian and Missionary Alliance congregation but was dissatisfied with what he perceived as a lack of productivity in his ministry and a lack of spiritual vitality in the churches with which he was familiar. During this time he read *God Can Do It Again* by famed healing evangelist Kathryn Kuhlmann. Her work whetted his appetite for a more powerful dimension in his ministry, which Price concluded would include "the demonstration of the power of the Spirit of God."[5]

Price had been pastoring for fifteen years before receiving the Pentecostal baptism of the Spirit in 1970. The next year, he founded Crenshaw Christian Center with nine members, five of them from his own family. Several months later, he began reading the teachings of Kenneth E. Hagin, founder of the Word-of-Faith movement, and incorpo-

---

[4]For an excellent discussion of this phenomenon, see Milmon Harrison, *Righteous Riches: The Word of Faith Movement in Contemporary African American Religion* (New York: Oxford University Press, 2005), pp. 131-34.

[5]"Ever Increasing Faith Ministries: Leaders – Dr. Price – Biography," www.crenshawchristian center.net/ccc-leaders.aspx?id=876.

rating elements of this teaching into his own ministry. As he did, his congregation began growing rapidly and soon required a move into new facilities.

In 1973, Price moved his three hundred parishioners from the West Washington area of Los Angeles to establish the Crenshaw Christian Center in the working-class community of Inglewood. By 1982, the four-teen-hundred-seat sanctuary was not large enough to contain the three worship services that Price was conducting each Sunday. One of the earliest and most visible black leaders within in the Word-of-Faith movement, Price is credited with introducing the Word-of-Faith message to the black community, though his ministry also draws on a significant segment of the white Word-of-Faith community.

Over forty more years, Price's ministry has grown to become Ever Increasing Faith Ministries, which includes radio broadcasts, a weekly television service that is viewed by millions across the country and throughout the world, tape and book ministries, and the Fellowship of Inner City Word of Faith Ministries (FICWFM). The organization, which Price established in 1990, provides financial assistance to approximately five hundred Word-of-Faith pastors in thirty-eight states and nineteen foreign countries.

In 1989, the congregation purchased the former campus of Pepperdine University and moved into the nine-million-dollar Faith Dome, a facility with a seating capacity of 10,146, which was at that time reportedly the largest church sanctuary in the nation.[6] By then, the ministry housed a Christian school, school of ministry, Bible school, bookstore, cafeteria, daycare center, alcohol- and drug-abuse program, and a twenty-four-hour prayer service, which is maintained by several hundred full- and part-time employees and a bevy of volunteers. In 2001, a Latino congregation began to hold its worship service concurrently with the English-speaking service each Sunday. The Crenshaw Christian Center-East was established the same year, twenty-eight hundred miles away, in Manhattan. Though Price would ultimately not serve as its senior pastor, only making irregular personal appearances, the congregation grew to more than eleven hundred members within a few years.

---

[6]Aldore Collier, "FaithDome: A Grand-Slam Homer for Jesus," *Ebony*, December 1, 1989, p. 42.

Throughout most of his years at the helm of the ministry, Price's teaching has centered on personal empowerment. This drew a multiracial congregation of middle-class and aspiring middle-class followers. But by the late 1990s the focus of his message would expand in an unexpected way. Following an incident in which Kenneth Hagin Jr., son of his mentor, made what Price considered disparaging remarks concerning interracial dating and marriage, he became an outspoken critic of racism, particularly within evangelical Christianity. The hard line he exhibited in his nationally televised series of teaching on the subject elicited strong reactions from both blacks and whites. Several television and radio stations canceled his broadcast, and almost half of the twenty-four black clergy on the FICWFM executive board resigned. But several prominent leaders supported Price and felt his frank criticism was on target. He was also given the Horatio Alger Award for "exemplify[ing] inspirational success, triumph over adversity, and . . . commitment to helping others," and the Southern Christian Leadership Conference's Kelly Miller Smith Interfaith Award for outstanding clergy.

Though later assisted by a cadre of paid staffers and host of volunteers, from the beginning Price has shared his ministry's leadership responsibility with his family. His wife, Betty, heads ministry to the more than half of his constituents who are women, and his three daughters—Angela, Cheryl and Stephanie—as well as their spouses all play major roles. By the time he reached his late seventies, the senior Price was contemplating stepping down from leadership of his congregation. Frederick Kenneth Price Jr., his second son, who was called to the ministry at the age of seventeen, had moved alongside his father in ministry. First introduced as a member of the pastoral staff and an irregular speaker on his father's television broadcast, Fred Jr. was ordained and installed as pastor of the twenty-two-thousand-member Crenshaw Christian Center at its thirty-fifth-anniversary celebration on his thirtieth birthday in March of 2009.

Creflo Dollar and World Changers Ministries. When Fred Price Jr. heard the call to the ministry, he was attending a service at his father's Crenshaw Christian Center, but his famous father had not preached the message. Instead, another rising black leader in the Word-of-Faith movement, Creflo Dollar, was speaking for a special event. A relative latecomer to Word-of-Faith leadership, Dollar converted from Methodism to Pentecostalism as a teenager. After his hopes of playing professional football ended in injury, Dollar began witnessing to students on the West Georgia College campus. After accepting Christ, a student introduced ten others to Dollar, and by 1981 Dollar and his roommate were teaching a dorm Bible study that quickly grew to over one hundred people. By his graduation in 1984, that study had grown to three hundred students.

Dollar held the first services of World Changers International Ministries in 1986 in an elementary school cafeteria with eight people. Within two years, the room could no longer hold the growing congregation, and twenty years later, in 2006, Dollar's twenty-thousand-member congregation was among the largest in the movement. By then, the congregation was worshiping in the eighty-five-hundred-seat World Dome, on eighty-one acres in the Atlanta suburb of College Park. By that time, Dollar had become internationally known through his "Changing Your World" television broadcast, a publishing group, bestselling books and a recording label, Arrow Records. Six years earlier, in 2000, Dollar had started a second congregation in Manhattan, which quickly grew to more than five thousand members. Unlike Price, the younger Dollar regularly commutes between the two congregations, preaching at Madison Square Garden on Saturday evenings and using two private planes to return to his Atlanta pulpit by Sunday morning.

Dollar, whose International Covenant Ministry has offices in South Africa, the United Kingdom, Canada and Australia, has always insisted that his message is about more than finances. Rather, he teaches that Christians should pursue prosperity in all areas of life—spiritual, physical, mental and emotional, as well as material.

Keith Butler. Keith Butler of the Word of Faith International Christian Center in Southfield, Michigan, became a protégé of Kenneth Hagin when he and his wife, Deborah, graduated from Hagin's Rhema Bible Training Institute in Tulsa, Oklahoma. He then returned to his hometown to establish a new congregation, which expanded rapidly, outgrowing eight locations within fifteen years. Finally, in 1996, it settled onto a 110 acre site with a 5,000-seat sanctuary in the Detroit suburb. Butler began his first local radio broadcast in 1979 and in that same year organized the Word of Faith Bible Training Center. By 2000, his Word of Faith International Ministers Association had grown to include 600 members. As a political activist, Butler promoted a variety of conservative causes and in 1989 successfully ran for a seat on the Detroit City Council, becoming the first black Republican to do so since World War II.

Other black Word-of-Faith leaders. In 1984, Leroy Thompson renamed his seventy-five-member Mt. Zion Baptist Church in Darrow, Louisiana, Ever Increasing Word Ministries Church. Membership has since grown to seventeen hundred. Though Thompson was converted in 1972, had been in the ministry since 1973 and in the pastorate since 1975, he did not experience Pentecostal Spirit baptism until 1983. Thompson's message is unashamedly focused specifically on economic prosperity. He is probably most known in charismatic circles for coining the phrase "money cometh to me, now!"

Other black Word-of-Faith leaders include Michael Freeman, who leads Spirit of Faith Christian Center, a three-thousand-member congregation in suburban Washington, D.C., and Bill Winston, pastor of Living Word Christian Center in Forest Park, Illinois, with forty-five hundred members.

The Word-of-Faith message has so permeated black charismatic culture that it is evident in congregations and ministries that would not explicitly identify themselves with that label or even claim that theology as their own. Elements of the teaching color the sermons of charismatic pastors as much as Pentecostal spirituality colors the worship of their congregations.

Critique of Word-of-Faith theology. Over the last several decades, many Word-of-Faith congregations have led the charge toward the emergence of megachurches, with several pastors gaining international followings through mass meetings that gather thousands and electronic media that draw millions of viewers. The movement, however, has not escaped critique from large segments of the African American community, who find it lacking in substance and sociopolitical relevance. Many evangelical Christians—both black and white—decry its apparent tie to New Thought metaphysics (which evangelicals consider an expression of the occult and therefore satanic). Most black Word-of-faith leaders blatantly reject such a charge, insisting that it stems from a misunderstanding about teaching they contend is both practical and biblical.

One of the earliest and harshest critiques of Word-of-Faith theology came from black political scientist James Tinney, who claimed that the movement not only lacked doctrinal precision but is also heretical, unscriptural, and "regressive in terms of political economics."[7] Tinney claimed that Word-of-Faith doctrine was a "cultural theology, perpetuated by the American capitalist impulse to have more." According to Tinney, such theology has a degrading effect on the poor and a sinister element that appeals to the carnal, selfish nature of humanity.[8]

The critique of the movement's apparent abandonment of social justice for the poor has been echoed repeatedly, as well as that of its narrow concentration on raising the economic status of the only minority of blacks who are middle class. Robert Franklin, an ordained COGIC elder who is president of Morehouse University, calls Word-of-Faith leaders "spiritual entrepreneurs, who purvey a 'pseudo-religious' prosperity gospel."[9] He contends that Black Word-of-Faith leaders attempt to put distance between themselves and traditional African American worship and preaching styles. Word-of-Faith leaders counter that. such being highly emotive preaching, it is generally impotent. Their messages are aimed at bringing practical transformation to people's thinking that changes their life situation rather than eliciting a strong emotive response. Notepads and pens are not relegated to midweek Bible study but are a staple even in Sunday morning worship. Rather than a sermon, one receives instruction—"new revelation" that emphasizes appropriating God's promised provision through faith—on how to be a better, more prosperous Christian in all areas of life.

Word-of-Faith pastors have prospered from the generosity of congregations who believe that "sowing into good ground," providing material gain for their leaders, will produce abundant return for them "in this life." Many reason that, since the pastor is God's anointed representative, when they are giving to the pastor, church or ministry, they are giving to God, who is "obligated" to bless them in return. It is not unusual for congregations to present pastors with extravagant gifts such as expensive watches and jewelry, automobiles, aircraft, vacations, large sums of money and even homes. Besides obtaining large bank accounts, many Word-of-Faith pastors come to own multiple houses, multiple automobiles, boats and even airplanes.

[7]James S. Tinney, "The Prosperity Doctrine: An Accretion to Black Pentecostalism," *Evangelical Review of Theology* 4, no. 1 (1980): 88.
[8]Ibid.
[9]Robert Franklin, "The Gospel Bling: If Preachers are Preoccupied with Pursuing the Life of Conspicuous Consumption and Preaching a 'Prosperity Gospel,' Then Poor People are in Big Trouble," *Sojourners*, January 1, 2007, p. 46.

But it is not only through the generous giving of constituents that they amass wealth. The prosperity message is marketed through sophisticated television, radio and Internet advertising. Selling products ranging from specially annotated study Bibles to sermon tapes and self-help books have not only helped members of their congregations to a better life but have also proven to be particularly uplifting to the financial status of these leaders, such as Freeman and Price, who unabashedly insist that their wealth is the fruit of faithful ministry and personal enterprise. But Dollar also became among the wealthiest of Word-of-Faith preachers, maintaining a one-million-dollar home in Atlanta, which is owned by the church, and a 2.5-million-dollar apartment in New York. Reportedly, his two Rolls-Royces were gifts from congregants and admirers.[10]

BLACK CHARISMATIC CATHOLICS

At the beginning of the twenty-first century, the nearly 2.5 million black Catholics in America represent approximately 10 percent of the African American population and a tenfold increase over seventy-five years. Many of these live in seven black dioceses of Louisiana, in the three dioceses around New York, and in those of Chicago, Washington, Miami, Los Angles, Detroit, and Galveston-Houston and Beaumont, Texas. They are served by approximately three hundred black priests, six hundred sisters, seventy-five brothers and four hundred permanent deacons.

Charismatic renewal within the Catholic Church was made possible because of changes in Catholic liturgy and practice that resulted from the deliberations of the Second Vatican Council. These changes allowed African American blacks and other faithful to incorporate culturally sensitive elements into the Masses within their local congregations. But it also allowed them to explore new varieties of spirituality without the direct guidance of church leaders, opening the possibility for exposure to Catholic charismatic Christianity. For black Catholics particularly, such exploration put them in touch with other forms of Christian spirituality, such as Pentecostalism, that resonated with their roots in African spirituality.

Black Catholic theologian Diana Hayes uses the term "black Catho-

---

[10]Michael Luo, "Preaching a Gospel of Wealth in a Glittery Market, New York," *New York*, January 15, 2006, p. 1.

lic revivalism" to describe what she sees as a "new form that comingle[s]
the egalitarian Arminianism of evangelical Christianity with the insti-
tutionalized ritual of Roman Catholicism."[11] Not tying black Catholic
revivalism explicitly to an understanding Holy Spirit baptism, Hayes
sees it rather as a "throwback to African spirituality."[12] But spirited gospel Masses replete with choirs singing the latest soulful gospel tunes
appear throughout the Catholic landscape at churches such as St. Augustine and St. Benedict the Moor in Washington, D.C., Holy Angels
in Chicago, and St. Anthony of Padua in Atlanta. The copy from a flier
advertising a revival, "No Ways Tired," among Chicago's black Catholics is an example:

> Join us for three nights of Spirit-filled praise and worship as we celebrate
> who we are and whose we are! This revival in the Black Catholic tradition
> will speak to the heart of every Catholic and set your spirit on fire! Come
> and be blessed by three of the most dynamic preachers in the Black Catho-
> lic community from across the nation.[13]

Most black Catholic charismatics have remained within that tradition,
involving themselves in liturgical innovation made possible by Vatican II.
But once exposed to the new spirituality, some have opted to leave Catholicism. One of the most visible, though controversial, expressions of
black Catholic charismatic spirituality is the African American Catholic
Congregation (AACC), founded in 1989 by Father George A. Stallings,
who had pastored St. Teresa of Avila, a predominantly black Catholic congregation in inner-city Washington, D.C., for twelve years. That congregation became known for enthusiastic worship featuring a crucifix with a
black Christ, a full-immersion baptismal font and a gospel choir within
what became a three-hour Mass.[14] Its highly charismatic ritual drew many
former Catholics back to the church and enticed Protestants to explore

[11]Diana Hayes, "Black Catholic Revivalism: The Emergence of a new Form of Worship," *Journal of the Interdenominational Theological Center* 14, no. 1-2 (1986-1987): 87-107.
[12]Ibid., p. 106.
[13]Poster, "No Ways Tired," Mission Chicago, Chicago, Ill., September 2006. See also, "Old St.
Mary's to Host Black Catholic Revival 'No Ways Tired' at Chicago's First Catholic Parish,"
Archdiocese of Chicago news release, September 22, 2006, www.catholicdioceseofchicago
.com/news_releases/news_2006/news_092206.shtm.
[14]Tom Stabile, "Holy Rolling: Archbishop George Stallings Is Putting Race into the Race to
Represent Ward 6," *Washington City Paper*, April 18-24, 1997, www.washingtoncitypaper
.com/articles/12523/holy-rolling.

Catholic worship, increasing St. Teresa's membership tenfold—from two hundred to two thousand parishioners.[15]

But amid acclaim from new believers, Stallings's spirituality drew concern from the Washington diocese, especially when he defied James Cardinal Hickey, establishing "Imani Temple" as an independent congregation and celebrating a first Mass that drew an estimated twenty-three hundred people. A year later, Stallings was excommunicated by the Roman Catholic Church. That same year, he was consecrated bishop of the AACC by Richard Bridges, who was from another breakaway denomination, the Independent Old Catholic Church. Within a year, Stallings was elevated to archbishop. The new church attracted thousands of worshipers, who stood for hours every Sunday at a three-hour Mass that incorporated African music, black literature and traditional African rites including invocation of ancestor spirits into its liturgy.[16]

Stallings's provocative style drew more than just disenchanted laypeople. Some of the leading figures in black Catholicism were sympathetic to him. Seven years after the AACC founding, Cyprian Lamar Rowe, a Marist priest who had served as the executive director of the National Office of Black Catholics and the National Black Catholic Clergy Caucus, as well as on the board of the *National Catholic Reporter*, broke from the mother church to join Stallings and was subsequently ordained a bishop.[17]

Though Stallings never publicly referred to his blend of Catholic ritual and African traditional religion as charismatic or neo-Pentecostal, the trappings of Pentecostalism—music, dancing, emotive preaching, baptism by immersion[18] and ritual healing—are part of the worship of Imani Temple and the AACC. But so is the strong social witness of the Catholic Church. Benevolence and the political activism have been integral elements of Imani Temple's ministry from the outset. At the same time, Stallings has been a highly visible member of the Washington community. His run for city council, though ultimately unsuccessful, included a highly publicized campaign.

---

[15]Marjorie Hyer, "Black D.C. Priest Plans Separate Catholic Church," *Washington Post,* June 20, 1989, A1.

[16]"Rift in Stallings Rank," *Christian Century,* November 6, 1991, p. 1023.

[17]"Black Leader Leaves Church," *National Catholic Reporter* 33, no. 17 (1997): 8.

[18]Controversy was stirred when one of Stallings's assistants' infants accidentally died following a baptism that had been conducted by immersion instead of the traditional Roman Catholic mode of sprinkling.

Stallings proved to be controversial on a number of issues at the heart of Roman Catholic social piety when he announced, for example, that he had abandoned Catholic teachings against abortion, birth control, homosexual activity, remarriage after divorce, and the requirement for priest to be celibate.[19] In 2001, the fifty-three-year-old married twenty-four-year-old Sayomi Kamimoto in a mass wedding performed by the Unification Church's Reverend Sun Myung Moon. He associated with the Nation of Islam's Louis Farrakhan, who, along with members of the Inner Light Unity Fellowship, a predominantly gay congregation, attended the 1994 dedication of the cathedral into which Stallings moved his congregation.[20]

The AACC began with nine churches and eventually expanded to include thirteen congregations. By 1990, there were approximately five thousand members in congregations throughout New Orleans, Baltimore, Philadelphia, Norfolk and Richmond. While the Norfolk congregation had closed by the late 1990s, additional congregations rose up in Los Angeles and Richmond, leading to a now estimated seventy-five hundred members.

BLACK NEO-PENTECOSTALISM

Neo-Pentecostalism within the African American context can be defined as those persons and congregations who have embraced Pentecostal worship styles while remaining in their denominational structure within historically mainline denominations. The name on the signpost may say African Methodist Episcopal Zion (AMEZ), Baptist, Disciples of Christ, United Church of Christ or represent some other black mainline denomination; but the character of the worship inside is distinctively Pentecostal. Indeed, on leaving the worship service, one may be tempted to pause and reread the signboard to make sure that he or she did not inadvertently step into a sanctified congregation.

More than occasionally, the preaching is punctuated with an amen and hallelujah or other exclamations much louder and stronger than the call-and-response motif generally accepted in the black church. And it is not just the old mothers or deacons who engage in the exuberant exchange but also young, expensively but casually dressed professionals and business-people. Gospel music, which was once relegated to the occasional youth

---

[19]Richard N. Ostling, "Catholicism's Black Maverick," *Time,* May 14, 1990, p. 67.
[20]"Stallings Dedicates a Cathedral," *Christian Century,* September 7, 1994, pp. 809-10.

Sunday, has invaded the spot once held by anthems and traditional hymns. And "praise and worship" has supplanted the place of testimony service. Core values replace statements of faith in the church bulletin, and every congregation has a catchy vision statement that graces its high-technology media presentations.

African American neo-Pentecostalism represents the convergence of two streams of the black religious experience into a distinct worship style that forges together elements of Pentecostal spirituality such as speaking in tongues, emotive worship and a dynamic preaching style with elements of their respective mother traditions. The new form is as much aligned with historical Pentecostal forms as with the particular parent denomination.

Early black neo-Pentecostals, as represented in John Bryant in the African Methodist Episcopal Church, sought to identify the roots of Pentecostal spirituality in a return to the African roots of black spirituality and infuse this spirituality with a conscious attempt to engage issues of social justice as well as individual and community wholeness. In doing so they were incorporating some of the very elements of African spirituality that the earliest leaders of independent black denominations such as Richard Allen and Daniel Payne sought to downplay.

The most visible distinction of neo-Pentecostal churches from the more traditional congregations within their denominations is their embracing of emotive worship styles that were once relegated to lower-class African American congregations. When the "new wine" of the Holy Spirit is poured into the "old wineskins" of existing denominational structures and polity, it results in a transformation where robed clergy and choirs, hymnals, Hammond or pipe organs, and vestments give way to worship choruses projected on wide screens, multiple keyboards, drums, tambourines, liturgical or "praise" dancers, and worship teams dressed in casual attire.

But not all denominational structure is lost. In most cases, unlike their charismatic brothers and sisters, neo-Pentecostals retain their denominational identification. Even Paul Morton, who formed an entirely new denomination, was careful to maintain the label Baptist, and Reverend George Stallings maintained the designation Catholic in his breakaway group. For even as denominational affiliation and branding become less important, neo-Pentecostal leaders have felt it important to stay close to the historical linkages that framed them while adopting the language, gestures, and preaching and musical styles once shunned as inappropriate in their sanctuaries; and their congregations, which have shown exponential growth, are reaping the fruit. Further, they are also quick object to Pentecostals' exclusivist privileging of the experience of the Holy Spirit baptism as their own, for as Frank Madison Reid, who succeeded John Bryant as pastor of Bethel AME Church, insists, to be authentically Christian every individual "must have a Pentecostal experience. . . . There's no way around it."[21]

But this claim of a common experience of the Spirit has not always resonated with old-line classical Pentecostals, who have been quick to point out the distinctions between themselves and charismatic and neo-Pentecostal Christianity. Classical Pentecostalism's heavy emphasis on rigid doctrinal lines separates constituents into denominational camps, and the emphasis on personal asceticism prohibits involvement in "worldly" social activities such as dancing, moviegoing and outward adornment of women. But this type of pietism is less and less attractive to a younger, more-educated generation of Christian believers. They find the charismatic and neo-Pentecostal movement much more arresting and palatable for its emphasis on engagement with the Holy Spirit in a more personal way and are attracted to the neo-Pentecostal movement's emphasis on Holy Spirit empowerment for more productive living.

While African American Pentecostals have historically drawn their members from the lower classes, black neo-Pentecostalism draws the bulk of its membership from the working and middle classes. Their constituents are often more highly educated than their Pentecostal peers and more open to a variety of expressions of Christian faith. There is generally broad cross-pollination between charismatic and neo-Pentecostal clergy, who for the cause of fellowship tend to downplay rather than highlight doctrinal distinctives.

Within the newer movements, constituents have also found a more educated clergy who can respond to their personal and philosophical queries with a more nuanced consideration of a wider range of theological resources than raw Scripture alone, giving attention to the broader Christian tradition and to broader reflection on theological and practical issues.

---

[21]Adrienne S. Gaines, "Revive Us, Precious Lord," *Charisma*, May 2003, pp. 37-38.

For some of these clergy, the higher level of education was attendance at ministry institutes or Bible colleges.[22] Others graduated from the finest historically black colleges, mainline universities and state institutions; and several attended some of the most prestigious schools both in the country and across the Western world. Reid, for example graduated from Yale, earned his master's of divinity at Harvard and a doctorate of ministry at United Theological Seminary. Empowerment Temple's Jamal Bryant dropped out of high school and earned a GED but went back to school and finally completed a Ph.D. at Oxford University.

Further, black charismatics and neo-Pentecostals added two new emphases that are not found as explicitly in most of classical Pentecostalism. One segment of these movements continues to uphold the black church's prophetic witness on issues of social justice, instilling it with an understanding of Holy Spirit empowerment. At the other end of the spectrum is the emphasis on prosperity—both physical and financial—represented in the health-and-wealth movement.

Both of these emphases offer a promise of deliverance from the socio-economic malaise and oppression that has been the bane of the black community since slavery and the failure of Reconstruction. With some notable exceptions, traditional Pentecostal leaders generally shunned political involvement; however, neo-Pentecostalism's embrace of such involvement, drawing on the heritage of their denominations for social engagement, is also attractive. The AME and AMEZ Churches, for example, were started as a protest against racist treatment of blacks in white Methodism. Both continued that tradition throughout Reconstruction, the Jim Crow era and the civil rights movement and have maintained a vibrant presence in new struggles for social justice throughout the diaspora.

The initial reaction of classical Pentecostal leaders to the newcomers was mixed. Some older leaders critiqued the seeming lack of commitment to classical tenets that have defined the movement since Azusa Street. They perceived a lack of emphasis on personal morality or "sanctification." They were also put off by relatively less emotive forms of worship that exchanged shouting for raising of hands and incorporated other elements foreign to classical Pentecostals, such as infant baptism or the weekly cele-

---

[22]Since in the earliest days of the movement even this level of education was rare.

bration of the Eucharist. Particularly disturbing, however, were modes of reception of the baptism of the Holy Spirit in which tarrying and praying through were replaced with coaching and prompting with practice syllables. Most jarring was the option of other evidences of Spirit baptism such as prophecy, or other gifts of the Spirit as a replacement for the initial evidence of speaking in tongues.

While these particular elements were more evident among white charismatics, especially those from more liturgical traditions, they also appeared to separate black neo-Pentecostals from classical Pentecostals. Yet the broader renewal movement provided opportunities for classical Pentecostals, charismatics and neo-Pentecostals to engage each other in ways that had not previously been possible.

African American classical Pentecostal congregations have not been untouched by charismatic/neo-Pentecostal spirituality. As classical Pentecostals found themselves in meetings and worship services with others who also appreciated a "move of the Spirit" and operated in gifts that had begun to lay dormant in their own congregations, they were pulled into an "ecumenism of the Spirit" that crossed denominational lines and rendered these Christians open to each other in ways that proved to be fruitful. Indeed, several formerly classical Pentecostal pastors and congregations have shed their Pentecostal labels, moved closer to the center of evangelical spirituality and adapted their doctrinal statement to what they see as a more progressive approach to black spirituality and the realities of contemporary culture. Carlton Pearson, for example, a highly visible pastor with deep COGIC ties, launched his congregation as a nondenominational charismatic fellowship. Again, noting that worship styles of Pentecostals and African Americans have long been similar, Vinson Synan notes Pentecostalism's fastest growth in the United States is among independent charismatic churches and black neo-Pentecostals.[23]

SPECIFIC EXPRESSIONS OF NEO-PENTECOSTALISM

Neo-Pentecostalism in African Episcopal Methodism. While young African Methodist Episcopal seminary graduate John Bryant was serving in the Peace Corps in Africa in the mid-1960s, he was intrigued by the

---

[23]Gaines, "Revive Us, Precious Lord," p. 38.

"spirited" worship in which he saw people healed, going into trances and exercising spiritual power—all "without the [Western] notion of Jehovah God or Jesus Christ."[24] The experience led him to believe that was a "realm of the Spirit" that "could not be explained away"; it also led him to reexamine Christian Scripture's teaching about the spiritual dimension, which had been largely overlooked within his own African American Methodist tradition. This search brought Bryant to the conviction that "in Jesus Christ everything the Bible said could be accomplished," and the Holy Spirit is "the power base of Christian theology . . . who can 'liberate and empower.'"[25]

On returning to the states and entering the pastorate, Bryant, considered the father of African American neo-Pentecostalism, sought to incorporate this spiritual realm into his own ministry within the most conspicuously Afrocentric denomination in America. Beginning at historic St. Paul's AME Church in Cambridge, Massachusetts, Bryant infused AME teaching and worship with his newfound Pentecostal spirituality without giving up the denomination's historic affinity for involvement in social justice. He saw this new spirituality as the means to connect his congregation to their black cultural roots in Africa, identifying the Spirit as the liberator who could empower the African American community.

During Bryant's tenure, St. Paul's young, urban, highly educated, middle-class congregation grew from two hundred to over three thousand members. In 1975, he returned to his native Baltimore and assumed the pastorate of Bethel AME, where both his grandfather and father had served.[26] When he took over the pulpit, the historic congregation's membership was six hundred. Within two years, the congregation grew to over seven thousand members, making it the largest AME congregation in the nation and a catalyst for African American neo-Pentecostalism. He served there thirteen years.

Bryant characterizes the combination of deep spirituality that emphasizes the Holy Spirit and activism in the community as a "biblical, winning formula" and used these to engage the congregations of St. Paul's and

---

[24]Ibid., p. 39.

[25]Ibid.

[26]The civil rights veteran comes from a family with a long AME heritage. He is the son of a bishop, Harrison James Bryant; both his late sister, Rev. Eleanor Bryant, and his son Rev. Jamal Harrison Bryant continued that heritage.

Bethel in conducting numerous outreach ministries, including economic and community development and prison ministry. At the same time, he challenged assertions of Holy Spirit empowerment that failed to take concerns for social justice seriously, insisting,

> One must ask the question, "Holy Spirit for what?" . . . If all we are doing is jumping up and down in the air, speaking in other tongues, saying, "Yea, the Spirit is with us," that's fine. But I preach all the time that that is taking the gravy and leaving the Spirit. The meat of the Holy Spirit is for our empowerment. It's for our liberation and development. It's for our strength as a people. And it has been that.[27]

Bryant's leadership in the AME denomination and black community has drawn several commendations and landed him positions on boards of numerous civil, educational and religious groups including the Board of Regents of Morgan State University, the National Committee of Black Churchmen and the board of the World Methodist Council on Evangelism.

While many AME traditionalists were initially disturbed by what they saw as Bryant's push to import Pentecostal spirituality, neo-Pentecostalism's success in revitalizing this older denomination aided Bryant's bid for election as bishop in 1988. Further, the largest and wealthiest AME churches, like Bethel, which had grown to six thousand members by the mid-1980s incorporated neo-Pentecostal elements into their worship. The ten-thousand-member Ebenezer AME congregation, led by Grainger and JoAnn Browning in Fort Washington, Maryland, for example, went from twenty-five members to over a thousand in two years after incorporating the new spirituality. But the phenomenon also includes older, urban congregations such as First AME of Los Angeles; Bridge Street in Brooklyn, New York; Payne AME in Nashville, Tennessee; and Floyd Flake's Allen AME in Jamaica, Queens, New York which grew from fourteen hundred members to seventy-five-hundred members.[28]

[27]Quoted in Lawrence H. Mamiya, "A Social History of Bethel African Methodist Episcopal Church in Baltimore: The House of God and the Struggle for Freedom," in *American Congregations: Portrait of Twelve Religious Communities,* ed. James P. Wind and James Weldon Lewis (Chicago: University of Chicago Press, 1994), p. 266.
[28]See Vern E. Smith, "Where Do We Go from Here?" *Crisis,* July-August 2006, p. 31; Larry Mamiya, *River of Struggle, River of Freedom: Trends Among Black Churches and Black Pastoral Leadership,* Pulpit and Pew Research Reports (Durham: Duke Divinity School, 2006); and Tamlyn Tucker-Worgs, "Get on Board, Little Children, There's Room for Many More: The Black Megachurch Phenomenon," in *Journey Inward, Journey Outward,* a special book-length

An unanticipated benefit of neo-Pentecostal vitality within the more traditional black churches has been the attraction of younger, more educated and upwardly mobile black congregations, including more young black men. Additionally there has been an upsurge in the number of people going into the ministry from these congregations. C. Eric Lincoln and Lawrence Mamiya reported in 1990 that Bethel AME had more than fifty pursuing ministry.[29]

Neo-Pentecostalism in the AMEZ Church. Unlike the AME Church, elements of neo-Pentecostalism are less visible in its sister AMEZ denomination. Only a small number of the more than thirty-two hundred AMEZ congregations and 1.4 million congregants throughout the country would openly characterize themselves as charismatic or neo-Pentecostal. But the neo-Pentecostal movement has not entirely missed the denomination, which, like its sister denomination, traces its roots back to nineteenth-century protest of freedmen against unjust treatment in the Methodist Episcopal Church. The slow spread of neo-Pentecostalism within the tradition was not aided by the denomination's experience with one of the movement's earliest and most prominent proponents, John Cherry. Cherry's suburban Washington, D.C., Full Gospel AMEZ congregation grew out of a 20-person Bible study started in his home in 1981. Within a year, the congregation was meeting in a storefront facility, slowly having grown to 81 members. It tripled again to 243 by May 1983, moving into a "housefront" that was soon overcrowded and holding three services each Sunday. By the time the church purchased and moved into a school building two years later, it had grown to 1,500 members and had established a Christian School. By 1989, it had over 6,000 members, ultimately reaching the present estimated 27,000 members and becoming the largest congregation in Prince George's County, the wealthiest black county in the United States. Along with Pentecostal-style worship, within the denomination Cherry was known for his controversial polemics against the hierarchy of the episcopal structure. He had been in trouble with church leaders because he had been "ordaining" other ministers, a

---

issue of the *Journal of the Interdenominational Theological Center* on the ITC/Faith Factor Project 2000 Study of Black Religious Life, ed. Joseph Troutman 29, nos. 1-2 (2001-2002): 177-203.

[29]C. Eric Lincoln and Lawrence Mamiya, *The Black Church in the African American Experience* (Durham: Duke University Press, 1990), p. 388.

role that is reserved for bishops in the denomination.[30]

In 1999, however, Cherry disagreed with denominational leaders and pulled the then 24,000-member congregation out of the denomination, renaming it From the Heart Ministries. In the ensuing court battle, the denomination recovered the majority of nearly 49 million dollars in church-controlled in assets, including cash, a national television ministry, two buildings, a Learjet and an estimated 120 acres of land. Undaunted by the loss, Cherry has since garnered 18 churches in the United States and over 170 churches worldwide into From the Heart Ministries. Additionally, the local congregation has over 100 full-time employees, including those affiliated with the school, and television broadcasts on 11 stations.

After being burned by the Cherry episode, the AMEZ Church did little to encourage the neo-Pentecostal movement within its ranks, and the number of congregations is relatively small. Still, there are a few outstanding examples of this new spirituality with AME Zionism. W. Darrin Moore's Greater Centennial AME Zion Church in Mount Vernon, New York, for example, has grown from 800 people to more than 5,000—making it currently the largest of the more than 2,000 AMEZ churches in the country, and the only AMEZ congregation among the 1,376 congregations identified by Hartford Seminary as a megachurch.[31] Moore grew up in Greater Centennial, a congregation that had been pastored by his grandfather William Pratt. After his grandfather's death, in 1995, the congregation retained Moore as its pastor. Baltimore's Pennsylvania Avenue AMEZ Church boasts a membership of several hundred. By 2006, its pastor, Dennis V. Proctor, had served as pastor of the West Baltimore congregation for fourteen years. In that time, its neo-Pentecostal spirituality had not moved the congregation into megachurch status, but Proctor had become an outspoken defender of the new spirituality. Countering accusations from more traditional pastors who saw the black church's involvement in the civil rights struggle as crucial, Proctor asserted,

> The frustration [they] feel is we are not making as many placards, we're not holding as many rallies. . . . But on the other hand, we're having many more

---

[30]"AME Zion Megachurch Leaves Denomination," *Christian Century*, July 28-August 4, 1999, pp. 737-38.
[31]"Database of Megachurches in the U.S.," Hartford Institute for Religion Research, http://hirr.hartsem.edu/megachurch/database.html.

revivals and teaching sessions and seminars, trying to equip our people to be family, to have sanctity of family, have respect and reverence for the house of God and the people of God. And the balance is absolutely necessary.[32]

By the end of the twentieth century, the denomination's periodical, the *A.M.E. Zion Quarterly,* had published a few articles on the work on the Holy Spirit in the ancient and contemporary church[33] but gave no coverage to any resurgence of neo-Pentecostalism within its ranks. The tension caused by varying degrees of openness to neo-Pentecostalism within the AMEZ Church is evident in an article that appeared in a 1998 issue of the denomination's quarterly review.[34] In it, a local pastor, Orlando Dowdy, assessed the state of charismatic spirituality throughout the AMEZ denomination, calling attention to and welcoming what he sees as the myriad ways in which the Spirit operates within the church while at the same time challenging the classical Pentecostal assertion of the necessity of speaking in tongues.

Bishop George E. Battle Jr., who served for some time in the Central North Carolina Conference before moving to the Northeastern Episcopal District has been a voice for neo-Pentecostal renewal within the denomination. Battle has been an advocate of openness to the "full gospel,"[35] and some see him as "a breath of Pentecostal fresh air to the AME Zion Church."[36] He was joined in his assessment by retired AMEZ Bishop Ruben Speaks, an avid supporter of charismatic spirituality within the AMEZ Church. Yet Speaks is equally insistent that rigid classical Pentecostal definitions of Holy Spirit baptism as always accompanied by glossolalia are inadequate, stating explicitly that "some Christians . . . insist that speaking in tongues is the only valid proof of Holy Spirit baptism. That is not true, not all who receive the baptism of the Holy Spirit speak in tongues." Further, he was adamant that "speaking in tongues

[32]Rivera, "A Shift in Their Focus for Black Churches."
[33]See, e.g., Atheal Pierce, "The Filling with the Holy Spirit: An Indispensable Entity," *A.M.E. Zion Quarterly Review* 111, no. 4 (1999): 34; Ruben L. Speaks, "The Challenge of a Spirit Filled Ministry," *A.M.E. Zion Quarterly Review* 99 (1988): 2-14; Samuel Chuka Ekemam, "Address to the Thirteenth Episcopal District—A.M.E. Zion: Give the Holy Spirit a Chance," *A.M.E. Zion Quarterly Review* 102 (1990): 2-8.
[34]Orlando Dowdy, "Worship, Works and the Gifts of the Holy Spirit in the A.M.E. Zion Church," *A.M.E. Zion Quarterly Review* 110 (1998): 22-32.
[35]Rueben L. Speaks, *The Prelude to Pentecost: A Theology of the Holy Spirit* (Eugene, Ore.: Wipf & Stock, 2007)
[36]Dowdy, "Worship, Works and Gifts of the Holy Spirit," pp. 22-32.

must be judged by the life of the Christian."[37]

Black neo-Pentecostal United Methodists. Within the predominantly white United Methodist church, most of the congregations that swelled to megachurch status have been white. Still, several prominent black congregations and a number of smaller congregations have adopted a neo-Pentecostal-style theology and style of worship. Kirbyjon Caldwell's Windsor Village United Methodist Church in Houston represents such an expression. Caldwell, who graduated from Southern Methodist University and the University of Pennsylvania's prestigious Wharton School of Business, is known for Pentecostal customs like speaking in tongues.[38] When he assumed the pastorate in 1982, the average attendance at Windsor Village was twenty-five. By 2006, it had grown to seven thousand, making it one of the ten largest United Methodist congregations, and the largest African American congregation, in the denomination. Caldwell's "Gospel of Good Success" blends a Pentecostal spirituality and practical economic empowerment. A book he coauthored by that title with Mark Seal became a bestseller and promoted Caldwell to national prominence. In the late 1990s, while George W. Bush was serving as governor of Texas, Caldwell and Bush, who shared a common interest in seeing religious organizations and the government work together to tackle social issues, developed respect for each other. Bush started frequenting worship services at Caldwell's church and continued to do so through his presidency.

A. P. Shaw's church in the predominantly black Anacostia section of Washington, D.C., another black United Methodist congregation, embraced neo-Pentecostal worship in a big way. The inner-city congregation regularly held prayer meetings and evangelistic services that resembled those of classical Pentecostals and produced a number of ministers who adopted Pentecostal-style spiritual, though many remained within the United Methodist Church.

Anthony Muse's Gibbons-Resurrection UMC in Brandywine, Maryland,[39] profited from their involvement in the neo-Pentecostal move-

---

[37]Speaks, "Challenge of a Spirit Filled Ministry," p. 60.

[38]David D. Kirkpatrick, "Christian Conservatives Embrace Inauguration," *New York Times*, January 20, 2005, A1.

[39]Muse subsequently moved out of the United Methodist Church to found his own nondenominational congregation, Ark of Safety Christian Church, in neighboring Upper Marlboro, Maryland.

ment. Muse, who had been raised in a black oneness congregation, brought his spirited Pentecostal preaching style, which included shouting, jumping and running the aisles with him into the Methodist Church, and shortly grew a sleepy country Methodist charge into a congregation of thirty-four hundred.

The new openness to Pentecostal spirituality did, however, make it possible for individuals within the denomination to achieve a degree of success than would have been possible for them within the narrower confines of the movement. For example, former Pentecostal Violet Fisher joined the Methodist Church after completing an master of divinity degree at Eastern Baptist Theological Seminary in 1988. Within twelve years, she had advanced within the denomination to become a bishop—an achievement that would not have been possible as a woman within her classical Pentecostal body.

Black neo-Pentecostal Baptists. Black Baptist churches were latecomers to charismatic renewal and started on a smaller scale than was true within Methodism. A 1977 survey by the Southern Baptist Home Mission Board indicated that, at that time, only perhaps one hundred of the more than forty-two thousand congregations identified with the charismatic movement. Once Pentecostal renewal began in earnest, however, it quickly spread throughout the denomination. Two years after the Home Mission Board survey, a Gallup poll indicated that about 20 percent of all U.S. Baptists viewed themselves as Pentecostal or charismatic.[40] However, some Baptist leaders have struggled with this new spirituality within their ranks. One leader insisted that charismatic spirituality had spread within the Baptist community, in part, because it had found "a fertile field among church members whose level of maturity [was] woefully retarded,"[41] and that speaking in tongues was usually received by those who were "eagerly and earnestly seeking it" after being "psychologically conditioned."[42]

The polity of the Baptist Church allows individual congregations and believers leeway in religious practice, and there is no official stand against

---

[40]Kenneth Kantzer, "The Charismatics Among Us," *Christianity Today* 22, February 1980, pp. 25-29. However, the same poll showed that of these "charismatic" Baptists, only a minority confessed that they had ever spoken in tongues.
[41]J. Terry Young, *The Spirit Within You* (Nashville: Broadman, 1977), p. 51
[42]Ibid., pp. 97-98.

speaking in tongues. While predominantly white Southern Baptist leaders have long designated the practice as unbiblical, going as far as disfellowshiping clergy and churches that practiced or allowed it, black Baptist conventions such as the National, Progressive or Missionary Baptists have historically taken a more open posture. Within that context, a number of black Baptist congregations have adopted the new spirituality and shown phenomenal growth in the wake of that move, gaining the attention of the community and the secular press.

In 1986 Eddie Long assumed the pastorate of Atlanta's 300-member Morning Star Baptist Church. Under his leadership, which blended Pentecostal-type spirituality, political conservatism and social activism, the congregation quickly grew to 2,000 members. By the mid 1990s they boasted 11,000 members and by the year 2000 had purchased a 10,500 seat sanctuary on a 140-acre complex that is estimated to be worth 45 million dollars, and membership had surged to more than 20,000.

Long's political conservatism, such as his strong stands on family values and Christian sexuality, often put him at odds with generally more politically liberal black leaders. At the same time, his social activism has involved him in such efforts as leading a 2004 march in Atlanta to advocate for education, healthcare and economic reform, which protested a proposed constitutional amendment allowing same-sex marriage. Such stances have drawn criticism from more liberal black political and church leaders such as Atlanta's Concerned Black Clergy, who labeled him a black Jerry Falwell, and the American Civil Liberties Union, and insisted that a sermon Long delivered in an Atlanta school after the fatal shooting of a student violated tenets of separation of church and state.[43] In 2006, when he spoke at the graduation of Atlanta's Interdenominational Theological Center, some students considered a boycott, and although liberation theologian James Cone was scheduled to receive an honorary degree, Cone decided not to attend.[44] But conservatives also criticized Long for divorcing his first wife, leading some colleagues to discourage him from pursing ministry.

Long's church, which he renamed New Birth Missionary Baptist

---

[43]"School Isn't Proper Place for Religious Message," *Atlanta Journal-Constitution,* October 9, 1997, A22.

[44]See "Bishop Eddie Long Tackles Controversy" *New Pittsburgh Courier* 97, no. 20 (May 17, 2006), B2; or "Contested Speech" *Christian Century,* May 30, 2006, p. 6.

Church, offers a ministry training institute, a private school, outreach to the Latino community with a separate service, ESL classes and instruction on life skills. At the same time, the congregation appeals to young black professionals, including Bernice King, daughter of Martin Luther King Jr. Long was among the group of Baptist ministers who helped Paul Morton found the Full Gospel Baptist Church Fellowship International. After a short period, Long left the denomination to form the Father's House, with more than 240 Baptist and nondenominational churches under his leadership. He labels himself as "Bapticostal," noting that he was baptized in the Holy Spirit in the 1980s at a crusade led by evangelist Jimmy Swaggart.[45]

The Full Gospel Baptist Church Fellowship International. When the Full Gospel Baptist Church Fellowship International (FGBCFI) held its first convention in New Orleans, Louisiana, in 1994, more than thirty thousand Baptists attended. With Morton's eighteen-thousand-member Greater St. Stephen Baptist Church in New Orleans as home base, the denomination, by one estimate, had grown by 1997 to over one million members in five thousand congregations in primarily in thirty-five states, but also in the Caribbean, Africa, Asia, the Bahamas, Germany, India, Canada, Great Britain and Italy. Members came from traditional black Baptist conventions, including the National, Progressive and Missionary Baptists. In the beginning, some of these maintained dual alliance, and while a few still do, a growing number has come to be fully aligned with the FGBCFI. But FGBCFI polity and practice has been broad enough also to attract formerly Pentecostal, non-denominational or mainline congregations into its ranks.

The ethos of FGBCFI is captured by the concept of "the right to choose," which conveys Morton's call for the opportunity for free expression of spiritual gifts in promoting evangelism and worship. Essentially, Morton espouses the right to exercise speaking in tongues, along with such historically Pentecostal phenomena as praying to cast out demons and the laying on of hands to impart healing within Baptist worship structures. For Morton's followers, that right to choose does not signal abandonment of the Baptist Church.

---

[45]Jonathan L. Walton, *Watch This! The Ethics and Aesthetics of Black Televangelism* (New York: New York University Press, 2009), p. 128.

Twelve prominent Baptist bishops joined Morton in forming the new organization: Odis Floyd of Flint Michigan's two-thousand-member New Jerusalem Full Gospel Baptist Church; Larry D. Trotter of the five-thousand-member Sweet Holy Spirit Full Gospel Baptist Church in Chicago; Carlos L. Malone of Bethel Full Gospel Baptist Church in Miami; J. Douglas Wiley of Life Center Full Gospel Baptist Cathedral in New Orleans; K. D. Johnson of Little Rock, Arkansas; Larry Leonard of Morning Star Full Gospel Baptist Church in Houston, Texas; Kenneth Robinson of Antioch Full Gospel Baptist Church in College Station, Arkansas; Kenneth Ulmer, Pastor of the eight-thousand-member Faithful Central Bible Church in Inglewood, California; Fred Caldwell of Greenwood Acres Full Gospel Baptist Church in Shreveport, Louisiana; Robert Blake of Greater Love Missionary Full Gospel Baptist Church Dallas, Texas; Eddie Long of the twenty-five-thousand-member New Birth Cathedral in Atlanta, Georgia; and Alton R. Williams of World Overcomers Outreach Ministries Church in Memphis, Tennessee. Eventually, all except Floyd, who is bishop emeritus, and Caldwell pulled out to form their own organizations, though many stayed in fellowship with Morton's group.[46]

Canadian-born Morton, who was raised in the COGIC, began preaching in 1967. Five years later, while still in his early twenties, he became associate pastor of New Orleans's Greater St. Stephen Missionary Baptist Church. After then pastor Percy Simpson Jr. was killed in a car accident in 1974, Morton was installed as pastor. Fifteen years later, Morton founded the FGBCFI in the wake of a scandal within the 8.5-million-member National Baptist Convention USA. Its president, Henry Lyons, was charged with stealing several million dollars from the organization, and though Morton initially backed Lyons, who denied the allegation, his colleagues were not as generous in accepting Morton's belief in speaking in tongues and divine healing, and the two parted ways.

The FGBCFI's spirituality converges with other traditions at two important points: the COGIC, where Morton spent his childhood, and, more recently, the black Baptist tradition. While the FGBCFI shares the

---

[46]For an overview of the history of the denomination, see Kenneth Ulmer, *A New Thing: A Theological and Personal Look at the Full Gospel Baptist Church Fellowship* (Tulsa: Vincom, 1995).

majority of its doctrinal beliefs with a variety of other Baptists, its theology differs in a number of areas that more clearly resonate with its COGIC heritage as outlined in its statement of faith.

The principle distinctions from other Baptist are pneumatological, diverging from the cessastionist stance regarding contemporary operation of the spiritual gifts, while the Southern Baptist convention, for example, outrightly rejects the public display of glossolalia and faith healing. Other Baptist conventions are not as explicit in their rejection, but most don't give these gifts the central focus Morton and his associates felt they deserved. Morton and other Full Gospel Baptists found the tradition historically deficient in this area, and they regarded other Baptists as not making full use of the spiritual power available to them.

In contrast to other Baptists, the FGBCFI maintains a highly visible tiered hierarchy based on an episcopal, rather than congregational, form of government. There are bishops, overseers, elders and adjutants—each with specific responsibilities and corresponding clerical garb. There is also an intricate ecclesiastical liturgical structure in which robed clergy are joined by choirs, processionals and many of the ecclesial trappings of high church. But this liturgical structure does not automatically translate into government structure, providing room for autonomy. Bishops have no governmental authority over local congregations, which operate as independent entities regarding matters of congregational polity, operation and discipline.[47] Though the designation "bishop" is considered to be a biblical term, FGBCFI constituents consider Morton's position as presiding bishop to have more influence than judicatory authority, corresponding to the position of president, general superintendent or general overseer in other organizations.

The pneumatological distinction between the FGBCFI and classical Pentecostalism revolves around the FGBCFI contention that at the moment of salvation Jesus, as the Baptizer with the Holy Spirit, brings men and women into relationship with himself and the church. Further, they contend that the filling of the Holy Ghost is an ongoing ministry of the Spirit in the life of the believer that enables him or her to live a life of power, victory and glory to God, not a single experience with a single

---

[47]Ulmer, *A New Thing*, p. 90.

identifiable evidence. For while FGBCFI theology appreciates speaking in tongues as one of the gifts of the Holy Spirit, it does not make either Pentecostal contention that speaking in tongues is the initial evidence of Spirit baptism or a necessary element of salvation for all believers. FGBCFI holds, rather, that the dichotomy between being filled with the Holy Spirit and being baptized with the Holy Spirit is a false one. To them, all believers are filled with the Holy Spirit, and such indwelling validates the believer as a member Christ's body. Additionally they hold that all believers should live a Spirit-controlled life. Indeed, being filled with the Spirit is deemed a volitional act in that it results from the believer's being submitted to divine control.[48]

Another area of distinction from more conservative Baptist teaching has been the FGBCFI's greater openness to the leadership of women. While the "tiers of leadership" that support Morton includes the all-male Bishop's Council and College of Bishops, the general, state, and district overseers and directors can be held by men or women.[49] By 2006, at least ten women were district overseers. Several more women serve as senior or staff pastors, and numerous women serve as copastors, alongside their husbands, of some of the fellowship's most prominent congregations. Indeed, women are among the pastors and copastors of several widely recognized megachurches, such as Betty Peebles of Jericho City of Praise.

THE TELEVANGELISM EXPLOSION

At the end of the twentieth century, a new innovation in evangelical religious culture was having an unprecedented impact on the spiritual choices of mainstream America. Individuals who had already made a name for themselves on the revival circuit began to populate the television airwaves in unprecedented numbers, spurred by relatively cheap access to cable TV technology. Though network owners such as Jan and Paul Crouch of the Trinity Broadcasting Network and Pat Robertson of the Christian Broadcasting Network were predominantly white, they showcased up-and-coming black preachers, introducing them to broader audiences than could be reached by the revivals and radio broadcast that were previously the movement's mainstays. Secular cable networks were also open to selling

[48]Ibid., pp. 100-101.
[49]Only one woman, Aretha Morton, serves as a state bishop in Delaware.

access to nationally known charismatic preachers as well as smaller local congregations who were savvy and well-financed enough to appropriate the exposure televised broadcasting would bring them. These preachers regularly draw large multiracial audiences who tune in and support individuals and networks by attending various advertised events, donations to broadcasters, and purchases of study and inspirational materials.

Carlton Pearson. Among the earliest black charismatic personalities to avail themselves of the new media was a pastor from Tulsa, Oklahoma, Carlton Pearson. That move made him one of the most visible Pentecostal televangelists and what sociologist Shayne Lee calls one of the most recognizable African American religious leaders of the twentieth century.[50] At one time, Pearson and Word-of-Faith preacher Fred Price were the only nationally televised African Americans with ties to the Pentecostal/charismatic community. Pearson has been a strong proponent of racial and denominational unity among Pentecostals and charismatics, as well as a supporter of the ministry and leadership of women. Not only did he build his ministry into one of the largest black congregations in the country; but his prominence also allowed him to be a sort of kingmaker, able to help up-and-coming preachers such as T. D. Jakes rise through the ranks to national prominence. During the early 1990s, his commitment to racial and theological unity was promoted through his annual Azusa Conference that spotlighted the hottest preachers on the circuit and provided unparalleled opportunities for black and white Pentecostal and charismatic men and women within the wider evangelical arena.

Pearson, a fourth-generation Pentecostal minister from a prominent Church of God in Christ family, began preaching at an early age. After being ordained in that denomination, he attended Oral Roberts University (ORU), where, because of his musical ability, he became a member of the World Action Singers. The group gained recognition in the contemporary evangelical Christian music arena, and Pearson's involvement with them brought him to the attention of the university's founder, Oral Roberts, who took Pearson under his wing and mentored him. In 1975 Roberts commissioned Pearson to a two-year stint as an associate evan-

---

[50]Quoted in Selwyn Crawford, "The Fall and Rise of Carlton Pearson," *Dallas Morning News*, Mar. 3, 2006, www.dallasnews.com/sharedcontent/dws/dn/religion/stories/030406dnrelcarl tonpearson.1f8935f9.html.

gelist for the ORU association. Pearson traveled with Roberts's son Richard, serving as an opening act for Richard's concert performances. His work with the association kept him so busy, however, that he never completed his degree.

By 1977, Pearson left Roberts's ministry to travel as an evangelist and four years later founded Higher Dimensions Family Church in Tulsa with a white fellow minister, Gary McIntosh. The first service drew seventy-five people, mostly ORU students, but within a year the congregation grew to between eight hundred and one thousand, becoming one of the largest in Tulsa—a city already saturated with several megachurches.[51] From this strategic Bible Belt locale, Pearson became one of the first African American televangelists with classically Pentecostal roots to have a major slot on national television and garner a multiracial following. His Azusa Conference, first held in 1988, specifically attempted to revive the racial harmony that gave birth to the classical Pentecostal movement. It regularly drew crowds of seventy-five hundred to ten thousand people at nightly meetings to hear leading Pentecostal/charismatic speakers. Its popularity would allow Pearson to parlay his influence to become spiritual overseer for another six hundred churches through the Higher Dimensions Ministries. Along with his own broadcast, he regularly appeared on the broadcasts of other Pentecostal and charismatic televangelists, recorded music albums, wrote books and made guest appearances at some of the biggest congregations and conferences in the country.

But his meteoric rise and broad popularity ended abruptly, when he began to enunciate a doctrine that veered sharply from classical Pentecostalism and even charismatic and neo-Pentecostal soteriology. His "gospel of inclusion," or "theory of universal reconciliation," was prompted in part by the death of his father, who was not a believer. But Pearson was also losing some of his prominence to newcomers who burst on the scene, attracting audiences through their theological appeal and overshadowing Pearson's more traditional style.[52]

[51]These included Church On the Move, pastored by Willie George; Billy Daugherty's Victory Christian Center; Rhema Bible Church under the pastorate of Kenneth Hagin, founder of the Word of Faith movement; and three large United Methodist congregations (First United, Boston Avenue and Asbury).
[52]For a thorough discussion of these views, see Carlton Pearson, *The Gospel of Inclusion: Reaching beyond Religious Fundamentalism to the True Love of God and Self* (New York: Atria, 2006).

His theology echoed Karl Rahner's idea of the anonymous Christian[53] and the mystical theory of the atonement, in which we are saved simply because the incarnation ties all of humanity to God through Christ's taking on human flesh.[54] On several occasions, the outspoken evangelist emphasized that "the world is already saved, they just don't know it!"[55] Pearson, however, nuances this view, insisting that "[a] Christian can be a Universalist, but not all Universalists are Christians,"[56] further explaining that someone can exclude themselves from the offer of salvation by deliberately rejecting the work of Christ on Calvary, asserting that

> Christ's death accomplished its purpose of reconciling all mankind to God. The death of Christ made it possible for God to accept man and, in fact, and indeed, He has done so. The substitution[ary] death of Christ not only made it possible for God to accept mankind as totally clean before Him but, more importantly, it demonstrated or proved God's unconditional love for His own creative handiwork. . . . Whatever separation now exists between man and the benefits of God's grace is subjective in nature; it is illusionary, existing only in man's unregenerate mind, his unenlightened or uniformed way of thinking. . . . People need to hear . . . that they simply have an opportunity for Salvation, but that they, through Christ, in fact, have already been redeemed, reconciled and saved, and . . . this information (Good News) frees them to enjoy the blessings that are already theirs in Him.[57]

While Pearson's assertion of the possibility of salvation for all of humanity was jarring, he took his message even one step further by contemplating the potential of salvation even for Satan.[58] Such a strong position

---

[53]Rahner declares that people who have never heard the Christian gospel or even rejected it might be saved through Christ. Non-Christians could have "in [their] basic orientation and fundamental decision," Rahner wrote, "accepted the salvific grace of God, through Christ, although [they] may never have heard of the Christian revelation." See Karl Rahner, "Anonymous Christianity and the Missionary Task of the Church," in *Theological Investigations*, vol. 12, *Confrontations*, trans. David Bourke (London: Darton, Longman & Todd, 1974), pp. 161-78.

[54]Both ideas soundly rejected by Pentecostals and other evangelicals.

[55]See, for example, Carlton Pearson, "Jesus Will Save You—Whether You Agree or Not," Beliefnet.com interview, www.beliefnet.com/Faiths/2003/06/Jesus-Will-Save-You-Whether-You-Agree-Or-Not.aspx.

[56]New Dimensions International, "Gospel of Inclusion," unpublished manuscript available at www.newdimensions.us/content.cfm?id=2010.

[57]Carlton Pearson, *Gospel of Inclusion*, p. 38.

[58]Kirby Lee Davis, "Tulsa Christian School Buys Former Church for $5.19 Million," *Journal Record* (Oklahima City), April 18, 2007, p. 1.

assured that within a few months the majority of Pearson's members were deserting him, and by 2005 Higher Dimension's membership and weekly offerings fell substantially along with attendance at the Pearsons' annual Azusa Conferences and the allegiance of his viewing public and that of most of the ministers who belonged to his nondenominational fellowship. Prominent Pentecostal/charismatic leaders refuted his theology, and most completely distanced themselves from him after he refused their repeated demands to denounce the teaching. His famous mentee T. D. Jakes remained a personal friend but publicly insisted that Pearson's teaching was erroneous and heretical.[59]

Yet Pearson remained convinced that every human being, whether or not they ever come to faith in Christ, will eventually be saved. The continued decline of his congregation led to the eventual loss of his seventy-one-thousand-square-foot worship facility to foreclosure. Oral Roberts University removed him from its board of directors, and he was shunned by the majority of the charismatic community. Undaunted, he established a new congregation, New Dimensions Worship Center, which meets in a borrowed Episcopal sanctuary, and ultimately affiliated with the United Church of Christ. The new fellowship attracts people who formerly would have been uncomfortable with open involvement in Pentecostal and charismatic circles and makes room for those who are openly homosexual or living a "worldly lifestyle," people whom the classical Pentecostal movement would have shunned.

T. D. Jakes and the Potter's House. T. D. Jakes represents a classical Pentecostal who has used the neo-Pentecostal model to grow a once-fledgling congregation in the middle of West Virginia into one of the nation's fastest-growing, most visible congregations. Jakes and the Potter's House represent a phenomenon of traditional Pentecostal congregations that have broadened their missional scope to reach a wider segment of the community. Both Jakes and his Potter's House congregation have touched a constituency that would not have been attracted to the traditional classical Pentecostal tradition out of which he emerged. In doing so, as the twenty-first century unfolded, Jakes had become one of the most recognizable personalities within the United States or around the world. Far from Sey-

---

[59]Crawford, "The Fall and Rise of Carlton Pearson."

mour's humble beginnings in a rundown livery stable, the state-of-the-art facility that houses his thirty-thousand-member Dallas congregation underscores the increasing affluence of Pentecostals who are willing to embrace the neo-Pentecostal spirituality.

Jakes, a former Baptist, was introduced to Pentecostal experience of Holy Spirit baptism and spoke in tongues during his early teens. He left high school to care for his ailing parents but completed a G.E.D. and later went on to complete both bachelor's and an master's degrees through correspondence courses through Friends University. He eventually added a doctor of ministry degree. As a young man, Jakes's lisp was so pronounced that some discouraged him from pursuing ministry. Nonetheless, by the age of seventeen, he had already begun to preach. He was licensed in 1977 and ordained in 1979 and assumed his first pastorate at Temple of Faith Church, a small oneness congregation in Montgomery, West Virginia, twenty-eight miles southwest of Charleston, working part-time to support his family. A year later, he planted Greater Emanuel Temple of Faith—another small oneness Pentecostal congregation. The integrated congregation grew quickly under his leadership, moving twice—from Montgomery to Smithers and then to South Charleston—eventually reaching over three hundred members.

Jakes married his wife, Serita, in 1981, and the two struggled financially for several years. During this time, he began a radio ministry, the *Master's Plan*, which ran from 1982-1985. But the catalyst for Jakes's move into national prominence came from an unlikely project—a Bible study for forty women, which he began in the early 1990s. The group quickly doubled in size, launching a ministry that led to the 1993 publication of his bestselling book *Woman, Thou Art Loosed*, which Jakes used fifteen thousand dollars of his own money to publish. The work, which was addressed to women dealing with the pain of rape, sold over three million copies and would become the first of eighteen he had published by 2006. In that year, "Get Ready with T. D. Jakes," started airing on national television networks in major markets, and Jakes's ministry was poised to skyrocket.

In the mid 1990s Jakes convinced fifty families to follow him from Charleston, a city of fifty thousand, to Dallas, Texas, the nation's largest metroplex, to establish the Potter's House in a former sanctuary purchased from W. V. Grant Jr., a televangelist being sent to prison for tax evasion.

Jakes's congregation took off immediately. The first Sunday he opened the Potter's House for membership, fifteen hundred people joined the church.[60] Within a year it had grown to ten thousand members, and within three years to seventeen thousand. Ten years later, the church had grown to more than twenty-eight thousand members, more than half the size of the town he left.

The extensive outreach of the Potter's House involves more than fifty ministries, including a homeless ministry that offers people from Dallas streets not just a shower and clean clothes but also an invitation to worship. There is outreach to prostitutes, a G.E.D. literacy program, a drug- and alcohol-abuse treatment program, an AIDS outreach, a prison outreach, bilingual services, literacy programs, youth ministries, weight-loss programs, and mentoring and job-training programs. The campus also includes the Metroplex Economic Development Corporation (MEDC), and plans are underway for an education facility, offices, recreation and cultural centers, and retirement homes.

Though his multicultural, nondenominational congregation is far removed from his oneness beginnings, socially and theologically as well as geographically, Jakes has never removed himself from a oneness understanding of the Godhead. Instead, he nuances his theology, insisting that there is "one God, Creator of all things, infinitely perfect, and eternally existing in three *manifestations*:[61] Father, Son and Holy Spirit."[62] His ability to avoid the oneness-trinitarian schism has allowed him to attract people from both camps; most of his followers pay little attention to this distinction in assessing his leadership, and he also downplays other divisive elements, displaying a broader understanding of the true Church as being "composed of all . . . who through saving faith in Jesus Christ, have been regenerated by the Holy Spirit."[63] Insistence on the necessity for the experience of Holy Spirit baptism as outlined in classical Pentecostalism is absent. Rather, Jakes insists that "the ministry of the Holy Spirit is to glorify the Lord Jesus Christ and during this age, to convict men of sin, regener-

---

[60]Kelly Starling, "Why People, Especially Black Women, Are Talking About Bishop T. D. Jakes," *Ebony*, January 2001, p. 112.

[61]As distinct from the trinitarian conception of three "persons." Emphasis in original.

[62]"Belief Statement," The Potter's House, www.thepottershouse.org/Local/About-Us/Belief-Statement.aspx.

[63]Ibid.

ate the believing sinner, indwell, guide, instruct, and empower the believer for godly living and service."[64]

Jakes's charismatic leadership has drawn several pastors and their congregations into the Potter's House International Pastoral Alliance, a fellowship of several hundred churches throughout the United States, Great Britain and Africa. The fellowship fully supports and encourages women in pastoral leadership, both as senior pastors and as members of copastoral teams. Further, he has been able to cross the racial divide to attract pastors of white and Latino congregations. While his combination of entrepreneurial skill, dramatic teaching style and administrative sophistication is attractive to the black middle class and has drawn a multiracial constituency to his church and conferences, his reception within secular society represents a new openness for black Pentecostals and charismatics. Far from the disenfranchised, disinherited congregations earlier shunned by prominent people and ridiculed by the secular press and Christian media, Jakes and the Potter's House have become celebrities. He received a Grammy award for his "Woman, Thou Art Loosed" CD, and his release *Sacred Love Songs* was named one of *Billboard* magazine's 1999 top gospel albums. His books regularly make the top seller lists of major periodicals, which devote a substantial amount of print to almost everything he does. A *Time* magazine headline asked, "Is This Man the Next Billy Graham?"[65] In 2001 an article in both *Time* magazine and a commentary on CNN dubbed him as "America's Best Preacher."[66] *Christianity Today* labeled his multiracial Potter's House congregation one of America's fastest-growing churches, contending that among megachurches, its growth could be considered phenomenal.[67] His rallies have increasingly drawn record crowds, at one point even going beyond those of Billy Graham. One journalist referred to Jakes as "the Oprah Winfrey of popular preachers."[68]

---

[64]Ibid.

[65]*Time*, September 17, 2001, cover page.

[66]David Van Biema uses this designation in the byline of his title article "Spirit Raiser (America's Best Preacher)," in the table of contents (*Time*, September 17, 2001), and Ralph G. Zerbonia cites the CNN designation in *Contemporary Black Biography* 43 (April 2004): 102.

[67]Jim Jones, "Swift Growth Shapes Potter's House," *Christianity Today* (January 12, 1998), p. 56.

[68]Julia Duin, "Provocative Pentecostal (author and minister T. D. Jakes reaches thousands)," *Insight on the News*, September 14, 1998, p. 41.

THE MEGACHURCH PHENOMENON

Pearson and Jakes represent one of the largest trends spawned by the new African American charismatic/neo-Pentecostal spirituality: the rapid rise of a number of megachurch congregations with middle-class, formerly classical Pentecostal and mainline practitioners. According to one estimation, though "fifty-nine percent of US congregations have fewer than one hundred regular participants" of any age and "71 percent have fewer than one hundred regularly participating adults," amazingly, "10 percent of congregations contain half of all [the nation's] churchgoers."[69]

Gilkes contends that blacks are disproportionately attracted to megachurches and that 25 percent of the American megachurch constituency is black, while they make up only 10 percent of the country's population.[70] A study by Hartford Seminary indicates that black megachurches account for nearly 11 percent of these congregations, and many more blacks are found in racially diverse megachurch congregations under either black or white leadership. Most importantly, nearly all African American megachurches (those with more than two thousand members) are charismatic or neo-Pentecostal.[71]

These congregations are not without their detractors. Critique comes from several arenas, including traditional black mainline church leaders, black classical Pentecostals and scholars. Many traditional black church leaders and observers have been concerned that the embrace of Pentecostal spirituality and emotive worship has come at the price of the abandonment of engagement in issues of social justice, where the black church has historically been at the forefront. These leaders would respond that working on individual transformation to make individuals more prosperous and better citizens will lead to transformation in other areas. This is totally different from the way that mainstream Baptists and Methodists have viewed their role in social and political engagement. Further, since megachurches are more likely to be multicultural than are smaller congregations, some

---

[69]Mark Chaves, *Congregations in America* (Cambridge, Mass.: Harvard University Press, 2004), pp. 17-19.

[70]Lawrence A. Mamiya, *River of Struggle, River of Freedom: Trends Among Black Churches and Black Pastoral Leadership,* Pulpit and Pew Research Reports (Durham: Duke Divinity School, 2006), p. 39.

[71]Quoted in John Rivera, "Neo-Pentecostals: Traditional Congregations Bristle at Stress on the Individual Over Social Activism," *Baltimore Sun,* August 25, 2002, p. 1A.

black critics question whether multicultural megachurches are draining prospective members and resources from smaller black congregations.

The charismatic megachurch is at the convergence of two traditions—and they do not always converge neatly. Those from mainline churches are accused of having given up concern for the poor and disenfranchised as well as shifted their focus away from civil rights and social justice. Those from the more conservative Holiness/Pentecostal traditions have been accused of buying into a worldly concern for material goods in the here and now while giving up pursuit of moral purity and personal piety. The success of neo-Pentecostal churches—which have found a way to powerfully mix spirited worship with a message of black empowerment—has prompted debate in recent years about the nature and mission of the black church, since some estimate that the influence of neo-Pentecostal spirituality is evident in at least a third of black mainline Christians.[72] As neo-Pentecostalism began to take root in earnest in the late 1960s, just as the civil rights movement was beginning to implode and lose steam, some, such as womanist Bible scholar Renita Weems, cast neo-Pentecostal spirituality as a corrective to the shortcomings of the activist movements of the 1950s and early 1960s, which had left some feeling psychologically battered and spiritually parched. For Weems, the lesson that came out of that period was that, in order to fight for justice, you have to have a strong spiritual life.[73]

When the charismatic movement exploded, more than half these congregations, which had existed as small to moderately sized congregations, began experiencing phenomenal growth. By the early 1990s the five largest churches in the 2.2-million-member AME denomination, for example, were neo-Pentecostal; this included Bethel in Baltimore; Ebenezer in Fort Washington, Maryland; St. Paul's in Boston; Bethel in Baltimore; and First AME in Los Angeles, California.

Since the average age of neo-Pentecostal megachurch pastors is fifty-two, many did not witness the most severe years of American Jim Crowism. Racism has not had the same impact on them or their congregations as it did with older pastors of more traditional congregations. So these pastors have not taken on the more militant stances of their colleagues. They have adopted a more reformist approach to social realities, determining to

[72]Gaines, "Revive Us, Precious Lord," p. 38.
[73]Renita J. Weems, "Black America and Religion," *Ebony*, November 1, 2005, p. 123.

empower individuals to live more productive lives and to contribute to the uplift of the communities in which they serve rather than challenge the structure of society through more systemic involvement.

The collective economic resources of these middle class congregations allows them to be heavily involved in outreach that goes far beyond the usual benevolence that smaller congregations are able to pull off. Several, like Jakes's Potter's House, have been able to undertake extensive programs of training and job development, housing, community development, and entrepreneurship.

Bishop Kenneth Ulmer's Faithful Central Bible Church, whose for-profit arm now owns the Forum, the former home of the L.A. Lakers, is another example. William Winston's eighteen-thousand-member Living Word Christian Center blends spirituality and entrepreneurship. In 1998, the church purchased a deteriorating shopping mall in Forest Park, Illinois, and has transformed what was once a blight on the community into a thriving mixed-use complex. At the same time, its congregation doubled to fifteen thousand members. At the center of the mall is the thirty-five-hundred-seat sanctuary, where worshipers attentively listen as Winston preaches a sermon projected on giant video screens.

The church's mission is twofold: saving souls and modeling economic development for a largely black congregation. In order to accomplish the latter, the church established a business school, broadcast media center, Christian bookstore, kindergarten-through-eighth-grade academy and its own clothing store. The church owns Forest Park Plaza, which runs the mall and houses major commercial tenants like Kmart, Ultra Foods, a U.S. Cellular store and Old Country Buffet.

Megachurch congregations are primarily an urban phenomenon—found largely either within the inner cities (many of them regentrified) or in suburbs of larger cities. Employing church-growth methods such as market share and targeting, these megachurches tend to appeal to a largely middle-class constituency and have generally little attraction for lower-class African Americans. No major U.S. city has been untouched by the new trend, and most larger Metropolitan areas are home to several charismatic megachurches. The largest numbers are in the Atlanta and Washington, D.C., areas. Atlanta is home to Eddie Long's New Birth Missionary Baptist Church, Cynthia Hale's Ray of Hope Christian Center in

Decatur, Creflo Dollar's World Changers Christian Center in College
Park, Gary Hawkins's Voices of Faith Ministries in Stone Mountain and
Craig Oliver's Elizabeth Baptist Church among others.

More than ten megachurches make their home in one suburban Washington, D.C., county—Prince Georges—which is statistically the wealthiest black community in the nation. These include two AME congregations: Ebenezer and Reid Temple. It also includes Jericho City of Praise, a
former Baptist congregation that is among the largest African American
megachurches to have been led by a woman senior pastor, Reverend Betty
Peoples;[74] First Baptist Church of Glenarden; Cherry's From the Heart
Ministries; Anthony Macklin's Sanctuary at Kingdom Square (formerly
Glendale Baptist Church) in Capitol Heights; Church of the Lord's Disciples; and Ark of Safety Christian Church pastored by former oneness-
Pentecostal-turned-Methodist Anthony Muse. Within the county, there
are also two predominantly African American congregations with essen-
tially white leadership, National Church of God under Steve Lowery and
Evangel Cathedral under John Meares and his sons.

The majority of black megachurches are also located in sunbelt cities,
including Houston, Dallas, Atlanta and Los Angeles. In a study of sixty-
six black megachurches, 46 percent were Baptist, 29 percent were nondenominational, 9 percent were black congregations of white denominations
(United Methodist, Disciples of Christ and United Church of Christ), 8
percent were African Methodist Episcopal and 8 percent were classified as
sanctified churches (COGIC, Pentecostal Assemblies of the World, Bible
Way Church, and various Holiness or Apostolic denominations).[75] Few
classical Pentecostal congregations have become megachurches in the recent upsurge. Most that are considered megachurches are old-line congregations that have shown steady growth over several decades, such as Detroit's Greater Grace Temple and First Apostolic Faith Church in
Baltimore. But the largest classical black Pentecostal megachurch in the
nation is West Angeles Church of God in Christ, which opened its new
sixty-million-dollar, five-thousand-seat cathedral in 2001. The eighteen-
thousand-member congregation, home to COGIC presiding bishop
Charles Blake, represents a strand that has adopted styles of worship that

[74]Peoples died in October 2010 and the pastorate was assumed by her son.
[75]Tucker-Worgs, "Get on Board, Little Children," pp. 177-203.

are more charismatic than Pentecostal or exhibits a blend of the two traditions. Some classical Pentecostal black congregations go as far as reclassifying themselves among the 29 percent who are nondenominational, like former oneness Bishop Joseph Garlington, senior pastor of the very successful Covenant Church in suburban Pittsburgh. Though not all African American neo-Pentecostal congregation are megachurches, the neo-Pentecostal movement has certainly influenced and revitalized many formerly small, dying congregations and allowed them to reach a level of viability for which previously they could have only prayed.

CHARISMATIC INFLUENCE ON CLASSICAL PENTECOSTALISM

The charismatic movement has not left classical black Pentecostal congregations untouched. The realignment of a few megachurches with the designation nondenominational or interdenominational is only one way that once-reluctant classical Pentecostals have been influenced by the charismatic and neo-Pentecostal movements. Many African American Pentecostals were exposed to the charismatic movement through involvement with parachurch organizations such as the Full Gospel Businessmen's Fellowship International or Women Aglow or through exposure to the explosion of televangelists or through the proliferation of teaching books and tapes by white and black charismatics that became their staple reading fare. These challenged such long-held Pentecostal distinctives as initial evidence, sanctification and restrictive personal piety while introducing an emphasis on a broader range of spiritual gifts—words of wisdom and knowledge and a heavy dose of the prophetic, which had largely been ignored within classical Pentecostal worship. They also broached issues of social responsibility and justice that had ceased being a central focus of classical Pentecostalism.

Initially, Pentecostal leadership balked at the newcomers, seeing them as interlopers who had not paid their dues and were watering down important doctrinal distinctives regarding initial evidence. They also felt that these neo-Pentecostals and charismatics were benefitting from new interest in Pentecostal spirituality at their expense. Such denominational barriers, however, have given way to a new fluidity and rapprochement between classical Pentecostals and their mainline brothers and sisters who grace each other's pulpits with a regularity that would have been unimaginable a generation ago. In this new arrangement, not only have mainliners embraced a Pentecostal spirituality that their fathers and mothers in ministry would have found detestable; but Pentecostals have also come to appreciate some of the liturgical elements that have been the mainstay of mainline church worship.

As some traditional Pentecostals began to move into the middle class, they had already begun to gain a measure of respectability, often putting distance between them and their less sophisticated brothers and sisters, noting that "it don't take all that" to have church. Related, the number of younger people has begun to plateau in the classical Pentecostal church, which retains mostly a nostalgic older generation along with worship styles that have little relevance for younger generations. Further, many of the very elements that had made classical Pentecostalism initially so attractive had been routinized. Over the years, increasingly smaller numbers of Pentecostals have actually spoken in tongues, and many have never experienced the demonstration of prophetic utterances and the miraculous healings that had characterized early Pentecostal meetings. And where these were still occurring, the operation of spiritual gifts was often centralized among church leaders rather than among "whosoever will" within the congregation, as had been the practice during earlier years. At the same time, neo-Pentecostal worship services sometimes out-Pentecostaled Pentecostals, with their greater emphasis on the demonstrative aspects of worship. But they also mix a level of "spreaching"—preaching that also teaches. These churches have redefined the perimeters of African American Pentecostalism. Previously shunned as ignorant, overemotional "Holy Rollers" who spoke in strange tongues and were often possessed by demonic spirits rather than the Spirit of God, and also being the recipients of blatant racial discrimination and segregation both within and outside the church, these classical Pentecostals turned neo-Pentecostals are now hailed as people of authentically deep spirituality and looked to for spiritual insight and leadership by former detractors.

HIGH-CHURCH PENTECOSTALISM

A vivid example of the interplay between classical Pentecostal and charismatic/neo-Pentecostal spirituality can be found in the Joint College of

African American Pentecostal Bishops. The organization was founded in
1995 by Bishop J. Delano Ellis II, leader of the twelve-thousand-member
United Pentecostal Churches of Christ. It represents a small but rapidly
emerging trend that attempts to maintain the fervor of Pentecostal worship—its literal belief in the Bible, a personal baptism in the Holy Spirit
and other manifestations such as prophecy or laying on of hands for healing—while constraining some of the more emotive elements and introducing an order more typical of liturgical traditions, all while linking congregations to their African heritage.[76]

So far, the high-church Pentecostal movement has affected only a small
percentage of the nation's more than six million African American Pentecostals. About one hundred people attended its first conference in the
Washington conference, which aimed to teach the basics of being a high-
church Pentecostal bishop. Many attending the sessions at the elegant
Mayflower Hotel were newly consecrated or soon-to-be consecrated bishops. Others included overseers, who serve as bishops' assistants; adjutants,
responsible for ceremonial preparation; and bishops' wives. The bishops
were decked out in religious garb more reminiscent of Roman Catholicism
than the old time Pentecostal churches—including skullcaps and episcopal rings—as they joined in prayers with worshipers, raised their hands,
shouted and intoned hallelujahs. Since that time, it has grown to more
than seven hundred affiliated ministers representing more than one hundred independent black churches. Many more denominational leaders
have been influenced by Ellis's book, *The Bishopric*,[77] and have incorporated specific elements of his proposed polity and liturgical structure into
their organization.

Moreover, the Joint College of African American Pentecostal Bishops
symbolizes the new spirit of cooperation that is allowing Pentecostals and
charismatics to move past theological differences to form networks. While
doing this, it reverses what it sees as outdated Pentecostal practices such as
not allowing women full freedom to preach—though the organization was
at first was reluctant to ordain them as bishops.

---

[76]Adelle M. Banks, "Pentecostals Dress Like Catholic Bishops—High-Church Pentecostalism," *National Catholic Reporter,* February 24, 1995, p. 3.
[77]J. Delano Ellis, *The Bishopric: A Handbook on Creating Episcopacy in the African-American Pentecostal Church* (Victoria, B.C.: Trafford, 2003).

WOMEN IN BLACK CHARISMATIC AND
NEO-PENTECOSTAL TRADITIONS

According to womanist theologian Renita Weems, who describes herself as a "recovering Pentecostal,"[78]

> It remains doubtful that women's rise over the last sixty years to some top posts in mainline religious structures can be traced directly to the Neo-Pentecostal renewal movement. But . . . one teaching of this movement has had an effect on a significant portion of its membership, namely the teaching that says that in the spirit everyone is equal and the same.[79]

Weems's assessment affirms the reality that black charismatics and neo-Pentecostals are generally more open to restoring the historical pattern of gender equality in ministry than are the classical black Pentecostals. Within the newer movements, several black women have been able to move into positions of prominence and gain followings for themselves that rival those of male colleagues. These women hail from the same breadth of denominational affiliations as their brother clergy.

In 1966, *Gospel Today* magazine listed classical Pentecostal Jackie McCollough as one of "the most influential African-American ministers in the nation."[80] But she shares the limelight with other women such as Disciples of Christ pastor Cynthia Hale, who leads a flourishing congregation, Ray of Hope Christian Church, in Atlanta, Georgia. Hale's congregation of some four thousand members began as a bible study in her apartment. Other woman pastor include Pastor Gina Stewart of Memphis's Christ Missionary Baptist Church;[81] Barbara Amos, who moved out of Mt. Sinai Holy Church of America to form her own, nondenominational fellowship, Faith Deliverance Ministries; and Juanita Bynum, the widely known and controversial televangelist.

A number of charismatic and neo-Pentecostal congregations are led by husband-and-wife teams, with women serving as highly visible copastors. Former Pentecostal Claudette Copeland, for example, and her husband,

[78]Renita Weems, "The Prophetic Role in Difficult Times" (keynote address, 2009 Hampton Ministers' Conference, Hampton University, June 8, 2009).

[79]Weems, "Black America and Religion," *Ebony* 61, no. 1 (November 2005): 124.

[80]"The Most Influential African-American Ministers in the Nation," *Gospel Today* (October/November 1996).

[81]In 1995, Stewart was the first woman elected to serve as pastor of a Memphis Baptist congregation. Under her leadership the congregation has grown to more than three thousand members.

David, copastor New Creation Christian Fellowship in San Antonio, Texas, a congregation they founded in 1984. JoAnn Browning made history in the AME church by being the first woman officially appointed by the bishop to serve as copastor along with her husband at the twenty-thousand-member Ebenezer AME Church in Maryland. Other women, such as Elaine Flake, take on a secondary but no less visible roles as assistant pastor. Flake serves as assistant pastor with her husband, Floyd, who leads the twenty-three-thousand-member Greater Allen AME Cathedral in Jamaica, Queens, New York.

Unlike either the Church of God in Christ or the Baptist tradition, from which the former was derived, the newer denomination Full Gospel Baptist Fellowship has aggressively promoted women's leadership; and the degree of freedom offered to women is unprecedented even among earlier classical Pentecostals. Women serve at every level of ministry, including senior pastorates, administrative officers and bishops. While by 2006, no member of the eleven-member Executive Council or the eight member Bishop's Council were female, one of the twenty-six auxiliary bishops and two of the twenty-four state bishops were women.

T. D. Jakes's support for women goes far beyond his attack on issues of abuse and domestic violence. Jakes expresses open support for women in positions of leadership, including senior pastor. Among his ten associates pastors who oversee the affairs of his congregation, two—Rita Twiggs and Bonné Moon—are women. Twiggs serves as director of discipleship and is responsible for overseeing several ministries, including training and developing other ministers.

New charismatic/Pentecostal openness to women's leadership has pushed some mainline congregations and denominations to move beyond their existing "liberal" posture to allow women to land important leadership roles that had been previously unavailable or off limits to them. Bishop Vashti McKenzie, noted for her fiery, Pentecostal-style preaching, became the first woman bishop elected in the AME Church. Bishop Violet Fisher, a former Pentecostal, was elected to the bishopric in the United Methodist Church.

George Stallings's African American Catholic Congregation allows women to be ordained as priests. Reverend Rose Vernell, a fifty-year-old former Roman Catholic nun, is a teacher and social services administrator from Asbury Park, New Jersey.[82] Nearly eight hundred people attended the unorthodox ceremony in which Stallings installed her as pastor of the Philadelphia congregation: "There is a need for the Catholic Church to stop paying lip service and to enforce with concrete action the statement that men and women are created equal. . . . Therefore African American Catholic Congregation, in an act of self-determination and prophetic witness, in an historic Catholic church . . ."[83]

Indeed, one of the severest critiques of the new spirituality has been its openness to women's leadership. Such criticism has not, however, stopped women from taking advantage of new opportunities to pursue a variety of congregational and parachurch leadership positions. While, for a variety of reasons, most women have not achieved the same stature or economic reward of their male colleagues, the number of those who are is growing.

CONCLUSION

At its inception one hundred years ago, the Pentecostal movement was home to only a small, despised segment of the Christian church, largely confined to the "least of these" who were sometimes unaccepted by mainline churches. A century later, scholars note that Pentecostalism and related spiritualities is the fastest growing segment of the church. More importantly for our discussion, they see the fastest growing segment of American Pentecostalism as among independent charismatic churches and black neo-Pentecostals; the two groups, Vinson Synan insists, have similar worship styles.[84] Concurring with Synan, sociologist Lawrence Mamiya contends that with "Neo-Pentecostalism [being] the fastest-growing segment of Christianity among the black middle class . . . by 2050 half of all black Christians will have embraced some form of Pentecostalism."[85]

The rise of this new acceptability of Pentecostal spirituality in charismatic and neo-Pentecostal churches has not escaped the attention of the secular media and has brought a certain acceptability to classical

[82]Peter Steinfels, "Black Catholics In Splinter Sect Ordain Woman," *New York Times*, September 9, 1991.
[83]"Stallings Ordains Woman," *Christian Century*, September 18-25, 1991, p. 941.
[84]Quoted in Gaines, "Revive Us, Precious Lord," p. 38.
[85]Quoted in ibid.

Pentecostalism. But it has not been without criticism, and some of the harshest criticism, especially as related to megachurch ministries within the black community, can be heard in Shayne Lee's assessment of T. D. Jakes:

> Today's post-denominational religious landscape contains a host of black Neo-Pentecostal preachers who have built mega churches and national ministries as part of the emergence of . . . the new black church. These celebrity preachers are CEOs of international ministries that reach millions of people through television, radio, the Internet, and by satellite technology, and their churches have resources rivaling denominations. These pastors take advantage of our media age by marketing their books, videos, and tapes to secure personal fortunes . . . [and] compete for twenty-first-century souls among a growing black middle class and newly educated African Americans excelling in corporate America, a niche that has intriguing possibilities.
>
> . . . The fact that some [black megachurches] have exploded in membership is not surprising. . . . Some scholars may argue that [these churches] are not doing anything new. But the notion of a new black church sheds light on a shift that most researchers tend to miss in the context of contemporary black religion, which, taken together, can very well be called a "new" form in the legacy of the black church. In the last thirty years, the trend has been for traditional mainline churches to lose their prominent places in the market share to neo-Pentecostal churches, which have secured phenomenal growth because they encompass many of the trends of American popular religion.[86]

In spite of such critique, black charismatic/neo-Pentecostal congregations have given middle-class blacks an alternative as they move up the social scale. They no longer have to evade the primitive spirituality of raw black Pentecostalism or switch to white mainline evangelical congregations. Rather, across the country, a growing number of educated, affluent blacks are turning back to the church and at the same time are able to embrace both their African spirituality and a more intellectual approach to religion. Further, they are able to align themselves with a broader move of the Spirit that reaches around the globe.

---

[86]Shayne Lee, *T. D. Jakes: America's New Preacher* (New York: New York University Press, 2005), p. 159.

Table 9.1. Characteristics of Representative Charismatic/Neo-Pentecostal Associations and Denominations

Association/Denomination	Year Est.	Founder	Affiliation
Fellowship of Inner City Word of Faith Ministries (FICWFM)	1990	Fred K. C. Price	Nondenominational
World Changers Ministries		Creflo Dollar	Nondenominational
African American Catholic Congregation	1994	George Stallings	Catholic
Potter's House International Pastoral Alliance		T. D. Jakes	
Full Gospel Baptist Church Fellowship International		Paul S. Morton	Baptist
Faith Ministry Alliance		Bill Winston	
The Father's House		Eddie Long	Baptist

10

CONCLUSION

HISTORICAL REALITIES AND
THEOLOGICAL CHALLENGES OF
AFRICAN AMERICAN PENTECOSTALISM
INTO THE TWENTY-FIRST CENTURY

. . . which if . . . written in detail, I suppose that even the world itself would not contain the books that would be written.

JOHN 21:25 NASB

APRIL **2006** MARKED THE CENTENNIAL ANNIVERSARY of the Azusa Street Revival, the seminal event that challenged both the existing understandings of the activity of the Holy Spirit in the life of the believer and the church and the existing understandings of class, gender and race within the American religious context. After a short period, though, the revival's religious fervor would continue to spread, engulfing not only the American context but also much of the Western world and what was then considered the Third World. The movement it generated, however, would revert to race, class and gender politics as usual. Yet within that one-hundred-year period, this relatively young movement has evolved from one considered by many to be a marginalized, sectarian cult to one whose global influence throughout the church and society cannot be overlooked. As it has unfolded, every facet of that evolution would be touched by a deep African American spirituality.

The modest Holiness women gathered with William Seymour in a humble Los Angeles home in 1906 sensed something powerful was happening in their midst. They were not aware, however, that they were at the forefront of shaping the theology, worship and music styles of a movement that would forever change the face of American and global Christianity. The black evangelists, pastors and denominational founders within the antecedent Holiness movement who would eventually make their way into the Pentecostal movement would be joined by the blacks who made up a significant portion of the Azusa Street congregation, which fueled the Pentecostal movement's spread. Once their tongues were touched by the fires of Azusa Street and they felt themselves empowered by the Spirit of God, they left Los Angeles with others of every race and culture to take the message of the in-breaking of the Spirit in a powerful new way across the nation and the world, serving as missionaries both at home and abroad. They founded Pentecostal churches and denominations that, at first, dotted the West and the South, where they were largely confined, and then moved with them in the Great Migration to the major urban centers and every town and hamlet in between so that within twenty years no part of the American landscape and very little of the world remained untouched by the revival.

Holy Spirit empowerment did not ensure that black believers could overcome the social realities of early-twentieth-century American race politics, even within the religious context. Black Pentecostals suffered the double indignity of racial discrimination and religious persecution. Though labels of "brother" and "sister" denoted equal access to the family of God, white Pentecostals forsook the Azusa Street ideal of genuine interracial fellowship, denying black Pentecostals access to positions of influence or leadership. Black Pentecostals were also scorned as ignorant and uncouth by black mainline Christians, who wrote them off as members of a mysterious cult under the powers of unscrupulous charlatans. As hopes for racial unity dissolved into the reality of the segregated social landscape, black men and women made a separate place for themselves that gave them room for cultural expression. This was true even when that subculture existed within larger white Pentecostal bodies. Sometimes this subculture provided the only safe haven from Jim Crow business as usual and allowed them to live out a distinct understanding of who they were as the "sanctified church."

As racial attitudes had begun moderating by the mid-twentieth century, the infrastructure of black Pentecostalism was solidly in place. Yet, coming into its own during this period, alongside the racial upheaval that challenged existing understandings of appropriate social relationships between blacks and whites as well as understandings of women's appropriate place in the church and society, much would change regarding the face of the Pentecostal movement generally and the face of African American Pentecostalism in particular. By the end of the twentieth century the relative fluidity in racial intercourse opened avenues for the exposure of highly charismatic and intellectually astute black Pentecostal and neo-Pentecostals to carve out a place for themselves in the spreading spotlight that would thrust the exploding charismatic movement onto the center of the American religious stage. Names that in another time would have remained largely unknown became household words and graced the pages of the nation's most prestigious publications.

Perhaps what is most distinctive about African American Pentecostalism today is the variety of modes of expression that it developed over the course of its history—much of it fueled by schism within its ranks. These schisms would leave the movement splintered into more than thirty-seven major denominations and more than one hundred smaller bodies that identified themselves as Pentecostal. The earliest of these schisms would in some way revolve around race, but they would also involve personality differences among strong, charismatic leaders. The movement would further divide along geographical and theological lines, and though the majority of the major bodies would be trinitarian, an entirely new branch of the Christian tradition would embrace an understanding of the Godhead that rejected trinitarian formulations for what most would see as a modalistic interpretation. Within the United States a large number of those in the oneness or Apostolic movement would be African American.

In the end, far from being simply the monolithic, otherworldly "tongues movement" many have depicted, Pentecostalism exhibits a full range of responses to modern realities. Just as there is no one black Baptist or Methodist denomination, there is no one black Pentecostal movement. The variety of expressions of Pentecostal spirituality among African Americans has come to mean that we can no longer speak of a Pentecostal movement but instead of Pentecostal movements, or movements of the Spirit. African

American Pentecostals can be found in more than one hundred large and small bodies that extend from regional groups with a handful of congregations and less than one thousand members to those with international constituencies, such as the Church of God in Christ, with several thousand congregations and several million members. What these groups, and the antecedent Holiness movement and the charismatic and neo-Pentecostal movements that have emerged from it, have shared is a common openness to the immanent work of the Spirit within their lives and congregations. Yet, after a century of expansion spurred by schism, persistent evangelism efforts and enticing media exposure, those believers and women and men who joined them at the Azusa Street Mission would not recognize the contemporary expression of the movement they helped to birth.

A movement that began with a handful of people gathered in a home Bible study and quickly grew to a few hundred people gathered daily in a rundown, converted livery stable has grown to engulf an estimated 600 million people globally. African Americans account for approximately eight million of that number. Six million more would characterize themselves as charismatic or neo-Pentecostals. These believers represent the breadth of socioeconomic classes, educational and professional attainment, and theological backgrounds and worldviews. They also exhibit a full range of responses to social concerns and political views depending, as with other congregations, on the prophetic vision of their leaders and the particular political proclivity and social level and consciousness of their membership

This volume has attempted to capture the contributions of those individual movements that make up *the* movement; to highlight the circumstances of their origin and growth; to celebrate the men and women who conceived, birthed and nurtured them to viability; and to examine the various schisms that were so integral in shaping that differentiation. A fuller discussion of the themes developed during the history of these movements—its roots within African spirituality, the development of its variegated theology and unique worship forms, its engagement with the urban context in which it experienced its greatest expansion, its contribution to the black struggle for social justice, and the expression of progressive elements within its ranks—remain for a separate enterprise.

As the twenty-first century enters the end of its first decade, black Pentecostal, charismatic and neo-Pentecostal believers continue to solidly plant their imprint on a movement that is still relatively young. At this time the fruit of a centralized revival in Los Angeles one hundred years earlier under the leadership of a humble black preacher would be evidenced in the phenomenal growth in the number of peoples whose lives would be touched by the Pentecostal experience. It would also be seen in the fact that Seymour's desire for the body of Christ to be unified in love by the power of the Holy Spirit seems to be taking on flesh. What such unity would mean for black Pentecostal believers remains to be seen, but it is certain that their collective voice will increasingly be heard.

BIBLIOGRAPHY OF HISTORICAL SOURCES FOR AFRICAN AMERICAN PENTECOSTALISM

Apostolic Faith Mission. *The Apostolic Faith*. Vols. 1-13, September 1906–May 1908.

Christian, William. *Poor Pilgrim's Work, in the Name of the Father, Son, and Holy Ghost, no. 3*. Texarkana, Tex.: Joe Erlich's Print, 1896.

Cotton, Emma. "The Inside Story of the Outpouring of the Holy Spirit—Azusa Street—April 1906." *Message of the Apostolic Faith* 1, no. 1 (1936): 1.

Dabney, Elizabeth. *What It Means to Pray Through*. Philadelphia : E. J. Dabney, 1945.

Delk, James Logan. *He Made Millions Happy*. Lexington, Ky.: James Delk, 1945.

Fauset, Arthur Huff. *Black Gods of the Metropolis: Negro Religious Cults of the Urban North*. Philadelphia: University of Pennsylvania Press, 1944.

Fisher, Henry L. *The History of the United Holy Church of America, Inc.* (s.l.: s.n., 193?).

Foote, Julia. *A Brand Plucked from the Fire: An Autobiographical Sketch by Mrs. Julia A. J. Foote*. New York: George Hughes & Co., 1879.

Haywood, Garfield T. *Before the Foundation of the World: A Revelation of the Ages*. Indianapolis: Christ Temple, 1923.

———. *The Birth of the Spirit in the Days of the Apostles*. Portland, Ore.: Apostolic Book Publishers, s.d.

Jones, Charles Price. *An Appeal to the Sons of Africa: A Number of Poems, Readings, Orations and Lectures, Designed Especially to Inspire Youth of African Blood with Sentiments of Hope and Nobility as well as to Entertain and Instruct all Classes of Readers and Lovers of Humanity*. Jackson, Miss.: Truth Publishing, 1902.

———. *The Gift of the Holy Spirit in the Book of Acts*. 1903. Reprint, Chicago: National Publishing Board, Church of Christ (Holiness) U.S.A., 1996.

Lawson, Robert C. *An Open Letter to a Southern White Minister on Prejudice: The Eating Cancer of the Soul*. Statesville, N.C.: VisionQuest Media, 1995.

———. *The Anthropology of Jesus Christ our Kinsman*. Piqua, Ohio: Ohio Ministries, 1925.

Mason, Mary. *The History and Life Work of Bishop C. H. Mason and His Co-laborers*. Memphis: Church of God in Christ, 1924.

Pleas, Charles. *Fifty Years Achievement, from 1906-1956: A Period in History of the Church of God in Christ*. Memphis: Church Public Relations, 1991.

Seymour, William J. *The Doctrines and Disciplines of the Azusa Street Mission of Los Angeles, CA.* s.l.: s.n., 1915.

Shumway, Charles. "A Critical History of Glossolalia." Ph.D. diss., Boston University, 1919.

Smith, Amanda Berry. *An Autobiography: The Story of the Lord's Dealing with Mrs. Amanda Smith, the Colored Evangelist; Containing an Account of Her Life, Work of Faith, and Her Travels in America, England, Ireland, Scotland, India, and Africa as an Independent Missionary.* Chicago: Meyers and Brothers Publishers, 1893.

Tate, Mary Magdalena Lewis. *The Constitution, Government and Decree Book of the Church of the Living God Pillar and Ground of the Truth.* Chattanooga, Tenn.: New and Living Way, 1924.

Vanzandt, J. C. *Speaking in Tongues: A Discussion of Speaking in Tongues, Pentecost, Latter Rain, Evidence of Holy Spirit Baptism and a Short History of the Tongues Movement in America and Some Foreign Countries.* Portland, Ore.: J. C. Vanzandt, 1926.

Webb, Lillian Ashcraft. *About My Father's Business: The Life of Elder Michaux.* Contributions to Afro-American and African Studies. Santa Barbara, Calif.: Greenwood, 1981.

White, Alma. *Demons and Tongues.* Zarapheth, N.J.: Pillar of Fire, 1910.

Williams, Smallwood. *This Is My Story: A Significant Life Struggle.* Washington, D.C.: William Willoughby, 1981.

———. *Significant Sermons.* Washington, D.C.: Bible Way Church, 1970.

BIBLIOGRAPHY OF CONTEMPORARY SOURCES ON AFRICAN AMERICAN PENTECOSTALISM

Alexander, Estrelda. *The Women of Azusa Street*. Cleveland: Pilgrim, 2005.

———. *Limited Liberty: The Legacy of Four Pentecostal Women Pioneers*. Cleveland: Pilgrim, 2008.

Alexander, Estrelda, and Amos Yong. *Philip's Daughters: Women in Pentecostal-Charismatic Leadership*. Eugene, Ore.: Wipf & Stock, 2009.

Allen, Earline. *Go Tell My Brethren: Overcoming Changes and Challenges Facing Women in Ministry in the Church of God in Christ*. Hazel Crest, Ill.: Faraday Press, 2005.

Andrews, Sherry. "Black Pentecostals: Who Are They?" *Charisma*, September 1978, pp. 52-55.

Bean, Bobby. *This Is the Church of God in Christ*. Atlanta: Underground Epics, 2001.

Best, Felton. "Breaking the Gender Barrier: African-American Women and Leadership in Black Holiness-Pentecostal Churches 1890-Present." In *Black Religious Leadership from the Slave Community to the Million Man March*. Lewiston, N.Y.: Edwin Mellen, 1998.

Billingsley, Scott. *It's a New Day: Race and Gender in the Modern Charismatic Movement*. Tuscaloosa: University of Alabama Press, 2008.

Butler, Anthea. *Women in the Church of God in Christ: The Making of a Sanctified World*. Chapel Hill: University of North Carolina Press, 2008.

Church, Carlyle. "The Accommodation and Liberation of Women in the Church of God in Christ." *Journal of Religious Thought* 2, no. 1 (1996): 52-53, 77-90.

Clemmons, Ithiel. *Bishop C. H. Mason and the roots of the Church of God in Christ*. Bakersfield, Calif.: Pneuma Life, 1996.

Cobbins, Otto B., ed. *History of the Church of Christ (Holiness) U.S.A., 1895-1965*. New York: Vantage, 1966.

Collier-Thomas, Bettye. *Daughters of Thunder: Black Women Preachers and Their Sermons, 1850-1979*. San Francisco: Jossey-Bass, 1998.

Corum, Fred T., et al. *Like as of Fire: Newspapers from the Azusa Street World Wide Revival*. Washington, D.C.: Middle Atlantic Regional Press, 1994.

Daniels, David. "'Doing All the Good We Can': The Political Witness of African American Holiness and Pentecostal Churches in the Post-Civil Rights Era." In *New Day Begun: African American Churches and Civic Culture in Post-Civil*

Rights America, edited by Dre Smith, pp. 164-82. Durham: Duke University Press, 2003.

Davis, Arnor S. "Pentecostal Movement in Black Christianity." *The Black Church* 2, no. 1 (1972): 65-88.

DuPree, Sherry. *African American Holiness-Pentecostalism: An Annotated Bibliography.* New York: Garland Press, 1996.

———. *Biographical Dictionary of African American Holiness-Pentecostals, 1880-1990.* Washington, D.C.: Middle Atlantic Regional Press, 1989.

Gilkes, Cheryl Townsend. "The Role of Women in the Sanctified Church." *Journal of Religious Thought* 43, no. 1 (1986): 24-41.

Golder, Morris E. *History of the Pentecostal Assemblies of the World.* Indianapolis: s.n., 1973.

———. *The Life and Work of Garfield T. Haywood.* Indianapolis: s.n., 1977.

Gregory, Chester W. *The History of the United Holy Church of America, Inc., 1886-1986.* Baltimore: Gateway, 1986.

Hardy, Clarence G., III. "From Exodus to Exile: Black Pentecostals, Migrating Pilgrims, and Imagined Internationalism." *American Quarterly* 59, no. 3 (2007): 737-57.

Harrell, David Edwin. *White Sects and Black Men in the Recent South.* Nashville: Vanderbilt University Press, 1971.

Harrison, Milmon. *Righteous Riches: The Word of Faith Movement in Contemporary African American Religion.* New York: Oxford University Press, 2005.

Hayes, Diana. "Black Catholic Revivalism: The Emergence of a New Form of Worship." *Journal of the Interdenominational Theological Center* 14, nos. 1-2 (1986-1987): 87-107.

Irvin, Dale T. "Drawing All Together in One Bond of Love: The Ecumenical Vision of William J. Seymour and the Azusa Street Revival." *Journal of Pentecostal Theology* 6 (1995): 25-53.

Jones, Charles E. *Black Holiness: A Guide to the Study of Black Participation in Wesleyan Perfectionist and Glossolalic Pentecostal Movements.* Metuchen, N.J.: Scarecrow, 1987.

———. "The Color Line Washed Away in the Blood: In the Holiness Church at Azusa Street and Church Growth." *Wesleyan Theological Journal* 34, no. 2 (1999): 252-65.

Jones, Pearl Williams. "A Minority Report: Black Pentecostal Women." *Spirit: A Journal Incident to Black Pentecostalism* 1 (1977): 31-44.

Kenyon, Howard N. "Black Ministers in the Assemblies of God." *Assemblies of God Heritage* 7 (1987): 10-20.

Klaus, Byron. *We've Come This Far: Reflections on the Pentecostal Tradition on Racial*

Reconciliation. Springfield, Mo.: Assemblies of God Publishing House, 2007.

Kornweibel, Theodore. "Race and Conscientious Objection in World War I: The Story of the Church of God in Christ." In *Proclaim Peace.* Urbana: University of Illinois Press, 1997.

Lee, Shayne. *T. D. Jakes: America's New Preacher.* New York: New York University Press, 2005.

Lewis, B. Scott. "William J. Seymour: Follower of the 'Evening Light' (Zech 14:7)." *Wesleyan Theological Journal* 39, no. 2 (2004): 167-83.

Lovett, Leonard. "Aspects of the Spiritual Legacy of the Church of God in Christ: Ecumenical Implications." *Mid-Stream* 24 (1985): 389-97.

———. "Black Origins of the Pentecostal Movement." In *Aspects of Pentecostal-Charismatic Origins,* edited by Vinson Synan. Plainfield, N.J.: Logos International, 1975.

MacRobert, Ian. *The Black Roots and White Racism of Early Pentecostalism.* New York: St. Martin's, 1988.

Mason, Elsie. *From the Beginning of Bishop C. H. Mason and the Early Pioneers of the Church of God in Christ.* Memphis: Church of God in Christ Publishing House, 1991.

Maye, Warren L. *Soldiers of Uncommon Valor: The History of Salvationists of African Descent in the United States.* Nyack, N.Y.: Salvation Army, 2008.

Michel, David. *Telling Their Story: Blacks Pentecostals in the Church of God.* Cleveland, Tenn.: Pathway, 2000.

Nelson, Douglas J. "For Such a Time as This: The Story of Bishop William J. Seymour and the Azusa Street Revival: A Search for Pentecostal/Charismatic Roots." Ph.D. diss., University of Birmingham, 1981.

O'Quinn, Doretha A. *Silent Voices, Powerful Messages: The Historical Influence and Contribution of the African-American Experience in the Foursquare Gospel Movement.* Los Angeles: International Church of the Foursquare Gospel, 2002.

Owens, Rosalie. "Out on Mt. Sinai: How Bishop Ida Bell Robinson Loosed the Women: An Examination of Her Leadership Style." Doctor of Strategic Leadership diss., Regent University, March 2001.

Paris, Arthur E. *Black Pentecostalism: Southern Religion in an Urban World.* Amherst: University of Massachusetts Press, 1982.

Patterson, James Oglethorpe. *History and Formative Years of the Church of God in Christ with Excerpts from the Life and Works of Its Founder—Bishop C. H. Mason.* Memphis: Church of God in Christ Publishing House, 1969.

Payne, Wardell, ed. *Directory of African American Religious Bodies: A Compendium by the Howard University School of Divinity.* 2nd ed. Washington, D.C.: Howard University Press, 1995.

Pearson, Carlton. *The Gospel of Inclusion: Reaching Beyond Religious Fundamentalism to the True Love of God and Self.* New York: Atria, 2006.

Rayborn, Joel. *Race and the Assemblies of God Church: The Journey from Azusa Street to the "Memphis Miracle."* Youngstown, Ohio: Cambria, 2007.

Richardson, James C. *With Water and Spirit: A History of Black Apostolic Denominations in the U.S.* Washington, D.C.: Spirit, 1980.

Robeck, Cecil M., Jr. The *Azusa Street Mission and Revival: The Birth of the Global Pentecostal Movement.* Nashville: Thomas Nelson, 2006.

Sanders, Cheryl J. *Saints in Exile: The Holiness Pentecostal Experience in African American Religion and Culture.* New York: Oxford University Press, 1996.

Sanders, Rufus G. W. *William Joseph Seymour: Black Father of the Twentieth Century Pentecostal/Charismatic Movement.* Sandusky, Ohio: Alexandria Publications, 2001.

Sharpton, Al. *Go and Tell Pharaoh: The Autobiography of the Reverend Al Sharpton.* New York: Doubleday, 1996.

Simmons, Dovie Marie, and Olivia L. Martin. *Down Behind the Sun: The Story of Arenia Conelia Mallory.* Memphis: Riverside, 1983.

Sims, Jane Ann. *Telling Our Story: A Brief History of Women in the Pentecostal Assemblies of the World.* Indianapolis: s.n., 2003.

Strong, Douglas M. "William Seymour." In *They Walked in the Spirit: Personal Faith and Social Action in America.* Louisville: Westminster John Knox, 1997.

Taylor, Clarence. *Black Religious Intellectuals: The Fight for Equality from Jim Crow to the Twenty-First Century.* New York: Routledge, 2002.

Thompson, Paul H. "'On Account of Conditions That Seem Unalterable': A Proposal About Race Relations in the Church of God (Cleveland, TN) 1909-1929." *Pneuma* 25, no. 2 (2003): 240-64.

Tinney, James S. "William J. Seymour: Father of Modern-Day Pentecostalism." In *Black Apostles: Afro-American Clergy Confront the Twentieth Century,* edited by Randall Burkett and Richard Newman. Boston: G. K. Hall, 1978.

Trulear, Harold D. "The Reshaping of Black Pastoral Theology: The Vision of Bishop Ida B. Robinson." *Journal of Religious Thought* 46 (1989): 17-31.

Turner, William C. *The United Holy Church of America: A Study in Black Holiness-Pentecostalism.* Piscataway, N.J.: Gorgias Press, 2006.

Tyson, James L. *The Early Pentecostal Revival: History of Twentieth-Century Pentecostals and the Pentecostal Assemblies of the World, 1901-30.* Hazelwood, Mo.: Word Aflame Press, 1992.

Williams, Larry E. *The Way God Led Them: A Historical Study of the Mt. Sinai Holy Church of America, Inc.* Ph.D. diss., Howard University, Washington, D.C., 1998.

Name Index

Subject Index

Denominations and Institutions Index